NATIONALISM AND MINORITY IDENTITIES
IN ISLAMIC SOCIETIES

STUDIES IN NATIONALISM AND ETHNIC CONFLICT
General Editors: Sid Noel, Richard Vernon

Studies in Nationalism and Ethnic Conflict examines the political dimensions of nationality in the contemporary world. The series includes both scholarly monographs and edited volumes that consider the varied sources and political expressions of national identities, the politics of multiple loyalty, the domestic and international effects of competing identities within a single state, and the causes of – and political responses to – conflict between ethnic and religious groups. The books are designed for use by university students, scholars, and interested general readers.

The editors welcome inquiries from authors. If you are in the process of completing a manuscript that you think might fit into the series, you are invited to contact them.

Nationalism and Minority Identities in Islamic Societies
Edited by Maya Shatzmiller

Nationalism and Minority Identities in Islamic Societies

Edited by
MAYA SHATZMILLER

McGill-Queen's University Press
Montreal & Kingston · London · Ithaca

© McGill-Queen's University Press 2005
ISBN 0-7735-2847-4 (cloth)
ISBN 0-7735-2848-2 (paper)

Legal deposit second quarter 2005
Bibliothèque nationale du Québec

Printed in Canada on acid-free paper

This book has been published with the help of a grant from the J.B. Smallman Publication Fund, Faculty of Social Science, The University of Western Ontario.

McGill-Queen's University Press acknowledges the support of the Canada Council for the Arts for our publishing program. We also acknowledge the financial support of the Government of Canada through the Book Publishing Industry Development Program (BPIDP) for our publishing activities.

Library and Archives Canada Cataloguing in Publication

Nationalism and minority identities in Islamic societies/edited by Maya Shatzmiller.

(Studies in nationalism and ethnic conflict; 1)
Includes bibliographical references and index.
ISBN 0-7735-2847-4 (bound)
ISBN 0-7735-2848-2 (pbk)

1. Minorities – Islamic countries. 2. Ethnicity – Islamic countries. 3. Ethnology – Islamic countries. I. Shatzmiller, Maya II. Title. III. Series

DS35.625.A1N38 2005   305.5'6'091767   C2004-905564-X

Typeset in Palatino 10/13
by Caractéra inc., Quebec City

Contents

Introduction   vii
MAYA SHATZMILLER

1 From *Dhimmis* to Minorities: Shifting Constructions of the non-Muslim Other from Early to Modern Islam   3
RICHARD C. MARTIN

2 Copts: Fully Egyptian, but for a Tattoo?   22
PIETERNELLA VAN DOORN-HARDER

3 The Egyptian Copts: Nationalism, Ethnicity, and Definition of Identity for a Religious Minority   58
CHARLES D. SMITH

4 The Sheep and the Goats? Christian Groups in Lebanon and Egypt in Comparative Perspective   85
PAUL S. ROWE

5 The Christians of Pakistan: The Interaction of Law and Caste in Maintaining "Outsider" Status   108
LINDA S. WALBRIDGE

6 The Baha'i Minority and Nationalism in Contemporary Iran   127
JUAN R.I. COLE

7 Royal Interest in Local Culture: Amazigh Identity and the Moroccan State 164
DAVID L. CRAWFORD

8 The Berbers in Algeria: Politicized Ethnicity and Ethnicized Politics 195
AZZEDINE LAYACHI

9 Kurdish Nationalism in Turkey 229
M. HAKAN YAVUZ

10 The Kurdish Minority Identity in Iraq 263
MICHAEL M. GUNTER

Conclusion 283
MAYA SHATZMILLER

Bibliographies 289
Contributors 317
Index 319

Introduction

Violent ethnic conflicts in the Middle East, North Africa, and Asia in recent years have drawn attention to an agonizing process of erosion of ethnic minorities' peaceful existence within Islamic societies, a peaceful existence that had previously been a constant feature of most of these societies. As nation building in Islamic societies moved away from the secular and Pan-Arab models of the early twentieth century and toward a variety of "nationalisms," it was accompanied by a growing antagonism between the Muslim majority in the national state and ethnic or religious minorities. National Islamic states operating with ideologies varying from individual state nationalism, as in Syria, Iraq, and Egypt, to secular state nationalism, as in Turkey, or with an Islamic nationalism, as in the Islamic Republic of Iran, have all reacted with hostility, and at times fury, toward minority expressions of separate ethnic or religious identities. Some have engaged in state-sponsored reprisals against such manifestations.

Historically, minority identities in Islamic societies had distinguished themselves from the Muslim majority by features such as culture, language, religion, personal and last names, literature, material culture, symbols and communal memory rather than by distinctive political roles or outlooks. In recent years, however, minority identities have been politicized and radicalized. Identifying the factors that determine whether a minority identity will remain only a cultural and/or an intellectual force or whether it will become politically mobilized when faced with a particular brand of state nationalism is crucial for understanding current conflicts and requires the development of criteria and models by which to measure, understand, and respond to the phenomenon of nationalist reactions to minority expressions.

The papers collected in this volume set out to examine religious and ethnic minorities living in Muslim-majority nation-states. Each case was selected for its potential to shed light on one essential question: What activates and shapes the formation of minority identities? The volume aims to demonstrate and define the distinctiveness of each minority group and, at the same time, to develop a set of factors for a common and larger comparative framework. Two categories of minority groups are of particular interest in the development of such a framework. The first category, in which the main distinguishing characteristic is religion, includes ancient religious minority groups, such as the Copts in Egypt, and more recent religious minorities formed during the nineteenth century or later, such as the Christians of Pakistan and the Baha'is of Iran. The second category consists of Muslim ethnic groups that are split between two or more territorial nation-states but that claim their own independent languages and cultural identities; these are the Berbers in Morocco and Algeria and the Kurds in Iraq and Turkey. The authors – anthropologists, historians, and political scientists – bring new insights to the discussion of minorities in Islamic societies, and their papers generate a vast body of scholarly knowledge relating to minority identities. The following brief review does not do justice to the wealth of the empirical evidence offered in each chapter but is nonetheless necessary for the sake of introduction.

Among the religious minorities, the factors dominating the process of minority-identity formation were not solely religion or church institutions but varied considerably. In the case of the Copts in Egypt, carefully analyzed by Pieternella van Doorn-Harder, although separate-identity formation was invigorated through such powerful means as religious education, the pastoral movement (headed by the energetic Pope Shenuda III), and the monastic revival, the conditions for identity formation and the process that triggered it could be attributed to a variety of catalysts. Van Doorn-Harder concludes that the prominence of church institutions in the fabrication of the new Copt identity was a reaction to the growing Islamic discourse emanating from the supposedly secular Egyptian state. Charles Smith reviews the historical involvement of the Coptic community in both Egyptian nationalism and Egypt's bureaucracy from the beginning of the British occupation of the country in 1882. Through a comparative analysis of the identity components of the Copts who remained in Egypt and of those who emigrated and lived in the diaspora, he suggests that the religious revival in Egypt was directed against the threat of secular modernity, not self-generated from within the church. Paul Rowe, also using a comparative approach, notes how the Lebanese Maronites, another Christian Arab group, are perceived as militant, while the Copts are seen as docile, and shows how in these groups the role of the church and the nature of political activity evolved differently in recent years. In his view, the emergence of the Coptic Church as the communal representative of the Copt community after the 1952 revolution in Egypt was in fact a revival of, or a return to, an old religio-political system, the Ottoman *millet* system, which, in its modern form, he terms a neomillet system. The reverse happened in Lebanon, where the ascendance of certain groups led to the eclipse of the organized church in favour of nondenominational parties.

A different set of factors affecting the role of religion in minority-identity formation is introduced through the study of the Christians in Pakistan and the Baha'is in Iran. In the case of the Christians of Pakistan, analyzed by Linda Walbridge, conversion to Christianity through missionary work among the untouchables in Pakistan created a Christian community perpetually locked into a low social and economic status. Walbridge calls attention to the importance of caste in this case: "Caste is used by the majority community to further marginalize this minority." Even Christian churches elsewhere on the Indian subcontinent have tried to distance themselves from the poor Christians in Pakistan. Pakistani Muslims tend to view the Christians' poverty and low social standing as disqualifying them from full citizenship, and the government of Pakistan prevents them from participating in political life by enacting discriminatory electoral laws. As a result of the Pakistani Parliament's enacting the Islamic law of blasphemy, Christians in Pakistan have been forced to live a life that some critics have called "modern-day martyrdom." In the Baha'i case, separate identity was inspired both by the particular religious nature of the group and by the majority's standpoint on the Baha'i place within the Iranian nation-state. Under both the previous Iranian regime and the current Iranian Shi'ite state, the message of exclusion was dominant. As Juan Cole argues in his chapter, under the shah's regime, the Iranian secular nationalists viewed the Baha'is as a source of disunity, while the universalist view of the Baha'i religion regarded state nationalism with suspicion. The Khomeini regime's ascension to power "shifted the official basis for identity in Iran from nation to Islam," and the Shi'ite religious nationalists viewed the Baha'is as heretics. However, a political factor was added to the religious one when the Baha'is were identified as a foreign body supporting and being supported by colonial forces. Exclusion also took place when the Iranian state enacted secular measures, as these prevented the Baha'is from participating in and benefiting from state institutions, social programs, education, and economic activities.

Among the Berbers and the Kurds, the identity-formation process has involved strong claims for minority cultural and linguistic autonomy as well as the incorporation of secular ideologies, both of which place them on par with European cases. What unites all the cases in this group is how the adamant hostility of the modern Islamic nation-state toward any manifestation of minority identity has influenced identity formation. Factors ranging from the suppression of both the Berbers' and the Kurds' cultural distinctiveness to the all-out war against the Turkish Kurds strongly support the argument that, just as religious-minority identity cannot be separated from what is happening on the Islamic side and in the Islamist revivalist movement, so are the identities of Muslim ethnic minorities linked to the reaction of the secular state to their claims. The two "Berber" chapters complement each other by using different paradigms to explore the specifics of the Berber question. David Crawford discusses the language question in detail since this is more central to the Moroccan situation, while Azzedine Layachi focuses on political conditions, as the Algerian movement has politicized and radicalized to a greater degree.

Because of these differences, the Moroccan case is an outstanding exception in this context. David Crawford uses the Royal Decree of 2001, which created an academic institution to study the Berber language and to implement its instruction in the classroom, to argue that the Moroccan government actually engages in a process of inclusion by legitimizing the Berber language and culture and by incorporating it into Moroccan nationalistic discourse rather than seeing in it an element of discord that threatens to antagonize and disrupt the national identity, as in Algeria. The singularity of the Moroccan Berber case does not end here. Berber identity in Morocco is historical, structural, and linguistic, yet none of these factors in themselves are unified or unifying. The Berber language, being divided into three dialects, is certainly not unified; regional diversity among Berbers is clearly seen in the Berber community's political structures; and the historical record shows considerable conversion from Arab to Berber and vice versa. Yet all three factors are commonly used to define Berber minority identity. Rural poverty is a unifying factor for Berbers, being the dominant fact of life among the Berber population. Moroccan Berber identity, therefore, could turn political if poor Berbers opted to use their identity as a means of mobilizing behind an economic platform. "The poorest Imazighen [Berbers] are likely to be the ones educated in the new Tamazight [Berber] language curriculum," Crawford says, and they might well choose it as a tool to claim social and economic redress. In his analysis of the Algerian situation, Azzedine Layachi agrees with Crawford's point about the link between ethnicity and economic conditions and with others' comments about authoritarianism and weak elite cohesiveness, but Layachi also points to major differences between the Berber identities in Morocco and Algeria.

The Algerian case has a strong historical component because some Algerian Berbers (mostly those concentrated in the Kabylie region), as participants in the Algerian national movement fighting for independence from France, have in the past attempted to express the particular nature of their identity from within Algerian society. However, neither then nor now have they been able either to incorporate Berber identity into the Arab Islamic context claimed as the national ideology by their previous comrades at arms or to convince themselves of the justification for abandoning their own culture in favour of the state ideology. During the last ten years, the confrontational component of Berber identity in Algeria has driven the Berber community into an open clash with the Algerian state, although as Layachi points out, the Kabylie Berbers provided both the zealots for the Islamist fundamentalist movement and the most secular supporters of the protagonists for Berber cultural identity. The emergence in Algeria of a Berber movement that is in open defiance of the state is no different in essence from the emergence of a militant Islamic movement there since both are responses to a general decline in the Algerian citizenry's social, economic, and political power. Layachi argues that the two movements are intrinsically similar despite pushing in opposite directions: "The Islamists favour a quasi-hegemonic order characterized by strict Islamic rule and Arab identity, while the Berber movement seeks an essentially secular order in which the Berber language shares preeminence with Arabic." What they share is the fight against the authoritarian nature of their state and the economic deprivation that has been their lot.

The modern process of identity formation, which is markedly shaped by the nation-state and its handling of minority identity, increasingly involves the process by which cultural identity converts itself into a political organism. No group demonstrates this better than the Kurds of Turkey and Iraq, where the process is also shaped by outside intervention, whether through direct international involvement or through European secular ideologies. Even though the political order in the region is no longer inspired by secular nationalism borrowed from nineteenth-century Europe, it is manifestly the secular nature of the host countries, Turkey and Iraq, both of which have allowed the proliferation of ideologies such as socialism and communism, that has made the minority identity of the Kurds unique. Iraqi Kurds and Turkish Kurds, moreover, have been affected by outside intervention – by US military intervention in the case of the Iraqi Kurds and by political pressure from the European Union in the case of the Turkish Kurds. The Iraqi Kurds have progressed from separate identity to virtual statehood, crowning the process by achieving a "de facto" Kurdistan state in Northern Iraq. Their future statehood is far from certain, however, as Michael Gunter shows, because inclusion rather than exclusion, federation rather than independence, are also components of the Kurdish articulation of their nationalist aspirations.

Several authors refer to theory as they try to address the quest for a common ground in which to integrate their work, but it is Richard Martin's analysis that most explicitly demonstrates why neither Islamic nor Western scholarship has been able to develop a unified theoretical model for minority identity, whether of an ethnic or religious nature. Placed at the beginning of this volume, Martin's chapter acts as a framework for the rest by providing a historical and current context for the questions dealt with in the other chapters. Martin's framework is based on the theological and legal classifications that developed in the first centuries of Islam, which the modern discourse of the minority groups discussed in the individual chapters reflects.

The importance of establishing this framework is fully apparent when we realize how its usage dominates the minorities' discussion of status in Islamic states – in strong contrast to modern Western scholarship, which, as Martin notes, "thinks and argues in quite different terms." Hence the conflict between Islam's basic teachings about minorities and the major international agreements regarding human rights, which regularly fail to gain a foothold within Muslim states. Martin's chapter also draws attention to the dichotomy, not often mentioned, between the social realities of religious, ethnic, and national minorities and the theoretical or empirical studies of Western scholarship. He quotes recent modern theories dealing with minorities (Islamic and other) that have taken a comparative approach but that give precedence to the work of historians of religion who look at "how intellectuals and ordinary religious communities of religious persons negotiate the tension and sometimes conflict between normative and actual behaviour." Such an approach makes it possible to distinguish between Muslim thinkers who live in religiously pluralistic societies in North America and Europe, whose discourse about identify allows them to be optimistic, and those locked in "the rigid framework of *shari'ah*-minded discourse." Martin demonstrates why, given the multiplicity of paradigms, it is impossible for Islamic societies, even using the traditional Islamic laws, to develop a unified approach. I recommend rereading Martin's chapter again once you have read the whole book. His reflections and insights will be even more appreciated.

The essays collected in this volume were written for a conference held at the University of Western Ontario on 8–9 December 2001 to discuss current research and to analyze recent developments in the field of ethnicity in Islamic societies.

Many colleagues at Western contributed to the success of the conference: Professors Sid Noel and Richard Vernon of the Nationalism and Ethnic Conflict Research Group; Professors Clive Seligman, Brock Millman, and Tozun Bahcheli, who served as session chairs; and Professors Peter Neary and Ben Forester, who made financial and personal contributions. Their help is gratefully recognized.

During the past year, we have lost one of our contributors, Dr Linda Walbridge, to cancer. This volume is dedicated to her memory.

Maya Shatzmiller

NATIONALISM AND MINORITY IDENTITIES IN ISLAMIC SOCIETIES

1

From *Dhimmis* to Minorities: Shifting Constructions of the non-Muslim Other from Early to Modern Islam

RICHARD C. MARTIN

This chapter sets out to do two things. It explores in a general way the basic teachings of Islam about minorities, especially as these teachings and the social ethos they engendered developed in the early and medieval periods. It also looks briefly at scholarly work done on minorities in the Middle East and elsewhere in the Muslim world, and it discusses some of the theoretical approaches found in earlier work. By "minority," I mean both minority groups within Islamic socio-political contexts as well as Muslims living as minorities in non-Muslim states and socio-cultural contexts. In both cases, the *shari'a*, or Islamic law, places certain rights and obligations on Muslims in relation to the "other." Against this background, subsequent contributions to this volume will examine the themes of nationalism and Muslim minorities in particular parts of the Muslim world, with an eye toward establishing a deeper understanding of particular social and political cases of Muslims and minorities in the modern period.

In Islam, religion is theoretically the sole legitimate basis for defining minority status; thus minority status is defined by Islamic law. In theory, Islamic jurisprudence provides no ethnic, racial, national, tribal (kinship), gendered, or numerical basis for determining minority status in society. *Islam*, "submitting to the will of Allah," or rather *not* submitting to the divine will as set forth in the Qur'an and the Sunna of the Prophet, provided the main ground for identifying most minorities living within lands under Islamic rule and jurisdiction.

Muslims – usually, but not always, Sunni Muslims – constituted the legal majority in lands under Islamic rule. This was more or less the case from the time of Rashidun caliphs of the mid-seventh century until the collapse of the Gunpowder Empires (Ottoman, Safavid, and Moghul) under the impact of European expansion and colonialism in the eighteenth century. This sweeping historical generalization, it must be admitted, knows many exceptions. For example, in early and medieval Islam, ethnic and tribal identities provided grounds for treating non-Arab converts to Islam differently.[1] Nonetheless, Muslim intellectuals cast early and medieval Islamic discourse about minorities in theological and legal terms.

Why was this the case? Why was a precise conceptual and differentiating language about minorities and specific categories of friends and foes of Islam a necessary and compelling discourse among the successors of the Prophet Muhammad: those companions during his lifetime who led his community during the first generation after his death? A major reason was the rapid expansion of Islamic rule, which necessitated classifying dissidents and enemies, as well as non-Muslims who accepted Arab rule either willingly or willy-nilly, and determining the degrees of threat they posed. In the early Islamic worldview during this period, the known world was divided into *dar al-islam* (the abode of Islam; i.e., lands under Islamic rule) and *dar al-harb* (the abode of war; i.e., lands actually or potentially in conflict with Muslim rulers and their subjects). Within Dar al-Islam, a diversity of religious communities and worldviews was able to continue to thrive, including those of various Christian and Jewish communities, as well as those of Sabi'ans, Mandaeans, Manichaeans, Mazdaeans, tribal polytheists, and others. The classification of these non-Muslim religious communities became the theological basis for conceptualizing the "other."

According to the Qur'an, the most seriously rejected category was Pagan polytheism: the predominant cluster of religious worldviews in Arabia at the time of the Prophet Muhammad. The polytheists were charged with *shirk*, associating other deities with the one God, Allah. The *mushrikun*, as these tribal polytheists were called, were regarded as God's most serious rejecters and enemies, and they were allowed no theological tolerance or sanctuary in Dar al-Islam. In theory, the *mushrikun* were to be invited to accept Islam, and if they refused, they could be coerced, enslaved, or even killed. In the modern world, *shirk* is no longer a label for a definable religious minority, but it has taken on the significance of anti-Islamic and antireligious worldviews, such as secularism.

A second important classification of minorities included non-Muslims who nonetheless had divinely revealed scriptures, or *ahl al-kitab*, known as People of the Book. This category was also Qur'anic, and in its earliest application, "People of the Book" referred to Christians, Jews, and curiously, the Sabi'ans of Harran.[2] This was a significant minority in early Islamic religious, political, and cultural life. Jurists discussed the problem of the relationship of the People of the Book to the Islamic state under the concept of *dhimma*, or "protected," status. People of the Book (for the most part Christians and Jews, but also Zoroastrians and others in later periods) were also to be invited to accept Islam, but Islamic law offered the alternative of *dhimmi* status – that is, remaining within one's own religious community both physically and under its laws and regulations.

The Qur'an and the biographies of the Prophet record him as sympathetic to the Jews of Arabia during the Meccan period. After the Hijra,[3] however, relations with the Jewish tribes of Medina were spoiled by accusations of their deception and collaboration with Muhammad's Meccan enemies. Eventually, the Jews were forced out of Medina. The relationship between the Muslims and their non-Muslim subjects soon required greater diplomacy and social stability in the early decades of expansion and state formation. *Dhimmi* status received its first application as a result of a text known as the Pact of 'Umar, 'Umar being a companion of the Prophet Muhammad and military commander who served as the second caliph (634–44) in the Rashidun period.[4] Later refinement in Islamic law of these earlier practices became the basis centuries later of the celebrated *millet* system of legally defined and protected religious minorities within the Ottoman Empire during the late Middle Ages.

Qadis, or judges, granted *dhimmi* status to religious scripturaries, or Ahl al-Kitab (known as *kitabis* in legal discourse), living within Dar al-Islam. *Dhimmis* were granted independence in the practice and maintenance of their own religious and social affairs so long as they did not impinge upon Muslims.[5] In exchange for official tolerance and legal recognition under the law, all male, free, and sane *dhimmis* were required to pay a poll tax *(jizya)*, and those who were land and property owners were also obligated to pay the tax known as *kharaj*. Another group of non-Muslims, in this case from outside of Islamic lands, in what was legally termed Dar al-Harb (lands potentially and often actually in conflict with Muslim rulers), became known as *harbis:* unsubjugated non-Muslims against whom, in principle, Muslim rulers could make war. If, on the other hand, a *harbi* applied to the ruler for writ of safe passage, known as an *aman*, whether as an individual or as an entire community, he became a *musta'min* (one seeking or qualifying for safe passage). The *aman* allowed *harbis* to conduct business within lands under Muslim rule. A *musta'min*, like a *dhimmi,* belonged to an "intermediate category" between believers *(mu'minun)* and unbelievers *(kuffar)* in the normative Islamic legal discourse about the "other."

A third category of social and religious discrimination in early Islam was converts to Islam, known in the early days of Islam as the *mawali* (sing. *mawla*), or clients of Arab Muslim tribes. That most of the earliest converts of the Rashidun (632–61) and Umayyad (661–750) periods were not Arabs, linguistically or culturally, often made them appear to be awkward and thus not true insiders in the practice of Islam and in properly reciting the Qur'an and other Arabic religious formulas. Examples of African American converts to Islam being perceived as "different" among Muslim emigrants from the Arab world and South Asia will be mentioned below.

A fourth important foundation for the discrimination of minorities in Islam is sectarianism, which began during the Rashidun era of Muhammad's closest companions and led to civil wars and the Sunni/Shi'i separation. In fact, several lasting sectarian differences developed during the first generations of Muslims, and these had theological as well as political significance. The Kharijites and Murji'ites are well known to students of early Islamic history.[6] The name of the former sect, known in English as "Seceders," in modern times has been used for hard-line Islamists who reject governments in Islamic lands that do not govern according to the *shari'a*. The Kharijites seceded from the partisans *(shi'a)* of 'Ali, Muhammad's cousin and son-in-law. 'Ali was ultimately unsuccessful in gaining universal recognition as caliph. Political legitimacy at the end of the Rashidun period was retained by the Arabs but was now established outside the House of Muhammad. 'Ali's followers were to continue to claim that political and religious legitimacy derived from being descendants of Muhammad's family, and although they were persecuted, they grew and were reckoned with in several ways as a minority that, by the end of the first half-century of Islam (681), had become permanently ensconced within Dar al-Islam.[7] Their existence required that caliphs, governors, judges *(qadis)*, jurists, theologians, and heresiographers attempt not only to define what made the Shi'a different, but also to limit their influence and the violence that was often directed against them. The major branches of the Shi'a have roots in the political conflicts and theological debates of early and medieval Islam. These branches are known today as the Ithna-'Ashara (or Twelver), the Isma'ili (or Sevener), and the Zaydi (or Fiver).

In summary, the determinants of an Islamic vocabulary and concept of minorities were: (1) the contentious power politics of early Islamic expansion; (2) the religious identities that this highlighted and created; (3) such ethnic issues as the significance of Arab identity in claiming privileges in the Islamic social order; and (4) the message of scripture and the direction given to the Muslim community by the Prophet Muhammad. The textual record of modern discourses about Kurds, Armenians, 'Alawites, Baha'is, Hindus, Christians, Jews, and the Shi'a, among others, reflect the theological and legal classifications that developed in the first centuries of Islam. This language and these conceptions served two objectives that may seem at cross purposes but that, in fact, generally interacted symbiotically in maintaining a dynamic but stable social order. They helped to differentiate the true insiders from those who had less or no access to power. They also related the differentiated social and religious entities to a larger conception of state *(dawla)* and power *(sulta)* that the sovereign authority of the Muslim state had to manage. My use of the term "Islam," which in the political sense must now include non-Muslims living under Muslim rule as minorities, requires some definition and qualification, as Bernard Lewis and Marshall Hodgson have argued.

"ISLAM" DEFINED AND QUALIFIED

What, then, do we mean by terms like "Islam" and "Islamic" when analyzing the relationship of Islam to minorities? In a short but useful study of colour and race in Islam, Bernard Lewis warns that important distinctions must be kept in mind when applying the term "Islam" to a thematic study, such as the present work:

The word Islam is used with at least three different meanings, and much misunderstanding can arise from the failure to distinguish between them. In the first place, Islam means the religion taught by the prophet Muhammad and embodied in the Muslim revelation known as the Qur'an. In the second place, Islam is the subsequent development of this religion through tradition and through the work of the great Muslim jurists and theologians ... In the third meaning, Islam ... means not what Muslims believed or were expected to believe but what they actually did – in other words Islamic civilization as known to us in history.[8]

My discussion in this chapter presumes the first two meanings: those enunciated in the sacred words of the Qur'an and the Sunna and those adumbrated in the arguments and interpretations of jurists and theologians. Nonetheless, it has been and will continue to be useful to refer to the historical, political, and social realities that brought the problem of minorities in Islam into local discussion. An example of the problem Lewis alluded to, especially when it is approached across national, cultural, and religious boundaries, was witnessed by this author a few years ago.

In the early 1990s, the United States Information Agency asked the Binational Fulbright Commission in Egypt to organize a conference of American and Arab Muslim scholars to discuss religion in the United States and in the Arab Muslim world.[9] This was in the immediate aftermath of the 1991 Gulf War and was not unrelated to Washington's recognition that the United States government had a serious image problem in the Muslim world. One of the themes of the conference (which was meant to take place in Egypt in the spring of 1992 but was finally convened in Salzburg, Austria, in the summer of 1993 for security reasons) was the relation of the dominant religious traditions in America and in the Arab Muslim world to religious minorities. One American and three Arab scholars from the much larger Muslim delegation presented papers on religious minorities. The three Muslim scholars interpreted the problem as a normative one, reflecting the first two meanings of Islam distinguished by Lewis. Each made strong cases from Qur'anic, Sunna, and Islamic jurisprudence, arguing that in Islamic social theory there are no race or colour distinctions and that most religious minorities were in principle well protected and, indeed, liberated by *dhimmi* status under Islamic rule, especially in premodern (i.e., precolonial) times, when, in their view, Islamic law, or the *shari'a*, was in force in the great Muslim empires.

Prof. Albert Raboteau of Princeton University presented a paper on the history of religious minorities in America. Although not an

Islamicist, Raboteau, a historian of religion, was chosen to speak on this issue because of his work on the history of ethnic and religious minorities in America. His presentation focused on the two minorities in America to which he in fact belonged: African American and Roman Catholic. He began by briefly recalling the history of white Protestant dominance in social and political life in America and what it was like to live in America, as a member of a minority group, outside of this framework. He spoke in both personal and theoretical terms about the effects of racial and religious minority status, in contrast to the Constitutional idealism of the moral and legal equality of all human beings. He gave brief historical accounts of how black Protestant churches and Roman Catholics were dominated and discriminated against yet noted how they found ways to subvert white Protestants' political, social, and economic dominance in order to establish their own American identity and pockets of power within the establishment.

In the discussion that followed Raboteau's presentation, some of the Muslim scholars claimed that in fact the *dhimmi* system described earlier had worked well for non-Muslim minorities. Eventually, however, a North African Arab scholar spoke up and said something like the following to Raboteau: Your analysis of religious minorities in America is admirably candid, and it highlights problems that lie beneath the surface of democratic idealism. However, most of us are not yet ready to see non-Muslim minority status as a problem in Muslim societies, even though privately we recognize that problems exist and that these create social inequities and injustices for minorities living in predominantly Muslim societies, like those of Islamic states in North Africa.

An additional point bears upon the discussions in this volume: Whereas Muslim intellectuals and moralists have traditionally approached the problem of the Muslim majority in relation to non-Muslim minorities in legal and theological categories, modern Western scholarship thinks and argues in quite different terms. With respect to theory, social scientists have done the most work on the study of minorities. Historians have done considerable documentary research as well. With respect to moral and legal considerations, scholarship has been based on the history of the implementation of international accords and instruments. These include the UN Charter of 1945, the Universal Declaration of Human Rights in the UN in 1948, and the Declaration on the Elimination of Intolerance and Discrimination

Based on Religion or Belief, adopted by the UN General Assembly in 1981. The conflict between traditional Islamic theological categories and modern frameworks for analyzing and judging human rights has been the topic of several books, articles, and conferences by Prof. Abdullahi an-Na'im, an international human-rights lawyer and professor at Emory University.[10] An-Na'im argues that Muslims and other non-Western peoples must live under universal instruments of human rights but insists, nonetheless, that Muslims and others must be able to base the warrants for human rights on their own scriptures and traditional value systems.

MINORITIES AND ISLAM IN MODERN THEORY

In an early study entitled *Minorities in the Arab World*, Albert Hourani raised but did not discuss a philosophical problem that has baffled social scientists for several decades and has generated disparate theories: "Why are there so many religious and linguistic minorities in these [Arab] countries?" He goes on to say: "To answer this question fully would involve raising profound metaphysical issues: the cause, nature and necessity of man's diversity." He then turns to what he calls the "more superficial of 'historical explanations,'"[11] which include such factors as the fecundity of the Arabian Peninsula and the lands surrounding it. Hourani refers specifically to the rise of monotheistic and prophetic religions, the Middle East as a terminus for migrations of peoples from Asia and Africa, the divisiveness and tribalism that these religious ideas and movements of peoples generated, and the tendency toward local loyalties and identities among these different groups in the Arab world.

As a consequence of viewing the social data more broadly than in terms of religious categories as such, Hourani found thirty-one minority groups in the Middle East. Written in the late 1940s and published in 1947, on the eve of the formation of the state of Israel, Hourani's study gave to the term "minority" a broad definition. It included Sunni Muslims who do not speak Arabic (e.g., Kurds), Arabic speakers who are not Sunni Muslims (e.g., Muslim groups like the Shi'a and 'Alawis), Christians of various denominations, Jews, other religious groups (such as Yazidis and Mandaeans), and a variety of communities comprised of persons who are neither Arabic-speaking nor Sunni Muslims.[12] In Hourani's taxonomy of minorities, language was as important as religion and ethnicity and more important than nationality in determining minority identity.

In the more than half a century since Hourani's attempt to classify and catalogue the minorities living in the Middle East, more scholars have turned their attention to some of the same problems he identified. More recent scholarship has brought the tools of the social sciences to bear on analysis of the growing amount of data on these minorities and of the expanding conditions of conflict among minorities in the Middle East and elsewhere in the lands to which Islam spread. Social scientists apply comparative methods to the study of Islam and minorities based on theories about minority-group formation and about social identity more generally. This has the important effect of deconstructing Islam per se as the sole or most essential variable in the study of minorities in Muslim societies. In the introduction to a recent collection of essays on minorities and the state in the Arab world, Ofra Bengio and Gabriel Ben-Dor summarized the main theoretical approaches to the study of minorities. The older "economic and rational" school, going back to Karl Marx and Emile Durkheim, believed that economic development inevitably created larger communities at the expense of smaller, more exclusive ones, which eventually and necessarily would be integrated into modern capitalist social economies. In the 1960s and 1970s, "modernization" theory argued that the rise of literacy, communication, technology, and mass participation in the political process would create new opportunities for minority groups and thus diminish the need for traditional minority identities. Other theorists saw more conflicted outcomes of modernization, such as dislocation and challenges to premodern traditional authority as well as an increased tendency among "minorities" in the modernization process to escape into stronger ethnic and religious identities.[13] The prevailing view of the Fundamentalism Project, led by Martin E. Marty and Scott Appleby, is based on this "modernization-conflictual approach" to explaining fundamentalism, whose adherents are often considered a category of religious minorities in the contemporary world. According to this theory, all religious fundamentalists, including Muslims, are reacting against modernism and secularization.[14] "Without modernity," wrote Bruce Lawrence, also a proponent of the modernization-conflictual approach, "there are no fundamentalists, just as there are no modernists." He continues: "The identity of fundamentalism, both as a psychological mind set and a historical movement, is shaped by the modern world. Fundamentalists seem bifurcated between their cause and their outcome; they are at once the consequence of modernity and the antithesis of modernism."[15]

Bengio and Ben-Dor argue that more recent scholarship has returned to another theory that emerged in the 1960s, which they call the "primordial, or authentic ethnic," approach. The concept of primordialism had been introduced by Clifford Geertz. In his 1963 essay entitled "The Integrative Revolution," Geertz argued that under the impact of political upheaval and the breakdown of traditional society, people turn to the most primordial ties that establish identity and provide security, namely ethnic ties. Ethnic ties are real and less susceptible to manipulation by national leaders and outsiders than, say, modern civic or national ties.[16] Geertz elaborates:

By a primordial attachment is meant one that stems from the "givens" – or, more precisely, as culture is inevitably involved in such matters, the assumed "givens" – of social existence: immediate contiguity and kin connection mainly, but beyond them the givenness that stems from being born into a particular religious community, speaking a particular language, or even a dialect of a language, and following particular social practices. These congruities of blood, speech, custom, and so on, are seen to have an ineffable, and at times overpowering, coerciveness in and of themselves ... the result not merely of personal affection, practical necessity, common interest, or incurred obligation, but at least in great part by virtue of some unaccountable absolute import attributed to the very tie itself.[17]

Bengio and Ben-Dor remind us that even though one is less able to overcome ethnic than nonprimordial identities, "ethnic groups themselves 'are constantly created and recreated anew. In establishing the political boundaries of Asia and Africa, for example, colonial powers redefined the size and the scope of the ethnic groups: as old groups disappeared, new ones emerged, while others simply merged and split.'"[18]

A recent summary of minority studies more generally has been published by Arnold M. Rose in the third and latest edition of the *International Encyclopedia of the Social and Behavioral Sciences*. Because Rose incorporates both social and cultural considerations, the following is broadly representative of most definitions. A minority, Rose writes, "is a group of people, differentiated from others in the same society by race, nationality, religion, or language, who both think of themselves as a differentiated group and are thought by others as a differentiated group with negative connotations."[19] Minority status within a society is not necessarily determined by relative size; indeed, it is a common mistake to think of minorities always as small groups differentiated within larger groups. Relative size of the minority to the host or predominant society is less important than determining what ideas and convictions cause the differentiation and social fact of minority status. Another way of putting this is that minority social groups are not "naturally" or inevitably differentiated. Variables such as political and cultural factors play analyzable roles in determining the minority status of groups. For example, with respect to the issue of relative numbers, blacks in many parts of the American South outnumber whites and have done so for over a century. Thus a minority, as in the case of blacks in the South, may form a numerical majority of the population that is dominated by a white minority. In this case, dominance rather than numerical superiority differentiates whites from blacks.

The point about relative size and considerations of dominance and power applies to early Islamic history as well. Richard Bulliet estimates that it took three to four centuries for Muslims to outnumber non-Muslims in most lands under Muslim rule.[20] During the Umayyad caliphate (661–750), Arab Muslims were clearly in the numerical minority, at first even in Syria, but they nonetheless quickly became politically and militarily dominant. Nevertheless, for nearly a century, they were able to dominate Christian, Jewish, and other religious and non-Arab groups living under their rule. However, cultural dominance was neither achieved nor even sought by Arab Muslims for several generations, except in the militia staging areas, or camp towns *(amsar)*, to which the Arab Muslims restricted themselves and to which some converts migrated. Urban rule in Syria, Iraq, and Iran depended heavily in the first century of Islam upon the literati and other bureaucrats writing in Greek, Persian, and other Imperial languages. It was not until the caliphate of 'Abd al-Malik b. Marwan (685–705) that Arabic began to replace Greek, Syriac, and Persian in the scribal chanceries of the Umayyad caliphate. A century and a half after 'Abd al-Malik's language reforms in Damascus, the secular Shu'ubiyya literary controversies under the new rule of the Abbasids in Iraq and the writings of al-Jahiz (d. circa 868) offered a rich indication of the culture wars among Arabs, Persians, and others as both Muslim and non-Arab populations continued to increase within the total population of lands under effective Muslim rule.[21]

Within the context of more general theoretical considerations, to which I now return, *minority status* often involves some form of exclusion from the dominant society or assignment to a lower status in one or more of four areas of life: (1) economic, (2) political, (3) legal, and/or (4) social-associational. *Dominance*, on the other hand, is based on (1) power, which enables the dominant group(s) to exploit the minority; (2) ideology, which rationalizes the claims that the dominant group has a monopoly over the minority (for example, Hindus over Muslims in India); and (3) racism, which argues for biological superiority.

Minorities often play a role in the social change of the larger society. For example, they may serve as an irritant that provokes social change, and they may provoke or be provoked into clashes with the dominant culture, causing social dissatisfaction and unrest. Research on minorities in the social sciences has been conducted within two main frameworks. *Ethological and ethnographic* research has focused on the social and cultural description of minority groups, while *sociological* research has dealt more with the relationship of majority or dominant groups to minority groups than with their cultural characteristics. These frameworks of research are not mutually exclusive, however. Historians of religion tend to draw on both kinds of research. In religious studies in particular, the *tension* between legal and theological constructions of minority status and actual social patterns of dominance and minority behaviour is of particularly interest. Historians of religion are generally interested in how intellectuals and ordinary communities of religious persons negotiate the tension and sometimes conflict between normative and actual behaviour, between worldviews and the social ethos. It is very often in the interstices of what ought to be and what actually is, nourished by hermeneutics, that religious communities – majoritarian or not – are able to effect and survive historical change. The dialogue between traditional ideas about minorities in Islamic law and the norms of modern international accords for the human rights of minorities can be seen as occurring between two value systems with overlapping moral concerns and areas of conflict. Both systems are challenged by the social realities of religious, ethnic, and national minorities.

MUSLIMS AS MINORITIES

I turn now to a consideration of Islamic views of Muslims living outside of Dar al-Islam – that is, Muslims living as minorities among non-Muslims.[22] This condition already existed in the time of the

Prophet, when a group of Muslims were sent to live under the protection of the Christian negus of Ethiopia to escape Meccan persecution of the nascent religion. It continues to apply to Muslims today around the world in such disparate regions as Southern Africa, Central Asia, North America, and Europe. Indeed, Muslim minorities living as diaspora communities in Europe, North America, South Africa, and elsewhere are almost inevitably thrown into conflict with the dominant, non-Muslim culture.

The Qur'an itself does not actually stipulate that Muslims must live within Islamic territory. The familiar language of Dar al-Islam, Dar al-Harb, and Dar al-Sulh (lands under treaty with Muslim rulers), to which I referred earlier in this chapter, developed later in the discussions of the early jurists, especially in the context of the problem of converting Dar al-Harb into Dar al-Islam through *jihad*. The Qur'an more significantly stresses that under certain conditions Muslims should migrate *(hijra)* to non-Muslim territory; in the paradigmatic case it was to join the Prophet in Medina after the Hijra.[23] Those who emigrate, or *muhajirun*, are valued over those who do not in such cases. As Khaled Abou El Fadl points out, however, it is not clear whether such verses establish a general principle that Muslims should move from lands under Islamic rule to lands governed by non-Muslims.[24] The Qur'an does require Muslims to stay out of or to leave non-Muslim lands under oppression. A passage in the Qur'an (4:79–100) echoes others by giving eschatological import to the requirement to emigrate: "As for those whose souls are taken by the angels (at death) while in a state of injustice against themselves, they will be asked by the angels: 'What state were you in?' They will answer: 'We were oppressed in the land.' And the angels will say: 'Was God's earth not large enough for you to migrate?' Whoever migrates in the cause of God will find many places of refuge and abundance on the earth." Indeed, oppression *(zulm)* that prevents Muslims from practicing their religion could happen even in Muslim territories, and under those conditions Muslims were enjoined to move to non-Muslim countries where they were free to practice their faith.[25] Moreover, some later jurists and theologians saw, in Muslims living as minorities in Dar al-Harb, an opportunity for *da'wa*: dissemination of the Muslim religion in order to bring converts to Islam.

Living in non-Muslim lands is a problem discussed in the Hadith literature, which comprises the oral teachings of the Prophet, although contradictory guidance can typically be adduced in the Hadith in support of divergent legal opinions. Some Hadith teachings forbid Muslims to live among unbelievers, and a few such teachings go on to require that such Muslims migrate to Muslim lands, an obligation that is said to be in force until Judgment Day. Abou El Fadl cites early authorities who note that the duty to migrate "ended with the conquest of Mecca and [who] argue that it is better to live under a ruler who is just (though not a Muslim) than a Muslim ruler who is unjust."[26] In fact, fleeing from unjust Muslim rule was justified because the chief legal argument in early and medieval Islam for emigrating to non-Muslim lands was the need to escape Muslim tyrants. Among the earliest examples of Muslims so forced to choose minority status in a foreign land to escape injustice occurred in the Umayyad period, when Muslims fled to the Malabar Coast of India to escape the wrath of al-Hajjaj b. Yusuf.[27]

The early jurists of the four Sunni and three Shi'i law schools did not have much to say about the permissibility of Muslims living in non-Muslim lands. Rather, some of the founders of the traditional schools of legal interpretation *(madhahib)* and their followers seem to have presumed that a Muslim living in Dar al-Harb was required to migrate to Dar al-Islam. This position was reportedly held by Malik b. Anas (d. 796).[28] Hanafi jurists, as is often the case, provided the exception. The early Hanafi jurists permitted travel to non-Muslim lands for the purposes of trade or diplomacy. Although Abu Hanifa (d. 768) is reported to have ruled that Muslims should not seek permanent residence in non-Muslim lands, his follower, al-Shaybani (d. 804), held that this requirement had been abrogated in the time of the Prophet.[29] Abou El Fadl observes that, in the absence of actual cases to rule on, the literature nonetheless records debates on the hypothetical case of a Muslim who has converted to Islam in a non-Muslim land: The question was whether such a person was under obligation to migrate to an Islamic land?[30] Actual case studies appear in the legal discussions after around 1050 C.E.

As time passed and as more and more Muslims came to live under non-Muslim governments, the requirement to migrate to a Muslim land lapsed, although the practical problems of practising Islam without the protection of Islamic law and a Muslim ruler continued to worry Muslim jurists. It was not until the twelfth century that trends within the major schools of legal interpretation solidified into firm positions. This was probably because by now many lands conquered by the Umayyads and Abbasids had fallen to non-Muslim armies and rulers, thus leaving a large number of Muslims under non-Muslim rule. Differences among the schools and jurists hardened. For example, the Maliki grandfather of the philosopher Ibn Rushd (Averroes), Abu l-Walid ibn Rush (d. 1122), held that Muslims who lost territory to Christian armies and rulers in the Iberian Peninsula should immediately migrate to Muslim territory; any Muslim who did not was to be suspected of immorality and corruption. Other Maliki jurists were only slightly more lenient. Later Hanbali and Shi'i jurists, on the other hand, argued that if a Muslim in a non-Muslim land were able to meet the ritual requirements of the Muslim faith, he was not required to emigrate. In the Eastern Islamic lands, which were partially overrun by Christians beginning in the eleventh century and by the Mongols in the thirteenth century, Hanafi jurists ruled that lands conquered by Mongols or Christians remained Muslim "so long as Muslims are allowed to practice their religion."[31] The Shafi'is, too, in the late Middle Ages held that Muslim territory lost to non-Muslim conquers, for legal purposes, became non-Muslim in appearance only. Legally, such lands remained Islamic, and Muslims were allowed to emigrate only for their own safety.

This brief and partial survey of legal discourse about Muslims living as minorities in non-Muslim lands yields two important conclusions. First, theological differences accounted for some of the differences among law schools, especially with regard to the leniency or stringency of the requirement to emigrate. Second, historical change and local political conditions also produced new interpretations, even within the same schools. Nonetheless, as supported by premodern legal and historical texts, a high degree of concern existed in predominantly Islamic societies about Muslims living as minorities beyond the reaches of Islamic governance. On the whole, practical considerations of the safety and prosperity of Muslim minorities who were able to practise their religion often determined how the laws were interpreted and applied. Basically, *fiqh,* or "legal reasoning," on the issue of Muslim minorities evolved from an early requirement that Muslims must emigrate to Dar al-Islam to more practical determinations of how to live Muslim lives in non-Muslim lands when necessary.

MUSLIMS IN AMERICA

Muslims living in Europe and America provide a contemporary and extended case of the legal and theological questions raised by

Muslims living under non-Muslim rule. If this is the case, then one may ask if America is part of Dar al-Islam or Dar al-Harb. This question has been particularly relevant since 11 September 2001 in light of the attention that the media have given to Muslims in America and to the question of their potentially conflicted identities as both Americans and Muslims. Recall that a view held by some medieval jurists was that wherever Muslims are living, even as minorities in non-Muslim lands, if the Islamic faith is practised freely and without oppression, these lands may be considered part of Dar al-Islam. After the fall of the caliphate and the rise of sultanates, whom the *ulama*, or Islamic scholars, accused of being corrupt, protecting the Islamic way of life rather than preserving Islamic rule as such became increasingly the criterion among religious authorities. Just and non-oppressive non-Muslim rulers were to be preferred to unjust and oppressive Muslim heads of state. This criterion has opened the way for Muslim diasporas in the twentieth century, when fully one third of all Muslims live as minorities in non-Muslim states, to seek a voice in their own affairs as Muslim communities. In Europe and the Americas – the "West" – Muslim minorities have recently experienced various forms of cultural conflict with, as well as accommodation by, the dominant non-Muslim society. Especially since 11 September, Muslim individuals and communities in the United States have experienced mindless verbal and physical attacks as well as sympathetic support and appreciation from some North American political and religious leaders.

Muslim majorities in Islamic Asia and Africa are predictably reluctant to relinquish traditional categories, such as *dhimmi* status, in maintaining their worldviews about minorities. Ali Kettani, for example, regrets the lack of overall unity and organization of Dar al-Islam that religious memory attributes to societies under "the Caliphs of Baghdad, then of Cairo and then Istanbul," for these caliphs "were not only the temporal and spiritual leaders for the territories which were under their control but also the spiritual leaders of all the Muslims of the world, irrespective of whether they lived as minorities or as majorities."[32] Kettani's project is not to deal with non-Muslim minorities living within Muslim lands, but rather with Muslims who live as minorities in the contemporary world. For him, the worldwide *umma*, or Muslim community, without the caliphate is nonetheless unified by individual Muslims everywhere in their attachment to the Qur'an and the Sunna of the Prophet. Abdullahi an-Na'im and other liberal modernists seem to be arguing that this is precisely the point: Dar al-Islam is an "imagined community" of global Islam with something to contribute to the international debate about human rights and minorities.[33]

In support of this more liberal and democratic strain of Islamic thinking about social democracy, Muslim minorities in Europe and the Americas often find themselves freer to reinterpret Islam; in the North American environment, they can more freely reflect on and experiment with Islamic ways to relate to the rest of society beyond the rigid framework of *shari'a*-minded discourse inherited from the days of empire in early and medieval Islamic civilization. It may be that Muslim jurists and intellectuals in those regions of Dar al-Islam where Muslims are in the numerical minority but part of a legally established religious pluralism, such as in the United States and Canada, among other countries, will be the most successful in establishing Islamic grounds *(usul)* for universal human rights and religious tolerance of minorities. This matter, however, is not for me to determine or predict in this chapter. Rather, it is my hope that this brief history of Islamic conceptions of minorities, as well as more recent theories in minority studies, will provide the reader with a useful background to the chapters that follow.

NOTES

1 One thinks immediately of the early, mostly non-Arab converts to Islam, known as the *mawali* (sing. *mawla*), who often complained of being subjected to lower social status than that enjoyed by Arab Muslims.

2 Qur'an 2:62, 5:69, and 22:17 identify them as believers with scriptures, along with Muslims, Jews, Sabi'ans, and Christians (in that order). The Sabi'ans were classed by later Muslim heresiographers as Pagans with Helenistic philosophical teachings.

3 The Prophet's departure from Mecca to Medina in 622, marking the beginning of the Muslim era.

4 Regarded by most historians as apocryphal, versions of this document appearing in later texts may nonetheless reflect early attempts to come to some accommodation of Christians and Jews. For a discussion of the Pact, or Covenant, of 'Umar, see A.S. Tritton, *The Caliphs and Their Non-Muslim Subjects*, 5–17. On this in the larger context of the history of the *dhimmi* system, see Xavier de Planhol, *Minorités en Islam*, 30–42, esp. 36ff.

5 See Claude Cahen, "Dhimma." A very tendentious study by the pseudonymous Bat Ye'or, *Islam and Dhimmitude*, is based on a considerable amount of textual and historical data; the work provides useful information on this topic if read cautiously and in light of the author's blatantly Islamophobic views.
6 See the discussion of these sects in H.A.R. Gibb et al., eds, *Encyclopaedia of Islam*, 2nd ed., and in Ye'or, *Islam and Dhimmitude*; on the Murji'a, see Wilferd Madelung, "The Murji'a and Sunnite Traditionalism," 13–25, esp. 13–19.
7 It is more appropriate to term the Shi'a a minority, or a cluster of subgroups (although this must be qualified, as in the cases of Fatimid Egypt and of both Safavid Iran and its successor governments), than to apply the notion of heterodoxy to the Shi'a, as some Sunni and Western scholars are inclined to do. Nor do the social scientific notions of denomination and sect really apply in this case. It is true that Sunni scholars have often levelled charges of heresy against the various branches of the Shi'a at different moments of Islamic history. Thus the underlying historical narrative of this chapter is that when the Shi'a lived among Sunnis under Sunni Muslim rule, they were usually treated as a minority.
8 Bernard Lewis, *Race and Color in Islam*, 5–6. See also Marshall G.S. Hodgson, *The Venture of Islam*, 3 vols, 1:57–60.
9 I had recently completed an eighteen-month research fellowship with the Binational Fulbright Commission in Egypt and was asked to help organize the conference, working with an Egyptian co-convener.
10 See, for example, Abdullahi Ahmed an-Na'im, "Toward an Islamic Hermeneutics of Human Rights," 229–41; and an-Na'im, *Human Rights in Cross-Cultural Perspectives*.
11 Albert H. Hourani, *Minorities in the Arab World*, 15.
12 Ibid., 1ff.
13 Ofra Bengio and Gabriel Ben-Dor, eds, *Minorities and the State in the Arab World*, 2.
14 Martin E. Marty and Scott Appleby, eds, *Fundamentalisms Observed*, 827–28, and index under "modernity" and "modernism."
15 Bruce B. Lawrence, *Defenders of God*, 2.
16 Clifford Geertz, "The Integrative Revolution."
17 Ibid., 259.
18 Bengio and Ben-Dor, eds., *Minorities and the State*, 3 n. 15.
19 Arnold M. Rose, "Minorities." In the discussion that follows, I rely heavily on Rose's helpful intellectual history of minority studies.

20 See Richard W. Bulliet, *Conversion to Islam in the Medieval Period*, wherein he presents data and estimates on conversion and Islamization rates by regions.
21 For a succinct summary of the Shu'ubi movement and literary expressions of cultural conflict, see Hamilton A.R. Gibb, *Studies on the Civilization of Islam*, 62–73; and more recently, S. Enderwitz, "Shu'ubiyya."
22 The most important works on this topic are Khaled Abou El Fadl, "Legal Debates on Muslim Minorities"; Abou El Fadl, "Striking a Balance"; and Abou El Fadl, "Islamic Law and Muslim Minorities." I have also consulted M. Ali Kettani, *Muslim Minorities in the World Today*.
23 See Qur'an 2:218, 4:89, 4:100, 8:72, and 16:41.
24 Abou El Fadl, "Legal Debates," 130–1.
25 Ibid., 131.
26 Ibid., Hadith references cited at bottom of page 131.
27 Ibid., 132–3.
28 Ibid., 133–4.
29 Ibid., 134.
30 Ibid., 133.
31 Ibid., 139.
32 Kettani, *Muslim Minorities*, 243.
33 See an-Na'im, *Human Rights in Cross-Cultural Perspectives*; and Farid Esack, *Qur'an, Liberation and Pluralism*.

2

Copts: Fully Egyptian, but for a Tattoo?

PIETERNELLA VAN DOORN-HARDER

INTRODUCTION

Older generations of Muslims and Christians agree that relations between their religions used to be more relaxed before the 1960s. Some fondly remember: "We used to have a beer with Muslim friends to celebrate the beginning of Ramadan."[1] And others: "Our neighbours were Muslim; they were honest, deeply religious people. We had good relationships; we shared in happiness and misery. The misery was much stronger than the religion."[2] The younger generation – those who were born after the 1940s – observe that a different mood has penetrated Egyptian society: "Nowadays the Muslim children grow up with a big wall against Christians. Children in the street become arrogant toward Christians. It used not to be that way. They get this from the teachers who are influenced by fanatic ideas that consider Egypt to be for Muslims only."[3]

These remarks testify to a change in the Egyptian religious climate. Private beliefs have moved into the public sphere, where they shape the cultural and political climate. This process was influenced by several developments within Egyptian society and came to the fore in 1967, when the Arab armies were defeated by the Israelis. To cope with the traumatic feelings of loss and failure, Egyptians, both Muslims and Christians, turned to their respective religions. Among one segment of the Islamic circles, increased religiosity moved toward the form of Islam born in the 1930s with the emergence of the Muslim Brotherhood, known now as "political Islam" or "Islamism."

In some circles, the newly found Muslim identity expressed itself in growing intolerance toward Christians that at times culminated in incidents of violence and religious strife. This reality forced the Copts to reconsider their position in Egyptian society. They realized the need to strengthen their church from within, not only in spiritual and liturgical spheres, but also in the social, cultural, and political areas of life. Pope Shenouda III, who has reigned since 1971, especially reshaped the church's hierarchy into what became a seemingly impenetrable bulwark of Copticism, led and guarded by clergy. In retrospect, during the past three decades, Coptic leadership, both lay and clergy, has laid the building blocks for what Anthony D. Smith calls "ethnic survival potential."[4] While fortifying the church from within, the Coptic leadership also had to reconsider its environment – that is, its relationship with the Muslim majority and its role and place in Egypt's nation-state.

This chapter focuses on the religious, cultural, and educational aspects of Coptic life that have proven crucial for the formation of a specific Coptic identity, one that shapes the Coptic attitude toward the Islamic environment and the Copts' self-definition as Egyptian nationals and that has ultimately formed the key to Coptic survival.[5] The leading Egyptian sociologist Nabil 'abd el-Fattah observed that little has been published about these elements of Coptic life and about the main influences on Coptic interaction with the Muslim environment.[6] Most studies of the Copts focus on their place in public life or on "safe" topics such as liturgy, history, and Coptic art. Aspects of Coptic life that shape its survival potentials and influence the social relations between Copts and Muslims, such as folk religion, folk stories, the role of religious authority, children's education, and the various Coptic social groups, are seldom studied.[7] True, it is the Copts themselves who resist such studies, treating them with great disdain. Ultimately, these studies do not receive the Coptic patriarch's approval – an essential seal of blessing for the work to be read by Copts.

Here I try to point out what have been the strongest forces to shape the Coptic identity. To place this development in the larger frame of Egypt's history, I provide some observations of where this history directly influenced the Coptic community. But first, I will briefly describe who and where the Copts are.

COPTIC COMMUNITY AND CULTURE

The Copts of Egypt constitute a religious minority that descends from the original, pharaonic inhabitants of Egypt. They are members of one of the oldest Christian churches, the Coptic Orthodox Church, which started sometime during the first century B.C.E. when St Mark the Evangelist arrived in Alexandria. The church's patriarch, currently Shenouda III, is the 117th successor to St Mark.

Nobody knows exactly how many Copts there are. The Egyptian census of 1986 estimated their number at 6.3 per cent of the population.[8] Copts themselves and others observing Egypt say that the state underrepresents the Copts statistically and that their number is at least 10 per cent. In 2003 Egypt's population was around 68 million, with a yearly growth rate of 2 per cent. This means that there are between 4 and 7 million Copts in Egypt. The Coptic growth rate is lower than that of the Muslim population due to lower birth rates and conversions to Islam. There are no hard figures for the number of Copts who become Muslim, but some estimate that the Coptic Church in Egypt loses over 6,000 members a year.[9] At the same time, the number of Copts outside Egypt has grown to over one million. These new communities are the result of emigration to the West, of Coptic missionary activities in various African countries, and of new members in the West, mostly women marrying Coptic men. At the time of this writing there are over 180 Coptic churches outside Egypt. Countries with substantial Coptic communities, such as Germany, the US, and Australia, have their own bishops. In the US there is a budding Coptic seminary, and elsewhere, too, Copts have built several monasteries outside Egypt.

The majority of the Copts in Egypt live in the south, while the largest concentrations of Copts live in Cairo and Alexandria. As Coptic families tend to be small, they stress the education of their children, resulting in an average educational level higher than that of Muslims. Copts are present in all social strata of society, but those with university degrees tend to occupy work in the private sector – for example, in the areas of medicine, finance, and engineering. As is the case with the rest of the Egyptian population, many Copts are poor and work in menial jobs such as garbage collection.

Coptic culture, language, and history were shaped on Egyptian soil; Copts share numerous identity markers with Muslim Egyptians, whose numbers have grown rapidly since the Arab invasion of Egypt in 642. During the Middle Ages, Islam replaced Coptic Christianity as the majority religion in Egypt, and Arabic became the dominant language. From an *ethnie* (i.e., an ethnic community that represented the dominant community of Egypt), the Copts became a vertical *ethnie* (i.e., a subject community held together by its members' exclusive bonds).[10] On the surface, the only difference between Copts and Muslims seems to be their religious affiliation. To understand how the Copts have survived since the Arab invasion, we need to look more deeply into Coptic life, including its social and cultural aspects, since religion alone does not guarantee the long-term survival of a community.

Woven through the tapestry of Coptic life are questions about the Copt's continuity and survival, about openness to the surrounding and dominant culture while preserving the boundaries erected to define their own culture. What does the Coptic "portable protective shell" consist of? How does it protect the community without smothering it into fossilization and slow decay? According to Anthony D. Smith, ethnic self-renewal is driven by four mechanisms: (1) religious reform, (2) cultural borrowing, (3) popular participation, and (4) myths of ethnic chosenness.[11] Remarkably, all four mechanisms are strongly developed in the Coptic community, starting with the religious reform that drives the others. The Coptic Church went through this reform for the greater part of the twentieth century, fashioning a new Coptic identity that, although separated from its environment by religion, claims a clear role in the Egyptian nation.

COPTS AND EGYPT

Coptic national consciousness awoke around the beginning of the nineteenth century when Muhammad Ali (1805–48), requiring skilled tax collectors, scribes, and land purveyors in order to develop Egypt's agriculture, brought many Copts into the public service.[12] Christians officially gained equal status with Muslims after the introduction of the 1856 Hamayouni Decree. Now that their *dhimmi* (minority) status had been abolished, the Copts were free to participate at all levels of Egyptian society, including in high administrative offices, albeit with a fluctuating sense of permanence. Twice, a Copt has served as prime minister: Boutros Ghali from 1908 until his assassination in 1910 and Yusuf Wahba Pasha from 1919–20. Muslims and Copts resisted British colonialism in unison, jointly staging the 1919 revolution and adopting a concept of one nation and one people. Their main vehicle was the mostly secular Wafd Party. The majority of Copts involved in politics were from the higher classes and underestimated the sensitivities of many Muslims, especially those of the lower classes, who suspected Copts in positions of power of interfering with the Islamic goals of the state. When Egypt proclaimed independence in 1922, Copts felt so secure in their quest for national equality that they opposed a clause in the Constitution guaranteeing their protection as a religious minority, while another clause made Islam the state religion.

The First and Second World Wars caused grave economic instability, and frustration ran high among Egypt's younger generations. Liberal Nationalism had failed, creating an opportunity for greater influence by Islamic-oriented groups, such as the Islamist Muslim Brotherhood, which offered alternative solutions to the country's moral and economic woes. The brotherhood criticized the secular Wafd and questioned the legitimacy of Copts in places of authority. Their rhetoric instigated frequent harassment of Copts, who started to realize that the government was doing little to protect them.

After the Second World War, the Arab world as a whole became increasingly frustrated by the defeat of Palestine by Zionist forces. Gamal 'Abd al-Nasser came to power in this volatile climate after the 1952 revolution. His policy focused on building Arab nationalism, and he nationalized agricultural lands and businesses, creating an "Arab socialism." The Copts suffered in ethnic, political, and material ways. They did not consider themselves Arab but "true sons of the pharaohs, who are the descendants of indigenous Egyptians."[13] They lost their political representation, their seats in Parliament fell to less than 1 per cent, and no Copt ever rose to political prominence during the Nasser era. Because many Copts worked in the private sector, the massive loss of approximately 75 per cent of their wealth led to the closing of Coptic schools and to the impoverishment of churches and monasteries.

These schools had served both Christians and Muslims. Many Muslim leaders, among them President Nasser, had graduated from Coptic schools. For Muslim children, there were now fewer opportunities to become familiar with Christian models of life. In 1957 Islamic religious education became obligatory in Egyptian schools. Over time, intensified Islamic education led to a renewal of faith among Muslim youth. At the same time, Coptic children in public schools also had to memorize parts of the Qur'an. Maurice Martin has observed that, while this education gave birth to a sense of Islamic national pride, it also created in its wake an Islamism that lacked consensus on the role of religion at the national level. The government assumed Islam to be a social force and avoided any discussion with those who had political aspirations based on Islam. Eventually, this intentional ambiguity polarized Egyptian Islam.[14] At the same time, the Nasser government kept potential religious conflicts at bay by imprisoning or executing Islamist leaders and banning the Muslim Brotherhood.

The Six Day War of 1967 with Israel exposed the level of disillusion among Egypt's population. The Liberal Nationalism of the Wafd Party, Nasser's socialism, and Pan-Arabism had all failed to spur on the masses. For the lower and middle classes, in particular, Islam became the most viable alternative. Sana Hassan describes Islam at this time as a power functioning as "a solid moral grounding for the youth" that could "infuse them with zeal in combat."[15]

This zeal became apparent during the 1970s, when members of extremist Muslim groups imprisoned under Nasser were released by President Sadat. They started to dominate the universities, the mosques, and the media, propagating an Islamic nation, preaching an Islamic nationalism, and arousing latent Muslim fears of Christian dominance. Attacks on Coptic persons and property increased.[16] Groups such as Jama'at Islamiyya felt insulted by Coptic expressions of cultural identity and interpreted church building activities as attempts to propagate the Christian faith and provoke Muslims. In their opinion, Christians could peacefully enjoy their *dhimmi* status until, inevitably, they would see the truth of Islam and convert.[17] The Copts, traumatized and fearful, rallied even more closely around their church.

Sadat saw it expedient to use the Islamic groupings as a means to legitimize his own power. He did not protect the Copts against their violence and ignited Muslim animosity by accusing Patriarch Shenouda of scheming to set up a separate Coptic state. This led to some of the most violent incidents in the Cairo district of Zawya al-Hamra (1981). While the Copts buried their dead, Sadat accused the patriarch of inciting the interreligious strife and banned him to his Monastery of Bishoi, where he stayed until President Mubarak released him in 1985.

Attacks on the Copts continued under Mubarak, who came to power in 1981, after Sadat was shot by the Islamists he had fostered himself. His regime remained lukewarm about protecting the Coptic minority until the 1990s, when the Islamists started to target tourists and high state officials. At this time, the tide turned, the government becoming aware that allowing marginalization and vilification of the Christians could have serious repercussions for national stability. By this time the reform of Coptic church life had already resulted in the strengthening of its institutional, social, and spiritual life. As part of this process of renewal, Copts had reflected on and designed new strategies for improving communications between Muslims and Christians. In other words, the Copts were ready to participate in this climate of renewed openness.

As Copts had started to emigrate to the West in search of freedom and work, the church had also developed a new self-image, which was independent of the Egyptian boundaries and based on a newly found international role. Inside Egypt a new vitality set in among Copts that led to a virtual renaissance. Their Sunday School Movement became a leading force in recreating ethno-religious boundaries, and the ascension of a truly holy man, Patriarch Kyrillos VI (1959–71), marked the new beginning. By the time Shenouda became the patriarch, the Copts had learned to negotiate the permanent ambivalence they experienced from the state. They also realized that a similar ambivalence was present in the Islamic discourse concerning non-Muslims.

COPTS, STATE, AND ISLAM

From the state's point of view, Copts do enjoy full rights as citizens. They are not considered a minority, and they form part of the Egyptian human fabric, sharing the problems of Egyptian society with Muslims. The Egyptian state is not based on Islamic laws and calls itself secular. However, Islam is the official state religion and the primary source of some state legislation, such as the personal status laws. Egypt recognizes only the religions of Islam, Judaism, and Christianity; all others are forbidden. As there are only around 200 Jews left in Egypt, Christians form the largest minority group, which is the case not only in Egypt, but in the entire Middle East.

The state system, although fair in theory, is fraught with ambiguity for non-Muslims. For example, in 1972, in the midst of discussions to introduce the *shari'a* (Islamic law) as the country's sole source of legislation, the National Assembly passed the law of national unity, which stipulates freedom of belief. Around the same time, Sadat called himself "a Muslim president to a Muslim country" and tried to silence Patriarch Shenouda, whom he viewed as a rebellious leader, by exiling him to a desert monastery (September 1981 to January 1985).

Apart from the question of religion, one of the most unsettling problems in Egypt is the oppressive, antidemocratic character of the state.[18] It can be violent toward groups it tries to control, such as the extremist Muslims. For most of the 1980s and 1990s, it sustained a fragile balance between maintaining peace and simultaneously pleasing both extremist Muslims and the moderate segments of society. The result is a secular state with an Islamic discourse that lacks any creativity when it comes to improving relations between Christians and Muslims. Its singular focus has been on maintaining security by locking up suspected dissidents and then suppressing public debates about the situation. The ongoing court case of Dr Saad Eddin Ibrahim, who is accused of, among other things, "defaming Egypt" with his lectures and writings on religious freedom and minority rights, is a telling example of the government's attitude. Observers of the case agree that the initial sentence of seven years given in 2001 was rather severe, as Dr Ibrahim's greatest infraction was monitoring the 2000 elections.[19]

Confusion about minorities is exacerbated when neither the state nor the Islamic establishment is willing to enhance national unity by producing clear statements or by taking firm stands concerning Christians. The state promotes public displays of "equality" and fiercely denies any problems with the Christian population. Resulting positions are often hyperbolic and counterproductive. We are told, for example, that "since the Byzantine period Copts have ... continued to occupy leading posts and offices in the state."[20] In 2000, when the Egyptian government nominated Pope Shenouda III for the UNESCO-Madanjeet Singh Prize for the Promotion of Tolerance and Non-Violence, Egypt's ambassador to the UN, Mrs Tahani Omar, commented that the prize "refutes the claim that discrimination against the Copts is institutionalized."[21] Indeed, it is not institutionalized but ingrained in society. The *Country Reports on Human Rights Practices*, published by the US government, reiterate annually that in Egypt "Women and Christians faced discrimination based on tradition and some aspects of the law." It confirms this observation with an analysis of the percentage of Copts who have positions of significance within the official state structure. In 2002:

There were no Christians serving as governors, police commissioners, city mayors, university presidents, or deans. There were few Christians in the upper ranks of the security services and armed forces. Discrimination against Christians also continued in public sector employment, in staff appointments to public universities, in failure [with the exception of one case during the year] to admit Christians into public university training programs for Arabic language teachers that involved study of the Koran, and payment of Muslim imams through public funds [Christian clergy are paid with private church funds].[22]

Unofficially, women and Christians indeed seem to be on the same level when one considers their political representation. Of the 264 seats in the upper house of Parliament (the Shura Council), the president can appoint forty-five members. In 2001 these included eight women and four Christians. Eleven women and seven Christians were in the People's Assembly, two women and two Christians served among the thirty-two Cabinet ministers, and no women or Christians were on the Supreme Court.

Despite the state's positive statement about the Copts, the state allowed preachers such as Sheikh Sha'arawi to use their time on government sponsored television to deliver vicious criticisms of Christianity. In 1982 and 1983, Sha'arawi discussed his derogatory views on the life of Christ and the crucifixion during the primetime slot of Friday afternoon. The government failed to ban his books, which are filled with spiteful language about Christians and are available on every street corner in Cairo. Such discourse poisoned the mindset of those born after the 1960s and exacerbated negative attitudes toward the Copts. Several generations of youngsters grew up hearing and believing that Christians "are not really human," "stink," and "have secret knowledge of magic and possess hidden resources."[23]

When Christians and their property are attacked, the state is slow to provide protection.[24] The lack of a clear penal policy, in combination with oppressive and arbitrary laws, often ends in favour of the aggressors. A case in point is the outcome of a trial in January 2000. After riots had started with a private quarrel between a Muslim and a Copt, twenty-one Copts and one Muslim were murdered during three days of sectarian violence in the village of Al-Kousheh, 250 miles south of Cairo. (The Muslim was killed by other Muslims who mistook him for a Copt.) The State Security was slow to restore order. Initially, only four of the ninety-six defendants (of whom fifty-eight were Muslims and thirty-eight Christians) received mild punishment, and all were acquitted of murder charges. A Muslim journalist summarized this state of affairs, saying "We [Muslim Egyptians] have a philosophy according to which we burn the Copts' homes and churches and then apologize to their clerics ... Be grateful to Allah that we do not annihilate you!!"[25]

Finally, the state contributes to interreligious strife – especially in the southern provinces, where 60 per cent of the Coptic population lives – by decreeing that civil servants must be employed in their areas of origin. This means that those assuming positions of local power remain embedded in age-old, traditional (some say "tribal") socio-political structures that perpetuate old rivalries and vendettas.

Muslim clerics add to the confusion surrounding their views on Christianity by preaching contradictory opinions on the position of Christians in Islamic countries. Their opinions, of course, depend on their specific interpretations of the authoritative texts of Islam, as evidenced by the disagreement between the Muslim Brotherhood and Sayyid Qutb. Whereas Qutb did not allow Christians full rights to citizenship, the majority of the Muslim Brotherhood considered Christians equal to Muslims, albeit as long as they kept a low profile.[26] Examples of this perspective can be found in the interviews with high-ranking Muslim clerics that appeared in the 24 November 2001 issue of the Egyptian magazine *Al-Musawwar*. In an article entitled "Is the West Still Home to Infidelity?" several authorities on Islam are interviewed about the definition of the term "infidelity."[27] The article has to be read in the context of the 11 September 2001 tragedy in New York.

According to the Islamist-minded Sheikh al-Qardawi, one form of infidelity is "the denial of Islam, and the message of Mohammed. All those who do not believe that Mohammed is Allah's prophet, and that the Qur'an was Allah's words revealed to him, are infidels, even if they are people of the Book, i.e. Jews, or Christians." According to al-Qardawi, their infidelity does not make these people apostates or heathens; it means only that they do not recognize the religion of Mohammed. The sheikh emphasizes that the Qur'an never calls any of its opponents "Infidels." Rather, it refers to the polytheists of

Mecca as "O people" and calls Jews and Christians "O people of the Book." Quoting the Qur'an, he points out that it teaches "infinite tolerance with its conclusion 'you have your religion and I have mine.'" Al-Qardawi's teaching leaves room for multiple interpretations, depending on which of his statements readers focus on.

Later in the interview, Sheikh al-Qardawi states: "As to the non-Muslim in an Islamic nation, they are citizens, sharing the same rights and duties as the Muslims. Their blood, their property, their honor, and sacred places are protected. No one may attack them without reason. Those who do so deserve to be punished in this life and the hereafter."

Others quoted in the article perform similar hermeneutic acrobatics, presenting contradictory opinions within the same interview. Of course, in the Islamic tradition of interpreting the holy texts, it is valid and recommendable to provide different sources and opposing opinions. But it is also customary to provide a conclusive answer. The statements made in the article leave room for multiple interpretations, a potentially dangerous road to follow.[28]

When, by the mid-1990s, the attacks by extremist Muslims began to harm the Egyptian state (with, for example, the collapse of the tourist industry), its attitude toward the Christians changed. It realized that the extremists were directly undermining the state's own systems and started to clamp down viciously on those of the Islamist mindset. The state realized that the benefits of protecting its minority community carried over to its own wellbeing. This led to an intensified campaign not only to arrest extremist elements, but also to address the pressing issue of the national discourse, which was fraught with intolerance of Christians. The state started to monitor the Friday sermons in the mosques and announced that the history books used in the state curriculum would be changed to contain more information about the Coptic community. It also encouraged increased coverage of Christian subjects in the mass media.

Not only did the Coptic Church welcome these initiatives to change the prevailing mindset, but it had been instrumental in preparing the foundations to facilitate their introduction. Through private schools and community-development projects, it had quietly prepared methods of reconciliation that directly served the government. While many Copts had opted to leave Egypt, those who stayed behind never doubted their Egyptian identity and nationality. While their first allegiance was to their church, Copts remained firmly entrenched in the Egyptian soil. Illustrations of their allegiance to

Egypt can be observed in the stands that the Coptic Church takes on issues such as international politics. For example, it supports the official Egyptian position on relations between Palestine and Jerusalem rather than the worldwide Christian allegiance to the holy places in Israel. This means that it excommunicates church members who make the pilgrimage to Israel.

Even Copts in the West see their identity as profoundly Egyptian. In the safety of Western countries, they can criticize the Egyptian government's treatment of their fellow Christians in the homeland. At the same time, they confess their allegiance to Egypt: A young Copt in the US has written, "No Copt is 'outside' Egypt no matter where he or she lives. Egypt is the entity that gives us, the Copts our identity."[29] He expresses the sentiment of many Copts: They will always be Egyptian, even when they are born and raised in the US and have rarely visited their country of ethnic origin.

While seeing themselves as fully Egyptian, Copts have been aware for centuries that there will always be elements within Egypt's society that deny them full rights. Only since the end of the 1980s have Copts started to study and classify the various Muslim attitudes toward them. Acknowledging that the majority of Egypt's Muslims want to maintain peaceful relationships with the Christians, they have more or less isolated the violent groups and focus their energies on developing stronger relations with the tolerant segments of Muslim society.

How, then, should we understand the Copts' place in the Egyptian environment, where moderate and extremist Muslim believers coexist under the governance of the same state? Some – for example, Sana Hasan – compare the Coptic community to a ghetto.[30] In the minds of Copts, this analysis is not only entirely wrong, but even potentially dangerous, as Islamists would prefer to relegate Copts to ghettos. The Coptic condition is not analogous to that of the Jews in premodern Europe, the most salient example of ghetto dwellers. While living in their protective shell, Copts can be found in all strata of Egyptian society, and some have held or now hold high positions of authority. On the surface, their language and physical appearance are similar to those of Muslim Egyptians. The state, in principle, considers them equal to Muslims, and the Constitution guarantees their basic civil rights, which Copts reiterate, promote, and claim. Egyptian state violence does not single out Copts but is also directed at other citizens, such as Muslim extremists and homosexuals.

Copts consider themselves fully Egyptian, but their first and foremost allegiance is not to the state but to their faith. A practising Copt will not convert to Islam for the sake of getting a certain job, for example. In short, it is not the Coptic attitude that changed during the twentieth century but the Muslim environment, which became more Islamist in tone and discourse after a brief period of courtship that lasted only for around three decades. In principle, Copts can negotiate their standing; after all, they have centuries of experience with *dhimmi* status. However, when they become the nation's scapegoat or mistrusted community based solely on the hate talk of Islamists, their position becomes precarious. In the current context, the main problem is that the state ignored the potential threat of Islamism for too long, disregarding incidents of religious strife and allowing Copts to suffer for the sake of maintaining an artificial state of peace. As there were few moderate Muslim Egyptians who had the tools to speak up for the Copts, from the outside there seemed to be an all-out war going on between Christians and Muslims. Copts understood that this was a misrepresentation of reality; in fact, only a segment of the population was actively persecuting them. Copts and the rest of Egypt's Muslims, whatever their thoughts about non-Muslims, lived peacefully side by side. To be left alone, then, is one of the ultimate goals, but Copts do not desire to live in isolation from the rest of society as in a ghetto. Rather, they aspire to be granted the basic human rights that allow individuals freedom of religion, speech, and thought while understanding that not even all Muslim Egyptians can claim these rights. In fact, realizing that these rights would be respected neither by the state nor by most Muslims, the Copts started to build a system that strengthened their position from within. The rest of this chapter discusses how they went about doing this.

INVISIBLE STRENGTH

Between the 1930s and 1950s, the Copts were slowly rendered all but invisible. In particular, extremist forces in the Muslim environment systematically tried to reduce the Copts to the status of nonpersons. More tolerant representatives of society lacked the solidarity needed to counter this development. Whereas, in the past, Copts had been the foremost producers of journals and newspapers, they were slowly erased as actors in the official public media. Nowadays, distribution of Coptic media, journals, newspapers, videos, and cassettes is limited to church circles. National television broadcasts the Coptic Christmas celebrations and some other holy days (especially when Muslim dignitaries visit the patriarch at the cathedral in Cairo). Bishop Mousa, bishop of youth, has calculated that this exposure amounts to five hours a year for Coptic matters in contrast to 3,000 hours of Islamic teachings. Muslim-Christian discussion on television is not allowed. As a result, "A five-year-old Muslim does not know who a Copt is."[31]

Manuel Castells has observed that "nations are constructed in the minds and in collective memory by the sharing of history and political projects."[32] According to Castells, "ethnicity, religion, language, territory *per se* do not suffice to build nations, and induce nationalism. Shared experience does."[33] This experience generates myths and memories that create a shared human experience.[34] Starting with the Muslim Brotherhood in the 1930s, Copts had to come to terms with Egyptians whose experience – memory, history, and political projects – were primarily based not on their Egyptian identity but on a specific interpretation of Islam and the desire for a worldwide *umma* (Muslim community). Copts, of course, are excluded from any of these experiences. In order to create a sense of belonging for its believers, the Coptic Church was forced to construct its own community, which, like that of Islamists, was based on a shared Coptic textual tradition rather than on shared national history and territory. Copts, like Muslims, searched for a cultural authenticity, which they naturally sought primarily in the Christian message, in stories of the saints, in holy places, and in the glorious past.

Copts turned to developing building blocks for survival and divorced their religious realm from the Muslim environment, where they had once hoped to participate at all levels of society. Copts have developed, and continue to stress, their own time and space, which now moves past the spiritual to encompass the physical as well. The Coptic calendar directs one's movement through the year from fasts to feasts. Whereas Islam refers to the universal *umma*, Copts refer to the universe of those who have shared their struggle: martyrs, saints, and other holy persons from the earliest Christian centuries. This universe, however, is firmly rooted in Egyptian space: in the soil that holds the footprints of the Holy Family, on ground that absorbed the blood of the early martyrs, and where the Virgin Mary has regularly made her appearance over the past decades. Copts have also defined their community in exclusive terms, distancing themselves from the

Muslim environment through specific traditions, rituals, and liturgies. In this process, they have also distanced themselves from non-Orthodox Christians, especially the Protestants. I will return to this shortly.

The Coptic world and history were reconstructed as a sacred space and time that have their roots in pre-Islamic Egypt and are free of Muslim influence. Egypt's symbolic geography is now divided into two realms: Muslim and Coptic. The Muslim realm refers to the world with all its trials and temptations; the Coptic realm encompasses the holy and sacred places formed in the footsteps of the Holy Family, the graves of the early Christian martyrs, the saints, and the saintly church leaders who are alive today. This vision of transcendence is congruent with an Orthodox theology that sees humans as angels in the flesh all striving to get one foot into heaven before death. In this vision, the church victorious – those in heaven who have overcome strife and temptations – and the church on earth are one body. The prime centres to initially teach this new vision of a Coptic identity were the Sunday schools, which started to flourish in the 1950s. But before considering this aspect of Coptic identity, I will first look at where it converges with its Islamic environment.

MARKERS OF IDENTITY: EGYPTIAN COPTIC

Much is said about the experiences Copts share with Muslims: They speak Arabic, eat the same food, and share work space, and many Copts are just as poor as Muslims or have the same trouble finding jobs after graduation or apartments when they want to get married. Many Egyptians like to go on pilgrimage and share folk-religion practices. Cross-visits to graves of saints happen when they are assumed to confer benefits regardless of religion. All celebrate the Shamm al-Nasim holiday the day after Easter and other national holidays. Coptic church services are held on Fridays and Sundays, and the weekend spans from Thursday to Sunday for most Egyptians. Although there are profound differences in the family laws of Muslims and Christians, views on women are similar. Muslim and Coptic boys and girls are circumcised, and seventh-day rituals are held at birth and fortieth-day commemorations at death.[35] Families of both religions prefer to select spouses for their children.

What seems similar on the surface is actually marked off by subtle boundaries in orientation and standards that accumulate into markers of Copticness.[36] Dress has become a marker of identity. Even where rural and poor Copts and Muslims still dress in similar attire, Copts display subtle markers of Christianity, such as a small cross or a pendant with a saint's picture. Copts always have the cross tattooed on one wrist, which can be hidden if necessary. They carry pictures of saints in their wallets and on their key chains. Names often point to religious identity. Most significant for Coptic identity is the move away from mixed experience to more specifically Coptic or Muslim expressions. A young Copt has exclaimed: "We do not speak the same 'Arabic,' ... Muslims can tell I am a Copt after two minutes of talking with me."[37] Copts modify the Islamic greetings; for example, "*Al-Salaamu 'alaikum*" (peace be upon you) becomes "*Salaamu lakum*" (peace to you). In shock or surprise, Muslims cry out "*Bism-Allah*" (in the name of God) or "*Mashaa-Allah*" (what God wills), while Christians say "*Bism-Al-Salib*" (in the name of the cross). Copts say "*rabbina*" (our Lord) instead of "Allah," and on Christian feasts they greet each other with phrases such as the Greek Easter greeting "*Christos Anesti*" (Christ is risen).

Copts do not sing the same songs as Muslims. They might listen to them in mixed company, but most Copts sing or chant Christian songs in unmixed company. Of course, they do not watch any of the 3,000 hours per year devoted to Islamic matters on television. They have their own body of literature, movies, and videos that are circulated through church channels and are hardly available outside those closed circuits. Copts eat the same food as other Egyptians, but dishes have different meanings for them. They follow a liturgical calendar that includes around 200 days of abstinence from the consumption of animal products and certain additional types of food as well as from sexual intercourse. Copts associate beans, lentils, and other legumes with the preparations for Advent and Lent, two of the fourteen feasts celebrated by the Church. For Muslim Egyptians, these foods signify simple, local dishes that form the principal source of nourishment for the poor.

THE REVIVAL

An increased focus on church life, which started at the time of Patriarch Kyrillos VI, "christianized" Coptic cultural and social expressions. This process was not serendipitous but reflected a concerted effort – orchestrated by Coptic clergy and devoted laity, especially youth leaders – to strengthen the Coptic Orthodox identity. They were dissatisfied with what they considered the backward and lackadaisical mindset of their church leaders. As the revival process was centred on renewing the church leadership, the ensuing process has been called "clericalization," which began with clergy becoming involved in activities outside the liturgy: clubs, summer camps, and excursions organized by various churches. A priest would organize comprehensive programs of activities intended to make his church into a spiritual and social respite. At the same time, lay workers involved in the numerous activities were consecrated and incorporated into the official church structure.[38] This development resulted in and was facilitated by a swelling number of new monks and nuns entering the monasteries. At the basis of this process was the Sunday School Movement, which, from its inception in 1918 until 1938, was conducted entirely by middle-class lay people. During the 1960s, these individuals were gradually incorporated into the official church hierarchy, many becoming bishops or prominent priests. These multilayered efforts resulted in what is now considered the revival or reformation of the Coptic Orthodox Church.

The Coptic Church's revival expressed itself in the renewal and strengthening of three main areas: the pedagogical, the pastoral, and the monastic. These areas touch upon the whole of Coptic life – at home and in church, from cradle to grave – and shape the Coptic identity. The pedagogical revival was spearheaded by the Sunday School Movement, the pastoral revival expressed itself in increased involvement in economic and social-development work, and the monastic revival resulted in an increased focus on spirituality and Coptic identity. When the Sunday schools managed to inspire young Copts to join the monasteries, the monasteries became the heart of the church revival. Monks and nuns became producers of spiritual and religious literature and served as guardians of the Coptic symbols and traditions. They were a rich well of human resources with their experience in Sunday schools, professional diplomas, and advanced university degrees.

This was not the first attempt to revive the church. Since the nineteenth century, the renewal of Coptic church-life had been attempted several times. The genius of Patriarch Kyrillos VI (1959–71) drew these scattered attempts together into a single focus. After independence from Britain in 1922, more Egyptians had access to education that, by the 1950s, had started to yield new cadres of highly educated Copts. Kyrillos VI drew the brightest graduates into church service. This move was revolutionary since Coptic clergy tended to be poorly educated, giving prevalence to the ideal of the simple, unlettered desert monk. Kyrillos VI's brilliance lay in choosing the monk as one of the central symbols with which to revive the life of the church, infusing the notions of "simple" and "unlettered" with a spiritual meaning. The monk was simple and humble in his spiritual life; however, similar to many of the early church fathers, he had deep knowledge of the Christian texts and tradition. Thus he vested the younger generation of monks who came to the monastery, graduate degrees in hand, with the authority needed to become the leaders of the current revival. Some of the most prominent among them are Patriarch Shenouda III (formerly bishop of education); Bishop Samuel of the Bishopric for Social and Ecumenical Affairs (killed at the same time as President Sadat in 1981); Father Matta al-Meskin, abbot of the Monastery of St Macarius and a prolific writer on theology and spirituality; and Anba Athanasius (d. 2000), bishop of Beni Suef.

The lay person Habib Girgis started the Sunday School Movement in 1918 because Coptic children lacked Christian education in the general Khedive schools. He patterned the educational approach on the Protestant Sunday schools. By the 1950s, several former students from these schools, men and women, were finishing their university educations in Cairo. Their desire to apply academic knowledge for benefit of the church translated into new curricula for the Sunday schools. Such initiatives proved vital since Coptic children had to participate in lessons on Islam at school beginning in 1957. (This was also the case in Christian schools since these were under the supervision of the government). As challenges increased for Coptic youth in public high schools and universities during the 1980s, the Sunday schools appealed to them with special groups and classes.

To provide adolescents and young adults with a place of rescue and reflection, the Bishopric for Youth was set up in 1980. Its leader, Bishop Mousa, developed a holistic model for educating and entertaining Coptic youth: Via clubs, retreats, vacations, study groups, seminars, and the top priorities of marriage counselling and preventing Coptic-Muslim dating, he catered to needs that could not be met elsewhere in society.

In the bishopric, young Copts can discuss their problems and situate themselves in their Christian vocation. Copts believe that adversity is sent by God and that preparation for martyrdom is necessitated by such adversity. In Coptic theology, Islam is a temptation that, if resisted, leads one to self-improvement. In an interview about the challenge of the Islamic environment, Patriarch Shenouda answered: "The difficulties around us create a deeper spiritual life: prayers, fasting, contact with God, dependence on God. We feel a deep need for the divine help."[39]

LITTLE ANGELS: THE CHILDREN

Children are the building blocks of every church.[40] In order to prepare and protect future generations, the Coptic Church started to develop special rituals and educational materials for them. Copts consider children to be pure and holy beings who become full church members when baptized. Before "graduating" to the status of married person, the church guides them through the rites of passage and in Christian education. During the past three decades, new rituals have been created or old ones reinvented to underscore Coptic identity. Seven days after birth, a child receives its name in a ceremony practised by Copts and Muslims, the *subu'*. At the same time, Copts hold another ritual of blessing that derives from a Jewish Temple rite and commemorates Jesus' presentation in the Temple when he was eight days old. This uniquely Christian *salawat al-tisht* ritual – the prayers over the washbasin – has gained in popularity and is considered a confirmation of the child's Christian identity. At baptism the child becomes a full member of the church. Gender segregation becomes apparent here, as the child is often baptized when the mother is no longer ritually unclean: forty days after birth for boys and eighty days for girls. The male child is circumcised during the first eight days, whereas this operation is performed on girls between the ages of seven and twelve. At a young age, the cross is tattooed on the child's right wrist. This is the honourable and most pronounced sign of Coptic identity, being both permanent and visible, unless covered by a long sleeve.

After baptism the child officially belongs to "the bosom of the church." Its mother receives instruction on raising a Christian child, and in some cases a deaconess is assigned as godmother to assist with Christian upbringing. Between ages two and eighteen, the child will attend Sunday-school classes with its peers. The goal is to raise a generation of new Sunday-school teachers, monks, priests, nuns, deacons, and believers who, if need be, are willing to die for their faith. In an aggressive program of church socialization, families whose children fail to come to church are visited by volunteers and offered rides in the church vehicles. The child participates in all church celebrations, learning how to venerate saints, hearing their stories, and learning their feast days by heart. Children are present during the long services, which can last over five hours and always end with the Sacrament of Holy Communion. Many churches now conduct children's services parallel to their official services, in which children follow the same rituals but use simpler language.

In Sunday school, teachers discuss the Islamic faith with the children, tackling difficult topics such as the Trinity, so that they can answer questions posed by an adverse society. A sense of Coptic pride is instilled in the children that can be called upon if they feel discriminated against. The martyr is held up as the ultimate model of faith, and the stories of modern martyrs killed in recent clashes point at a higher goal. The Norwegian anthropologist Nora Stene once heard a Sunday-school teacher ask a group of four-year-olds if they were afraid to die as martyrs, the answer was, in one voice, "NO!"[41] The positive aspects of life are always stressed. Dwelling on violence and unpleasant incidents is considered unproductive, so children are also encouraged to hold an optimistic and unconditional belief in the power of prayer.

The contents of the curriculum are reflected in the topics discussed in *Magalet Madaris Al-Ahad* (the Sunday-school journal). Circulating since 1947, it covers themes such as spiritual and biblical reflections, essays on dogmatics, history, liturgy, sacred music, monasticism, the saints, Coptic celebrations, the Coptic status in Egyptian society, and current events within the church.[42] Practising the Coptic faith requires a vast knowledge of ritual, dogma, sacraments, the saints, prayers, and fasting. Texts from the Bible that are used in liturgy and prayer must be learned by heart. Sunday school is the only place to receive this knowledge, and in some ways the curriculum resembles that of the *madrasah* (traditional Islamic school). The younger generation that benefited from this system is now more adept in their Christian knowledge than their parents. Consequently, parents are at times considered "slack," or "not Coptic enough."

THE PASTORAL REVIVAL

In addition to resulting in more ordained clergy, the pastoral revival led to a strong youth ministry and a more prominent role for women in the church. The Bishopric for Youth, led by Bishop Mousa, was founded in 1980 to meet the needs of university students confronted by aggressive Islamist activities that encroached on their private existence. Coptic students created a system of groups or families (*usar*) to serve the Sunday schools and to meet on campus for Bible study and prayer. In the mid-seventies, Islamists started to hinder Christian gatherings, and they would force dorm residents to attend communal prayer five times a day. In the bishopric, students found not only a safe discussion forum, but also a platform for mobilizing people with a shared agenda.

The work of the bishopric flows through so-called "action groups," each focusing on activities ranging from Bible study and counselling to the renewal of the arts, the study of atheism, the study of citizenship, and research into societal problems such as drugs. The network of this bishopric reaches from the patriarch to priests in remote villages. It strengthens youth but also works as a catalyst in times of crisis – for example, when a Coptic woman wants to marry a Muslim man (the reverse happens less frequently due to the specific Islamic rule forbidding Muslim women to marry outside their faith). If the woman still wants to marry the Muslim man after the action group has monitored her, the group immediately finds her a Christian husband. If the woman was tempted into a relationship outside the church because of poverty, a fully furnished flat is provided. Once married, an intense period of counselling is undertaken to "build up her spirituality." If the group is too late and a mixed marriage has already taken place, the group will not sever contacts with the woman in case she ever desires to return to the church.[43]

From these action groups new movements emerged that now hold the potential to reshape the Coptic position in Egyptian society. The Coptic Centre for Social Studies, founded in 1994, is the brainchild of Samir Morqos, who started as a member of the so-called intellectual-development group. This group organized regular meetings with Muslim leaders to give a voice to moderate Muslims "who are not organized, unlike fanatic Muslims." The Coptic Centre now focuses on issues of citizenship, ecumenical relations, and contemporary social concerns, each of which will be discussed below.

The Sunday School Movement indirectly generated the restoration or renewal of powerful Coptic institutions and symbols, the most powerful being total dedication to the church. When, in the 1940s, its teachers searched for ways to convert their voluntary teachings on

Thursdays, Fridays, and Sundays into full-time occupations, the idea of dedication *(takris)* was born. Some of these teachers left their secular jobs to become the equivalent of deacons. Each received a blessing from the church and took a vow of obedience and celibacy that was not binding. Many went on to become monks, while others married, pursuing careers within the church. Combined efforts of the monastics and the "semimonastics" led to new developments in the fields of Coptic icon painting, church music, art, linguistics, archeology, and the study of patristics. These were acts of charity; all those involved had taken a vow of poverty or lived in a perpetual state of frugality.

An active role for women who opted for a career within the church was rediscovered through the introduction of *takris*. Until 1965 women who wished a life in church service rather than marriage had no other option but to become cloistered, contemplative nuns. The pastoral renewal provided Coptic Orthodox women with the opportunity to take on active ministry in the church again. The Sunday School Movement led to the consecration of deaconesses, an office that had existed in the early church but had gradually disappeared, probably due to the male hierarchy and the Muslim environment.[44] In 1965 Anba Athanasius established the first community for women devoted to active church ministry in Beni Suef. This community became a source of leadership for women and provided a model of relief work open to Christians and Muslims.

These various developments were consolidated into successful operations by a rapid increase in the number of religious and lay leaders who had solid educations, both professionally and in Coptic theology. Patriarch Shenouda, in particular, focused on building new seminaries throughout Egypt in order to strengthen the church with leaders well versed in its teachings. Today around 20 per cent of those graduating are women who work as deaconesses or Sunday-school leaders.[45] The brightest of the seminary students are encouraged to consider entering the monastery. A large pool of monks with advanced degrees in theology enabled Patriarch Shenouda to ordain more bishops than the Church had ever employed. When he became the patriarch, there were twenty-eight bishops. By the year 2000 this number exceeded eighty and was still rising. The extra bishops allow the church to divide dioceses into many subdistricts, guaranteeing more intense supervision of priests, better pastoral care, and closer monitoring of the Coptic theology and doctrine taught to parishioners. The bishops also organize activities of reconciliation between

Muslims and Copts, such as shared dinners to break the fast during the Muslim month of Ramadan.

THE MONASTIC REVIVAL: EVERY COPT A MONK

Traditionally, the Coptic leaders – bishops and the patriarch – begin their careers in one of the remote desert monasteries. Monks were and are the bearers of Coptic faith and tradition. Since the beginning of Christianity, stories have abounded of monks fighting devils in the desert. The core of a monk's identity is that of the spiritual man who keeps the tradition alive, alone if need be. Because of such monks, Egyptian monasticism never died out.

The heart of monastic life is the daily Eucharist, during which Copts confirm the core of their belief with the words "I believe, I believe, I believe and confess to the last breath, that this is the life-giving body that your only-begotten Son, our Lord, God and Savior Jesus Christ took from our lady ... St. Mary."[46] Copts believe that at the time of Communion, angels descend to hold the vessels with the bread and wine. Only baptized Copts may join in this holiest moment of the Eucharist. Communion excludes all who do not hold the Coptic theological stand (Muslims, Protestants, and Catholics, among others), cementing the bond between church and community. Allegedly, Kyrillos VI could discern when Muslims or non-Coptic Orthodox Christians tried to join Communion. Thus he preserved the holy body and blood from defilement by those not holding the proper beliefs. His discernment also reenforced the immeasurable distance between the core beliefs of Muslims and Christians and between the beliefs of Copts and Christians of other denominations.

Regular participation in the Eucharist, then, strengthened the community's spiritual and communal bonds, defining the borders between Copts and non-Copts. In order to revive the Coptic community, Kyrillos VI focused on intensifying the celebration of the Eucharist. Being a hands-on person, he travelled from village to village waking up local priests and convincing them to celebrate the lengthy liturgy, which can take up to six hours and, if necessary, be celebrated alone. The belief was that if one sanctified the environment, the parishioners would come. In 1959 the so-called rural diaconal project was launched that sent students of the Clerical College to villages that were without a church. These students provided basic education in the Christian faith and simple social services. Priests followed with portable altars to celebrate the Eucharist and to baptize children.[47]

Daily celebration of the Eucharist has always been a signpost of monastic life. Prayers of the Hours are expanded by continuous prayers and praises for the saints. These three monastic practices were introduced to regular church members through little booklets, sermons, and visits to monasteries. Bishop Athanasius compiled the stories of the saints in *Garden of the Monks*. Father Matta al-Meskin started his profuse publishing career with booklets about every aspect of Coptic life. His journal, *Morqos*, published by the Monastery of St Macarius, became one of the main vehicles of the Coptic spiritual revival. Bishops, furthermore, write spiritual reflections in the national church bulletin, *Kiraza*, while Patriarch Shenouda reiterates his teachings in a weekly public Bible study complemented by myriad publications with titles such as "The Release of the Spirit" and "Comparative Theology." Spiritual formation comprises the core of Coptic education. It is taught that strengthening one's spiritual life is a way to escape human vice and the deficiencies of the world. Renewal of the spirit is considered the only means of coping with possible hostility. Even lay people are encouraged to develop a monastic attitude in everyday life.

The ultimate examples of those who persevered in the demanding ascetic and spiritual exercises are the saints. Their presence looms large in the monasteries. Their relics grant protection and blessing. Living saints sustain believers with advice, often based on the gift of clairvoyance developed by a lifetime spent in prayer. Saints protect the monastery, the Copts, and the faith. Both dead and living saints attract large crowds who visit the monasteries for refuge from the world outside and to "stock up" on the protective power of blessing. The veneration of saints culminates in the yearly *maulids*, celebrated all over Egypt. Originally these folk celebrations were a combination of Christian rituals and an array of other events, such as fairs with merry-go-rounds, story tellers, and puppeteers. They were equally popular with Muslims, who shared in the amusement, the blessings, and the occasional miracle of healing.

In line with church renewal, *maulids* have been stripped of non-Christian elements and turned into polished Christian meetings orchestrated by church officials. Pilgrims nowadays are guided in their prayers and given booklets with the "definitive biographies" of the saints. These contain the proper songs to praise and commemorate each saint *(tamgid)*, thus transforming myth into fact. The transformation of folk events was also influenced by reformist Islam, which attacks the veneration of saints, regarding it as un-Islamic.

Copts living in the metropolitan areas of Cairo and Alexandria are receiving more attention from the church hierarchy since many are from the countryside and have only recently settled in large cities. Although hard data are lacking, this part of the Coptic population is considered most at risk of conversion to Islam. Thus the church has initiated special services, such as counselling, relief drives, and vocational training.

During the 1990s, as part of this new focus, a new holy place came into existence on the outskirts of Cairo itself in the midst of the poorest Coptic population: the ministry of Father Samaan on the Muqattam hill. His church is situated in the middle of the *zabbalin* (garbage collectors). Every Thursday, Father Samaan holds meetings of prayer and praise that also attract thousands of middle-class Copts, who drive up from the city. For one night Copts escape the anxieties of daily life to join the extensive singing sessions. They feel spiritually uplifted, and the strong stench of garbage in their cars as they return home allows them to identify with the poor. Father Samaan has gained a reputation as an exorcist and deeply spiritual person. He started his ministry on the Muqattam hill after experiencing an inspiration based on Acts 18:9, 10.[48] The location is laden with significance. Today Copts hold emotional religious gatherings where Khalif Mu'izz challenged the Copts in the tenth century to prove the truth of the Bible verse stating that faith can move mountains. According to the tradition, the Muqattam hill moved four kilometres after several days of fervent prayer by the holy patriarch and a tanner called Samaan.[49] The earnest belief of the contemporary Father Samaan is that miracles abound, especially in times of adversity.

By means of the monasteries and holy places, old and new, a part of Egypt has been claimed and appropriated as Coptic and infused with a spirit of holiness and chosenness. Coptic believers shuttle between the desert and the inhabited world, between physical rituals and spiritual practices, from home to church. Both living and dead have a place in this universe, and these movements are protected and guided by the church hierarchy, which sustains Copts in their daily struggle, strengthens their Coptic identity, and provides meaning in times of adversity. Copts live in two worlds: the Coptic universe, where they can rejoice in their symbols, songs, and beliefs; and the Egyptian world, where a Copt covers the cross on his or her wrist. Each world has its own language and symbols, which Copts learn to keep separate from an early age. They are like aliens in their own country, which has been overtaken by a majority that fails to understand the Coptic core beliefs and rituals. It is a dual existence that some cannot tolerate. They trade it for another type of duality: living as a Copt in the West.

THE LANDS OF EMIGRATION AND THE OTHER CHURCHES

Having churches outside Egypt has added a whole new dimension to Coptic identity. Copts looking in from the outside started to question age-old rituals and to regard the forbearance of those suffering in Egypt as too meek a reaction to what in terms of universal laws could be considered acts of blatant violence and terrorism. Emboldened by freedom of expression in their new homelands, the Copts of the diaspora have become openly critical of the Egyptian government. This has not been well received by those remaining in Egypt, who often feel exposed to risk by those who have forgotten that the Egyptian political climate is not free.

The Coptic Church takes pride in the rapid development of communities outside Egypt. Since 1971 the number of Coptic churches in the West has grown from only 7 to over 180. Another source of pride is the active mission that the Coptic Church has developed in Africa, setting up churches from Sudan to South Africa.[50] Prosperity in the West flows back into Egypt, where the contributions of emigrants have become influential in promoting the cultural and academic life of the Copts. The *Coptic Encyclopedia*, for example, was the brainchild of Aziz Souriyal Atiya, a us-based Copt who dedicated most of his career as a historian to the preservation of the Coptic heritage. A group of wealthy Copts from the us funded the establishment of a program for Coptic studies at the American University of Cairo, while the Association of St Mark dedicates itself to the publication of books in Arabic and English about Coptic history, art, and culture.

Using new modes of communication, the Copts abroad have taken on a specific role in defending the Coptic community in Egypt. Through websites and pamphlets, they keep alive the memory of violence past and current, documenting in detail every incident of anti-Coptic behaviour. They also provide information on other groups experiencing discrimination in Muslim countries, including Berbers, and on the plight of Christians in Indonesia, Pakistan, and the Philippines. In this way, the Copts have joined the global community of those suffering for faith and ethnicity.

Some perceive this new development as long-lost momentum regained. Well remembered are the days before the Council of Chalcedony in 451, when the Coptic Church was a main player in the ecumenical scene. After it split from the Imperial Church and was cut off from the rest of Christianity, it fell into a state of oblivion. Now the days when Coptic leaders were shining stars in the Ecumenical Councils are being relived. The US-based website for *Copts Digest* proudly remembers: "During the first Ecumenical Council held in the Nicea (321) with 318 bishops the Church of Alexandria had a leading role through its Pope Alexandros 'the most knowledgeable and educated,' and his deacon, Athanasius, who wrote the Creed adopted by the Council."[51]

Being Coptic means accepting the whole package. Christians of other, non-Orthodox denominations wishing to marry a Copt must accept rebaptism. As the Coptic Church strengthens its identity, voices are more often heard that disapprove of marriages between Copts and Catholics or Protestants. Recently a Coptic priest in the Cairo suburb of Ma'adi started an initiative to visit all Copts living in a mixed marriage in order to impress upon them that their marriages were "invalid and thus they were living in sin."[52] In a similar vein, a rural priest near Minya threatened his parishioners in February 2000 with excommunication if they watched the visit of Pope John Paul II on television. Unlike the *umma*, the Coptic community is self-contained and not inclined to actively link up with what could be a formidable ally: the worldwide Christian community. Although there are official ecumenical relations (the Coptic Church is a member of the World Council of Churches), Christians of other denomination are noticed mostly when, like the Copts, they suffer from Muslim violence.

With respect to Coptic nationalism, it appears that the first loyalty of the Copts is to the church, which directs not only the spiritual but also the national allegiance of the community. Coptic protest – for example, against the government – takes place under the aegis of the patriarch. Their second loyalty is to the Egyptian state and environment, not to a worldwide Christian community. Thus Copts are loyal, first and foremost, to their Muslim compatriots; others, even non-Coptic Christians, rank a distant second. A recent example of this loyalty emerged when Copts joined the rest of Egypt in protesting the US invasion of Iraq. This loyalty to Egypt is part of the Copts' success at integrating into Egyptian society on their own terms. If Copts were to become semi-Western Christians, for example, their battle for acceptance would surely be lost.

TOWARD A NEW IDENTITY

Coptic self-renewal serves as a model illustration of Anthony D. Smith's theory regarding the potential for an ethnic minority's revival. Coptic religious reform is now firmly situated within the Egyptian culture. Reforming the church did not mean withdrawal from society but allowed for a deeper participation in the life of Egypt. Rural-development projects, for example, allow Copts and Muslims to work together.

Coptic self-renewal was so successful that it created a new, proactive identity that Manuel Castells calls the "identity for resistance." He discerns three forms of identity building that contribute to the development of societies and nationalism: (1) the legitimizing identity that generates civil society and in due time takes over the state without a direct assault; (2) the identity for resistance that forms the basis for building communes or communities; and (3) the project identity that is formed when social actors build new identities that redefine their positions in society. As an example of the third identity, Castells mentions women's rights groups that have left the trenches of resistance to challenge an overwhelming patriarchal structure. Castells sees the identity based on resistance as the most important.[53] Only briefly in their history were Copts allowed to participate in building Egyptian civil society. For the longest part of their existence, they were in resistance and forced to build their own community, with the church and the sacred as safe haven.

Peaceful resistance through prayer has partially transformed the Coptic community into a nonviolent civil-rights movement similar to Mahatma Gandhi's. They have no territorial ambitions – after all, the whole of Egypt is their Motherland – and they ask only for the right to be visible as Christians. With the problems created by Islamists, Egypt knows that, in an odd way, it needs this type of peaceful community. As I noted, the state has started to use certain occasions to introduce modest improvements to interreligious relationships. The millennium celebrations and the ensuing visit of Pope John Paul II in February 2000 were opportune moments to put the Coptic community in the limelight. The Egyptian minister of tourism produced a booklet called *The Holy Family in Egypt*, stating in bold script that "the unity of the Egyptian people, both Moslems and Copts, is the backbone of the entity of the Nation-State of Egypt." The visit of Pope John Paul II received elaborate descriptions in the media and several hours of television coverage. After this visit, state-controlled media started to allow a few more hours for Coptic news, views, festivals, and religious rituals.

Other moves by the government to improve the position of the Copts have included:

- allowing for increased Coptic participation in public life, culminating in the election to Parliament of three Copts in 2000, fifty years after the last public election of a Copt, and continued appointments by the president of an additional number of Copts to Parliament
- after four decades, the return of Church endowments confiscated under Nasser
- revision of schools' curricula to render them more sensitive to Coptic concerns, culture, and history and to improve relationships between Muslim and Christian children[54]

As with other developments described in this chapter, these were based on careful preparations. Copts realized that the key to regaining a position in Egyptian national awareness was to create a real dialogue focused on social and cultural issues. Dwelling on dogmatic questions of the differences between Islam and Christianity had never been a productive approach to dialogue between the two faiths. In 1985 Patriarch Shenouda started to hold breaking-of-the-fast *(iftar)* gatherings during the Muslim fasting month of Ramadan, reviving an old tradition of friends visiting each other to create a spirit of love as remembered by Dr Rushdi Said, whose words open this chapter. The gatherings became successful all over Egypt.

The Coptic Centre for Social Studies focused on creating solid foundations for the question of Coptic citizenship by producing three books about this topic, authored by teams of Copts and Muslims.[55] The books address in detail the Egyptian, Islamic, and constitutional bases for citizenship. A division of this project researched the disastrous results of the 1995 elections, when not one of the many Coptic candidates managed to win.

To create a new, less fanatic generation of Muslims that might serve as a buffer zone, Bishop Athanasius of Beni Suef started to build one school a year in his diocese, which was the largest in Egypt before he passed away and it was subdivided. The goal is to create a space where Muslim and Christian children can learn together and develop a spirit of friendship. The novelty of the schools is their English-only curriculum and that, even though the schools are private, children of poor families are allowed to attend, paying only a nominal fee for tuition. The long waiting lists show that the schools are a solution for many Muslim parents who realize that creating a climate of bigotry does not improve their children's condition in any way.

The bishop for youth, Anba Mousa, encouraged young Copts to meet with Muslims during interfaith discussions that started in 1985 and intensified after 1989. "There is a gap we have to cross; we should not sit and wait but move with Christian love. Push the young Copts to be among their Muslim brothers so that they do not become isolated but find their place in groups and clubs. If we close up and withdraw, we are going to lose."[56] A special subject addressed by the Bishopric for Youth is how to cope with extremism. The bishopric has prepared a model that divides Muslims into five categories: representatives of the government (i.e., the Islamic state), liberal Muslims, moderate Muslims, extremist Muslims, and terrorist Muslims. Relationships with the government take place via the Coptic hierarchy, guided by the patriarch. The dialogue with liberal and moderate Muslims is a continual process that never really stopped and finds expression in scores of official discussions and unofficial grassroots events. According to the bishopric, it is useless to waste energy on terrorists since it is part of their agenda and identity that they refuse to converse with those who are not Muslim. Muslims of extremist tendencies, however, receive the bishopric's close attention. As they do not comprise a homogenous group, it is considered useful to seek out those who are willing to engage in dialogue with Christians. Since the participants in the interfaith activities are already bound together by their youth, they have a foundation for mutual regard. Moreover, they constitute Egypt's future and thus can never be ignored.

There are, however, limits to Coptic interest in dialogue with Muslims. The Catholic priest Yuhanna Kulta, on the occasion of Ramadan, wrote an article in which he praised the Prophet Muhammad. While receiving praise from Muslim sides, some of the Coptic comments were vicious. In Coptic eyes, Father Kulta had crossed the line that keeps the two faiths apart. In an interview I had with him shortly after this article appeared, he defended his writing as follows: "This was the first time that a Christian in Egypt spoke about the Prophet Muhammad in a positive way. After a while my article will be understood. You never have to talk with Muslims about the divinity of Christ, you talk about love. Islam can never replace Christianity since the Christian religion is based on God's love."[57]

Another youth-generated project studies how culture influences Coptic and Muslim patterns of thought concerning women. Headed by Vivian Fouad, the project members, comprising both Copts and Muslims, analyzed sermons and writings of 700 Christian and Muslim leaders, such as Patriarch Shenouda, Father Matta al-Meskin, and Sheikhs al-Azhar and Sha'arawi. The team's motivation was its dissatisfaction that "current discourse assigns women specific roles only and is limited to the middle-class level."[58]

The preliminary findings of the study are that there are fundamentally few differences in men's attitudes toward women, whether the men are Copt or Muslim. Armed with these results, a team has started to address the custom of female circumcision, or Female Genital Mutilation (FGM). The entrenchment of the traditional mindset they are battling became evident when they presented the project to Patriarch Shenouda. When Vivian revealed that it was her dream to ban the practice of FGM, he asked her "Why?"

The main aim of the project is to fill the vacuum that exists in Egyptian feminism and to contribute to the creation of a religious, feminist discourse for women. The leading Muslim feminists are mostly secular, and few are working on the development of an indigenous Muslim discourse. The Coptic Church does not have feminist theologians, although several women have graduated from the Coptic seminaries. According to Vivian and her team, a lack of fundamental knowledge on both sides about the place of women in the respective religions obstructs fruitful dialogue on the status of women.

CONCLUSION

Although outwardly impeccable citizens, in reality Copts live in a state of resistance that is peaceful but not passive: They resist being pushed from Egypt's national scene, and they resist their religion being rendered obscure by intolerant Muslims trying to enforce their claim to the truth. While outwardly accommodating the Egyptian environment, Copts hold on to their Christian identity, which is anchored in the reinvented universe of the Coptic Church and its beliefs. Their unique tradition, which goes back two millennia, provides the signposts for the Coptic map of Egypt.

In particular, the tradition of stressing the spiritual life has provided the roots for the Coptic renewal. Modelling themselves on the holy men (and women) of early Christianity, who could look beyond the visible now and here, Coptic Church leaders such as Patriarchs Kyrillos VI and Shenouda III, Bishops Samuel and Athanasius, and Father Matta al-Meskin searched for inspiration beyond the obvious to recapture the vigour their church once had. They could do this because they were no longer reduced to the state of *dhimmis* and because they had the intellectual and professional tools. Copts regard the adversities with which they must live as a blessing in disguise. Remembering that their church produced its best thinkers, theologians, and desert fathers in times of duress, they identify with its leaders of old, such as Clement of Alexandria (b. circa 150), Athanasius (patriarch, 328–73), and the famous desert father St Anthony (250–356). The names of the contemporary leaders express their desire to emulate the courage and creativity of these early fathers.

By fortifying their counteridentity with scores of spiritual, social, ritual, and educational initiatives, Copts have succeeded in giving their existence in Egypt new meaning. Just as the early fathers were unbendable concerning their doctrines but flexible concerning methods, Copts have borrowed new models of teaching and grassroots development work from Protestants and the West, they have allowed women to participate in the new projects, and they do not shy away from using the newest technologies. Nevertheless, even though tradition is reinvented, holy sites are rediscovered, and new hagiographies regularly surface, the core message of Coptic Christianity may not be tampered with. Copts are, for example, not allowed to read the popularized translation of the Bible: the Good News version.

Whether the Coptic project to find full equality in Egypt will ever succeed depends on many variables, the most important being the introduction of true democracy. For Copts to leave Egypt all together has never been an option. They belong to the Egyptian soil and need it as much as Egypt needs them. Thus, if the law of the land cannot protect them against hate crimes and bigotry, the most powerful defence the Copts have is to regain their space in Egypt's public life, to keep the lines of communication with Muslims open, to try to change the biased public mindset, and to provide alternative models that are beneficial for both groups. It is true that Coptic children will never stop singing the words from a popular song "I am a Christian, a Christian ... [Look at] the tattoo on my hand!" but this tattoo will hinder the Copts' full integration only as long as Egypt does not have a fully democratic system that guarantees freedom of expression and belief for all.

NOTES

1 Interview with Dr Rushdi Said (born in the 1920s), Cairo, 26 February 2000.
2 Interview with Catholic bishop Yuhanna Qulta (born in the 1930s), Cairo, 15 February 1998.
3 Interview with Sister Rauth (born in the 1950s), an active Coptic Orthodox nun, Cairo, 18 February 1998.
4 Anthony D. Smith, *National Identity*, 33.
5 "Copts" here are the members of the Coptic Orthodox Church, the original, indigenous church of Egypt. There are a small number of Protestants and Catholics in Egypt who share in the fate of the Orthodox Copts. Their churches are, however, of foreign origin.
6 Nabil 'abd el-Fattah (editor-in-chief) and Diaa Rashwan (managing editor), *The State of Religion in Egypt Report 1995: Summary*.
7 An exception is the book by S.S. Hasan, *Christians versus Muslims in Modern Egypt*.
8 *General Census of Population and Housing, all Egypt*. See also E.J. Chitham, *The Coptic Community in Egypt*.
9 It is almost impossible to verify this number, as it is based on interviews with church workers, bishops, and observers of the Coptic Orthodox Church such as the Jesuit father Maurice Martin. All agree that there are conversions to Islam due to intermarriage and because poor Copts from rural areas who move to the cities are recruited by Muslim groups with promises of work and prosperity.
10 Smith, *National Identity*, 21, 62.
11 Ibid., 35–7. The term "portable, protective shell" was coined by Smith, 62.
12 See Hasan, *Christians versus Muslims*, 32–53; and R.B.L. Carter, *The Copts in Egyptian Politics, 1918–1952*.

13 Aziz Souriyal Atiya begins his life work, the *Coptic Encyclopedia*, by stressing the Coptic pharaonic roots (lxi-lxiii). Around 90 per cent of the current Egyptian population is of Coptic origin either through intermarriage between Copts and Arab occupiers or because many Egyptians' Coptic ancestors converted to Islam.
14 Maurice S.J. Martin, "The Coptic-Muslim Conflict in Egypt," 38.
15 Hasan, *Christians versus Muslims*, 105.
16 For lists of the various incidents from the 1970s to the mid-1980s, see Nadia Ramsis Farah, *Religious Strife in Egypt*. See also Hasan, *Christians versus Muslims*.
17 Gilles Kepel, *The Prophet and the Pharaoh*, 158.
18 Some of the latest information about state violence is based on the Egyptian issue of *Country Reports on Human Rights Practices 2002*, published by the Bureau of Democracy, Human Rights and Labor, (Washington DC, 31 March 2003).
19 Among others, see the *New York Times*, 22 April 2001, and Dr Ibrahim's letter of 20–23 March 2001 to the US Embassy in Cairo. Dr Ibrahim was released temporarily early in the seven-year sentence but was retried several times before being exonerated.
20 Tarif Khalidi, "Religion and Citizenship in Islam," 36.
21 *Al-Ahram Weekly*, no. 506 (2–8 November 2000), http://weekly.ahram.org.eg.
22 *Country Reports on Human Rights Practices: Egypt*, 2002, section 2c.
23 George Eshaq, the director of a Coptic school in Cairo, heard these remarks during a meeting with members of the Gama'at Islamiyyah in 1992. See also Pieternella van Doorn-Harder, *Contemporary Coptic Nuns*.
24 A list published by the Ibn Khaldoun Centre for Development Studies shows that during the 1950s, 6 incidents of religious violence and attacks on Copts occurred, 2 during the 1960s, 49 during the 1970s, 111 during the 1980s, and 368 between 1990 and 1993. Saad Eddin Ibrahim et al., *The Copts of Egypt*, report for Minority Rights Group International, 22.
25 "Egyptian-American Writer: The Egyptian Regime Encourages Persecution of Christian Copts," The Middle East Media Research Institute, Egypt Reform Project, 3 August 2002, no. 352 (writer anonymous; first published in *Al-Quds Al-Arabi* [London], 7 March 2002, 9).
26 See Christiaan van Nispen tot Sevenaer, "Changes in Relations between Copts and Muslims," 32.
27 The three main authorities interviewed were: Sheikh Yusuf Al-Qardawi, Dr Mohammed Ra'fat Uthman (dean of Al-Azhar University's College of Shari'ah and Law), and Dr Mohammed Nur Farahat (a law professor).

28 For a summary of the foundational Muslim Arabic writings about this topic, see P.J. Vatikiotis, "Non-Muslims in Muslim Society."
29 *Copts Digest,* 13 August 2001, Coptsdigest.com.
30 Hasan, *Christians versus Muslims,* 266.
31 Interview with Bishop Mousa, bishop of youth, 18 February 1998.
32 Manuel Castells, *The Information Age,* vol. 2, *The Power of Identity,* 51.
33 Ibid., 29.
34 See Anthony D. Smith, *Myths and Memories of the Nation.*
35 The seventh-day ritual stems from a time when many babies died shortly after birth. By the seventh day, the child has received its name and been presented to a wider circle than that of its immediate family. It is greeted by a special procession of children holding candles and singing songs. On the fortieth day after death, family and friends gather to say special prayers in front of a picture of the deceased.
36 Among others, see Fredrik Barth, "Ethnic Groups and Boundaries," 75–82.
37 Nathan Kater, "On the Arabhood of the Copts," *Copts Digest,* 20 September 2001, Coptsdigest.com.
38 See, among others, van Doorn-Harder, *Contemporary Coptic Nuns,* 24.
39 Interview with Patriarch Shenouda III, 19 February 1998.
40 This paragraph is based on Nora Stene, "Becoming a Copt: The Integration of Coptic Children into the Church Community," on my book *Contemporary Coptic Nuns,* and on observations made during fieldwork.
41 Van Doorn-Harder, *Contemporary Coptic Nuns,* 79.
42 Wolfram Reiss, *Erneuerung in der Koptisch-Orthodoxen Kirche,* 149.
43 Interview with Bishop Mousa, 18 February 1998.
44 Van Doorn-Harder, *Contemporary Coptic Nuns,* 37–9.
45 For the seminaries and the numbers of students graduating, see *Al-Kiraza* 21 (1993), nr. 45/46.
46 Translation from Christian Cannuyer, *Coptic Egypt,* 104–5.
47 Maurice Assad, "Prägung der koptischen Identität," 114ff.
48 Acts 18:9, 10: "Do not be afraid, but speak and do not be silent; for I am with you, and no one will lay a hand on you to harm you, for there are many in the city who are my people."
49 Iris Habib el-Masri, *The Story of the Copts,* 359–61.
50 See His Grace Bishop Antonius Markos, *Come Across ... and Help Us.*
51 From the sermon of the departed Anba Youanis, *Copts Digest,* 19 March 2001, Coptsdigest.com.
52 Interview with Dr Christiaan van Nispen tot Sevenaer, February 2000.
53 Castells, *The Power of Identity,* 8–10.

54 These observations are based on: (1) Letter by Dr Saad Eddin Ibrahim on the Occasion of the Visit to Egypt by the US Commission on International Religious Freedom, *Copts Digest,* 20–23 March 2001, Coptsdigest.com; and (2) interviews with Dr Nabil 'abd el-Fattah and several representatives of the Coptic community.
55 Isma'il Sabri 'Abd Allah, William Sulaiman Qilada, and Muhammad Salim al-'Awa, *Al-Muwatina*; Amir Nasr, *Al-Musharika al-Wataniya lil-Aqbat fi al-'Asr al-Hadith,* vol. 1.; and William Sulaiman Qilada, *Mabda'u-l-Muwatina.*
56 Interview with Bishop Mousa, 18 February 1998.
57 Interview with Father Yuhanna Kolta, 15 February 1998; see also *Al-Ahram Weekly,* 24 February to 1 March 2000.
58 Interview with Vivian Fouad, 4 March 2000.

3

The Egyptian Copts: Nationalism, Ethnicity, and Definition of Identity for a Religious Minority

CHARLES D. SMITH

INTRODUCTION:
SELF-DEFINITIONS OF IDENTITY IN NATIONAL
AND INTERNATIONAL CONTEXTS

The literature on minorities has exploded in recent years, influenced primarily by events in Europe during the 1990s. This scholarship should afford Middle East specialists the opportunity to test hypotheses found in their own research against conclusions based on data drawn from other regions, especially with respect to questions of nationalism and ethnicity. A welcome contribution to the study of Middle East minorities was that edited by Ofra Bengio and Gabriel Ben-Dor, *Minorities and the State in the Arab World*, although presentation of theoretical matters was mainly limited to Ben-Dor's introduction, and most of the sources used by contributors date from the 1980s. Equally useful is the collection of empirical studies edited by Andrea Pacini, *Christian Communities in the Arab Middle East: The Challenge of the Future*, and the recent comparative essay on the status of minorities in Egypt and India by C.A. Bayly.[1]

This chapter considers the question of the Egyptian Copts within the frameworks of nationalism, ethnicity, and identity. It also examines the changing role of the state in contributing to the definition of the identity of a particular minority. Finally, I address the problem of disparate and occasionally conflicting information offered by sources.

Whereas ethnicity is often associated with "subnational units" and minorities in relation to the majority, I argue here, following Thomas Hyland Eriksen, that the term in social anthropology refers to groups considering themselves culturally as well as racially distinctive. In short, I introduce the term ethnicity because of its usual link to consideration of minority status but also to argue that it is not a term easily applicable to consideration of Egyptian Copts and their relations with Egyptian Muslims; other than religion, they are neither culturally nor ethnically distinctive today. Further complicating matters is Copts' identification of themselves as Egyptians sharing a national identity with Egyptian Muslims. Is there any element that defines for Copts, and for non-Copts, their uniqueness within Egypt other than their status as a religious minority?[2]

With regard to identity, not only do the Copts of Egypt define themselves with respect to the Egyptian state and the Muslim majority in this state, but they also insist that their Christianity is the true Christianity and hold views that depart from all other Christian beliefs concerning the divinity of Jesus.[3] They do not appear eager to identify themselves with other Christian minorities in the Middle East; when they do, they note that they are the largest of the Middle Eastern Christian communities.

Although framed in religious terms, this appears to be an Egyptian *national* assertion of Christian religious preeminence within the framework of minority identity in an overwhelmingly Muslim country. Copts, as well as Egyptian Muslims, retain, as I have argued elsewhere, a predominant identification with Egypt; neither group subsumes this identification within broader, competing national loyalties. That such national loyalty linked to a territorially bounded state can coexist with retention of religious identities challenges basic assumptions underlying the arguments of Benedict Anderson in his *Imagined Communities: Reflections on the Origin and Spread of Nationalism*.[4]

To be sure, these arguments do not deny the possibility of broader identities that link a particular minority to outside movements, but it is important to consider whether the impulse for such linkage comes from within the state or region or from outside.

For example, the Coptic community, especially the church leadership *in Egypt*, insists on representing itself to the outside world, despite its travails, and is clearly alarmed at efforts elsewhere, especially in the United States, to politicize the question of its status by labelling it a persecuted minority in an Islamic state. This has resulted from the expansion of Coptic dioceses overseas, following Copts who emigrated possibly because of recent persecution, but also over the past half century for better economic opportunities, especially after President Nasser's nationalization decrees of 1960. These dioceses are concentrated mainly in Canada, the United States, and Australia, and by 1995 included an estimated 300,000 in the United States, 50,000 in Canada, and 35,000 in Australia; the first church in the US was established in Jersey City, NJ, in 1964. A survey in 2002 lists ninety-two Coptic Orthodox parishes in the United States and twenty-two in Canada, suggesting ongoing growth.[5]

The expansion of overseas dioceses clearly reflects the desire of the church to minister to its flock abroad, but it also indicates patriarchal determination to represent the Coptic community to others in terms agreeing with the directions emanating from Patriarch Shenuda III in Cairo (installed as patriarch in 1971). Consolidation of Coptic Church authority has been going on for over half a century (to be discussed below) but has been spurred in recent years by alarm at representations to the US Congress by independent Coptic publicists demanding outside intervention in Egyptian affairs. It is noteworthy that this alarm at the prospect of such external intervention has been expressed not only by the Coptic Church in Cairo, but by Sadd Eddin Ibrahim, recently released from prison in Egypt, whose critical essays on Egyptian politics have been used by Copt publicists and their political allies in the United States to justify intervention and criticism of the Egyptian government.

These developments illustrate what as been called "the growth of transnational religious movements" and their offshoots, which add global dimensions to what were formerly considered statist issues or particular religious concerns within a given state. It also demonstrates the impact of new information technology on this subject. If print culture, for Benedict Anderson, removed control of the printed word from overarching religion-based governmental systems, facilitating the expansion of secular nationalism beginning in the sixteenth century, then the computer and the fax machine serve analogous functions today but with different results. They can be used by both sides, by the church as well as by its opponents, contrary to Anderson's thesis, which presumes that print capitalism signifies a unilateral direction away from loyalty to religious identity.[6]

The Coptic lobby in the United States is "electronically savvy and well-connected" and not under church supervision; conversely, clergy distrust lobby efforts by those described as "secular Copts." Matters have developed to the point where the website "Copts.com," based in the United State, has as its subtitle "Home of the Persecuted Copts in *Egypt*" (my emphasis); dissident Copts are represented by the American Coptic Association, founded in 1998.

In riposte, a website under the title "Copts in Egypt and Abroad" is actually sponsored by the Egyptian government. In its material on Copts, it features a series of interviews with Patriarch Shenuda, summarizing the book by Rajab al-Banna (cited in note 6) *The Copts in Egypt and Abroad: Conversations with Patriarch Shenuda*.[7] The book is intended to "confront those who trifle with and conspire against Egypt and Egyptians." The faithful in Egypt and overseas should be "on the alert and ... aware of the conspiracy," meaning that undertaken by dissident Copts.

In chapter 3, "Expatriate Copts," Shenuda specifically rebukes overseas Copts for blaming the Egyptian government for terrorism and for publishing harmful materials without consulting the church; these individuals should seek approval from pastors of Egyptian churches overseas who give guidance and would never publish an attack on Egypt. Indeed, those who publish such blasphemous material against the Egyptian state and President Mubarak "can no longer be identified as *Egyptian* [not as a Copt; my emphasis] ... [especially because] the western media take for granted the talk of these sick-minded, vengeful, and disillusioned persons." Finally, with respect to identity, Shenuda said that the "Copts are no minority. They do [not] [sic] qualify for the definition of minority. They are not the blacks of the USA nor the Muslims of Germany. They are part of the texture of society, part of the history of Egypt."

Official Copt alarm is understandable given the exploitation of this question by evangelical Christians in the US, allied to dissident Copts but also linked occasionally to right-wing pro-Israeli forces in Congress, which seek levers to influence American policy makers against current Arab allies of the US. A book that has served as a rallying cry for Christian activists is Paul Marshall's *Their Blood Cries Out*, which has been used by groups such as Christian Solidarity International and the Center for Religious Freedom and which has focused on Sudan as well.

These groups banded together to gain passage of the Freedom from Religious Persecution Act of 1998, with lobbying assistance from Copt activists in the US. Such activism, often backed by Christian evangelicals, is reflected with respect to Pakistan in a recent book by

Warren Larson titled *Islamic Ideology and Fundamentalism in Pakistan: Climate for Conversion to Christianity?*, and Christian evangelical groups have entered Iraq in the wake of the American occupation to seek converts there.[8] Although these groups can be viewed as opposing all types of religious persecution and oppression, there is an anti-Islamic tone, as witnessed in the above title, that has intensified since the al-Qa'ida terrorist attacks of 11 September 2001 against the United States. Calls for the nuclear destruction of Mecca and Medina, the two holiest sites in Islam, and possible conversion of the survivors to Christianity, have been proclaimed on conservative websites such as the "National Review," and a former Reagan official, Fred Iklé, called for "nuking" Mecca and Medina in an op-ed in the online *Wall Street Journal*; these statements were headlined in newspapers in the Arab and broader Muslim world.[9]

Although these lobbying activities were undertaken well before the terrorist attacks of 11 September, this event has served to encourage such protagonists, who are often allied with the pro-Israeli lobby to discredit the American scholarly community specializing in Middle East affairs in the eyes of Washington policy makers.[10]

Beyond the question of these tensions is a specific dispute within the Coptic community that exceeds the framework of expatriates vs the church. It involves church efforts to embrace all members of the community, in a sense a Coptic version of the *umma* (Muslim community), and anger that the church's wishes are defied. Conversely, some Copts in Egypt and more clearly overseas resent that Patriarch Shenuda has made his peace with the Egyptian government even though attacks against Copts in upper Egypt, admittedly more isolated occurrences than before, have continued. That al-Banna's *The Copts in Egypt and Abroad* was published initially in Arabic and addressed to all Egyptians is itself significant, but its exploitation in English on the Internet signifies the effort to include expatriate Copts in a single transnational religious community under the guidance of the Cairo patriarchate.

To a degree this dispute centres on the question of minority identity and its assertion, with the leader of the community denying its status as a minority. That the Egyptian state and the Coptic Church have reached a truce and agreed to unite against radical Islam has in turn split elements of the Coptic émigré community from the church – especially, it would appear, in the United States. If one's status as a minority includes, as much scholarship argues, a sense of collective persecution based on memory of discrimination, real or perceived, Copt persecution is asserted as deeply felt more by those living overseas, who are free of it, than by those living where it supposedly exists, in Egypt; Shenuda insists that the Copts are thoroughly integrated within the Egyptian state and national entity.

An obvious retort is to say that Patriarch Shenuda has no choice but to make such claims, but this is the same patriarch who openly defied President Anwar al-Sadat on behalf of his flock in 1980 in the midst of major Muslim-Copt clashes in Cairo as well as Upper Egypt. Sadat accused Shenuda in May 1980 of plotting a Coptic secession from Egyptian rule, with Assuit as the capital of a Coptic state, and removed Shenuda from the patriarchate in September. Placed under house arrest and then isolated in a desert monastery, Shenuda remained there until his release by President Husni Mubarak in January 1985.

With respect to questions of territorial nationalism and the role of the state, other observations can be offered, based in part on other essays in this collection. Berbers, for example, are reasonably well-integrated within the Moroccan polity when compared to their compatriots living in Algeria. Clearly, territorial nationalism does not explain the identity formation of the Berbers, but the tolerance of the Moroccan state for Berber activities contrasts sharply with that seen in Algeria, where the question of the existence of a functioning state itself appears open to question. The situation of Kurds begs comparison in certain respects because no state with generally acknowledged boundaries embraced the Kurds partially or fully; most lived within the Ottoman Empire as loyal Sunni Muslims until after the First World War. To be sure, Kurdish national ambitions have been articulated since then, but they have foundered and have served mainly to instigate devastating reprisals, particularly in Turkey and Iraq, the latter itself an artificial state. Iraqi Kurdish efforts to acquire autonomous status for a Kurdish region in the north of the new Iraqi state that will emerge are no longer as sure of success as originally appeared, despite general acknowledgment of long-standing Kurdish settlement in and claims to the area.

In contrast, the Copts have had their religious and historical identity within the land of Egypt acknowledged by Egyptian Muslims and the Egyptian state despite the violence inflicted upon them by Islamic extremists in recent years. The question for the Copts is not so much that of identity but of the status derived from their identity;

are they to be given equal treatment before the law or, according to some extremist Islamist claims, forced to revert to *dhimmi* (minority) rank in a state ruled by the *shari'a* (Islamic law), issues to which I will return in the conclusion.

THE COPTS:
RELIGION AND SOCIAL PRACTICES

The Copts qualify in Anthony D. Smith's phrase as an *ethnie*, the original core of the Egyptian nation, the descendants of the Egyptians of the Pharaonic era.[11] It is arguable that a majority of Egyptian Muslims are themselves descended from Coptic blood and that this process continues; there are estimates of at least several hundred conversions to Islam annually, for reasons I will note later. The Copts generally stress that they are an integral part of an Egyptian nation, a secular identification designed to minimize the impact of being designated a religious minority set against a Muslim majority.

In terms of numbers, how much a part of Egypt are the Copts; what percentage of the Egyptian population is Copt? Copts argue that they comprise 10 to 12 per cent of the population, a figure accepted by some scholars. Most studies, however, adopt official Egyptian-government statistics, which place the proportion at between 6 and 7 per cent. This figure has remained relatively constant for the last fifty years, despite emigration by Copts and, as noted, conversions to Islam.[12]

There is also no agreement on other matters pertaining to the Copts. Who, for example, are the Protestant Copts and Catholic Copts referred to by scholars, including Saad Eddin Ibrahim? Are they actually members of a specific Protestant denomination or members of the Roman Catholic Church? If so, why do they continue to refer to themselves as Copts?

Copts have always retained pride in their distinctiveness vis-à-vis other Christians, noted earlier. According to Edward Wakin, whose book was published in 1963, Copts disliked being labelled "Christians" on their identity cards because it lumped them together with other Christians and blurred their identity. Even Copts who converted to other branches of Christianity "retain[ed] an ambiguous allegiance to their original identity that confounds any Western missionary in search of total conversion." A prominent Catholic Copt woman informed Wakin that her father told her she could follow the

Catholic Church but should be "baptized Orthodox, marry Orthodox, and die in the Orthodox Church." A convert to Protestantism and wife of a high official in the YMCA told Wakin that "We are still Copts [despite the family conversion of 50 years before] ... Many of my cousins are [also] converted to Protestantism. But they will have their children married in the Coptic church."[13]

Some scholars believe that such converts should be identified as part of the broader Catholic or Protestant denomination, but it seems clear that the Copts do not agree. Nevertheless, such linkage was and still is convenient at times, especially with respect to the question of marriage and divorce. Here again sources differ.

Marriage in the Coptic Church is regarded as being of such sanctity that it resembles the union of Jesus with the church. Is divorce possible? This depends on one's source. It is either impossible or possible, although very difficult, with a waiting period of seven years that makes it virtually impossible.

It is here that the matter of conversion, while significant, must be linked with historical interactions between Copts and Muslims as well as current practices. Conversions to different Christian denominations or to Islam appear to be motivated frequently by a wish to end the marriage, notably on the part of the husband, and especially in urban communities. That this then weakens the man's ongoing self-identification as a Copt is doubtful, but it does remove him as a statistic. According to Saad Eddin Ibrahim, however, when either partner in a marriage converts to Islam or another Christian sect, the Coptic marriage is automatically annulled. This opinion differs from that of Mohamed Afifi, who asserts that the Christian wife of a convert to Islam can remain married to him, authorized by Patriarch Shenuda himself. Otto Meinardus makes no mention of such circumstances; nor does he insist that divorce requires such stringent conditions and a seven-year waiting period. He does note, however, that the reverse, a Copt marrying a Christian of another denomination, has varying conditions attached: A Protestant must be baptized in Coptic Orthodoxy, whereas a Catholic or other Orthodox may merely state in writing his or her intent to practice the Coptic rites.[14]

What further confuses the issue is evidence that, historically, Copts of certain classes often adopted Muslim practices, including polygamy, and that Copts have in the past contracted marriages according to the *shari'a*. Indeed, practices found in Islamic contracts, such as conditions stipulated by the bride, including prohibiting the husband from taking a second wife, entered into Coptic marriage arrangements – even though such contracts contradicted the idea of marriage as an unbreakable sacrament. To be sure, such incidents reflected life in urban communities among relatively wealthy families, as they did among Muslims, but they indicate a blending of arrangements that apparently seemed quite acceptable and were clearly contrary to Coptic doctrine. Although such incidents would not occur today, they do reflect a much closer interaction between elements of the Muslim and Coptic communities before the modern era.[15] In addition, Copts historically practised female circumcision, as did Muslims, especially in Upper Egypt, where Coptic rural communities are concentrated.[16]

COPT-MUSLIM RELATIONS IN HISTORICAL PERSPECTIVE, 1800–1914

Government Posts and Muslim-Copt Charges of Favouritism

It is clear that the Copts' status as a minority has been problematic at times in the modern era with respect to their national identity and legal standing within Egypt, but the sources disagree as to the position of Copts during foreign occupation. At times Copts aligned themselves with foreign rulers against fellow Egyptians despite the proclaimed or assumed favouritism shown by these occupiers to the Muslim majority. For example, Napoleon declared himself a Muslim on the eve of his invasion of Egypt, a transparent propaganda device that supposedly endangered the Copts' security. Still, he retained the services of Copt fiscal experts who had served the Mamluk rulers, and Copts formed a Coptic Legion that followed the French army back to Europe and served in campaigns there.[17]

Following Napoleon's departure, Copts maintained an apparently significant presence in Muhammad Ali's and subsequent Egyptian administrations, especially in financial affairs. With the British occupation in 1882, Copts expected preferential treatment and were resentful when it was not forthcoming. Many felt that the British deposed them of their jobs in favour of Armenians and Syrians. Historical accounts suggest that British officials took pains not to antagonize either community, Muslim or Copt, but would at times naturally favour the Muslim majority, seeking to quell nationalist resentment, especially in the first decade of the twentieth century. Perceptions were critical then as now. Muslims suspected the British of favouring fellow Christians. Copts believed the opposite but welcomed British intervention in times of communal tensions.[18]

In this instance, it is clear that those of the minority identity retained the sense that they were subject to discrimination, whether real or perceived, although those who were accused of discrimination were the British, not Egyptian Muslims. However, perceptions are not always accurate, and statistics for the period 1882–1914 suggest otherwise. Jeffery Collins argues that non-Muslims were "disproportionately represented on all levels of the government bureaucracy" after 1882, with Christians as numerous at some levels as non-Egyptians. It appears that Copts began replacing Turko-Circassian ministers after 1882 and that significant posts at the middle level of bureaucracy, such as inspector and judge, were opened to them so that they "could act to extend the power of their British co-religionists." Nevertheless, entry into lower-level posts, such as that of clerk, was facilitated for Muslims, and the non-Muslims' representation in government of 25.77 per cent from 1891 to 1899 probably "decreased to perhaps seventeen percent through 1907." Although the category of non-Muslims included foreigners, Copts constituted a significant percentage, outstripping their population ratio of less than 7 per cent.

Such evidence seems to bear out the assertion in 1911 of the British proconsul, Sir Eldon Gorst, that "The figures indicate that the Copts are represented in the Egyptian Civil Service both as to numbers and salaries to altogether disproportionate extent" as well as further findings that Copts, and Christians generally, significantly increased their status as part of the Cairene socio-economic elite from 1882 to 1894 as indicated by property and mortgage records.[19]

This evidence also challenges the statements made by those sympathetic to Copts that Muslim charges of Copts collaborating with foreign rulers were unfounded or that with the British occupation Copts were denied the right to hold certain posts such as that of *mudir* or *mamur*, being the governor of a province or the chief administrative officer of a district. Still, that this relative prosperity in terms of representation in higher offices did decrease, according to Collins, from 1900 to 1907 likely furthered Coptic anxieties in a period of heightened nationalist tensions when Copts were perceived as siding with Britain against the goals of Egyptian nationalism.

Nonetheless, Copt alarm during these years did not prevent Copt leaders from continuing to press for preferential treatment from the British, including an attempt to have the British declare Sunday the official day of rest instead of Friday, as observed by Muslims, a demand that Gorst rejected out of hand, resulting in severe criticism by leading Copts. In addition, Butros Ghali Pasha, a leader of the Copt reform movement discussed below, had presided over the trial of the Dinshaway peasants that resulted in the hanging of four of the accused. The 1906 Dinshaway incident, subsequent trial, and carrying out of verdicts greatly inflamed Egyptian nationalism and mobilized opposition to British rule. Some Copts joined this opposition, but Ghali retained his links to the Residency, later became prime minister, and was assassinated in 1910 by a member of the Egyptian nationalist party, a Muslim militant, further inflaming tensions.[20]

Copt Church Reform and the Question of Foreign Interference

In retrospect, it appears that the Copts, despite the nationalist upheavals noted, experienced a new "golden age" after 1882 with regard to access to political office and expansion of wealth that extended to 1914. This assessment is based in part on analysis of developments within the Coptic community itself and invites comparison to similar events since the Second World War. In 1874 lay members of the Coptic Church had succeeded in gaining Khedive Ismail's approval for establishing a religious council *(majlis al-milli)*. Staffed primarily by communicants who were not church officials and who were often regarded as holding "secular" views, this council claimed to supplement church authority even though its existence was due to deep lay concerns about church laxity in overseeing affairs, including administration of Coptic religious endowments *(awqaf)*. Despite ostensible approval by Coptic patriarchs, the general tenor of patriarchate-council relations remained tense and mutually suspicious until a rapprochement was effected only with the accession to office of the current Patriarch Shenuda.

Equally noteworthy is that the lead in representing the Copts to the British after 1882 was not taken by church officials but by members of the Copt community, among them Butrus Ghali. It was Ghali who, with a letter to the khedive, had instigated the *majlis al-milli* movement in 1874, who had been appointed foreign minister by the British in 1895, who was the first Copt to be rewarded with the title of pasha, and who as acting minister of justice had overseen the trial of Egyptian peasants accused of murdering a British officer in 1906, already discussed.[21] Ghali had been an exceptional mediator between British imperial officials and Egyptian officialdom, including at times Khedive Abbas Hilmi, but he was viewed by most Egyptian Muslim nationalists as too pliant and too willing to serve British interests.

The crisis engendered by Ghali's murder inflamed Copt passions. They deeply resented Gorst's attempts to engage Egyptian nationalists in dialogue, which they viewed as casual disregard of their interests. Gorst's attitude intensified the condescension Copts' perceived in the pronouncements of Gorst's predecessor as proconsul, Sir Evelyn Baring (Lord Cromer), before his hasty departure from Egypt in 1907, encouraged by outrage over the Dinshaway incident. Cromer had sought to manipulate Christian sentiments in order to quell nationalist resentment, efforts that call attention to the role of foreign Christian missionary activities at the time.

Cromer, and on occasion the Copt reform movement, which was tied to the religious council rather than to the church, approached the British Church Missionary Society to seek its intervention on the Copts' behalf. Whereas Copts sought the society's aid to encourage Coptic Church reforms by the laity, Cromer hoped to use it to lobby his interests in London. The society's director in Egypt, Bishop Rennie MacInnes, seized the opportunity to impress upon Cromer the extent of Copt grievances. It is clear, however, that this aid could engender a backlash. The Copts, hard-pressed by Egyptian Muslim anger at apparent collaboration with the British, had also been embarrassed by Anglican and Presbyterian missionary activity arguing their case not only religiously but nationally as the only true Egyptian race. These latter arguments, building on the science of eugenics, gave the impression of foreign backing of the Copts as those truly deserving of governing Egypt, further inflaming Egyptian Muslim passions.[22]

The events of this period illustrate how foreign societies, pursuing their own interests, could be seen as useful by opposing groups within Egypt. They also serve as a forerunner to the example of Coptic propaganda in the United States today. In both cases, Copts can point to specific incidents of violence against them, certainly more numerous during the 1980s and 1990s but clearly existent in open threats and harassments following Ghali's assassination.[23] But the perception also exists that there is ongoing discrimination, which may not be borne out by the facts. Copts had seen the Ghali assassination as the culmination of anti-Christian propaganda by Muslims, ignoring its basis in charges that Ghali and others had served British imperial interests. Prominent Copts called a congress in Assuit in 1911 to declare their grievances and also lobbied members of Parliament in London to reverse what they perceived as Gorst's prejudice against them, rivalling a similar congress called by Muslims. Despite extensive publicity, abetted by a book published by a Coptic activist (and republished in the US in 1971), the British government held firm; the author, Kyriakos Mikhail, argued the case of racial purity for the Copts to British officials. With the start of the First World War, passions subsided, and in the war's aftermath Copts would gain prominence as members of the premier Egyptian nationalist party, the Wafd.[24]

Finally, one can point to the activist role played by secular Copts both within the reform movement of the church and in political activity during the occupation period until 1914; the church played virtually no part in either endeavour. In contrast, since the Second World War, an expanded and revitalized Coptic Church has energized the Coptic community and represented it to the Egyptian state and abroad, with the caveat that it objects to the propaganda emanating from outside, rather than encouraging it as did some members of the secular elite before the First World War.

Discrimination: Its Variables and Its Application in Comparative Perspective

A key consideration is the extent to which the Coptic experience past or present has represented what can be called discrimination. In some definitions, religious discrimination is regarded as distinct from either political, economic, or cultural discrimination. A factor in considering any type of discrimination is the degree to which the government, or the state, is involved in or tolerates such discrimination; we can distinguish here between actively encouraging or mandating this discrimination as opposed to taking a passive stance toward it. With respect to religious discrimination, a factor is "the extent to which religious practices are restricted due to either public policy or to widespread social practice, here taking into account the nature of that discrimination and state involvement."[25]

It seems clear that Copts were discriminated against in all of these categories at one time or another in the twentieth century, but it is also the case that many Copts have perceived themselves as suffering from ongoing intentional discrimination when circumstances have suggested otherwise. The question remains as to whether this was deliberately inspired at a given moment, whether it was institutional, reflecting traditional practices that had not been addressed for rectification, or whether the hardship resulted from decrees that included Muslims as well. Traditional discrimination is not in itself *persecution*, but deliberately inspired discrimination could be regarded as such, an important variable since it seems clear that during the 1970s persecution did occur with President Sadat's tolerance.

We must also recall that matters deemed discriminatory today, such as assigning non-Muslim minorities second-class status, were matters of tolerance in communities defined by religious identity that lasted into the twentieth century. Here, too, the appearance of secular states in the nineteenth and early twentieth centuries did not and could not erase cultural assumptions that had been part of state practice when the state was Islamic. Finally, another variable for analysis is the extent to which such practices mirrored actions taken toward elements of the Egyptian Muslim community, although not necessarily against the entire Islamic population. In any case, recent events have their precursors, establishing elements of continuity in the realm of political exploitation of religious issues as well as in that of intentional discrimination.

POLITICAL AND LEGAL ISSUES IN THE MODERN ERA

The 1919 revolution and struggle for independence highlighted disputes within the Coptic community, some Copts fearing, but most welcoming, calls for Egyptian independence, which would necessarily result in a government with a Muslim majority. The Wafd Party of Saad Zaghlul was renowned for its fusion of Copts and Muslims in what was proclaimed the truly *national* party, but this unity led to divisive arguments. When the British declared Egyptian independence in 1922, they reserved for themselves certain rights, including that of protecting minorities in Egypt. Some Copts welcomed, but many condemned, the clause because it included the Copts, not just foreign communities. Those Copts who decried the provision argued that they were Egyptians, not a minority and certainly not foreign, whereas some Muslims saw the clause as indicating special preference for the Copts arranged in advance.[26]

Similar difficulties arose in 1923, when Saad Zaghlul declared that Egyptians should be considered "neither Coptic nor Muslim, but Egyptian." As Bernard Botiveau observes, the Constitution did not stipulate that the *shari'a* was the basis of Egyptian law. Nevertheless (and this is not discussed by Botiveau), the Constitution did declare that Islam was the state religion. Therefore, even though the Constitution proclaimed that all Egyptians were equal before the law and that "liberty of religious opinion was absolute," national identity in constitutional terms was linked to Islam, whatever the hoped-for national unity Zaghlul extolled. Moreover, Copts were listed under the rubric of protected minorities despite their unease with a designation that technically, although not literally, excluded them from the national community.[27]

More specific challenges followed promulgation of the 1971 Constitution, which declared that "the principles of *sharia* law will be a main source of legislation." This phrase was vague enough to be evaded, but the 1980 amendments to the Constitution stipulated more firmly that "The Islamic *sharia* is the main source of legislation," a statement that put both the Egyptian state and the Coptic community on notice.[28] Both institutions have found themselves seeking, by often conflicting means, to block the literal application of Islamic law despite parliamentary instructions mandating such an application because it might once again relegate Copts to *dhimmi*, or protected-minority, status within a religious framework.

Ironically, at precisely this time Anwar al-Sadat, threatened by Islamist movements seeking his overthrow, turned against Patriarch Shenuda when the latter complained about Muslim assaults on Copts. Sadat was a victim of his own policies. Once in office as president of Egypt, he encouraged the resurgence of Islamic activity, notably on behalf of the Muslim Brotherhood, to counter anticipated opposition from the Egyptian left, which had supported Nasser. This approach backfired when the brotherhood and more radical groups began to condemn corruption in the Sadat regime, largely inspired by Sadat's other initiative, his *infitah*, or economic opening to the West, notably the United States. Coupled with these developments was the outbreak of Muslim incitements of violence against Copts in Upper Egypt, tolerated if not encouraged notably by the appointed governor of Minya and secondarily by Sadat.

Major incidents of violence against Copts began at this time, ultimately sparking the open confrontation between Sadat and Patriarch

Shenuda; there were serious clashes and casualties in Cairo as well as in the Sa'id from 1979 to 1980. Perhaps not given sufficient attention is that the sites of these assaults in Upper Egypt, Minya, and the Assuit provinces were precisely those places where the extremist Muslim organizations Islamic Jihad and the Gama'a Islamiyya originated. Inspired by the writings of Sayyid Qutb, their vision of an Egypt ruled by the *shari'a* incited both their activities against the Sadat regime and incidents of violence against Copts in their midst.[29]

Less well known are analogous incidents from the early 1930s, inspired (as was Sadat's behaviour in the 1970s) by political calculations for domestic support. In this case the Liberal Constitutionalist Party, containing the most openly secular politicians and intellectuals, had come under fire for defending publications attacking Islam. The two most prominent books were *al-Islam wa Usual al-Hukm* (Islam and the principles of government) by 'Ali 'Abd al-Raziq and *Fi al-Shi'r al-Jahili* (On pre-Islamic poetry) by Taha Husayn. The furor over these publications led the Wafd to suggest that the party was anti-Islamic. In reply, the party newspaper, *al-Siyasa*, and its weekly, *al-Siyasa al-'Usbu'iyya*, began reconsidering their secular emphasis for political reasons and by late 1929 had turned to defending Islam. Under the leadership of the papers' editor, Muhammad Husayn Haykal, they also accused the Wafd of harbouring a Coptic conspiracy against Muslim Egypt because of its Copt membership and, in one instance, of seeking to "use the nationalist movement to gain power over Muslims," charges taken up by other papers.[30]

It is clear, therefore, that manipulations of minority issues for political gain by persons known to be secular was not new. New in the 1970s was what could be called sustained, rather than sporadic, violence and persecution resulting in numerous deaths, with the apparent tolerance of the state at the time. How representative was the behaviour of the state under Sadat and how representative was the reaction of the Coptic community? Can Copt action in general be linked solely to state actions considered to be aimed at the Coptic community?

THE COPTIC RENAISSANCE: THE CHURCH, THE STATE, AND PATRIARCH SHENUDA

In order to answer these questions, I must return to the immediate post-Second World War period, when a Coptic renaissance began.

With the Nasser-led Officers' Coup in July 1952, parliamentary life in Egypt essentially ended, as did active political involvement for most Egyptians. Although the punitive land laws passed by Nasser and the nationalization of businesses from 1960 to 1961 severely punished the Copts, these laws were not directly aimed at Copts but at the wealthy elite generally. This did mean, however, that Copts who had been prominent politically as well as economically before 1952 often had no financial basis for such prominence in the future – and no Copts had been members of the officers' group that took power. Nevertheless, the Nasserite decree placing all charitable endowments (waqfs) under a Muslim Ministry of Religious Affairs could have been seen as a direct challenge to Copts simply because the state ministry represented the majority religion.

At precisely this time, however, the Coptic renewal was gaining ground within the Coptic community. It had begun in the late 1940s within the church among a group of younger clergy and involved not simply the creation of a new sense of unity among clergy serving the community, but also a renovation of the monastic communities. For the first time, stress was placed on accepting educated candidates for monastic orders, many with university educations who were multilingual and who in earlier times, such as before the First World War, would have been part of the secular Copt elite. New journals were also published.

The movement sought to embrace the entire Coptic community of Egypt within the protective sphere of the church, which would represent it. This meant church insistence on the community being drawn into the religious life of Coptic Christianity as well as a daily round of community activities organizing existence in religious terms defined by the church. Great stress was placed on the martyrdom of the founders of the church and on the sacrifices made by leaders over the centuries. During this period, especially beginning in 1960, the cleric who would become Patriarch Shenuda was deeply involved in these developments and, between 1960 and 1990, would publish some seventy books on church affairs and the unity of the faithful.

This renewal began as a response to modernization, rather than to political threats, and can be traced back to the late 1920s, with earlier manifestations apparent. Like the Muslim Brotherhood founded in 1928, this effort was inspired by devout Copts who were not necessarily members of the clergy but deeply concerned about the impact of secular ideas on adherence to religious values. Reforms were focused on strengthening religious education to counter modern education, stressing religious identity as opposed to a secular state identity, and a concern for the community and its welfare. In short, we see parallels between how elements of the Muslim and Coptic communities reacted against perceived foreign cultural threats to religious identities. Indeed, the Coptic community of the late 1920s and from the late 1940s onward stressed an adherence to "religious precepts" that were identified with the "historical experience of the first four centuries [of the Coptic Church], established by the actors of the renewal as an example to follow."[31]

This appears to be the introduction of a Coptic movement analogous to the Muslim Salafiyya, which called for a return to the model of the Prophetic era as the basis for action in the present; in the 1920s two major journals represented this Muslim trend: *al-Manar*, edited by Muhammad Rashid Rida, and *al-Fath*, edited by Muhibb al-Din al-Khatib. However, whereas the Islamic movement was undertaken by actors outside the dominant Muslim institution, al-Azhar University, the Coptic movement was aimed at restoring the strength of the church, its dominant institution, as the means to represent the community.[32]

The Coptic renewal's stress on using journals and religious literature in the broadest sense to spread this reform further refutes Benedict Anderson's assumptions about print culture and the expansion of secularism. But was this only a religious movement, or could it be seen as a national expression of identity as well? Partha Chatterjee rightly challenges Anderson's assumption that the secular nation is "part of the universal history of the modern world." Chatterjee argues that this is a Eurocentric reading of nationalism that extends the European experience to the non-European world, which, unlike Europe, was colonized. For him, anticolonial nationalism had two domains: the material, or Western, which was rejected, and the spiritual, by which one sought to retain the essence of indigenous spiritual culture. Chatterjee uses the term "spiritual," rather than "religious," to argue that such nationalisms seek to create a modern national culture that is not Western.[33]

To what extent was this Coptic renewal in its earliest stages "political"? There is little evidence of political motivation, but it was clear, as it was with respect to the Muslim Brotherhood, that such activities could have political ramifications. Still, this renewal, with its insistence on the unity of the Copts within the framework of Mother Church, became more "political" in the 1950s, having been fostered by efforts to undermine the Nasser regime's broader political activities. Commitment to church activism meant acceptance of individual noninvolvement in political life, what Dina el-Khawaga calls a "withdrawal," but she asks whether this withdrawal represented "a constant phenomenon typical of minority communities"(i.e., a deliberate depoliticization) or a defensive reaction against the increasing Islamization of Egyptian society?[34]

Initially, this withdrawal was sponsored by the church itself to strengthen its hold on the community, particularly from the late 1940s; this church-initiated withdrawal for internal reasons later enabled the church to provide a strong institutional response to Islamization from the mid-1970s onward. At this time, too, Patriarch Shenuda resolved the church's problematic relationship to the religious councils by agreeing to chair their meetings, drawing them more fully into church activism. Moreover, this restructuring of the community under the aegis of the church also amounted to a restructuring of the "political dynamics of the Copts," who would now be represented to the state by the church; this in itself represented a reassertion of religious identity that had increasingly important political implications, as it provided Copts with a mechanism to resist state actions.

El-Khawaga's argument recalls the work of James C. Scott, although Scott is more concerned with rural actors than with urban institutional responses; nonetheless, the title of Scott's book, *Domination and the Arts of Resistance,* calls to mind the types of responses open to those seeking to carve out areas that the state or dominant force cannot penetrate or in which the state finds it prudent not to intervene.[35] The nature of this resistance involves the creation of political fields of representation and defence (i.e., spaces defining limits and establishing boundaries) rather than necessarily direct involvement in politics.

Not so paradoxically, the church's renewal movement allowed the church itself to become a meaningful *political* actor vis-à-vis the state in the absence of other mediating institutions. Indeed, as el-Khawaga argues, the failure of various instruments of civic representation to influence the state makes the use of "religious spheres" all the more attractive in the absence of alternatives.[36] Shenuda and his backers argued that the church had the right to provide social services to Copts in the place of the state: The church was asserting its right to take over presumably state functions "in return for recognition of the Church as spokesman for the community."[37]

The Coptic renewal, therefore, was not initially inspired by state or Muslim persecution but indicated a response to the challenges of secular culture, which were also felt at the time by sectors of the Muslim community. However, the result of this renewal (i.e., the focus on the church as the representative of the community) did serve as the bulwark of the response to the challenges and Muslim-incited violence that the Copts initially faced under the Sadat regime and then more sporadically, but to a degree still constituting a threat, during the Mubarak era.

It is precisely here, however, that we can discern the reasons for dissension within the Copt community today. Although there was always resentment among some educated Copts at the extent of church dominance, this dominance was accepted as the price for protection and for the articulation of community grievances. But from the early 1990s, Patriarch Shenuda reconciled with the Mubarak regime (i.e. the state) because they had a common enemy: the Islamist movements. This tactical alliance infuriated many Copts, particularly abroad, as incidents of violence lessened but did not cease. Consequently, overseas Copts have instigated publicity not only against such violence, but also against their own leadership, which they view as having withdrawn from the fray.

Nevertheless, the entrance of the church into such a relationship with the regime has led to a number of concessions on issues that had been deemed prejudicial: Difficulties in gaining permission to build new churches have been alleviated, and monies taken in the absorption of Coptic *waqfs* (endowments) by the state in the mid-1950s have been returned to the church. In sum, the Coptic Church's political alliance with the state has resulted in the state granting more freedom to Copts as a religious community within an ostensibly secular state.

CONCLUSION

This chapter has raised a number of issues dealing not merely with the Copts, but also with questions of how to interpret minority relations with a state whose overwhelming majority population is of a different religion. Modern Egyptian history suggests the existence of ongoing tensions in the Copts' relationship with the state and with the Muslim community, the latter two entities not always being identical. Throughout the twentieth century, Copts and Muslims expressed suspicions of each other that were at times manipulated for political purposes by secular as well as religious factions seeking to exploit religious identities for political goals.

This is not new. What was new was the emergence of radical Islamic movements seeking the overthrow of the state in the 1970s, thus focusing attention on vulnerable Coptic communities in Upper Egypt. With the state, in the person of Sadat, seeking to exploit these tensions for its own benefit, not always successfully, the salience of religious identity came to the fore among both Christians and Muslims. Moreover, the consolidation of religious identities as communities in the face of modernization enabled these communities to represent themselves politically as well.

The Coptic experience suggests that the status of minorities should be examined in terms not only of how they are acted upon, but also of how they respond to such actions and whether they are able to respond effectively. Do the minorities studied have the capacity and scope for a reply? The Egyptian example would suggest that they do, as does the assertiveness of Copts themselves both within Egypt and without as well as against each other at times. Changes in the status of the Copts over time reflect the influence both of internal community dynamics and of developments in the broader public realm. Today, the Coptic patriarch can define the Copts' identity in national terms, linking it to their identity as Egyptians, thereby openly rejecting the designation of "minority" used by members of his flock, particularly outside Egypt, who assume this identity for their own political reasons.

What relevance does the Copt experience have for analysis of other minority communities generally or within the Islamic world? Perhaps very little, and it is important to note that most Copts in Egypt would likely agree. They insist on their uniqueness not only as a Christian minority in the Islamic world, but also as Christians in a national context despite sharing common historical experiences with other minorities. These experiences have entailed long periods of mutual tolerance and accommodation within an ongoing framework of lingering suspicion of the "other" as defined by religion. These periods have been and are still being disrupted by upheavals of violence instigated by religious or state actors seeking to restructure existing patterns of identity and self-definition for specific goals.

In the case of Copts, their sense of identity as Egyptians coexists with their identity as Copts, but each identity functions in a different sphere. If, as Tobin Siebers has argued, "there can be no political community without a serious conception of borders," such communities can exist within states as religious communities, establishing borders in terms of identities and relationships with other majority or minority communities that regulate interactions and have political as well as religious implications.[38] What is crucial is the recognition of these borders by the state and their acceptance, however grudgingly, by other communities. This recognition seems to characterize the Copts' standing today and, despite the inevitable continuance of tensions seen in the past, should continue to do so in the future.

NOTES

1. Ofra Bengio and Gabriel Ben-Dor, eds, *Minorities and the State in the Arab World*; and Andrea Pacini, ed., *Christian Communities in the Arab Middle East*, notably the articles by Bernard Botiveau, "The Law of the Nation-State and the Status of non-Muslims in Egypt and Syria," and by Dina el-Khawaga, "The Political Dynamics of the Copts"; el-Khawaga's article derives from her doctoral dissertation, *Le renouveau copte*. See also C.A. Bayly, "Representing Copts and Muhammadans."

   For stimulating approaches to minorities generally, see, for example: Gubernau i Berdun and Maria Montserrat, *Nations without States*; T.K. Oommen, *Citizenship, Nationality, and Ethnicity*; Terry H. Pickett, *Inventing Nations*; Jennifer Jackson Preece, *National Minorities and the European State System*; Edward Mortimer, ed., *People, Nation, and State*; Michael Keating, *Nations against the State*, 2nd ed.; Thomas Hyland Eriksen, *Ethnicity and Nationalism*; Geoffery Hosking and George Schopflin, eds, *Myths and Nationhood*; George Schopflin, *Nations, Identity, Power*; and Jerry Everard, *Virtual States*.

2. See the remarks of Thomas Hyland Eriksen in his *Ethnicity, Race, Class, Nation*, 3–7, cited in John Hutchinson and Anthony D. Smith, eds, *Ethnicity*, 28–34.

3. Copts hold that Jesus had a divine and human nature but that these were indistinguishable, thereby opposing Orthodox belief in Jesus' two distinct natures and the Monophysite belief in only his divine nature. On these

and other matters, see Aziz Suryal Atiya, ed., *The Coptic Encyclopedia*, 8 volumes.

4 Benedict Anderson, *Imagined Communities*, 2nd ed. Anderson considers nationalism to be a territorially bounded "cultural artefact" (his spelling) that emerges from two "cultural systems" that have collapsed: the religious community and the dynastic realm (20). Anderson assumes that such nationalism has to be secular – that is, expressed in language that has broken away from the "sacral-based" languages that express religious values. For further discussion, see Charles D. Smith, "Imagined Identities, Imagined Nationalisms," in which I challenge the arguments of Israel Gershoni and James Jankowski, *Redefining the Egyptian Nation, 1930–1945*, with respect to Anderson's views. Gershoni and Jankowski's reply and my rejoinder are in the *International Journal of Middle East Studies* 31 (1999) along with a relevant bibliography. For a recent article arguing the nationalist identity of modernist Islamic movements, see James Gelvin, "Modernity and Its Discontents." Earlier rebuttals of the argument for a "supra-Egyptianism" that erased a sense of territorial identity as Egyptian are the articles by Gabriel Piterberg, "The Tropes of Stagnation and Awakening in Nationalist Historical Consciousness," and James Jankowski, "Arab Nationalism in 'Nasserism' and Egyptian State Policy, 1952–1958."

5 The estimate of the number of Coptic dioceses in the US, Canada, and Australia comes from Nabil 'Abd al-Fattah, ed., *Taqrir al-hala al-diniyya fi Misr, 1995* [Report on the religious situation in Egypt, 1995], 216–17, and is reported in Ami Ayalon, "Egypt's Coptic Pandora's Box," 69 n. 6. My 2002 estimate of the number of Coptic parishes comes from consulting the website www.coptic.org/north_am.htm. One can also consult the website "Coptnet." These numbers significantly exceed Otto Meinardus's estimate in 1999 of over 80 churches in the US and Canada combined, as this figure now appears to stand at 114 combined; See Meinardus, *Two Thousand Years of Coptic Christianity*, 81.

6 Paul S. Rowe, "Four Guys and a Fax Machine? Diasporas, New Information Technologies, and the Internationalization of Religion in Egypt." Other sources of particular interest in this vein are Dale Eickelman and James Piscatori, *Muslim Politics*; and Jeff Haynes, ed., *Religion, Globalization, and Political Culture in the Third World*. For unflattering comments on independent Copt lobbyists in the United States, see Saad Eddin Ibrahim et al., *The Copts of Egypt*, 22. Published by the Minority Rights Group, this book attracted much attention, as has Ibrahim because of his imprisonment by the Egyptian government for his criticism of the Egyptian political process.

A good Egyptian account of the spread of the parishes abroad and Patriarch Shenuda's travels to establish dioceses and oversee religious instruction is Rajab al-Banna, *al-Aqbat fi misr and al-mahjar* [The Copts in Egypt and abroad], especially chapter 3, which provides extensive coverage of this subject.

A note on transliteration: In Arabic the word "Shenuda" is "Shanuda." However, the universal use of "Shenuda" in English leads me to follow this practice.

7 See the website www.sis.gov.eg/online/coptic.
8 Some activities of the International Coptic Federation, the umbrella organization including the American Coptic Association, and its pressure in Washington are noted in H. Scott Kent Brown, "The Coptic Church in Egypt."
9 Fred Iklé was formerly undersecretary of defence in the Reagan administration. His article "Stopping the Next Sept. 11: Intelligence Is One Element, Offense and Defense Are the Others" appeared in the *Wall Street Journal,* 2 June 2002, www.opinionjournal.com/?id=110001790.

Having discussed various forms of terrorism and the threat posed by new technologies and means of delivery, Iklé concluded by referring directly to Saudi Arabia and its financial backing for fundamentalist institutions: "Those who out of cowardice use their wealth to pay danegeld to the preachers of hate and destruction must be taught that this aggression will boomerang. A nuclear war stirred up against the 'infidels' might end up displacing Mecca and Medina with two large radioactive craters."

Such sentiments are not unique among neoconservative backers of the Bush administration. Rich Lowery, editor of the National Review online, (nationalreview.com), which calls itself "America's Premier Conservative Website," wrote on 7 March 2002:

> Lots of sentiment for nuking Mecca. Moderates [sic] opt for something more along these lines: 'Baghdad and Teheran would be the likeliest sites for a first strike. If we have enough clean bombs to assure a pinpoint damage area, Gaza City and Ramallah would also be on the list. Damascus, Cairo, Algiers, Tripoli and Riyadh should be put on alert that any signs of support for the attacks [against the US] in their cities will bring immediate annihilation ... Mecca seems extreme of course but then again few people would die and it would send a signal. Religions have suffered such catastrophic setbacks before ... And, ... the time for seriousness – including figuring out what we would do in retaliation, so maybe it would have some slight deterrent effect – is now rather than after thousands and thousands more American casualties.'

A staff writer, Rod Dreher, chimed in that as for Mecca, "well it would feel good, but then we'd have every Muslim on the planet enraged unto ages of ages."

Another neoconservative, Ann Coulter, had published similar sentiments on the National Review website in September, calling for invading Muslim countries, killing their rulers, and converting the survivors to Christianity. Coulter also expressed these views at an annual meeting of American conservatives with Lynne Cheney, wife of Vice President Dick Cheney, and William Bennett in attendance.

10 For example, Martin Kramer, *Ivory Towers on Sand*. Published by the Israeli lobbying group, the Washington Institute for Near East Policy, this book is aimed at Washington policy makers, as the directors of the institute acknowledge in their preface. Daniel Pipes, founder of Campus Watch, which seeks to monitor presumed criticisms of Israel on US campuses, was recently appointed to the board of the US Institute of Peace by President George W. Bush, who bypassed congressional consideration of the matter to do so. Legislation backed by the Washington Institute is now being considered that would permit courses taught by American academics to be monitored for their political content.

11 Smith's classic statement of his argument is in Anthony D. Smith, *The Ethnic Origin of Nations*. For a discussion of the Pharaonic theme in Egyptian nationalism during the 1920s, see Israel Gershoni and James Jankowski, *Egypt, Islam, and the Arabs*, and my discussion of the applicability of Smith's theories to Egypt in Charles D. Smith, "Imagined Identities, Imagined Nationalisms."

12 Conflicting estimates can be found in the following sources: Philippe Fargues, "The Arab Christians of the Middle East," 59, has the Copt population as a percentage of Egypt's declining from 8.14 per cent in 1886 to 5.87 per cent in 1985, a statistic buttressed by fuller discussion in Youssef Courbage and Philippe Fargues, *Christians and Jews under Islam*, 180–1; Edward Wakin, on the other hand, accepted Coptic figures of about 16 to 18 per cent in his *A Lonely Minority: The Modern Story of Egypt's Copts*, 24–5. Ayalon, "Egypt's Coptic Pandora's Box," 53, summarizes the debates, but the most recent statement, in Jonathan Fox, "The Copts in Egypt," 138–42, accepts a figure of 10 per cent. A Coptic population of 6 per cent of roughly 65 million Egyptians would amount to 3,900,000, nearly 3 million less than a Coptic population of 10 per cent.

13 Wakin, *A Lonely Minority*, 25–6.

14 Otto Meinardus, *Christian Egypt, Faith and Life*, 283; see also his discussion of divorce on page 284. Compare Ibrahim et al., *The Copts of Egypt*, 24–5,

with Mohamed Afifi, "Reflections on the Personal Laws of Egyptian Copts," 202–15. Afifi also argues (202) that while Coptic Christianity does not recognize divorce, the Coptic Church in practice does, a distinction left unclarified. See my discussion below of Coptic polygamy in previous centuries, also taken from Afifi.

15 On the Copts, see Mohamed Afifi, "Reflections on the Personal Laws," 202–18. On similar practices among Muslim families, see Nelly Hanna, "Marriage among Merchant Families in Seventeenth-Century Cairo," 143–54, whose title indicates the elevated status of families in which women could claim such contractual obligations from their prospective husbands.
16 Meinardus, *Christian Egypt*, 318ff.
17 Meinardus, *Two Thousand Years*, 66–7.
18 F. Robert Hunter, *Egypt under the Khedives, 1805–1879*, 22, 85; and B.L. Carter, *The Copts in Egyptian Politics*, 58–9. A good summary of Copt and Jewish participation in public life during the Ottoman period can be found in Michael Winter, *Egyptian Society under Ottoman Rule, 1517–1798*, especially 203–24.
19 For employment statistics, see Jeffery G. Collins, *The Egyptian Elite under Cromer, 1882–1907*, 240–3; his survey of land-holding and mortgage records is on pages 113–31. Gorst's remarks came in his report to the Foreign Secretary, Sir Edward Grey, F.O. 371, vol. 1111, files 8011, 9057, 10869, 10, 11, and 18 March 1911, cited in Peter Mellini, *Sir Eldon Gorst: The Overshadowed Proconsul*, 293 n. 6.
20 Collins, *The Egyptian Elite*, 243, finds Christians holding bureaucratic offices at a rate disproportionate to their population of 6.3 per cent, except in the office of *'umda*, or village headman. For claims of Copts being barred from offices, see S.H. Leeder, *Modern Sons of the Pharaohs*, 329–30. Wakin, *A Lonely Minority*, 9–13, appears sympathetic to Copt complaints of discrimination during British rule. A still relevant discussion of Egyptian nationalist demands and tensions over the Dinshaway trial is Arthur Goldschmidt, Jr, "The Egyptian Nationalist Party, 1892–1919." See also Samir Seikaly, "Prime Minister and Assassin: Butrus Ghali and Wardani."
21 Meinardus, *Two thousand Years*, 71–4. On Coptic reform, see also Samir Seikaly, "Coptic Communal Reform, 1860–1914."
22 Mellini, *Sir Eldon Gorst*, 124–7. A basic source for Mellini's discussion, which I have been unable to find, is the unpublished doctoral dissertation by Samir Seikaly, "The Copts under British Rule, 1882–1914." See also Bayly's discussion of race and Christian missionary activity in "Representing Copts and Muhammadans," 170–81.
23 Ibid., 178–9; and Seikaly, "Prime Minister and Assassin."

24 The book in question was Kyriakos Mikhail, *Copts and Moslems under British Control*. For a useful summation of events, see also Goldschmidt, Jr, "The Egyptian Nationalist Party."
25 This discussion is derived from Jonathan Fox, "Religious Causes of Discrimination against Ethno-Religious Minorities," especially 426–7.
26 Carter, *The Copts in Egyptian Politics*, 66–72.
27 Bernard Botiveau, "National Law and Non-Muslim States," 114. See also Brown, "The Coptic Church in Egypt," 1052–4.
28 See Botiveau, "The Law of the Nation-State," 123–5.
29 See relevant articles in Joel Beinin and Joe Stork, eds, *Political Islam: Essays from Middle East Report*, which illustrate Islamic attacks on Copts and the attitudes behind them.
30 Carter, *The Copts in Egyptian Politics*, 77–8. See also Charles D. Smith, *Islam and the Search for Social Order in Modern Egypt*, 83–5, 126–8.
31 el-Khawaga, "The Political Dynamics of the Copts," 181. Much of my following discussion is derived from el-Khawaga's essay.
32 On the Salafiyya, see the survey with extensive bibliography in *The Encyclopedia of Islam*, new edition, vol. 8, fascicules 145–6 (Leiden: Brill, 1995), 900–9.
33 Partha Chatterjee, "Whose Imagined Community?" 216–17.
34 el-Khawaga, "The Political Dynamics of Copts," 173.
35 James C. Scott, *Domination and the Arts of Resistance*.
36 el-Khawaga, "The Political Dynamics of Copts," 182.
37 Ibid., 188.
38 Tobin Siebers, *The Subject and Other Subjects*, 132.

4

The Sheep and the Goats? Christian Groups in Lebanon and Egypt in Comparative Perspective

PAUL S. ROWE

In any assessment of ethnic and religiously inspired conflict, it stands to reason that some measure of blame will be levelled against one or both sides or, upon reflection, against grievances or situations within the control of various actors. In the case of radical groups based in some way on religious imagery and devotion, this seems only more likely, particularly in the wake of the events of 11 September 2001.[1] A popular (instrumentalist) perception is that religious groups provide opportunities for nationalistic groups to defend territory, wealth, and status. However, not all religious groupings are strongly nationalistic or eminently political, particularly in places where they remain in the minority. Clearly, most appear either benevolent and constructive if not more or less irrelevant to the larger issues of politics. Where religious groups are involved in politics, pointed fingers often give way over time to questions of who, how, and what specifically are the sources of conflict that are not entirely black and white. They lead the analyst to realize that one needs to consider conflict sparked among religious groups in greater detail and with greater sensitivity to the issues and beliefs involved.

Where they exist, Scholarly comparisons of the activities of Christian minorities in the Egyptian and Lebanese contexts tend to draw strong distinctions between the passive and cooperative spirit displayed among Egyptian Christians and the aggressive and at times militant participation of Christian sects in Lebanon.[2] One group appears to accept the secular nation of which it is a part, whereas the other has been seen to chafe against any formulation of nationalism that is not linked to Christian dominance. Typical adjectives used for Christians in Egypt, known popularly as Copts, are "quiescent" and "apolitical," whereas the Christian population in Lebanon is often considered "militant" and "uncompromising." Such assessments tend toward hyperbole, but it is certain that the Christians in Lebanon are markedly more politically active than their counterparts in Egypt.

In *The Arab Christian: A History in the Middle East*, an important work published in 1992 comparing the history of Christian populations throughout Middle Eastern countries, Bishop Kenneth Cragg formulates a theological critique of Christian approaches to Muslim dominance in the Middle East. He argues that divergent types of political activism are related to different historical and cultural imperatives internalized by the Christian populations of Middle Eastern countries. In Lebanon "[a]n ingrained belligerence and a sense of Western church tied into the emotions and the power equations of the East took root in the Maronite soul."[3] He thus (albeit gently) takes the Maronite community to task for maintaining a strongly particularist and unilateral strategy with regard to its neighbours in Lebanon, from the "Crusader mentality" forged in past interaction with the Oriental kingdoms of Western Christendom and the creation of a greater Lebanon designed to enhance Maronite leadership in the region to the "patriotic" groups that were founded prior to the Lebanese civil war. The outcome was a nationalistic church unwilling to deal with the demographic challenges of Palestinian exiles and the surge of Pan-Arabism and Islamism that followed Arab defeat in the 1967 Middle East War. "Such was the church, self-crucified on its own intransigence, which – perhaps more than any other factor – polarized Lebanon into tragic anarchy."[4] The result, according to Cragg, was the continuing trauma of the Lebanese quagmire and protracted civil war.

Unattached to the Western ties that characterized Lebanese Christianity and resigned to their minority status since the early part of the last millennium, Egyptian Copts were not given to the initiation of widespread intercommunal violence. According to Cragg, the Copts were always resigned to their status as "protected peoples" (or *dhimmis*) under Islam and became a truly "easternized" church, as it were.[5] They possessed a level of Eastern authenticity that allowed them to integrate over the course of centuries into a predominantly

Islamic milieu. The threats to identity and autonomy that plagued Lebanese Christianity were not common to the Coptic Christians of Egypt, something that should comfort Egyptian Christians in what may appear to be their second-class status. "Lebanon may suggest to Copts a wry gratitude that the fact of their being a minority was never, through all the Islamic centuries, pretentiously in dispute."[6] Although a passive reaction to *dhimmitude* is revealed in the Egyptian case, Copts should not be complacent, as the religiosity infusing political and communal issues in the Middle East is prone to escalate the mundane concerns that divide groups of people; it is a region that "is prey to the tyranny of lesser causes made absolute."[7] The theme that emerges is the irresponsibility of a religious activism that defends a militant reaction against perceived besiegement and tyranny.

After the publication of *The Arab Christian*, Habib C. Malik's review of the book was published in the *Beirut Review*. Malik is a former member of the Lebanese Front and a professor at the Lebanese American University who has consistently supported a free Lebanon under traditional sectarian authority. He registered vociferous criticism of Bishop Cragg's work, excoriating the book for condoning submission to *dhimmi* status and taking issue with what he perceived as Cragg's tendency to condemn Western influence in the Maronite church over and against an innate "Easternism."

Sycophancy and sincerity merge strangely in the depths of the *dhimmi* psyche, which is fundamentally conditioned by fear. Thus being a *dhimmi* produces an insidious form of existential degradation. Cragg, who elevates Arabism to the level of a metaphysical necessity, is unable to detect, for instance, the pathetic romanticism mingled with personal tragedy in someone like [Pan-Arabist Ba'ath Party founder Michel] Aflaq.[8]

To be fair, Malik's reading portrays Cragg as a figure not entirely recognizable in the chapters of *The Arab Christian*, where the reality of *dhimmi* status is acknowledged and the struggle that it presents for Arab Christians is the proper subject of the book. Nonetheless, Malik presents an argument that is significant to understanding comparative experiences of Middle Eastern Christians.

The debate thus summarized is this: Should one understand the Christian minority of Lebanon as a warlike group bent on dominating Lebanon at all costs, while the Egyptian Copts are long-suffering sacrificial lambs subject to the vicissitudes of majoritarian politics? Or are both tragic victims of the *dhimmi* status foisted upon non-Muslims in Muslim society, the former forced into a defensive reaction and the latter consigned to an enforced lackeyism? Are the two reactions to their larger Arab nations functions of internal logic or of external pressures to conform to an Arabist national impulse? In fact, either conclusion is overdrawn, and it is important to understand the activity of Christian groups in Lebanon and Egypt as a function of pressures native to these countries and as resulting from the internal belief systems of specific organizations among these Christian minorities rather from the operation of minorities collectively.

DISAGGREGATING RELIGIOUS GROUPS

Among the many criticisms that have been levelled against scholarship of Middle Eastern politics, there are continual objections to a caricatured cultural homogeneity tailored by Islam, traditional ties, and other "cultural" traits.[9] In fact, this very tendency to equate religion with monolithic Islam is partially responsible for a general ignorance of the existence of minority groups of Christians and others in the "Islamic world" of the Orient. In response to this phenomenon, modern scholarship has been preoccupied with the disaggregation and deconstruction of larger groups and societies that in the past were judged to be monolithic.[10] So it is with the analysis of religious movements. A fluidity and transcience of larger categories of religious movements must be considered. Radicals and moderates, militants and revivalists: All are distinct types and are created and recreated through the ebb and flow of popular belief and environment. History has proven that today's radical can soon become tomorrow's moderate. The scholar must be careful not to fall prey to assuming reified cultural organization or to assuming that modifiers of belief and practice are irrelevant.

When considering the activity of Christians in Middle Eastern countries, this observation is just as relevant. No matter their shared experience, Christian groups are divided on the bases of historical development, shared beliefs, official doctrine, and application. One must not fall into the trap of minimizing the difference between apples and oranges, as it were. The experience of Coptic Christians and Lebanese Christians, although similar due to their shared status as descendants of *dhimmi* populations in Muslim societies of the

Middle East, should not be considered consanguine. In addition to divergent environmental factors, basic differences in belief have characterized some, but not all, of the Christian groups involved in Lebanese and Egyptian politics over the last three decades. As a result, different types of groups representing different sets of beliefs and priorities have arisen.

These observations highlight the ascendence of specific groups among Lebanese and Egyptian Christians with widely divergent avenues of political participation. In Egypt this has meant the maintenance of a community in solidarity under the banner of a single united organization, the Coptic Orthodox Church. It has allowed the church and the regime to maintain the autonomy of church devotees and institutions under the officially recognized authority of the traditional patriarch, harping back to the *millet* system used by the Ottomans in the imperial period. Under the ostensibly republican regimes following the Revolution of Free Officers in 1952, Egyptian Christian participation was characterized by the recognition on the part of the regime of the singular importance of the church leadership in determining the status of the Christian community, what might be called a neomillet system. In Lebanon the ascendence of certain groups has favoured the eclipse of the organized churches in favour of non-denominational parties and, throughout the 1970s and 1980s, militias. Only since the end of the civil war and the imposition of the Ta'if regime of 1990 has a more traditional neomillet system taken hold.

EGYPT: THE COPTIC ORTHODOX CHURCH AND THE NEOMILLET SYSTEM

One must keep in mind relative proportions when considering the Egyptian Christian population. Whereas at the time of the Muslim conquest of Egypt in 640 the majority of the population of Egypt was of the Coptic Orthodox faith, over the course of ten centuries, conversions to Islam resulting from the privileges granted to Muslims over non-Muslims left a small minority who claimed the Christian religion. Today the number of Copts is a matter of significant controversy, but one might (generously) estimate their number at around 10 to 12 per cent of the Egyptian population in order to confirm the point that they are a relatively marginal minority.[11] Of course, this makes them the largest Christian minority in the Middle East by sheer numbers, at around 5 to 8 million. Yet given that they form a unified but small minority among a population that is 90 per cent Sunni Muslim, it is understandable that Copts should expect an influence proportional only to their numbers at best. Additionally, although it is difficult to know for certain how long this proportion has obtained, one can logically assume that it has been thus for several centuries given a lower infant mortality rate in the 1800s and the likelihood that they have been in the minority since the Fatimid period. In the final analysis, the Copts have been marginal in terms of numbers for a significant period, even as their persistence speaks to a latent survival instinct.

Another consideration of importance to understanding the operation of Christianity in Egypt has already been intimated: the singular unity of the Christians in Egypt under the banner of the Coptic Orthodox Church. Approximately 95 per cent of the Christian population consider themselves devotees of the Coptic Orthodox Church, and many of the others are converts from the Orthodox Church who maintain a familial or sentimental allegiance to the church. The reasons for this are rooted in historical isolation from the outside church since its division in the fifth century over the nature of Christ as well as in a strongly nationalistic association of the church with the nation of Egypt. As a result, there are effectively no challengers to the authority of the church in the spiritual realm, and there has been little need for ecumenical or secular consciousness to unite Christians politically.[12] On the surface, this might suggest a more active and confident church; in fact, it translates into a deferential organization that is conservative and defensive about its status among Christians. Religious rivalry is just as likely to stem from the Roman Catholic and evangelical churches as it is from organizations of the Muslim majority, with other Christian organizations occasionally perceived to be wolves in the henhouse preying upon the Christian population for converts.[13] The centrality of the church and its mission to minister to all Egyptian Christians also confers a high degree of influence on the Coptic patriarch both inside and outside the community.

That the Coptic Orthodox Church is the single most important source of authority among Christians in Egypt may also be attributed to the relatively low level of democratic development obtaining in the country more generally. Egyptian domestic policy regarding the development and improvement of civil society has become increasingly repressive over the course of the last decade. Whereas President Mubarak began his time in office with a spate of liberalizing initiatives and the release of many of the revolutionaries and moderate opponents of the regime that had been imprisoned by his predecessor, he has spent the last decade reversing much of the liberalizing program he embarked upon in the 1980s.[14] The country has remained in a semipermanent state of emergency that gives the government powers to override the Constitution. In an effort to maintain strong state autonomy and to limit pressure from internal opposition groups, the Mubarak regime has continued (albeit in different forms) many of the repressive tactics used by its predecessors. At first, this was aimed directly at clamping down on the activities of radical Islamist organizations such as Islamic Jihad and the Gama'a al-Islamiya. In 2000 and 2001, however, the government prosecuted and imprisoned prominent intellectual Saad Eddin Ibrahim on charges that he had illegally received funds from foreign governments and, rather nebulously, that he had "defamed Egypt." Around the same time, draconian legislation was enacted to maintain control over advocates of civil society through limits on funding and restrictions on ties to foreign organizations. Furthermore, the relatively irresponsible activity of the Egyptian press in recent years – which, most importantly, opened up an emotional and political debate over the publication of the book *A Banquet for Seaweed* in spring 2000 and over the publication of a supposed exposé on Coptic monastic life in the *en-naba'a* newspaper in June 2001 – have given the government a strong excuse to clamp down on freedoms of speech and association.[15]

In the midst of this situation, political parties have languished, nongovernmental organizations have remained in a state of stunted development, and emigration and continuing economic crisis have led to a continuing brain drain and to a stunted intellectual and cultural infrastructure. For Copts the restrictions remain especially egregious given that they are systematically eliminated from key positions in the government and that the construction of churches and religious schools has been dramatically circumscribed for years. Nonetheless, the *relative* strength of Coptic civil society has been increasing in scope. A revival within the Christian community dating back to the creation of the Sunday School Movement in the 1930s and 1940s brought a new and more assertive leadership to the fore in the 1970s.[16] At the same time, President Sadat's appeals to Islamist sentiment accelerated Coptic agitation for equality and rights. In the midst of the furore that attended Sadat's last days in office, the Coptic Orthodox Church shared radical Islamists' fate as a target of armed crackdowns and detention.[17] This came to a head with the imposed exile of Coptic Patriarch Shenouda III to a western desert monastery in 1981.

However, since the accession of Hosni Mubarak as Sadat's successor, the Coptic Church has been able to escape the repression levelled against Islamist radicals. It continually stresses national unity through cooperation with the regime, but it has been no less active and important in representing Christian interests. This has meant an increasingly visible role for the Coptic Church and the continued spread of church services to the Christian community. Moreover, there has been a recent tangible increase in the number of building permits and a loosening of restrictions on church construction within the last five to ten years, the number of new churches having skyrocketed from an average of less than ten per year to hundreds.[18] In terms of its institutional spread and ability to provide services for those in need, the Coptic Orthodox Church is unique. In fact, it is arguably the strongest and best financed nongovernmental organization in the country. Christian citizens used to the effective service of the church under the constraints established by the regime are generally not enticed nor motivated to create rival organizations.

That the Coptic Orthodox Church operates as the single most important representative of Coptic interests is significant. The church subsists on a high level of deference, and it developed an entrepreneurial interest in providing basic social services for Christians in Egypt through community clinics and centres established as early as the 1970s. Its focus on social networking and revivalism is displayed through its integration of the monastic order within the hierarchy, its development of a large-scale elementary spiritual education network known as the Sunday School Movement, and its sponsorship of an activist and relatively evangelical hierarchy over the course of the last three decades. The direction of the monastic order can be considered key to the direction of the larger church. Monks are singularly loyal to the Coptic Orthodox Church and form the foundation of the church hierarchy, and the most famous recent church leaders and modernizers (Patriarchs Kyrillos VI and Shenouda III and Father Matta al-Meskin) have come from the monasteries and have sponsored a relatively passive revivalist spirit among their disciples. Overall, the apolitical and socially aware monastic order has become the backbone of the church and has led to its revival over the last few decades, even as it has strengthened a neomillet partnership between the Egyptian regime and the church.

Finally, one must observe the nonterritoriality of Coptic claims. While Copts are largely geographically concentrated in Upper Egypt (particularly in Asyut, Minya, and Sohag) and in certain suburbs of Cairo, there is no isolated region of the country in which they form a vast majority. Rather, they are scattered throughout the country and are not ethnically or culturally distinctive from their Muslim neighbours. As a result, there is no logic in territorial or irredentist claims, as Egyptian Christians consider themselves to be descendants of the ancient Egyptians and thus to comprise the native population of the country every bit as much as (if not more than) their Muslim compatriots. Whereas Coptic religious loyalty derives in part from a strong ascriptive nominalism, this is not associated with direct political claims to an area of the country. Rather, it is channelled into a communal consciousness and a loyalty to the hierarchy and leadership of the church itself.

Each of these factors tends to contribute to the relatively conciliatory and centralized nature of Coptic political activism. In general, Copts are not fixed on territorial acquisition or on the defence of a certain geographic position. Patriarch Shenouda III, current leader of the church, has responded to attacks on the Coptic population with praise for the attempts of authorities to bring Islamist vigilantes to justice and with an encouragement to nonviolent reactions, stating publicly that "Christianity without the Cross isn't Christianity."[19] The relative size of the Copt population argues for the general limitation of their demand for representation in government to tokenism and for official state secularism rather than sectarian rights. The former goal has generally been achieved, as the government has traditionally appointed several Coptic members to the People's Assembly, where individual Copts rarely gain more than two or three seats. Progress toward the latter goal has been set back by official sanction of the *shari'a* (Islamic law) as the major source of Egyptian law in the constitution. But in 2000 the church was consulted on the redrafting of personal status laws, and it has seen the restoration of historic churches throughout the country and has managed to regain properties absconded by the regime during the 1952 revolution.[20] Moreover, the increasing number of church permits and the declaration of Coptic Christmas as a state holiday in early 2003 have pointed toward a more friendly state policy of listening to Coptic concerns.

The general tendency of Copts to trust their cause to elite negotiations between the church hierarchy and the regime is a direct result of the relative unity of the Coptic Orthodox Church on the basis of official doctrine and popular belief. The church is not strongly divided between an official and popular doctrinal position: In many ways, the attitudes of those in the street match the official positions adopted by the church leadership. Part of this relates to the unity that obtains between the monastic movement, the Sunday School Movement, and the patriarchate. All the major organs of the Coptic Orthodox Church subscribe to a unified version of Orthodoxy and exhibit a relatively free attitude toward evangelical movements within the church. Outside the church, there are no strong rivals to Christian loyalty. Since the church is thus essentially the sole organization and voice of Copts both spiritually and politically, it reinforces a neomillet style of bargaining with the secular (or, perhaps more accurately, secular Muslim) authorities.

LEBANON: SECULAR-SECTARIAN PARTIES AND NATIONALISTIC COMPETITION

One can observe significant differences between the Lebanese and Egyptian cases. Of highest importance, Lebanon has a demographic and intersectarian history that is significantly different from Egypt's. The religious communities of Lebanon date back to the early Muslim conquest of larger southwest Asia. Over the course of centuries, at least four major ethnic/religious communities settled the area now known as Lebanon. Mount Lebanon, a term used for the northern mountainous region of Lebanon, from Beirut on the coast upward as far as Jebel Sannine near Bsharré, was a sanctuary for the settlement of a mixture of different Christian groups who fled from the persecution of both Christian and Muslim tyranny over the course of the sixth to tenth centuries. Among these were the Maronites, named for a eponymous monk or patriarch (a matter of some dispute) dating back to the Byzantine period.[21] It is conjectured that this group was originally composed of monothelite refugees who made their home in the Beqa'a and Qadisha Valleys. Maronites came into communion with the Roman Catholic Church as early as 1215, creating the first Uniate Church (that is, "reunited" with the Roman Catholic Church) in the region. Today they form the largest single Christian group in Lebanon, boasting about 21 per cent of the population of the country and about 60 per cent of all Christians. The remaining 40 per cent are largely devotees of the Greek and Syrian Orthodox and Melchite

Churches. Today the largest confessional group in Lebanon is the Shi'a, at around 35 to 40 per cent of the population, with Sunni Muslims and Druze standing at around 23 per cent and 7 per cent respectively.[22] The general trend over the last thirty to forty years has been a decline in the proportion of Christians of all sects within the Lebanese population at large and a corresponding increase in the proportion of the Shi'ite population.

Consideration of the relative numbers of Lebanese Christians originally set the foundation for the Lebanese confessional system, which was created under the National Pact *(mithaq al-watani)* of 1943 to privilege the Christian population. Under a 1937 census, Christians were said to compose over 50 per cent of the population, resulting in a National Assembly where six seats were set aside for Christians for every five granted to other sects, including Sunni, Shi'a, and Druze. This system was subject to a rigid policy against innovation despite the growing gap between the dwindling number of Christians and the increasing number of Shi'ite Muslims in particular. Most analysts would relate this rigidity to the continuing crises that beset the Lebanese state, especially in 1958 and 1976, and to the descent into civil war throughout the 1980s.[23]

It is important to note that Lebanon was effectively created for the Christians by the French colonial mandate. However, even the mandated separation of Lebanon from Syria was by no means the beginning of Christian rule over the region. During the years of the later Ottoman period, loose control over the area of Lebanon led to semiautonomous regimes known as the emirate and the *mutassarifiya*. During the century before Lebanese independence, semiautonomous *millet* rule created by the Porte and the local administration gave Christians an important role in the government of the country. Ascriptive loyalties fostered by the Muslim milieu and the natural tendencies of Maronites, Shi'ites, and Druze (most importantly) to remain tribally (although not always geographically or culturally) separated fed into the idea of the sectarian democratic system adopted under the National Pact. Christians in Lebanon had long shared the experience of participation in political intrigue and in the political direction of the country because they comprised the largest ascriptive religious group in Lebanon and later because they retained their privileged position under the National Pact. There was also a continuing European interest in the region, relating to the Ottoman capitulations to European interest in the Christian populations and to the intervention of European powers, particularly the French, during the sectarian crises that beset Lebanon in 1860.

The National Pact system led to simultaneous secularizing and sectarianizing efforts among Lebanese political parties. At first glance, this appears paradoxical; in fact, it is quite logical. Christians are divided in Lebanon between different denominational groups. To form stable political alliances between Christians of various sects, thereby maintaining the structure of the National Pact, Christians (more than Druze, Shi'ite, or Sunni groups) needed to provide sectarian, yet nondenominational, political alternatives since they were divided among the various Roman Catholic and Eastern-rite churches. Furthermore, they needed to garner intersectarian consensus through building secularized parties to defend the confessional status quo. This developed into a greater imperative as the Christian population began to decline proportionately in the later twentieth century. Ghassan Salamé writes, "in order for me to better assert myself as a Christian, I am not only in need of the Christians' solidarity, but also of that of the Muslims who define themselves as Muslims first, and can thus participate in the assertion of my Christian identity, in an uninterrupted game of mirrors."[24] Thus, within the notionally sectarian (or "confessional") system, Christians created secular political movements that would serve to unite the Lebanese (most importantly various Christian sects) on secularist bases. However, secular-minded parties could not challenge the sectarian system and the ascriptive notion of religion on which it was founded, for that might in effect have challenged their own place within the institutions of the National Pact.[25] Separate churches and sectarian identities remained, but they were eclipsed by the rise of the secularist movements dominated by Christians of all stripes.

The result was the ascendence in the late 1960s and early 1970s of political parties that, despite a notionally secular outlook, supported the demands of ascriptive loyalty between sectarian groupings. Among the more prominent were *hamula*-based parties – that is, parties gathered around major kinship networks tied to prominent local leaders known as *zuama*. These included the National Bloc of the Eddé family of Jbeil, the Liberal Party gathered around the Chamouns of north Lebanon, and the independent grouping surrounding President Sulaiman Franjieh of Zghorta. Added to these was a mass movement, the Phalange. The Phalange was distinctive in that it began as a nationalist youth social movement in the 1930s established by the Gemayel family of Bikfaya.[26] While the Phalange had obvious subaltern roots and gathered a mass following for a formerly unestablished family, it did not challenge the basic terms of the sectarian system and sought, perhaps more than other parties, to attach a secular outlook to its mass appeal to the Lebanese state.

The incompatibility between the secular notion of freedom of religion and belief and the ascriptive loyalty to religion made these parties contradictory, ultimately leading to a crisis of legitimacy and the downfall of the Christian-dominated parties. Nonetheless, prior to and during the civil war, the parties remained the chief representatives of Christian political activism and managed to effectively downplay the role of the church hierarchies in representing Christians, as had been the tradition under the *millet* system of Ottoman times. The general pattern of representation came in the form of aggressive nationalistic claims backed up by local and regional militias. Such movements were attached to religious ascription and family ties gathered around the important *zuama*, strengthening a competitive nationalistic system of religious communalism.

Religious communalism in Lebanon was based on more than just the existence of significant religious divisions. Lebanese Christianity is closely attached to territorial claims, as compared to the nonterritoriality of the Egyptian Copts. Communal allegiances are tied very clearly to specific regions of the Lebanese countryside. Maronite Christians dominated Mount Lebanon and portions of the Chouf and the south, and as a result of worsening sectarian divisions throughout the nineteenth century up to the civil war of the 1980s, this cantonization has been exacerbated such that Maronites are largely confined to the coastal regions of Kesrouan, Mount Lebanon, and West Beirut.[27] In the case of Greek Orthodox and Melchite adherents, regional concentration has not been so marked. Nevertheless, they are concentrated in the cities of the coast and in the central Beqa'a Valley towns, such as Zahle, Chtaura, and Qabb Elias. In addition, Lebanese Christianity is inculcated with a strong ethnic distinctiveness, what might be considered the inevitable outcome of the *millet* system enforced under Ottoman suzerainty and of their status as *dhimmis* under Islamic Law. The result, particularly among the Maronites, was a culture dominated by the understanding of a people under siege in their own land, inheritors of the ancient Phoenician traditions favouring Mediterranean culture and European colonial-era contacts.[28] As a result, Lebanese national identity became a code word for a Lebanese state dominated by Christians, often specifically Maronites,[29] whereas the non-Christian as well as the Eastern and Oriental Orthodox Lebanese were more likely to accept Pan-Arab and Syrian national claims.

A relatively vibrant associational life and relatively libertarian system was in evidence in Lebanon from the 1940s to the 1970s, incubating the Christian political parties and providing them with tribal and confessional bases that survived their entry into the civil war. In particular it gave impetus to the upward mobility of an unestablished family, the Gemayels. Their party, the Lebanese Phalange, was particularly important to gathering Christian Lebanese into a united coalition based on a Christian version of Lebanese nationalism. Even so, it was only one of several groups that had their roots in a paramilitary reaction to the influx of Palestinians. Pan-Arab nationalism, as championed internally by Nasserists and pro-Palestinian apologists, was thus anathema to the hardened "Christian nationalism" of the militias. Their creation was made possible by the relatively free associational life of the Lebanese, but clearly the specifically militant nature of the organizations was peculiar to the nationalistic and territorial claims of the popular theology of Lebanese Christians, particularly Maronites. Over time, the organizations were taken over by a new generation of more militant leaders who viewed themselves to be Christians in strongly ascriptive terms.

At the same point in history came the breakdown of the Lebanese state under the increasing divisions caused by the paramilitaries and parties in the 1970s. The outbreak of hostilities that erupted in Beirut in 1975 led to a civil war that enjoyed a lull of sorts before the Israeli invasion of 1982. However, throughout these years, the state rapidly broke down with the defection of military officers to the militias, the inability of police and basic service providers to do their jobs, and the creation of extortion networks that rivalled the state apparatus in areas such as port authorities and transport. The decline of public order and the rise of vigilantism in opposition to the presence of Palestinian refugees in Lebanon fed into the rise of factional militias based on defending the confessional system and Lebanese nationalism. Many of these, such as the Tanzim and Abu Arz's Guardians of the Cedars, were not officially related to the Christian-dominated parties and rose as *ad hoc* networks in the late 1970s, some with covert supplies and training coming from Israel. Others, such as the Phalangist militia and the National Liberal "Tigers" militia, were at first closely associated with the parties and specific *zuama*. The consolidation of these militias into the Lebanese Front (and joint Lebanese Forces militia, or LF) in the late 1970s culminated with Phalange militia leader Bashir Gemayel's internecine quarrels with the rival groups.[30] This brought the Christian militias into a theoretically unified force by the early 1980s and propelled Bashir to the presidency in September 1982.

It is important to note that these organizations were dissociated from the sects and churches by choice. It was necessary for them to develop secularized organizations that had no clear ties to any one church in order first to attract Christians (and some secular Muslims) of all stripes and second to detach themselves from the leadership of the churches in order to avoid the criticisms that might possibly come from the hierarchies. This was of particular concern when it came to the Maronite Patriarchate, which was beholden to the diplomatic efforts of the Vatican, such as friendly moves toward the Palestine Liberation Organization in the early 1980s.[31] This is not to say that church elites and ecclesial authorities had nothing to do with the parties to the Lebanese civil war. In fact, the monastic movement, in particular, was vociferously in support of the Lebanese Forces throughout the early 1980s. However, the official position of the Maronite Church, and certainly that of the hierarchy of the Greek Orthodox and Melchite Churches, supported a negotiated solution in favour of altering the National Pact as well as acquiescing to a united Arab front in favour of Palestinian national rights. This led to the continuing detachment of the Lebanese national movement (dominated by Christians) from the ecclesial authorities of the churches, despite the contention of the LF and other groups that they were friendly and obedient to the church leadership.

The culmination of a nonecclesial secular-sectarian system was the ascendence of organizations based not on the official organs of the churches of Lebanon but on ascriptive claims as defended by the Christian-dominated parties and militias. Although there is a clear connection between the nominal Christian population of Lebanon and the parties of the Lebanese Front, it was not in effect a religious organization. Over the course of the civil war (i.e., from 1976 on), the Phalange increasingly took on the role of a secular national institution that sought to govern Lebanon not as a Christian party per se but as a secularist party *dominated by Christians*. With the violent elimination of all of its strongest rivals (aside from the ZLA militia of the Franjiehs), the Phalange leadership managed to establish a state within a state in central-north Lebanon.[32] Yet the definition of this state as a nationalist entity dominated by Christians was effectively irreconcilable with the officially secular philosophy of the Phalange. When the Phalangist leaders of the LF were implicated in the September 1982 Sabra and Shatila massacres of Palestinian refugees, it provided ample evidence that the professed mission of the Phalange was at odds with its militant and self-aggrandizing tendencies.

Over the next few years, the leadership of the LF was divided and factionalized by the creation of rival fiefs and power constellations. During the late 1980s, leadership crises and divisions, and the concomitant rise of the Maronite Church both as the voice of a resurgent traditionalist elite and as a force in favour of moderation, resulted in the disintegration of the Lebanese Front. The secular and anticonfessional vision of General Michel Aoun, appointed prime minister in an emergency decision in September 1988, was popular with Christians but eventually lacked the support of major organized interests.[33] Finally, Syrian intervention to force General Aoun out of the country with the tacit and deliberate support of nearly all the combatants brought an end to the civil conflict and installed a regime controlled from behind the scenes by Syria.

Under the Ta'if Agreement, which brought an end to the civil war, the LF was officially banned, and since then Christian-dominated mass parties have languished, marking the end to their secular-sectarian version of Lebanese nationalism. Instead, the Maronite Patriarchate has emerged as the major pole of Christian loyalty and the primary representative of Christian political activity within Lebanon, closely paralleling the neomillet system obtaining in Egypt. Whereas most of the remaining Christian-dominated parties have either cut deals with Syrian authorities for influence in the Lebanese government or exist only in exile, the patriarchate continues to speak independently for the Christian population.

What is remarkable about the activity of Lebanese Christians is how irrelevant and apparently powerless the churches remained within the Christian community prior to the close of the civil war. In 1977 then patriarch Qureish disavowed any political role for the church hierarchy, stating that "when we had our own republic in 1943, the Patriarch's function and role changed."[34] However, with the end of the civil war and the transformation of the Maronite Church under the leadership of the new patriarch, Cardinal Nasrallah Butrous Sfeir (beginning in 1987), evolutions in popular theology brought about by the ravages of war encouraged a sea change. Today the Maronite Church is by far the most important representative of the Christian community. Cardinal Sfeir has been given increasing credence in his defence of Lebanese independence versus Syrian intervention, calling for Syrian withdrawals both personally and in consultation with the Council of Maronite Bishops.[35] He has also proven instrumental in encouraging Christian resettlement of the Chouf region in concert with the Druze community and in calling for fairness in judgments handed down against former Christian militia leaders. Nor has this role been exclusively critical of the regime. A growing neomillet partnership has appeared more stable since the onset of the crisis over Iraq in 2003, with the patriarch receiving strong words of praise for his criticism of American actions from both the Lebanese authorities and the Syrian president, Bashar al-Assad.[36] The durability and stability of such a partnership is a matter for future consideration.

CONCLUSIONS: REGIONAL IMPLICATIONS AND POLICY PRESCRIPTIONS

What accounts for the distinction between Egyptian political quiescence and the rigid religious politicization of Lebanon as regards the Christian population in each country? Clearly, there are a number of factors to consider. First is the history of communal rule in Lebanon, as compared to a marginal Christian group submerged in an Egyptian Sunni Muslim majority. Second is the attachment of Lebanese Christians to specific regions of the country, as compared to a geographically dispersed Christian population in Egypt. Finally, one must note state weakness and the relatively open associational life that obtained in Lebanon up to the civil war, as compared to a restrictive central administration in Egypt. All of these observations should not obviate the need to realize significant differences in the way politically active organizations of Christians were constituted.

It is important to point out the significance of the peak organizations that emerged as the representatives of Christendom in each country. In Lebanon a series of Christian-dominated secularist-yet-sectarian parties based upon ascription led to a competitive nationalistic system based on confessional allegiances. Since the close of the civil war and the application of the Ta'if Agreement, most of the Christian-dominated parties have been eclipsed by the Maronite Church, which in turn has emerged as the single most important representative of the Christian community. In the absence of the parties and militias, the church has favoured a move toward a neomillet system. In Egypt the most important organization representing Christians has been and remains the Coptic Orthodox Church, which encourages a continuing neomillet-style subordination of the Christian community to elite negotiation between the hierarchy of the church and state authorities.

Significant differences between the popular theologies observed among Lebanese and Egyptian Christians lead to distinctive models of engagement with the larger nation in the two cases. Both are based largely upon an ascriptive loyalty to the church, although there remains a strong evangelical element. However, the Egyptian case is based on a positive reaction to the present institutional order, whereas the dominant theme in Lebanon is a negative reaction to popular innovations within the institutional order. Whereas the Coptic Orthodox Church stresses a this-worldly and sacrificial attitude toward Christian mission, Maronite popular theology has been based in a transformative and often confrontational approach to religious pluralism. Even so, it is important to distinguish popular street support from the official doctrines of the church and the operations of the patriarchate, which throughout the 1970s and 1980s, as the sole representative of Lebanese Christians, were at best lukewarm toward the parties and the LF. While the Copts have emphasized community organizations, nonsectarian workshops and training initiatives, and social services for communities in Egypt, Christian activity in Lebanon has been geared toward the development of more instrumentalist educational and institutional services specifically aimed at the Christian community. Whereas Copts see themselves as part of the "fabric of Egypt," Lebanese Christianity, particularly Maronitism, is attached to the perpetuation of the communal identity and the secular-Christian state. Copts tend to embrace a pluralistic Arab nationalism, while Lebanese Christians have sought a more sectarian-inspired and particularistic vision of the nation.

Distinctions between Christian populations on the basis of popular and official theology remain a barrier to the development of both regional cooperation between Christian groups and a coherent Arab "Christian Nationalism." Despite the apparent possibilities of establishing regional links between the churches of Lebanon and Egypt, there is little in the way of a regionwide movement on par with Pan-Arabism or Islamism. One significant manifestation of regionwide organization is the Middle East Council of Churches (MECC), founded in May 1974, an ecumenical organization representing a regional offshoot of the World Council of Churces.[37] This organization serves to bolster the regional presence of individual church hierarchies by giving them a forum in which to be heard on the basis of the partnership of all. It thus operates as a support for the neomillet system now common to both Egypt and Lebanon. Nevertheless, the significant doctrinal disputes and innate competition between most Middle Eastern churches, especially between the more evangelical boosters of MECC and the more traditional churches that dominate Middle Eastern states, tends to limit ecumenical efforts outside of posturing and basic relief organizations. What is remarkable is that diaspora groups have become more and more aggressive in recent years (particularly among the Coptic groups in the US and Australia), setting a precedent for new regional challenges. Among these groups, there have been occasional outbursts of ecumenical unity against *dhimmi* status and the lack of democratization in Arab states of the *mashreq* (Near East). Nevertheless, the eminent differences between the Lebanese and Egyptian cases underline common disagreements over how to address the larger political order.

In the twenty-fifth chapter of the gospel of Matthew, Jesus Christ is quoted predicting a final judgment, in which his self-professed followers are to be divided as a shepherd separates sheep from goats. Those who were true followers would be rewarded and those who were not would be consigned to punishment. Doubtless for the devotee, ultimate justice will exonerate both the good deeds and indiscretions of the past. But for the scholar, it is not sufficient to write off entire minorities as "sheep" or "goats." There are obvious dangers implicit in the politicization of religion, but this does not need to translate into the generic condemnation of a widely based minority religious group. The difficulty is the attachment of such a group to a hardened line of group consciousness and identity.

For all the differences that are apparent in the Egyptian and Lebanese cases, there is one startling unifying theme: the strong reliance upon an ascriptive version of religion that makes the line between Christian and non-Christian a hardened and potentially politicized and nationalistic one. In Egypt this has not yet created a widespread violent reaction to Arab nationalism, whereas it had an important part to play in the Lebanese civil war. In a concluding chapter of *The Arab Christian*, Bishop Cragg writes that "[p]oliticization of religious causes is not seldom the atrophy of religious conscience."[38] Here is an important lesson, for religion cannot be held responsible for the faults of religious ascription. Similarly, Habib Malik's call to emphasize the psychological and sociological effects of *dhimmitude*'s roots in an identity-based apartheid system should not neglect the very problematic association of communal identity with religion. Created by hardened ascriptive religion that has been strengthened via *millet* and neomillet systems and political parties, the status of the Christian minority in Middle Eastern countries remains subject to an ongoing paradox. Secularization in terms of an official neutrality toward religion seems *both* impossible *and* imperative.

I offer here one attempt to rationalize the contradiction. Rather than emphasize the role of religion in forging communities of purpose, it behoves the policy maker to seek to strengthen the role of traditional religious groups themselves as bulwarks of debate and cultural renaissance, thereby simplifying but not ruling out the impact of religion on politics. It is indeed unfortunate that the most plural society and pluralist country in the Middle East, Lebanon, has also proven in the past to be its greatest political failure. Quite possibly Egypt, short of the continuing unification and strengthening of the Coptic Orthodox Church against identity-based interest groups and parties, may not be so far away from the Lebanese example. The deconfessionalization of politics in Lebanon has long been a stated goal. It will not obtain there, or in Egypt, until religion has been confined to the realm of free choice. This is not to say, however, that religion must be confined to the realm of private life. Religion is a shaper of interests, a mindset that remains prior to political decisions, and in most cases it cannot be distilled out of the individual.[39]

Nevertheless, the extent to which religion is a shaper of "imagined community" can be eliminated through the free communication of ideas, a premise that is shared by all major religions. A true continuing dialogue on the bases of religious conviction, with free communication as a starting point, is the only likely solution to interreligious discord.

NOTES

1 See Lester R. Kurtz, *Gods in the Global Village*, 214ff. Elsewhere, observations of this sort come from Kay B. Warren, ed., *The Violence Within: Cultural and Political Opposition in Divided Nations*, and from Robert Cox, "Civil Society at the Turn of the Millenium," which identifies "exlusionary populist" movements, hermetic religious cults, and underground activities as elements of weak state reactions to the spread of civil society.

2 There are few substantive comparative surveys of the politics of Christian minorities in the Middle East. Two that stand out are Robert Brenton Betts's (now dated) work, *Christians in the Arab East*, and William Dalrymple's travelogue entitled *From the Holy Mountain*. Minorities more generally are covered in Ofra Bengio and Gabriel Ben-Dor, eds, *Minorities and the State in the Arab World*.

3 Kenneth Cragg, *The Arab Christian: A History in the Middle East*, 215.

4 Ibid., 227.

5 Ibid., 194–7.

6 Ibid., 197.

7 Ibid., 290.

8 Habib C. Malik, "Review of *The Arab Christian: A History in the Middle East*," 116.

9 Certainly, this was a key part of the critique of Western scholarship of the region offered by Edward Said in *Orientalism*. A newer debate has been set up against the perceived notion that religion guides the operation of fundamentalist groupings in Muslim societies as well, a pattern of thought known as neo-Orientalism. See Yahya Sadowski, "The New Orientalism and the Democracy Debate."

10 Perhaps best known for this perspective with regard to Islamist groups is John Esposito. See, for example, *Islam and Politics*, 3rd ed., or *Unholy War: Terror in the Name of Islam*.

11 The Ibn Khaldoun Center estimated the Copts' numbers at approximately 10 per cent of the Egyptian population in 1996, but statistics of any sort are dubious at best. Saad Eddin Ibrahim et al., *The Copts of Egypt*, 6.

12 While the Coptic Orthodox Church has been an important partner in the ecumenical Middle East Council of Churches, this participation is most important at the regional and international level. Ecumenical partnership within Egypt is ongoing but largely centred on attempts by Western and evangelical movements. Recent examples include the development of the Forum for Intercultural Dialogue at the Coptic Evangelical Organization

for Social Services (CEOSS) and the papal visit of early 2000, which appealed to a wide Egyptian audience.
13 This observation should not be taken too far: Certainly, the various Christian organizational groups remain cordial and cooperative, at least at the level of their hierarchies and leadership.
14 Eberhard Kienle discusses multiple sources of deliberalization in a recent article, "More Than a Response to Islamism: The Political Deliberalization of Egypt in the 1990s."
15 Khaled Dawoud, "Precarious Politics," *Al-Ahram Weekly*, 25–31 May 2000; Shaden Shehab, "Tabloid's Outrageous Toll," *Al-Ahram Weekly*, 21–27 June 2001.
16 For a consideration of the roots and nature of the Coptic renewal, see Pieternella van Doorn-Harder, *Contemporary Coptic Nuns*, 23–4. A more detailed assessment is Dina el-Khawaga, *Le renouveau copte: La communauté comme acteur politique*.
17 Hamied Ansari, "Sectarian Conflict in Egypt and the Political Expediency of Religion."
18 Statistics have been provided to the US government in response to questions on human-rights practices in Egypt. See US Department of State, "Country Reports on Human Rights Practice for 1999."
19 Warren Cofsky, "Copts Bear the Brunt of Islamic Extremism," *Christianity Today*, 8 March 1993, 47.
20 "Interview with Patriarch Shenouda III: Marriage, Politics, and Jerusalem," *Al-Ahram Weekly*, 1–7 April 1999.
21 Matti Moosa, *The Maronites in History*, 7–9.
22 William Harris, *Faces of Lebanon*, 83, provides an excellent breakdown of statistical evidence for the rise of the Shi'ite population and the relative declining proportion of the Christian population of Lebanon.
23 See, for example, Michael Hudson, *The Precarious Republic: Political Modernization in Lebanon*, and "The Problem of Authoritative Power in Lebanese Politics: Why Consociationalism Failed."
24 Ghassan Salamé, *Lebanon's Injured Identities*, 2.
25 Kamal Salibi, "Community, State, and Nation in the Arab Mashriq," 45, describes religious groups in Lebanon as "clects," meaning half-tribes, or clans, and half-sects.
26 See John P. Entelis, *Pluralism and Party Transformation in Lebanon, Al-Kataib, 1936–1970*.
27 Among others, Augustus Richard Norton, "Lebanon After Ta'if: Is the Civil War Over?" has produced an effective graphic representation of the increasing territoriality of sectarian affiliations in Lebanon.

28 Asher Kaufman, "Phoenicianism: The Formation of an Identity in Lebanon in 1920."
29 Hilal Khashan, *Inside the Lebanese Confessional Mind*, 13–20, notes serious misgivings among the various non-Maronite devotees to Lebanese national claims and the confessional system.
30 Lewis W. Snider, "The Lebanese Forces: Their Origins and Role in Lebanon's Politics," 5–10.
31 George Emile Irani, *The Papacy and the Middle East*, 118–46, has pointed to the Vatican's tendency to subordinate the interests of Maronite communities in its control of Lebanese politics to the dictates of its regional interests in rapprochement with other religious groups and its desire to see a settlement in favour of Palestinian national rights.
32 The institutionalization and development of a full state apparatus, and its role in consolidating the interests of individuals involved in the Lebanese Forces militia in the late 1980s, is covered well by Marie-Joelle Zahar, *Fanatics, Mercenaries, Brigands ... and Politicians*.
33 Aoun himself shared much of the blame, unable to bring even the leaders of his own Christian community to conclude a settlement with the government to end the civil war. Annie Laurent, "A War Between Brothers: The Army-Lebanese Forces Showdown in East Beirut."
34 Moosa, *The Maronites in History*, 296.
35 For example, in September 2000, the council issued a strong critical statement against Syrian occupation, arguing that it "embarasses" the Lebanese people, and also denounced government economic policy. "Bkirki's Blast Could Spark Unity Dialogue," *The Daily Star* (Beirut), 21 September 2000.
36 This was most clearly in evidence with a "national unity rally" that took place in March 2003, at which representatives of the church and both Syrian and Lebanese authorities displayed a united stand. Badih Chayban, "March to Damascus Draws Thousands," *The Daily Star* (Beirut), 10 March 2003.
37 The ecumenical drive has been present in the Middle East for over a century, but the council has been in existence since 1974. See the history of the ecumenical process on the MECC website at www.mecchurches.org.
38 Cragg, *The Arab Christian*, 292.
39 This is properly the topic for a far larger project. Early comments on the role of religion in "secular" nationalistic societies along these lines (with regard to the case of India) come from T.N. Madan, *Modern Myths, Locked Minds*, 233–79.

5

The Christians of Pakistan: The Interaction of Law and Caste in Maintaining "Outsider" Status

LINDA S. WALBRIDGE

After the Second World War, societies throughout Asia and Africa, freed from colonial rule, had the unenviable task of constructing nations and national identities. Clifford Geertz has pointed out that the people involved in this process had two related but conflicting motives: One was "a search for an identity, and a demand that that identity be publicly acknowledged as having import"; the other was "a demand for progress ... for an effective political order" – that is, the desire to be part of a nation that is recognized by other nations in the world.[1] Geertz goes on to say that the tension between these two motives is severe in new states "both because of the great extent to which their people's sense of self remains bound up in the gross actuality of blood, race, language, locality, religion or tradition, and because of the steadily accelerating importance in this century of the sovereign state as a positive instrument for the realization of collective aims."[2]

In Pakistan we see the effects of a number of the "primordial bonds" to which Geertz refers. To varying degrees and in different parts of the country, both political and physical fighting is carried out in the name either of protecting a group's right to use a particular language or of asserting tribal or ethnic privileges. In some cases, groups or regions have attempted to break away from the state. In other cases, we find groups simply demanding that their language, their traditions, and their values be the ones that define people as

Pakistani. The case of the Mohajirs in Karachi is such an example. An Urdu-speaking people, they wish to maintain Urdu as the dominant language in Sindh and have been willing to fight both in the political forum and in the streets for their position. In other words, the Mohajirs, along with other groups, wish to be part of a nation recognized and respected by other nations in the world but do not want to sacrifice their other loyalties and their own strong sense of self in the process of nation building.[3]

Religion, more than any other factor, is at the core of Pakistani identity. Whether one accepts Samuel Huntington's main thesis or not, he makes a compelling point when he observes that "in the modern world, religion is a central, perhaps the central, force that motivates and mobilizes people."[4] This certainly appears to be true for Pakistan. From its inception there has been a struggle over the role that Islam was to play in the new state of Pakistan. In the years preceding the birth of Pakistan, the subcontinent had been centre stage for the development of a new Islamic ideology. One of the major ideologues in the struggle for Islamic purity was Mawlana Sayyid Abu 'l-'Ala Mawdudi, who was born in 1903 in Delhi. In 1941 he founded the foremost Islamic organization in Pakistan, the Jama'at-i Islami. Mawdudi was at loggerheads with Mohammad Ali Jinnah and his Muslim League over the type of society that Pakistan would become. The secularist approach of the Western-educated Jinnah was unacceptable to Mawdudi. He is quoted as having said, "No trace of Islam can be found in the ideas and politics of the Muslim League. [Jinnah] reveals no knowledge of the views of the Qur'an, nor does he care to research them ... All his knowledge comes form the western laws and sources."[5]

Jinnah supposedly did become religious in the latter part of his life. His religiosity, however, was not such as to pass muster with the *ulama* (Muslim scholars). Certainly he had no intention of turning over the running of the government to them. From his speeches, we can see that he intended for Pakistan to be a nation built on tolerance. When prohibition was proposed in the new state, Jinnah protested that since drinking was already banned in Islam, no further action was needed on the part of the government.[6]

Jinnah had little say in the future shaping of Pakistan, as he died soon after Partition. The years that followed were turbulent and included coups, wars with India, and a civil war that split West Pakistan from East Pakistan. Throughout the years, however, how to define Pakistan – whether as a homeland for Muslims or as an Islamic state – has been a core issue, one that intensified during the administration of General Zia al-Haq, who made common cause with those promoting an Islamic state. During his days in office, religiously based organizations were founded, organizations with a far weaker intellectual basis than Mawdudi's and some of which blatantly advocate violence. The current world focus on Pakistan due to the US campaign against the Taliban in Afghanistan and to the threat of war between Pakistan and India has highlighted some of these radical groups. An example of such an organization is the Harakat-ul-Ansar Pakistan (Movement of the Helpers of the Prophet), closely linked with the Deobandis. It emerged in the 1980s specifically to fight the Soviet Union in Afghanistan, where its members received military training, including lessons in bomb and explosive making and in the use of light and heavy weapons.[7] They attacked "infidels" in both Afghanistan and Pakistan and lent their support to efforts to overthrow the Governments of Egypt, Algeria, Tunisia, and Jordan. Harakat-ul-Ansar Pakistan was also a supporter of the most notorious of all anti-Shi'i groups, the Sipah-e-Sahaba.

The Anjuman Sipah-e-Sahaba (Society of the Soldiers of the Prophet's Companions, or SSP) was founded in September 1984 by a member of the *ulama*, Maulana Haque Nawaz Jhangavi, who had been an active member of another Islamic group in Pakistan, the Jamiat-i-Ulema Islam (Union of the Learned of Islam). Sipah-e-Sahaba's manifesto specifically calls for "action against the Shi'a sect." Any Muslim who regards the Shi'a as infidels apparently is entitled to membership in the organization. They have written and distributed pamphlets, one of which declares the Shi'a to be *kafirs* (infidels) and forbids any of their members from having any contact with them whatsoever. Such organizations demand that Pakistan be not only an Islamic state, but a state that promotes the most radical of Wahhabi Islam, that which was practiced by the Taliban.[8]

The debates – or the battles – over the role of Islam in society and the type of Islam that should predominate have left little room for concern about non-Muslim minorities. Census reports show that Pakistan's population is 97 per cent Muslim, although non-Muslim minorities protest that they are undercounted. Whatever the case, minorities tend not to loom very large in the Pakistani consciousness. The Christians comprise the largest of these communities. How they identify themselves, how they see themselves fitting into a larger

Pakistani identity, and the ways they have been marginalized so as to prohibit them from becoming full citizens in Pakistani life are the subject of this chapter.

CHRISTIAN CONVERSION AND THE ISSUE OF CASTE

Prior to the nineteenth century, the British rulers in India were relatively tolerant of other religions, contributing to Muslim processions, administering Hindu temple funds, and supervising pilgrimages to holy places. But this sort of tolerance turned to open contempt in the nineteenth century as a new wave of religious fervour took hold in both Britain and the United States. Fear swept over the Indians that the British government was about to forcibly convert the population, especially as the number of missionaries in India increased. Missionary zeal motivated Parliament to pass the Charter Act in 1833 approving the permanent presence of missionaries in India, a charter that was not popular among the antimissionary element in the British administration in India.

Missionaries did not have brilliant success in converting the natives. Still they persevered, as they assumed that Western education would eventually overcome any obstacles to the process of civilizing and Christianizing the Indian people.[9] They set up schools directed at the higher castes in the belief that these people would eventually lead all of India to Christianity.

It should be noted that the missionaries' attitudes were in contrast to those of the clergy serving the spiritual needs of the British stationed in India. The cathedrals they built were for the British and Irish, not for the Indians. The people they served are memorialized, at least within the Anglican cathedrals and churches, with metal and wooden plaques engraved with the names of soldiers and their family members who died in battle or from disease or were killed during the "Great Mutiny." The present congregants of these churches pay little heed to the memorials. The plaques are a reminder, however, of the enormous changes that have taken place in the Christian population of the subcontinent. These changes began when the United Presbyterian missionaries, mostly from America, entered the scene. Seeing the immense variety of humanity that they were called to evangelize, they decided not to limit themselves to the upper castes; instead, "their purpose was to win anyone whose heart was open to God's Word."¹⁰ In many respects, they continued to follow the tactics of other missionaries. They established schools for high-caste non-Christians, convinced that through them they would win India as a whole to Christ. They, like other missionaries, believed that the entire system of Hinduism would crumble before Western science and philosophy. They also preached in the city bazaars, thus limiting their contacts mostly to urban men. The Presbyterian missionaries – men and women – were an educated group of people but had a narrow view of the world shaped largely by their small-town American upbringing. Their American education stressed the individual's commitment to Christ, a commitment that would require a long period of education and preparation. Their approach to teaching was also rather cerebral. Once again, the educated upper castes were the most likely to be drawn to their sermons. They did indeed win converts, but as these converts were generally on the fringe of society, they were willing to break their family ties. A Hindu, Muslim, or Sikh convert faced ostracism and worse from his or her extended family and caste members. Generally, converts had to remain in the church compound for a proper Christian education and to protect themselves from their own families.

Where the United Presbyterians differed from other missionaries was in their readiness to take advantage of the social changes occurring in India. During this period of British rule, there was a loosening of social ties. These ties, while oppressive, had at least provided some security for the most depressed classes. Freed from some of their traditional constraints and protections, those from the lowest castes looked for new patrons. They found them in a variety of places, but a significant number found them in the church.

The missionaries called the conversion of large numbers of untouchables "the Mass Movement of the Punjab." Missionaries report that in western Punjab in the 1870s, they began winning converts among the Chuhra, or sweeper caste.¹¹ The Chuhras were a new experience for the missionaries. Sir Denzil Ibbetson, in his exhaustive work *Punjab Castes,* refers to them as "the sweepers and scavengers par excellence of the Punjab."¹² They were village people who, if they were living among Hindus, were obliged to live outside of the village proper. While some worked as landless labourers, most worked in jobs considered polluting to Hindus and Muslims, such as removing dead animals from fields, skinning animals, removing the bodies of the unclaimed dead, executing condemned criminals, and cleaning latrines. They also ate carrion and other people's leftovers. Thus, to caste Hindus, even their shadows were polluting. They were known for their "abject dependence, lack of ambition and initiative, carelessness, deceitfulness, extravagance, drunkenness, insolence and harshness in dealing with others" of the Chuhra caste.[13]

At first, the United Presbyterian missionaries were reluctant to baptize Chuhras since they had no instruction in Christianity and since it was difficult to assess their sincerity. There was also fear that untouchables would drive away other prospective converts. Finally putting these fears aside, the Presbyterians began to accept untouchables. Soon thereafter, other missionaries followed suit. According to their accounts, a majority of these converts were identified as Chuhras.[14]

Just as the missionaries feared, Indians of caste were repulsed by seeing a missionary share a meal with a ritually polluting untouchable. In spite of this, the Protestants continued to work among the Chuhras, enlisting 20,729 converts between 1881 and 1891. They no longer required a "high standard of knowledge and moral attainment as a pre-requisite for Baptism," as earlier missionaries had done.[15] They learned the Punjabi language, the local language of the illiterate, as opposed to Urdu, the language used when addressing higher-caste people. Eventually, Catholic missionaries, particularly Capuchin friars, followed the example of the Protestants. Missionaries of all backgrounds came to accept family and group conversions, seeing these as a way to protect converts from persecution by other family members, a problem that converts from higher castes commonly faced.

This does not mean that the new converts were free from harassment. Hindus and Muslims expressed their displeasure at the new conversions. The missionaries believed that caste Indians feared the disruption of the caste system since Chuhras and other untouchables began to take advantage of missionary schools with the hope that they could escape the degrading but essential work that they had been assigned as a birthright.

Again, returning to the discussion of caste, there is no doubt that many converts were Chuhras. The amount of agreement among missionaries leaves little doubt of this. The question arises of whether the missionaries also included other poor Indians in this category, ones who were not untouchables. The issue becomes particularly relevant when studying the settlement of the Christian canal colonies, those started by the missionaries when land became available with the building of the irrigation canals in the Punjab. Many of the Christians who live in the canal colonies today deny that they are of Chuhra backgrounds. They say that since Chuhras could never have done agricultural work, being unaccustomed to it, the missionaries would not have settled such people in these places. The people I met from the colonies said that they were either from the Jat or Rajput castes, which are highly represented among all religious groups in the Punjab.[16] The people in the Catholic canal colonies with whom I worked claim that it is the Christians in the cities who are Chuhras, not they themselves. Certainly, some of them do not resemble the common image of Chuhras as small and dark. This description does fit many Christians but not all of them.

If a large proportion of Christian converts were indeed Jats and Rajputs, then why do the missionary accounts not tell us this? They were extremely eager to bring in "respectable" members of society and were very caste conscious. Most Christians to whom I spoke cannot trace their ancestry. Most do not even know who the first Christian was in their families. They simply say that their families have "always" been Christian, "for at least one hundred years." In contrast, we do find a few Christians, relatively speaking, who know something of their heritage and can identify a recent ancestor who converted from Hinduism or Islam. Often these people, unlike the ones who know nothing of their ancestors' religious background, are more educated and hold relatively high positions in the Christian community. My observations and reading of historical documents suggest to me that, when people were baptized into a Christian denomination, the missionaries knew something about the background of the convert. And, as mentioned above, they were especially conscious of whether a convert was a member of a caste or not.

The topic of caste is fraught with difficulties. However, an explanation of the disagreements surrounding it might be found in the fact that these "scheduled caste" people (a term often used in preference to "untouchable") themselves were a diverse group. "Chuhra" is actually a term describing the work that people do. As mentioned above, they clean latrines, sweep, remove dead bodies, and so forth. However, some also work on land as common labourers. The term usually used to refer to these untouchable agricultural labourers is "Kammis." Actually, as it was explained to me, Chuhras are counted in this group but are considered the lowest members of the Kammis.

Therefore, Kammis would differentiate themselves from Chuhras despite both groups being untouchables.

The picture is further complicated by the fact that people can "lose caste." That is, they might be of a caste background but have become polluted and thus relegated to untouchable status and to the work that such status involves. It seems, therefore, that Chuhras and other untouchable groups cannot be classified as being of one particular type or background.

When in 1898 the Catholic and Protestant missionaries were able to persuade the government to allot them a small area of land along the new irrigation canals, they referred to settling "selected Christians." It is most probable that these Christians were selected from among people who had some experience at agricultural work. This does not mean that they owned land themselves but that they worked the land. While untouchables, their experience as agricultural labourers would have given them an advantage over the sweepers in turning the canal colonies into successful enterprises. Once they received their own land, the idea of being an untouchable would have seemed impossible, since land ownership is a mark of high status. We also know that people came to the canal colonies as labourers seeking work on the land of the new Christian landowners. These people would have been designated Kammis, underscoring that the Christian landlords were now of a higher rank (or caste) than the people who worked for them. They could now begin to call themselves Rajputs and Jats. On the subcontinent, self-anointed status is not uncommon, and after awhile this self-designation may gain acceptance in the larger community.

I will not be able to settle the issue of caste among Christians, but it is imperative to understand that a large number of Punjabi Christians do work as sweepers or sanitation workers, jobs that are associated with "untouchability." Those who own land in the canal colonies established by missionaries, or who have received advanced education, generally deny ever having had such lowly roots. However, to the larger Muslim population, Punjabi Christians, regardless of their current place in life, are usually referred to as "*chuhras.*"[17]

There is one other group of Christians who played an important role in Pakistani life but who are not part of the "mass conversion" period and are never associated with the "Chuhra" designation. These are Goan Catholics. There is not space in this chapter to discuss their interesting history. I will mention only that their conversion dates back to the sixteenth century, that their customs and attitudes are very Western, and that they came to the new city of Karachi, where they found work with the British doing jobs that Hindus and Muslims did not want. In general, they took advantage of educational opportunities and now form an elite among Pakistani Christians. Most of the Roman Catholic bishops in Pakistan have been Goan, for example.[18]

Of course, caste is a system we think of as associated with Hinduism, not Islam. Indeed, Pakistani Muslims often seem uncomfortable with the idea of caste because of its links with Hinduism and because Islam teaches equality among the believers. Despite this discomfort, the caste system does exist in Pakistan. The topic of caste is most likely to come up when there are discussions of marriage. No one wants to marry into the wrong caste. There is even a column in one of the English newspapers that satirizes, a little nervously, parents' obsession with marrying their sons and daughters to people of the appropriate caste.

I have spent a considerable amount of space expounding on the situation of caste among Christians because of the conflicting role it plays in defining the Christian identity and because caste is used by the majority community to further marginalize this minority, as should become clear later in this chapter.

CHRISTIANS AND THEIR EARLY RELATIONS WITH THE STATE OF PAKISTAN

The partition line dividing India and Pakistan cut across the territory of the Lahore Diocese, with a large section ending up on the India side. This was a difficult time for the church in Pakistan. The missionaries were helpless in the face of the disasters inflicted on people because of Partition. Children were separated from their parents and husbands from their wives. The indigenous Christians found themselves unemployed after the founding of the new state. To resettle the many thousands of Muslim refugees from India, the government divided up large tracts of land abandoned by Hindu and Sikh landlords and parcelled them out in small lots to the Muslim refugees. The services of the Christians who had worked for the large landowners were now no longer needed. Natural disasters added to the misery. Severe flooding brought famine and plague. In addition, world demand for Pakistani cotton diminished as synthetic materials replaced it. All of these factors set off an upsurge of migration to urban areas throughout the country and severely weakened Christian rural communities. Moving into the cities meant settling Christian ghettos *(bastis)*. These *bastis* would be fertile ground for the myriad social problems that plague the churches today. More often than not, the *bastis* were also temporary, being subject to bulldozing by the government.[19]

In the midst of all this misery, missionary nuns continued to open new schools and to improve the already existing ones. Other developments were soon underway as well. In 1951 the Roman Catholic Minor Seminary opened to train indigenous priests, and in 1954 a new translation of the Bible into Urdu began.[20] There was a growing awareness that the Catholic Church in Pakistan had to be turned over to the Pakistanis. Missionaries, both Catholic and Protestant, began to realize that they would be unwelcome in both the new states, associated as they were – at least in people's minds – with colonial rule. Hence they began to prepare local people to take over leadership roles.

Christians, who became the largest of Pakistan's minorities after Partition, were not targets of persecution. In fact, at this time, some low-caste Sikhs decided that it was in their best interest to convert to Christianity. While some people do recall, as children, their Muslim peers taunting them with the idea that they did not belong in Pakistan and should go to India, generally speaking, Christians continued to believe that there was a place for them in Pakistan. They were particularly optimistic when Zulfikar Ali Bhutto came to power in the 1970s. Bhutto seemed to have inspired hope that Pakistan would be rejuvenated and that conditions would improve for all Pakistanis. As one Protestant bishop told me:

We were talking about rights of people. Bhutto was talking about freedom for the people. We were experiencing a different Pakistan. We were turning to a situation where Pakistan was led by a bureaucrat and a politician. We had public rallies, public speeches, freedom of speech – for the masses. Our morale was low because of the 1971 war. So Bhutto had to give new input to the nation.

However, Bhutto's government was marked by extremes of conciliation and confrontation. For example, Christians held offices throughout the government, a fact that they have not forgotten. Nevertheless, it was also under Bhutto's watch, with his nationalization program, that they received their first substantial signal that their position was fragile. He nationalized agribusiness, which upset landlords, merchants, and rural politicians, but, more to the point, he nationalized schools. Some Christian leaders today say that his real targets were the centres of Islamic learning, the *madrasas*, as these traditional schools posed a threat to his political career. But the nationalization program also encompassed the schools run by the Christians – or at least the schools that would most affect poor Christians. As the Roman Catholic archbishop of Lahore explained to me:

There was a rule of thumb [for determining closures]: Those that charged fees of twenty rupees or more were not taken over. Those charging less than twenty rupees were taken over. It was quite arbitrary. The sad thing was that most of our Catholic children were in the lower-fees schools, and these became nationalized.

In other words, the Urdu-medium schools – the low-fee schools – were the ones most likely to be turned over to the government. The English-medium schools could remain in the hands of the owners. The Christians ran both. But the poorer Christians – at least those fortunate enough to have the opportunity – usually went to the Urdu-medium schools. The English schools were mostly for the elite. Bhutto himself had been educated in a Catholic school, as was his daughter Benazir, herself a future prime minister, and most other political and military leaders of the country. These schools were to remain in the hands of the church. However, the colleges opened by the Protestants were also nationalized. The nationalization of the schools dealt a serious blow to the Christian church in Pakistan.

Bhutto never seems to have been able to manage his government. Despite his increasingly autocratic rule, his control over the country was weak, leaving him vulnerable. As fate would have it, his most powerful foe was one of his own generals, Zia al-Haq, an admirer of Mawdudi and an Islamist himself. Zia led a coup that swept Bhutto and his People's Party from power in 1977.

The church in Pakistan was quite helpless. It represented a minority community whose leaders were still mainly foreign. Thus rebelling against the government would surely mean the expulsion of the foreigners and perhaps the demise of the church in Pakistan altogether. Besides, the state of Pakistan had not singled out Christians for persecution. However, as Zia's control over Pakistan grew and as the Islamist movements discussed above emerged, this sense of "not being persecuted" would evaporate. By the 1990s Christians certainly believed they were the targets of systematic oppression.

The oppression has largely come in the form of laws that have increasingly been used against them. When Zia took over Pakistan, he placed the country under martial law and pushed through legislation that has driven Pakistan in a direction diametrically opposed to the one Jinnah envisioned.

For Christians and other minorities in Pakistan, Zia al-Haq's rise to power marks the turning point from guarded hope to despair. The discriminatory laws he pushed through, his own sectarian biases, and his support of militancy to crush his enemies have led to bloody street violence between Sunni and Shi'a and to near civil war in Karachi. They have led to the flight of Ahmadis, Goans, and others who can afford to leave and to the proliferation of militant Islamic groups. To poor Christians the policies and the laws inaugurated during his regime have led to lives of fear and apprehension.

LEGAL AVENUES FOR THE MARGINALIZING OF CHRISTIANS

Pakistani Christians complain about numerous humiliations that they face in their daily lives. There are regular reminders that they are not part of true Pakistani society. It is not uncommon, for example, for a Christian to have to pay for his or her tea cup when visiting a tea shop. During Ramadan, when all restaurants are shut down and street vendors are forbidden to sell food, they are reminded of their marginal place in society. The loudspeakers broadcasting from the mosques underscore the fact that Christians are excluded not only from the physical building of the mosque, but also from the "space" created and monopolized by the preachers at their microphones. While Christian women wear the traditional *shalwar kameez*, the flowing dress worn by almost all women and most men in Pakistan, which helps them blend into Pakistani society, the Islamists are increasingly insisting that women wear burqas or some all-encompassing garment that would not be acceptable to Christian women. All of these factors and more remind Christians that they are not full members of Pakistani society.

However, their greatest concern is with the so-called blasphemy laws, as many of the attacks on them are framed in these laws, which were established during Zia al-Haq's tenure. These laws have been increasingly utilized since the early 1990s.

The roots of Pakistan's blasphemy laws can be found in British Indian laws established in 1860. The Indian blasphemy laws made it a criminal act to injure or defile a place of worship with the intent of insulting the religious sensibilities of other communal groups. A person found guilty of such a crime could be fined or sentenced to imprisonment for up to two years. This law shows just how ill-defined the concept of blasphemy is. Blasphemy is almost always a verbal offence – either written or spoken. Here, however, it is an action. It has its corollary in British history, when in 1850 there was a wave of "bible burnings" or at least alleged bible burnings. By adding actions to the definition of blasphemy, the British opened up the possibility of more draconian laws in the subcontinent.[21]

In Pakistan's short history, we have witnessed a series of mutations in the blasphemy laws and thus in the definition of what constitutes blasphemy. In 1980, Section 295A was added to the Penal Code. This statute prohibited the use of derogatory remarks "by words, or by imputation, innuendo or insinuation, directly or indirectly, about persons revered in Islam. In 1982, Section 295B was promulgated by a Presidential Ordinance. It stipulated life imprisonment for an offender who "willfully" defiles a copy or portion of the Holy Qu'ran. The law that has been most distressing to Christians is 295C. It has been the centrepiece of Muslim-Christian tension. Under this section, a person found guilty of "defiling" the name of the Prophet of Islam automatically receives a death sentence. What the defendant actually intended by his words or actions is of no consequence.

The Section 295 laws do not openly target any particular group as potential blasphemers. Muslims themselves have been charged under 295A, B, and C. But Christians have become associated with the law and feel the most vulnerable. The suicide death of the Roman Catholic bishop John Joseph, is now eternally linked with 295C for good reason. When the bishop shot himself in front of the Sessions Court in the city of Sahiwal, a young Christian man named Ayyub Masih was in prison under charges of blasphemy under 295C. He had been found guilty in Pakistan's lower court. During the bishop's last days, he was seeking an attorney who would present the case before the high court. Ayyub Masih, the son of illiterate sweepers, had been charged with praising Salman Rushdie's *The Satanic Verses* and for using the Prophet's name in a "familiar" sort of way. These crimes were sufficient to merit the death sentence under Section 295C of the Pakistan Penal Code. After the guilty verdict was read, while Ayyub Masih was being escorted through the corridors of the Sessions Court of Sahiwal, he was fired upon at close range. The police took no action against the assailants.

There are common patterns in blasphemy cases involving Christians. Often the accused has acquired a small piece of land or even something of far lesser consequence. Alternatively, the accused might be an educated Christian who has opened a private school and found himself in competition with a Muslim who has done the same. Or he may have a reputation for curing and attract a clientele. Thus jealousy of relative success is a factor. Almost invariably the accusations have been instigated by a member of a militant Islamist group – more often than not, the Sipah-e-Sahaba. It appears that the threat of a Christian *"chuhra"* climbing the social ladder and perhaps surpassing his Muslim neighbours is simply unacceptable. The blasphemy laws serve to silence and intimidate the weak. People told me that before these laws were put into effect, there was much more intercourse and discussion among communal groups. Now Christians tell their children never to mention religion when speaking to Muslims for fear they will be accused of blasphemy. Furthermore, they feel additionally vulnerable because lawyers and judges have been reluctant to handle their cases since the assassination of a judge who overturned a blasphemy case involving a Christian.

Thus the blasphemy laws serve as a constant reminder that Christians are not like the rest of Pakistanis. They must avoid Muslims as much as possible for fear they might say something that could be used against them in a blasphemy case. Yet it can be argued that an even deeper indication of division between Christians and Muslims in Pakistan is the separate electoral system.

The separate electoral system also has its roots in the Zia era. In Pakistan very few Christians serve in the provincial or national assemblies. In fact, that there are any at all is probably due to the separate electoral system, which is why some Christians were enthusiastic about its inauguration. Under this system, the members of each minority get to elect representatives from their own religious communities on a proportional basis. Thus, in the National Assembly, Christians have four seats; Hindus and people belonging to the scheduled castes have four seats; Sikh, Buddhist, and Parsi communities and other non-Muslims have one; and Ahmadis have one. The system is similar for the provincial assemblies. Christians and other non-Muslims can vote only for these at-large reserved seats and do not vote in the elections for local members of the provincial and national assemblies. In reality, the few Christian seats represent Christian voters scattered across the entire province. Members of these minorities cannot vote for any other representatives. Therefore, the average Christian rarely has an opportunity to meet with his or her own provincial or national representative. With few exceptions, Christians do not have any direct representation, as they commonly live in Muslim villages or in sectors represented by Muslims. Thus the representatives for these areas have no interest in the fate of these Christians, who are not part of their constituencies. While Christians might once have been swing voters in marginal constituencies under the joint electoral system, they can now be safely ignored by all but their own handful of representatives.

The results of the separate electoral system were driven home to most Pakistani Christians when Muslim mobs attacked several Christian *bastis* (ghettos). The attacks were either ignored or actually encouraged by members of Parliament in districts where Christians lived. Since the Christians could not vote for them, they felt no obligation to intervene on their behalf.

The separate electoral system and the use of the blasphemy laws have served to send the message to Christians that they will never be defined as true citizens of the Islamic Republic of Pakistan. While their status as true Pakistanis has been a troublesome question since the birth of Pakistan, they have found their position eroding over the past couple of decades. They must increasingly turn to sources of identity other than Pakistani nationality in order to feel that they are part of something larger than themselves.

THE ROLE OF CASTE IN ISSUES OF IDENTITY

As I explained in an earlier section, the majority of Christians in Pakistan do menial work that has traditionally been associated with low-caste status. They are regularly referred to in a derogatory sense as *"chuhras."* Yet there are Punjabi Christians who have either risen in status or were not from a lowly background to begin with. In addition, there are Goan Catholics, who have dominated the church hierarchy and have had a very different history in Pakistan. Those who consider themselves to be of higher caste often resist identifying with the poorer members of the Christian community. By word and action, they have made attempts to distance themselves from the plight of the poorest Christians, sometimes blaming them for their difficult circumstances. It has taken considerable effort by Christian human-rights workers – led by the late Bishop John Joseph – to develop any sense of a unified Christian identity. The discriminatory laws described above have had a contradictory effect in this identity formation. On the one hand, there are Christians who insist that the charges of blasphemy against poorer Christians are a result of their lack of discretion and unwillingness to behave in a way that will not draw negative attention to themselves. On the other hand, the sophisticated crusade led principally by Christian human-rights workers against the separate electoral system and the blasphemy laws has drawn in a larger spectrum of the Christian community who see a need to protect the interests of all Christians. One important variable that has affected this shift is the recruitment of liberal, secular Muslims in the fight to abolish discriminatory laws, giving the battle a greater sense of respectability.

The issue of caste is a far more important factor, however, in how Muslims view the right of Christians to full citizenship in Pakistan. If Pakistani Christians were generally of a higher caste (and social class), their right to be considered full-fledged members of Pakistan might still be questioned, but they would not face virulent reminders of their marginal status on a daily basis. Goans are a case in point. Goans have not been accused of blasphemy. Nor are they discriminated against in restaurants or other public places, as poor Christians are. Their elite status generally protects them from dangers and humiliations. They are certainly unhappy with the Islamization program in Pakistan, and many of them have opted to live abroad, but this choice is based on the fact that they live according to a Western model of life and do not like the restrictions forced upon them due to the Islamization of Pakistan. Their experiences are far different from those of *"chuhras."*

That Punjabi Christians are referred to as *"chuhras"* is important to the discussion of national identity formation. Benedict Anderson discusses the use of these kinds of "racist" terms and the way they are used to "erase nation-ness." The word *"chuhra,"* to use his argument, is like the word "nigger." An American "nigger," regardless of his or her passport, was not considered an American.[22]

The use of the term *"chuhra"* is becoming a more important designation in impoverished Pakistan as Muslims move into some of the "dirty" occupations traditionally filled by Christians. Because they are now competing for some of the same jobs, further means of differentiating themselves from untouchable Christians has become increasingly necessary. In addition, a significant number of Christians have managed to educate their children. Once people matriculate (achieve the equivalent of two years of high school education), they believe that they should not do physical – and certainly not "degrading" – work. Resentment toward Christians who have matriculated or even gone to college can be palpable and has led to accusations of blasphemy against the "successful" Christian. Thus Muslims are competing with Christians either for "Chuhra" jobs or for jobs that take Christians out of their "Chuhra" status. In either case, this can be threatening for people in an economy that offers so few options and opportunities.

I do not wish to reduce the tensions between Muslims and Christians to economics. Research has shown that economics does play a role in the perceived status of low-caste peoples on the subcontinent.[23] But certainly, the religious ideology being promoted in various strata of Pakistani society – an ideology that promotes violence and oppression – does not have a simple economic explanation. Yet in discussing the upsurge in violence and animosity toward the Christian community – violence that has involved people who are not directly connected with militant organizations – one needs to look at the structure of Pakistani society in order to determine what sorts of influences changes in this structure can have on overall issues of national identity.

More to the point, if discriminatory laws and practices could be abolished at the state level, Christians and other minorities would not be marginalized in a way that prevents them from seeking political and legal assistance for their grievances. With a joint electoral system, they could turn to a Muslim member of Parliament because they would be part of his constituency. If the blasphemy laws were not in effect, Christians would be more likely to make common cause with Muslims on a wide range of social and political issues. But the threat of blasphemy accusations tends to further ghettoize the Christian population.

Finally, there is one other point of particular concern. The Pakistani Christians are generally either Roman Catholic or mainstream Protestant. In the eyes of Pakistanis, and indeed as viewed by most of the world, they belong to religions that are "Western." Although

Europeans or North Americans living in Pakistan are always assumed to be Christian, they are not mocked or treated in a degrading fashion. However, indigenous Christians are ridiculed not only because they are poor and "untouchable," but also because they don't even have the protection of their powerful co-religionists. Their loyalty to Pakistan is always questioned because they are accused of siding with the West, yet this loyalty brings them no apparent benefits. The church teaches them that they are members of a universal church and that their way of life is alien to their Muslim neighbours. Yet they experience little benefit from this larger identity; it offers them no protection. Generally speaking, their identity as members of a "Western" religion and their existence as the lowliest of Pakistan's population have the effect of marginalizing them even further.

Under current circumstances, a Christian's primary identity is that of a Christian. Human-rights activists might keep reminding Christians that they are Pakistani, but the current situation in Pakistan raises serious questions about whether this is so. As long as the separate electoral system prevails, as long as the blasphemy laws are in effect, and as long as the practice of designating Christians *"chuhras"* continues, Christians will simply have to resort to their "primordial" identity.

NOTES

1 Clifford Geertz, "The Integrative Revolution," 280.
2 Ibid., 281.
3 Feroz Ahmed, *Ethnicity and Politics in Pakistan.*
4 Samuel P. Huntington, *The Clash of Civilizations and the Remaking of World Order*, 66.
5 Vali Reza Nasr Seyyed, *The Vanguard of the Islamic Revolution,* 20.
6 S. Ahmed Akbar, *Jinnah, Pakistan and Islamic Identity*, 83.
7 Musa Khan Jalalzai, *Sectarian Violence in Pakistan and Afghanistan*, 227.
8 For an account of the formation of such groups, see, for example, Musa Khan Jalalzai, *Sectarianism and Ethnic Violence in Pakistan*; James Warner Bjorkman, ed., *Fundamentalism, Revivalists and Violence in South Asia*; and Afzal Iqbal, *Islamisation of Pakistan.*
9 Jacob E. Dharmarja, *Colonialism and Christian Mission,* 58.
10 Frederick and Margaret Stock, *People Movements of the Punjab,* 18.
11 Denzil Ibbetson. *Punjab Castes.*

12 Ibid., 293.
13 Edmund Lucas De Long and F. Thakur Das, *The Rural Church in the Punjab*, 13. For a discussion of non-Brahmin castes, see G.A. Oddie, "Christian Conversion among Non-Brahmans in Adhra Pradesh, with Special Reference to Anglican Missions and Dornaka Diocese, c. 1900–1936."
14 Duncan Forrester, *Caste and Christianity*, 74.
15 Frederick and Margaret Stock, *People Movements in the Punjab*.
16 Peter R. Blood, ed., *Pakistan: A Country Study*, 6th ed.
17 "Chuhra" can designate a particular caste, or it can be used in a nonspecific, derogatory manner. When used in the latter sense, I do not capitalize the term.
18 An article that discusses the adaptation of the Goans in Pakistan is Raffat Khan Haward, "An Urban Minority: The Goan Christian Community in Karachi."
19 Pieter Streefland, *The Sweepers of Slaughterhouse: Conflict and Survival in a Karachi Neighbourhood*.
20 Emmerich Blondeel, *A Short History of the Catholic Diocese of Lahore*.
21 For interesting accounts of the historical development both of concepts of blasphemy and of laws relating to the concept, see David Lawton, *Blasphemy*; and Leonard W. Levy, *Blasphemy*.
22 Benedict Anderson, *Imagined Communities*, 148–9.
23 See Robert Deliege, "At the Threshold of Untouchability."

6

The Baha'i Minority and Nationalism in Contemporary Iran

JUAN R.I. COLE

The Baha'i religious minority would on the surface appear to have been well placed to benefit from the rise of modern Iranian nationalism. As one of only four extant religions that arose on Iranian soil (the Zoroastrian, the Ahl-i Haqq, and the Babi comprising the other three), it has the advantage of being indigenous and thus, in the terms of romantic nationalism, presumably authentic. Its scriptures are largely in the Persian language, the vehicle of modern Iranian nationalism. It also has a generally modernist orientation. It has suffered, however, because nationalism in Iran has tended to be either secular, and thus suspicious of any sectarian division in the body public, or religious, coding non-Shi'ites as somehow un-Iranian. The issue of nationalism and the Baha'i religious minority has been complicated by the emergence of the Islamic Republic of Iran insofar as it is a clerically ruled state and among the few real theocracies in the contemporary world.[1] As a theocracy, Iran rejects – on the surface at least – many of the premises of nationalism developed in eighteenth- and nineteenth-century modernity. In addition, a theocracy is premised upon a state ruling on behalf of a specific religious community, which raises difficult questions about the position of religious minorities. From the point of view of both the Enlightenment and the twentieth-century elaboration of a human-rights discourse, it is expected that all citizens of a state, regardless of religious adherence, will enjoy the same rights under the law. This ideal is at odds with the Islamic

Republic of Iran's treatment of religious minorities, including even sects of or orientations within Shi'ism, all of which have faced varying degrees of discrimination or persecution. The Baha'i minority is unique, however, insofar as the Islamic Republic does not recognize it as a religious minority at all, instead designating it a political party in defiance of everything social scientists know about the movement. It is true that a significant contemporary group within the Baha'is is itself comprised of theocrats who envisage a Baha'i-ruled state in the future, but this utopian hope, which in any case directly contradicts the Baha'i prophet's own teachings, hardly qualifies them as a political party.[2]

Theocracy challenges both of the major nationalist traditions that developed in the eighteenth and nineteenth centuries. The "revolutionary" or "civic" tradition in eighteenth-century France and the United States equated the nation with the people in a democratic society, regardless of their language or ethnicity. Often even the individual's religion was declared irrelevant to membership in the nation. Of importance was one's commitment to a set of secular ideals and, at most, one's willingness to acquire the national language, criteria that authorized a pluralist conception of the public. The later Central and Eastern European ideals of exclusionary nationalism based on language and "race," which emerged in the mid-nineteenth century, envisioned a singular source of national identity.[3] Benedict Anderson has argued that nationalisms in the global South were modular, having been modelled on nations in South America and Europe.[4] He has been challenged on this point by Partha Chatterjee, who maintains that nationalisms in the colonized world outwardly adopted the techniques of colonial power (political parties, nationalist discourse, newspapers, etc.) but inwardly demarcated a "spiritual" realm of difference from the colonizer concerned with domesticity, the place of women, and religion.[5]

Iran's theocracy turns Chatterjee's perspective on its head insofar as Rohu'llah Khomeini transformed the latent "spiritual" realm that distinguished Iranian nationalism from that of the North Atlantic imperial powers into the public realm, displacing Western-derived discourses of nationalism in the process. Iran's theocracy mixes elements of both civic and exclusionary nationalist traditions while appearing to reject nationalism altogether. It defines members of the nation by their willingness to accept the rule of the supreme jurisprudent and to be subordinate to the apparatus of Islamic law, over which he presides. In a sense, only Shi'ite Muslims are full citizens (only a Shi'ite may be president), with minorities being ranked in the following order: Sunni Muslims, Christians, Jews, and Zoroastrians. Baha'is and secularists have at many points been defined as persons outside the nation altogether because by definition they cannot sincerely accept the rule of the jurisprudent and because he cannot define a legitimate Islamic niche for them to occupy. There is thus both an ideological and an ethnic element in Iranian Muslim nationalism. Yet Iran's nationalism also appeals to nativist authenticity since Iranian Shi'ism gives a distinctive identity to members of the nation, who either were brought up within the Shi'ite faith or are encompassed by it culturally and politically.

Many of Iran's clerical leaders have rejected the notion of nation-states altogether and see the international conception of human rights as a Western invention or a hypocritical means for corrupt imperialist powers to meddle in the internal affairs of an Islamically ruled nation. Antinationalism in the tradition of Khomeini has been tempered over time even though he founded the republic. It has been widely noted that the Islamic Republic has passed through distinct phases of governance. I will characterize these as a radical right-wing populism during the Khomeini era (1979–89), conservative theocracy during the presidency of Hojjatu'l-Islam 'Ali Akbar Hashimi Rafsanjani (1989–97), and polarization (a struggle between radicals, conservatives, and reformists) under President Mohammad Khatami (since 1997). During the Khomeini era of radical theocracy, many religious minorities were treated with extreme harshness. During the succeeding era of conservative theocracy, policies became less draconian (although on the whole they remained unsatisfactory to the international human-rights community and to many members of the religious minorities themselves). Here I concentrate on the 1990s and investigate the question of minority and nation in Iran. How did changes in regime policy affect the conception of the nation and the place of the Baha'is within it in this period of great change? The Iranian Baha'is are, among all the minorities, perhaps the most anomalous in contemporary Iranian law and politics, and from their case we may therefore expect to learn a great deal about the considerations driving Iran's minorities policy more generally.

The issue of the place of religious minorities in the Iranian nation is more important than it might appear on the surface. Non-Muslim religious minorities probably account for only 1 per cent of Iranians today (around 600,000 persons). But in fact, the proportion is much higher if we take into account that Sunni Muslims are a religious minority in Iran that, although traditionally estimated at only about 7 to 8 per cent of the population, some observers put at 10 to 20 per cent. (Sunnis belong to tribal groups on Iran's periphery, such as Kurds, Lurs, Arabs, Turkmen, and Baluch, and many are pastoralists who have probably been undercounted in censuses; they also include the some 2 million Afghan refugees in Iran, many of whom seem unlikely to return to Afghanistan.) It should also be remembered that Shi'ism itself is differentiated into Sufi orders such as the Ni'matu'llahi and theological schools such as the Shaykhi, both of which have been persecuted in Khomeinist Iran. The heterodox Ahl-i Haqq sect, being syncretic, coexists uneasily with Shi'ism. Religious minorities are therefore a more pressing national issue than the undifferentiated social statistics might suggest.

Ofra Bengio and Gabriel Ben-Dor have distinguished between "compact" minorities in the Middle East (Druze, Maronites, Kurds) and diffuse minorities. They note that groups such as the Eastern Orthodox Christians in Syria and Lebanon lack a strong regional base or close political connections with centres of power. They have an impact on culture and in private business. Elaborating upon the observations of Bernard Lewis, they also point out that the melding of Islamic themes with Middle Eastern nationalisms in the past thirty years has had the effect of excluding or marginalizing Christians and others. This problem has been especially acute for the Christians of Southern Sudan, who are neither Arab nor Muslim in a state that has increasingly defined itself as both.[6] The Baha'is in Iran resemble the Eastern Orthodox Christians in being such a dispersed minority with no strong regional base (although they are significantly concentrated in a few towns, such as Sangesar). They benefit from being Persian-speaking Iranians in the main, although there is a substantial Azeri minority among them. The rise of the Islamic Republic, however, positioned them unfavourably, just as Islamically tinged nationalisms in the Arab world tend to exclude Eastern Orthodox and Coptic Christian minorities. Understanding the position of Iranian Baha'is in contemporary Iran requires an understanding of how nationalism now manifests itself in this country.

NATIONALISM AND THE BAHA'IS IN IRAN

Iran as a nation, like most other modern nations, was first imagined into being in the nineteenth century. Prior to this time, the Iranian plateau had been ruled by polyglot empires that, despite having a conception of the peoples who had dwelt on the plateau (e.g., Persian-speaking "Iranis" and Turkic-speaking "Turanis"), had no conception of the nation-state in the modern sense. The Achaemenids kept their records in Elamite or Aramaic for the most part, even though they themselves spoke Old Persian. The plateau was ruled by Arabs from the Muslim conquest to the rise of the Buyids in the tenth century and then by ethnically Turkic dynasties such as the Saljuqs, Safavids, and Qajars for much of the rest of the medieval and early modern period. Even in what is now Iran, only about 51 per cent of the population speaks Persian as its primary language, with Turkic dialects, such as Azeri, Qashqa'i, and Turkoman, being spoken at home by at least a third of Iranians. Other Iranian languages, such as Kurdish, Luri, and Baluch, are also significant. Some intellectuals in the nineteenth century began to fall under the spell of romantic nationalism, which posited nations as eternal essences intimately linked to land, blood, and tongue and which sought ancient origins for modern polities. A few Iranian thinkers found these ideas attractive insofar as they underlined the greatness of the Achaemenid Empire in antiquity and constituted Iranians not as backward Muslim tribespeople and villagers but as cosmopolitan heirs to Cyrus the Great. Ominously, many of these early nationalists were especially attracted by the scientific racism of Joseph-Arthur comte de Gobineau, and others,[7] which put "Aryans" at the pinnacle of a racial hierarchy. By becoming nationalists, Persian speakers could thus hope to join the system at the top (although in actuality the idea of Europeans accepting Iranians as equals in the age of empire was foredoomed to failure). Thinkers such as Akhundzadih and Mirza Aqa Khan Kirmani excoriated the Arab Muslims for having, in their view, ruined the ancient and proud Iranian Aryan civilization, characterized by Zoroastrianism and empire.[8] Needless to say, this view of things struck most Iranian Shi'ite Muslims as bizarre.

The Baha'i faith has its roots in the nineteenth-century millenarian Babi movement, which around 1849 may have had as many as 50,000 to 100,000 adherents in a population of around 6 million.[9] However, it was brutally suppressed in the 1850s, and these numbers, if they were really this high to begin with, certainly declined dramatically during the persecution launched after leading Babis attempted to assassinate the shah in 1852. Baha'i numbers in Iran have always been a matter of informed guesswork.[10] From the late 1860s, the movement was reinvigorated and transformed by Baha'u'llah, who founded the Baha'i faith, which from all accounts grew rapidly in Qajar Iran. His modernist message of world peace, world unity, and adoption of both parliamentary democracy and Western technology struck a chord with many Iranians.[11] It would not surprise me if there were 200,000 Baha'is by 1900 in a population of 9 million, and the movement appears to have garnered enormous numbers of adherents and sympathizers in the early twentieth century under the charismatic, liberal, and universalistic leadership of 'Abdu'l-Baha (head of the religion from 1892 to 1921). By the 1920s an internal census conducted by the Baha'is is said to have found that about a million persons in Iran came at least occasionally to Baha'i meetings. This number seems surprisingly high, but it is plausible given that it reports only attendees, not actual members of congregations, and that it includes many persons who would now be categorized as vague sympathizers, as friends of believers, or perhaps even as idly curious.[12]

Because the Baha'i faith originated in the mid-nineteenth century on Iranian soil, it could conceivably claim advantages over the "foreign" Islam of the Arabs. In actuality, the movement out of which it developed, Babism, was a form of hyper-Shi'ism focused on the advent of the Shi'ite Mahdi, or promised one. In contrast, the Baha'i faith itself shed most of the particularistic practices of Shi'ism and Babism, seeking instead to engage modernity by emphasizing values such as globalization and world unity. As neither Shi'ism nor Babism lent itself to modern nationalism, both sects were often dismissed by nationalists. Akhundzadih, a Voltairean who deeply disliked Islam, sniffed that given what the Bab's grandfather (the Prophet Muhammad) had achieved, it seemed unlikely that the "grandson" (Sayyid 'Ali Muhammad Shirazi, the Bab [1819–50]) had founded a beneficial movement.

Mirza Husayn 'Ali Nuri (1817–92), known as Baha'u'llah, the founder of the Baha'i faith, was deeply suspicious of modern European nationalism. He said, "Glory does not lie in loving one's nation but rather in loving the whole world." Still, he took pride in Iran's ancient civilization and urged Iranians to adopt modern institutions, such as parliamentary democracy, and to embrace science in order to recover their honoured place among the nations. In 1891, during the Tobacco Revolt against a European monopoly, he wrote, "O people of Persia! In former times you have been the symbols of mercy and the embodiments of affection and kindliness. The regions of the world were illumined and embellished by the brightness of the light of your knowledge and by the blaze of your erudition. How is it that you have arisen to destroy yourselves and your friends with your own hands?" He added, "How strange that the people of Persia, who were unrivalled in sciences and arts, should have sunk to the lowest level of degradation among the kindreds of the earth."[13]

Much earlier, in a book published in Bombay in 1882, his son 'Abdu'l-Baha 'Abbas, later the leader of the movement from 1892 to 1921, had written words about Iran that any romantic nationalist would recognize:

O people of Persia! Look into those blossoming pages that tell of another day, a time long past. Read them and wonder; see the great sight. Iran in that day was as the heart of the world; she was the bright torch flaming in the assemblage of mankind. Her power and glory shone out like the morning above the world's horizons, and the splendor of her learning cast its rays over East and West. Word of the widespread empire of those who wore her crown reached even to the dwellers in the arctic circle, and the fame of the awesome presence of her King of Kings humbled the rulers of Greece and Rome. The greatest of the world's philosophers marveled at the wisdom of her government, and her political system became the model for all the kings of the four continents then known. She was distinguished among all peoples for the scope of her dominion, she was honored by all for her praiseworthy culture and civilization. She was as the pivot of the world, she was the source and center of sciences and arts, the wellspring of great inventions and discoveries, the rich mine of human virtues and perfections. The intellect, the wisdom of the individual members of this excellent nation dazzled the minds of other peoples, the brilliance and perceptive genius that characterized all this noble race aroused the envy of the whole world.[14]

He went on to recount legends, based on Firdawsi's epic, *Shahnameh*, of how "the first government to be established on earth, the foremost empire to be organized among the nations, was Persia's throne and diadem" and then to speak of the glory of the Achaemenids, who ruled much of the ancient world.[15] The Baha'i emphasis on peace and globalism led outside observers, such as E.G. Browne, to assume that they would side with foreign powers against the interests of their own nation, but there seems little evidence for such an allegation.[16] The Baha'i leaders were more critical of Europe and European imperialism than Browne realized.

With the rise of the Pahlevi dynasty in the mid-1920s, ideas of race and nation began to be spread through the modern school system. On the one hand, nationalists such as Reza Shah and his supporters attempted to reduce the power of Shi'ite Islam and to foster a civil Iranian identity. Many Baha'is saw this emphasis as beneficial to them at least in the short run. On the other hand, strong secular nationalists such as Ahmad Kasravi attacked the Baha'is and other religious groups as a source of disunity for the Iranian nation. Throughout the twentieth century, Shi'ite religious nationalists saw the Baha'is as dangerous heretics and as channels by which dangerous Western ideas, such as equality for women, entered Iran. Insofar as the Baha'i faith was a post-Islamic religion, its legitimacy was rejected by the Shi'ite clergy, who could not recognize any religion arising after Islam as a real religion. They categorized it as a political movement, a somewhat bizarre characterization given the Baha'i leaders' quietism.[17] It is true that in the 1930s some Baha'i leaders turned their back on the earlier scriptural principle of separation of religion and state championed by Baha'u'llah and 'Abdu'l-Baha and began to advocate a theocracy in which Baha'i institutions would ultimately supplant civil governments and impose censorship and Baha'i law on the populace. Such theocratic dreams, however, were not regarded as a practical goal to be implemented but as a mystical vision that God would bring about by visiting sudden catastrophes on humankind. From the 1960s, the Baha'is' bestowal on these apocalyptic motifs of a patina of anticlericalism, modernism, and cosmopolitanism made them hated among Shi'ite activists, such as the Hujjatiyyih movement, which was dedicated to fighting Baha'i influence and disrupting the religion and which cooperated with the shah's SAVAK, or secret police, in order to do so.

The Baha'i faith has no trained formal clergy and deals with its affairs by electing or appointing lay officers. From the late 1920s, a rigid administrative structure was imposed on the Iranian Baha'i community involving elections in which nominations or overt campaigning were forbidden. While such a system worked relatively well in small local communities where everyone was known and interaction was face to face, the newly invented electoral system of the 1920s and 1930s posed great problems at the level of national elections, and administrators, despite their wide popularity, gradually discovered that incumbents could almost never be unseated and could, behind the scenes, create a "buzz" around informal candidates they favoured to fill open seats. This openness of the system to such irregularities and authoritarian tendencies at the national level was reinforced by the Baha'i authorities' insistence that these institutions be obeyed implicitly and never publicly criticized and by the creation in 1951 of a body, the "hands of the cause," charged with both propagation and "protection" of the Baha'i faith. In the view of the more narrow-minded "hands," the latter function authorized them to conduct a standing Inquisition against Baha'is with innovative ideas. They were empowered to suggest excommunication and shunning as punishments for thought crimes, giving them great informal power. Strict prepublication censorship was required of adherents who wrote anything for publication about their own religion, and Baha'i books and histories, even some scriptures, were routinely suppressed by the Baha'i leaders. That is, the universalist and liberal principles of the founders of the religion had by the mid-twentieth century been reduced to an attractive facade for a movement that now had a secret authoritarian agenda. It is instructive that several of the religion's major intellectuals in twentieth-century Iran ended up being largely marginalized or even shunned inside the community, which produced only a handful of writers willing to brave such opprobrium.

From the mid to late 1920s, Baha'is in Iran were forbidden by their ecclesiastical authorities to maintain dual membership in the Baha'i faith and any other religion, to belong to political parties, to hold political posts, or to belong to organizations such as the freemasons or Sufi orders. Baha'is were excommunicated and shunned for declining to relocate from their homes to some other region when ordered to do so by the Baha'i authorities. An anti-intellectualism emerged that alienated many Baha'is who entered higher education as students or professors. These policies had the effect of transforming an open and universalistic movement of great popularity, with many adherents and sympathizers, into a closed, quietist, and somewhat narrow-minded ethnic community that sometimes sought inordinate control over the lives of the faithful. Among the few high positions open to Baha'is in Iranian society were those in the Pahlevi military, and many became officers. Prominent Baha'i military men emerged as power brokers within the community and began to impose almost military-style discipline at Baha'i meetings and study classes. Because of the Baha'i administration's rigidity and controlling tendencies, as well as the hatred many Iranian Shi'ites entertained for the new faith, many Baha'is left the religion in the course of the twentieth century. By 1978 there were only about 90,000 registered Baha'is in Iran and perhaps another 200,000 ethnic Baha'is and sympathizers who never declared formal membership. Many of the sympathizers who did not formally join were unwilling to submit to the degree of control over their lives or isolation from Iranian political and civil society demanded by Baha'i leaders of formally registered believers. In addition to regimentation inside the community, Baha'is faced occasional attacks from outsiders and even, in 1955, a nationwide pogrom.[18] Many of these developments devastated the movement in Iran, where most supporters and many members voted with their feet by melding into secularist groups.

In his book on nationalism in Iran, based in part on interviews with Iranians in the 1950s, Richard Cottam maintains that the nationalist movement of Muhammad Musaddiq curbed those in its religious wing who wished to attack the Baha'is in the early 1950s. He argues that nationalism can benefit indigenous groups such as the Zoroastrians and Baha'is, while those religious minorities identified with a foreign state (Armenians and, after 1948, Jews) are hurt by it. Musaddiq, who nationalized Iran's oil industry and sent the shah into exile, was overthrown by a CIA-backed coup in 1953. Two years later, the conservative clerics who had been allied with the shah launched a major campaign of persecution against the Baha'is. Cottam suggests that Muhammad Reza Pahlevi thereby rewarded those Shi'ite clergymen who had supported him against the nationalist Musaddiq. What Cottam does not know is that the shah also owed debts to the Baha'is. His royal physician, a Baha'i who had grown fabulously wealthy from court patronage, supported him while he was in exile in Italy in 1953. Thus the shah allowed only symbolic damage to be inflicted on the Baha'i centre's dome in Tehran in 1955, which nevertheless served to establish his bona fides with conservative clerics, such as Ayatollah Burujirdi.

But Muhammad Reza Pahlevi then gradually included the Baha'is in his policy of favouring minorities for court patronage as a way of offsetting the demands of nationalists and dissident Shi'ites. He extended a certain amount of protection to minorities in return for their support of his corporatist state. Baha'i industrialists, such as Habib Sabet, benefited enormously from royal patronage, as did bankers, such as Hozhabr Yazdani. (Employees in Sabit's enterprises tended to dominate the National Spiritual Assembly of Iran.) The

Iranian airline bureaucracy came to be staffed disproportionately by Baha'is. This minorities policy of the 1960s and 1970s, which benefited Baha'is, was a source of Khomeini's most vehement denunciations of the shah's regime. Cottam reports that the Iranian Baha'is he interviewed in the late 1950s professed themselves to be strong supporters of the Iranian nation, but he seems ambivalent about whether to believe them.[19] There is no strong reason to dismiss these expressions of fervour. I have been told by older fallen-away Iranian Baha'is that they first experienced an intellectual and cultural awakening during the Musaddiq crisis. In the 1970s, at the height of the minorities policy, Iranian Baha'is frequently told this author that the shah's so-called White Revolution was based on Baha'i teachings, and they were universally proud that "Hadrat-i Baha'u'llah" (His Holiness, Baha'u'llah) had sprung from Iranian soil.

Khomeini's ascension to power in the winter of 1979 shifted the official basis for identity in Iran from nation to Islam. This shift disadvantaged all the religious minorities since a Zoroastrian could be an exemplary Iranian but could be nothing more than an infidel in fundamentalist Islamic terms. Among many other things, the 1979 revolution represented for many committed Shi'ite activists, including Khomeini himself, the opportunity finally to take measures against the Baha'is. Under Khomeini, many activists within the Hujjatiyyih movement, which was obsessed with destroying the Baha'i faith, gained great power in the new government. Among them was Muhammad 'Ali Raja'i, who was elected president briefly before being blown up by the Mujahidin-i Khalq guerrilla movement. In 1979 the Baha'i headquarters was invaded and confiscated, and the membership list naming some 90,000 registered believers was found. Between 1979 and 1989, nearly 200 Baha'is were executed and thousands jailed.[20] Among those killed were the members of the Baha'i national spiritual assembly. A Muslim judge and head of the Revolutionary Court in Shiraz gave a newspaper interview in 1983 in which he maintained that "The Iranian Nation has risen in accordance with Quranic teachings and by the Will of God has determined to establish the Government of God on earth. Therefore, it cannot tolerate the perverted Bahais who are instruments of Satan and followers of the Devil and of the superpowers and their agents."[21] This passage evinces a confusing mixture of nationalist and religious language: It is the "Iranian nation" that has established the Islamic theocracy, and the Baha'is are excluded because of their alleged cosmopolitan links to the superpowers. They are depicted as both demonic and foreign, whereas true Iranians are Muslim and godly. Even at the height of Khomeini's Pan-Islam, some Iranian clerics saw a role for "the Iranian nation" in the enterprise. In the same year, the Islamic Republic circulated a twenty-page document attempting to justify its treatment of Baha'is, insisting that the Baha'i faith constituted a political movement fashioned by powerful anti-Islamic colonial forces, such as the British, and supported by the neocolonial Government of Israel. They said, moreover, that the Baha'is had been a pillar of the overthrown Pahlevi regime and were thus deeply implicated in human-rights violations of the 1960s and 1970s.[22] Of all the charges made, only this latter has a kernel of truth, and then only if it is applied to a handful of the shah's Baha'i cronies, not to the entire community.

It should be noted, however, that the political context of the early 1980s, when most of the killings of Baha'is occurred, was the Great Terror that accompanied the repression of militant guerrilla groups and of ethnic minorities, such as Kurds and Turkmen. The vast majority of those who died during this revolutionary killing spree were not members of religious minorities but political dissidents. For instance, over 10,000 members and sympathizers of the Mujahidin-i Khalq guerrilla movement were killed (mainly by execution) in the 1980s, and hundreds, if not thousands, of Kurdish political and paramilitary activists were also mown down. The European Parliament estimated that between 1981 and 1990, some 90,000 Iranians (about 0.2 per cent of the population) were executed and that 140,000 (about 0.3 per cent the population) were jailed.[23] Political prisoners and prisoners of conscience formed a large proportion of those killed or incarcerated. As late as fall 1988, the Government of Iran admitted to having carried out large-scale executions.[24] Amnesty International said that Iran accounted for 1,200 of the 1,600 executions it recorded throughout the world during the first eight months of 1989.[25]

Nevertheless, the very innocuous character of the Baha'is, who constitute the Iranian equivalent of a "peace church," makes executing them seem particularly egregious. As a result of their persecution by the state, about 30,000 Baha'is emigrated during the 1980s. These were likely disproportionately drawn from the registered group since the regime had firm evidence of their membership and since the Baha'i authorities would validate for the us State Department and other international government agencies only registrants' claims to being genuine Baha'is deserving of asylum. Registered Baha'is who flew out of Tehran airport before about 1989, acquiring a visa by falsely declaring themselves Muslim, were uncompromisingly excommunicated by the Baha'i authorities in the countries to which they moved, nor would those authorities cooperate in their applications for asylum. This sort of behaviour belies the publicly stated concern of the Baha'i authorities for the welfare of the Baha'is and for upholding human-rights standards since maintaining control over adherents through strict behavioural requirements was clearly more important to them than saving lives.

Many of those formally registered Baha'is who remained in Iran were taken to mosques by Khomeinist fanatics and forced to apostatize; in some instances, the state abducted the children of those who refused to accept Islam and gave them to Muslim families to raise. The fate of the 200,000 or so Baha'i sympathizers inside Iran who had never registered is difficult to know, but it seems likely that many have dissociated themselves from the movement, even as others have stubbornly, if secretively, retained some allegiance to it. Although it may thus be posited that the Baha'i community, however defined, is much smaller now than it was in 1978, it is certainly still tens of thousands strong. The overall near doubling of Iran's population between 1978 and 1998 probably left the Baha'is behind because Baha'i families tend to be middle-class and small.[26] In the late 1980s, measures were undertaken to reduce some of the pressure on the community. In 1986 there were 650 Baha'is in prison as prisoners of conscience.[27] In 1987 there were still 200 Baha'is incarcerated in Iranian jails for their faith. In 1988 the number declined to 129, and signs emerged of a thaw more generally.

RAFSANJANI'S FIRST TERM, 1989–93

The year 1989 represented a major turning point for the Islamic Republic. The previous year, Imam Khomeini had reluctantly accepted a ceasefire in the long war of attrition with Iraq; thus, for the first full year since 1980, Iran was not on a war footing. Khomeini himself died of a heart attack on 3 July 1989, bringing to a close a decade during which he and his policies of authoritarianism and mass terror had dominated Iran. The clerical Assembly of Experts met and selected Hujjatu'l-Islam 'Ali Khamenei, who had served as president since 1981, as the new supreme jurisprudent. Presidential elections were then quickly planned for 28 July, with 95 per cent of the vote going to 'Ali Akbar Hashemi Rafsanjani, who had served as Speaker of Parliament since 1980. The radical wing of Iranian theocracy had advocated strident attacks on the West along with Iranian economic self-sufficiency and state ownership of much of the economy. Having for some time questioned this isolationism and statism, Rafsanjani, once in power, attempted to move the country away from radical right-wing populism and toward policies consistent with a general opening-up of the economy, such as a selective rapprochement with Western European countries and privatization of industry. He surrounded himself with Western-trained technocrats, dubbed the "California mafia," and increasingly moved toward a pragmatic conservatism that not only alienated him from the radical theocrats, but even created tension between him and the somewhat more xenophobic and reactionary supreme jurisprudent, 'Ali Khamenei.[28] Rafsanjani promised in his inauguration speech to respect the "freedom and dignity of individuals,"[29] and although his critics would have found such a pledge on his part laughable, it is remarkable that he should have spoken in such terms at all. This rhetoric was no doubt an attempt to signal the international community that he intended to undertake policy changes. Khomeini's persecuting society, with its ever-widening wave of taboo groups, began to subside in favour of a more selective use of repression.

During Rafsanjani's eight years in power, the absolute numbers of those jailed or killed annually declined. The improvement under Rafsanjani was relative, not absolute, and his regime was much worse than some of the other dictatorships in the second half of the twentieth century if one focuses on incarceration and executions of political prisoners and prisoners of conscience. It is still true that acts of official terror occurred far less frequently than in the frantically bloodthirsty days of the early 1980s. From 1989 to 1997, human-rights organizations continued to report widespread abuse in Iran, including substantial use of torture, arbitrary detentions, lack of fair trials, and restrictions on the rights of women and of workers. Members of the political opposition – such as the Mujahidin-i Khalq, the Tudeh communist party, the Kurdish parties, and others – continued to be brutally arrested and executed on a large scale. The number of political prisoners in Iran as late as 1996 was estimated to be several thousand by Amnesty International.[30] Most religious minorities, in contrast, began to be shown some clemency. By 1989, for instance, the number of Baha'is in prison as prisoners of conscience had fallen to 15, and this number remained the average in the succeeding decade. This change marked the Rafsanjani years as quite different from the situation under Khomeini.

In the 1990s some Baha'i students who had been expelled from state schools were allowed to resume their studies, and a small amount of property was returned to the Baha'is from whom it had been confiscated.[31] The relative tolerance of Baha'is coincided with a sharp drop in the influence of the Hujjatiyyih and of other radical right-wing Shi'ite populists on the Iranian state. The Baha'is incarcerated during the Rafsanjani period included Bihnam Mithaqi and Kayvan Khalajabadi, who were arrested in Karaj because of their beliefs in April 1989 and continued to be held at Gohardasht Prison without charge or trial for the succeeding decade.[32] The relatively small number of arrests after 1989 took the form of serial harassment of prominent or die-hard Baha'is. In 1990, for instance, fourteen Baha'is were arrested as prisoners of conscience, whereas nineteen were released. A few Baha'is were actually issued visas to leave Iran. Others were allowed to reopen private businesses.

A strong Khomeinist legacy of official discrimination against the Baha'is, who were branded a "misguided sect," did continue. The Baha'is' administrative institutions had been disbanded by official decree in 1983, and they continued to be banned from holding elections for local or national spiritual assemblies, which crippled the Baha'i "administrative order," a sort of one-party structure that normally controls important aspects of adherents' lives. They were also prohibited from proselytizing others to their faith.[33] The government continued to deny that the Baha'i faith was a religion at all. This religious community's property, including administrative offices and places of worship, had been confiscated by the Khomeinist government, and no restitution had been made. Baha'is were largely excluded both from attending universities as students and from teaching on their faculties as professors. In the mid-1990s some Baha'i youth were prevented from attending the final year of high school as well.

Given the position of modern education and of universities in nation-building and nationalist iconography, this exclusion clearly marked the Baha'is as somehow not a part of the Iranian nation. The government regularly ruled Baha'is ineligible for compensation for injury or criminal victimization on the grounds that only Muslim plaintiffs may receive compensation.³⁴ They were frequently denied public sector jobs, and the 10,000 Baha'i civil servants fired from the state bureaucracy in the 1980s continued to be denied government employment and the pensions they had accumulated. Indeed, even in the 1990s demands continued that they pay back to the government the salaries they had received while working for the state and that those too indigent to do so be jailed. Again, exclusion from positions in the state bureaucracy marked them as alien, as shapeshifters only pretending to be part of the Iranian nation. Most were not issued passports, although this began to change for a few. Baha'i marriages were not officially recognized. This nonrecognition had been used in the 1980s as a pretext to accuse Baha'is of adultery and the religious officials who married them of being pimps – both capital crimes – but such accusations appear to have become uncommon in the 1990s. The Baha'is allege that they suffer continued discrimination in the judicial system and that revolutionary officials pressure defence lawyers not to accept Baha'i clients, although the Iranian authorities deny this charge. Baha'is have had difficulty meeting together for worship because the government has insisted that no more than fourteen can gather at one time.³⁵

How the Baha'is were treated in the 1990s depended a great deal on the jurisdictions in which they lived, and some suffered more than others. Yazd, for instance, was a difficult place for Baha'is to operate businesses. The imprisonment and execution of Baha'is as well as the other acts of persecution to which they were subjected in the 1990s were symbolic, making a statement about the illegitimacy of the community in the eyes of the authorities rather than involving pogroms and large-scale judicial murder, as had occurred under Khomeini. In 1993, for instance, the Tehran municipal authorities tore up the Baha'i cemetery in order to build a cultural centre on the site. Grave markers were reportedly uprooted and sold off, and earthwork often involved desecrating gravesites.³⁶ This action created the problem for the Tehran Baha'i community of where to bury their dead and elicited widespread condemnation from Western governments and human-rights organizations. In the end, the Baha'is were assigned some wasteland by the authorities for their burials but were denied the right to place tombstones with names over the graves.³⁷ Like universities and bureaucracies, graveyards tend to have national significance, as repositories of past citizens, some of whom would inevitably be veterans or persons of national significance. Just as living Baha'is were defined out of the Islamic Iranian nation, so now even their dead were erased from history and dumped unnamed in wastelands.[38]

Some further executions of Baha'is did take place in this decade. Bahman Samandari, a Tehran businessman, was suddenly arrested and summarily executed in 1992. Samandari appears to have been punished in part for having acted as liaison for the leaderless Iranian Baha'is with the religion's officials in Haifa, Israel, and in part for having gotten word out to the United Nations about his arrest. The official reason given for his execution was "espionage," although Iranian officials also openly complained about his having contacted the United Nations about his arrest.[39] Although such executions came to be rare, at times Baha'is were sentenced to death, and a handful appear to remain on death row.

In 1991 Ayatollah Khamenei formalized many of these policies by approving a "blueprint" for dismantling the Baha'i presence and influence in Iran aimed at employing Shi'ite state hegemony gradually to extinguish the community rather than wiping it out through brute force. The document was drawn up by Sayyid Muhammad Gulpaygani, head of the Supreme Revolutionary Cultural Council, after this body consulted on what to do about the Baha'is. Ironically, as will be seen, this clerical plot resurrected key elements of secular nationalist Iranian identity. The policy decided upon a grudging and partial toleration of individuals but heavy discrimination against the community, the religion, and its organization. Baha'is were not to be arrested, imprisoned, penalized, or expelled from the country for no reason (i.e., for no reason other than that they were Baha'is). As Iranian citizens, they were to be provided routinely with ration booklets, passports, burial certificates, and work permits. They were to be allowed to earn a modest living but not to prosper in such a way as to encourage them to remain Baha'is. They could be schooled but only if they avoided identifying themselves as Baha'is, and they were to be sent especially to schools known for being able to indoctrinate students heavily into Khomeinist ideology. With regard to employment, they were to be denied government posts and university jobs and were generally to be kept out of education as a field. Baha'i attempts to proselytize others and to spread their religion were to be met with counterpropaganda. The memorandum advised, "a plan must be devised to confront and destroy their cultural roots outside the country." This paragraph appears to refer to the Khomeinist officials' bizarre belief that the Baha'i faith was founded as part of a British or other imperialist plot to divide Iranians. Finally, the document insists that "their political (espionage) activities must be dealt with."[40] This phrase refers to the officials' conviction that Baha'is systematically engaged in spying for Israel and the US, a charge that their apolitical quietism makes absurd and for which not even all the reconstructed shredded documents captured at the US embassy provided an iota of confirmation.

The general tenor of the plan submitted by Gulpaygani and signed by Khamenei was to treat the Baha'is as ordinary citizens of Iran for most purposes and to avoid making them martyrs in the eyes of the international human-rights community for no good purpose; rather, gradual and firm pressure was to be exerted on the community to force it into the ranks of the poor, with the aim of thus making it extremely unattractive to be a Baha'i. They clearly hoped that over the long run, such systematic discrimination would deplete the religion's ranks without any need for wholesale persecution of the sort tried during the early 1980s. Still, in recognizing that the Baha'is were Iranian citizens who should be treated like other citizens, the document found a new way of legitimating their existence as individuals in the country, even while it continued to deny the legitimacy of the religion to which they belonged. Remarkably, this legitimation appealed to the secular principles of Iranian nationhood and citizenship and left out reference to Islamic law altogether. Henceforth, individual Baha'is were to suffer discrimination similar to that visited upon African Americans in the days of Jim Crow in the American South or upon Jews in the Germany of the mid-1930s, but they would not face the sort of extreme persecution they had suffered under Khomeini.

RAFSANJANI'S SECOND TERM, 1993-97

Rafsanjani's second term, 1993-97, was marked by increased struggle between the three camps that had now emerged among the theocratic heirs of Khomeini: what I will call (1) the pragmatic conservative, (2) the reactionary, and (3) the radical. *Pragmatic conservatives*, such as Rafsanjani and his followers, continued to advocate economic privatization, an opening to Western Europe, and slightly greater cultural freedom inside the country. Houshang Amir Ahmadi has argued that the second Rafsanjani term witnessed the rehabilitation of key themes in Iranian nationalism and that the president himself intervened to foster it.[41] As of the 1992 parliamentary elections, the pragmatic-conservative faction held about 30 per cent of the seats in Parliament. It was weakened in the 1993 elections by a very low turnout. Although its candidate, Rafsanjani, received 63 per cent of the vote, only 50 per cent of eligible voters came to the polls, meaning that only a third of the electorate had actually voted for him. The pragmatic-conservative faction was further shaken by the failure of its policies to produce significant economic growth, by high inflation, relatively low oil prices, and continued high population growth as well as by the fact that the Lebanese hostage crisis did not produce any tangible reward for Iran (especially the release of billions of dollars embargoed by the United States because of the 1979–81 Hostage Crisis). The early 1990s were marred by squatters' riots, bombings allegedly carried out by the Mujahidin-i Khalq in places like the Imam Riza Shrine in Mashad, and an assassination attempt on Rafsanjani himself.

The *reactionary faction* associated with Khamenei supported privatization and free-market economic policies but continued to be suspicious of Western cultural influence and to reject extensive loosening of theocratic controls on politics and culture. This faction controlled about 40 per cent of the seats in parliament in the mid-1990s. The *radical theocrats* – who remained isolationists in foreign policy, advocated national self-reliance in economics, opposed privatization, and desired to reinstitute Khomeini's reign of terror against those they viewed as deviationists – held about 15 per cent of the seats in Parliament. Whereas from 1989 to 1993 the conservative and reactionary theocrats had cooperated against the radicals, moving the country in the direction of some liberalization, increasingly in Rafsanjani's second term, Khamenei and his reactionaries took stances redolent of the radical position. They outlawed satellite dishes and Western television, and they reconstituted the *basij* (irregular volunteers who had fought at the Iraqi front) as a civilian vigilante force with the power to harass and even summarily execute persons they viewed as deviating from Islamic norms. They elevated Khomeini's *fatwa*, or ruling of death, against Salman Rushdie to the status of an irrevocable law, or *hukm* (apparently in the knowledge that this would make it difficult for Western European nations entirely to effect a rapprochement with Iran).[42] The weakness of the pragmatic conservatives and their friction with reactionaries and radical right-wing populists was played out on many levels, including that of the treatment of religious minorities.⁴³

From 1993 through 1997, the Islamic court system, especially in the provinces, became the primary arena for symbolically sanctioning apostates, both Baha'is and others. As President Rafsanjani sought good relations with Western Europe and institutions such as the World Bank, he had a motivation not to engage in unnecessary and egregious human-rights violations on the old Khomeinist scale. A desire to continue to subject the Baha'is to punitive measures remained liveliest among the more radical clerics, who, although comprising only 15 per cent of parliament deputies, retained great power over the judiciary. Radicals could also pressure the private sector, as in Mashad, where businesses were discouraged by Khomeinist activists in the mid-1990s from employing Baha'is.

The UN High Commission on Human Rights denounced the practice in the second Rafsanjani term of "arresting Baha'is and detaining them for short periods and of summoning Baha'is to Ministry of Intelligence agencies on various pretexts" and noted that during the years 1994–97, "nearly 200 Baha'is were arrested and detained for periods ranging from two days to six months."⁴⁴ Religious beliefs affected sentencing. Police arrested a group of young men for misconduct and later released the Muslims among them. Two of the arrested, however, Arman Dimishqi and Kurush Dhabihi, were Baha'is, and the courts demanded that they recant their faith in order to obtain quick release as well. When they refused, both were sentenced to eight years in prison. Among those in prison in 1997 were Mansur Haddam and Kamyar Ruhi, who had been convicted of "being active in the Baha'i community, of gathering for Baha'i meetings in a private house and of working against the security of the country by organizing a Baha'i children's art exhibit." A Baha'i edifice in Urumiyeh was destroyed in 1997, Baha'is were occasionally summarily expelled by Revolutionary Guards from their homes, which were confiscated, and "it was alleged that the majority of the Baha'is in the city of Yazd were prohibited from conducting any business transactions."⁴⁵

But the courts were entirely capable of going well beyond mere judicial harassment on occasion. Bihnam Mithaqi and Kayvan Khalajabadi, two Baha'is arrested in April 1989 and held without charge or trial until December 1993, were sentenced to death.⁴⁶ A *New York Times* editorial explained, "The judicial judgment against two defendants living in Karaj, near Teheran, accuses them of a new kind of crime – transmitting information that they were on trial for their lives to the United Nations and to Bahai groups outside Iran."⁴⁷ In addition, the two were accused of holding religious ceremonies, owning books, and being "at war" with Islam. The government, however, managed to drag its feet on carrying out the sentence, so the two men simply languished in prison. Also late in 1993, a provincial revolutionary court in Rafsanjan sentenced another Baha'i, Ramadan 'Ali Dhulfaqari, to death for apostasy. He was released from prison on 6 January 1994, although the charge of apostasy "is said to remain outstanding."⁴⁸ This outcome appears to reflect a conflict between the provincial judiciary, who wanted Dhulfaqari executed, and other officials of the Islamic Republic, who seem to have effectively buried the case, even though it inevitably still hangs over his head.

In January 1996, Dhabihullah Mahrami (b. 1946) was sentenced to death by a revolutionary tribunal in Yazd, joining Bihnam Mithaqi and Kayvan Khalajabadi on death row. In February the Iranian Supreme Court confirmed the death sentences against Mithaqi and Khalajabadi, although one Iranian official floated the bald-faced lie that the charge against them was espionage rather than religious heresy. Their situation differed from that of Mahrami, however, insofar as they had been arrested in 1989 while Khomeini was still alive simply for being Baha'is. Mahrami, born a Baha'i, had succumbed in 1981 after the revolution to pressure to convert to Islam in order to keep his job in the Ministry of Agriculture in the Province of Yazd. His conversion under duress had been announced in the *Kayhan* newspaper in August 1983, and in 1985 he had signed a document at the ministry where he was employed indicating that he was a Muslim. Either because he could not bear the hypocrisy any further, or because he thought that Khomeini's death and Rafsanjani's election had made it safer to announce one's adherence to the Baha'i faith, or both, Mahrami had then apostatized from Islam in 1989.

However, he had not realized that under classical Muslim jurisprudence, such as had been made the law of the land in Iran, apostasy is a capital crime. The clerics might have overlooked those 60,000 or so formally registered, born Baha'is who had neither left the country nor adopted Islam. But apostasy was something they could not accept. For one thing, if citizens began feeling it was safe to say they were Baha'is after having affirmed a primary Muslim identity for over a decade, then not only might thousands of formerly registered

Baha'is return to their religion, but even the 200,000 or so former sympathizers with the religion might begin experimenting again with dual identity. Moreover, the possibility of the religion drawing new converts from Islam could not be ruled out. Mahrami's boldness presented the clerics in control of the judicial system with the difficult choice of either risking the reemergence of the Baha'i faith as at least an informal religious option for hundreds of thousands of people in Iran or provoking economic and diplomatic retaliation against Iran by the world community. They must have likewise been worried about the underground successes of Christian evangelicals in winning converts in northern Iran and about a renewed secularism, both of which would have been emboldened if they had allowed apostasy. The conflict between the radical Islamic republicans among the clerics and their enemies (the pragmatic conservatives) heated up and began to involve charges against an old and favourite scapegoat, the Baha'is.

Mahrami had been summoned to the Islamic Revolutionary Court in Yazd on 24 July 1995 and came before the court on 6 August 1995. In this session, he was questioned about his current religious beliefs. He affirmed he was a Baha'i. The authorities brought Mahrami back for three further court sessions. Each time, they requested that he reconsider, repent, and return to Islam. He repeatedly declined the invitation. As a result, he was charged with "national apostasy," a crime specified in the writings of Imam Rohu'llah Khomeini that had come to have the force of law for judges of the Islamic Republic. The inextricable intertwining of Shi'ite religion with the Iranian nation is underlined by this conception of national apostasy. The phrase implies that abandoning Shi'ism for any other religion is tantamount to renouncing Iranian citizenship, or to treason (also a capital crime). Despite the language of the Gulpaygani document cited above, which recognized Baha'is as Iranian nationals due the rights of citizenship, the conception of national apostasy that still dominated judicial thinking about them continued to define Baha'is as traitors to the nation.

After Mahrami had chosen a defence lawyer, the 2 January 1996 court session took place at which he was condemned to death. It is worthwhile quoting some of the verdict of the Revolutionary Court in Yazd against him:

Concerning the charges against Mr. Dhabihullah Mahrami, the son of Gholamreza, i.e. denouncing the blessed religion of Islam and accepting the beliefs of the wayward Baha'i sect (national apostasy), in light of his clear confessions to the fact that he accepted the wayward Baha'i sect at the age of maturity, later accepted Islam for a period of seven years, and then returned to the aforementioned sect; and because of the fact that, despite the most tremendous efforts of this court to guide him and encourage him to repent for having committed the most grievous sin, he remains firm in his baseless beliefs, he has, on three consecutive meetings, while being of sound body and mind and in absolute control, announced his allegiance to the principles of Baha'ism and his belief in the prophethood of Mirza Husayn-Aliy-i-Baha, he has openly denied the most essential [principle] of Islam [Prophet Muhammad's being the Seal of the Prophets], and he is not willing to repent for having committed this sin, the following verdict was issued, based on the investigations of the Department of Intelligence of the Province of Yazd, and the damaging consequences of his leaving the true religion of Islam and rejoining the Baha'i sect, which, according to indisputable principles accepted by reasonable people, is a clear insult to the beliefs of over one billion Muslims. By applying the tenth definition of "Nijasat" [ritual impurity] to be found in the first volume of Tahrir ol-Vasileh in defining an infidel and an apostate, as well as section ten of the book of Al-Mavarith (on the topic of inheritance) and sections one and four of al-Hudud (on the topic of apostasy) written by the great founder of the Islamic Republic of Iran, His Holiness Imam Khomeini, the accused is sentenced to death because of being an apostate. Furthermore, based on section one of al-Mavarith (on the topic of inheritance) and in light of the fact that he does not have any Muslim heirs, a verdict is issued for the confiscation of all his properties and assets [Mahrami's wife and children are Baha'is and this decree would disinherit them].[49]

Mahrami appealed the death sentence against him to the Supreme Court in accordance with a 1994 law governing public and revolutionary courts. Amnesty International reported that on 7 March 1996 the organization "received a letter from the Iranian Embassy in London ... which stated that the Supreme Court had quashed the death sentence against Dhabihullah Mahrami and referred the case back to a lower court for reconsideration." Mahrami's own family, however, may not have been informed that this was the case.[50] And then the "reconsideration" turned sinister, as Mahrami continued to be detained in Yazd while awaiting a new trial in a civilian (rather than revolutionary) court on the same charges![51] This turn of events suggests some technical flaw in the way the first Yazd Revolutionary Court proceeded against Mahrami or perhaps a conflict between the

Supreme Court judges in the capital and the provincial revolutionary officials in Yazd.

The clerics in the Isfahan judiciary drew the same sort of line in the sand when, in June 1996, they sentenced Musa Talibi to death for apostatizing from Islam to return to the Baha'i faith, in which he had been reared. He appealed the sentence but was reportedly told that it had been confirmed. Talibi had originally been arrested in Isfahan in October 1994 on charges unrelated to religion and sentenced to ten years imprisonment. He appealed, and in February 1995 his sentence was reduced to eighteen months. The prosecutor for the Islamic Republic objected to the reduction in sentence on the grounds that Talibi was an apostate, which had not been taken into account by the courts. The prosecutor's demand for a retrial provoked the June 1996 death sentence.[52] In 1996 there were about 10 Baha'i prisoners of conscience in Iranian jails, including Mahrami and Talibi.

On 14 May 1996 Chief Justice Ayatollah Mohammed Yazdi gave an address in the holy city of Qom, in which he alleged that "The Bahai sect is not a religion, but a web of espionage activities." Here again, deviant religion and treason to the nation are collapsed into one another. It should be underlined that the punishment in Iran for espionage is death. He accused the West of "using the human rights issue as a means to pressure other countries." He added that Iran would "never abandon the application of Islamic law just to please international organizations." He further alleged that recognized Iranian religious organizations "enjoy freedom of faith."[53] Given that the Supreme Court had confirmed the death sentences against Mithaqi and Khalajabadi the previous February but had in March overturned Mahrami's death sentence for apostasy, it is difficult to interpret this speech. Was he announcing a reconsideration of his leniency toward Mahrami and saying that he was now determined to see apostates from Islam to the Baha'i faith punished and that he would attempt to find a fig leaf such as espionage that would not require an open admission that apostasy is a capital crime in Iran? Was he throwing down a gauntlet before Rafsanjani, whose government, eager for good relations with Western Europe, had been hurt by the bad publicity over Mahrami? Or was he simply employing bluster, reminding them that he had reaffirmed the two earlier death sentences in an attempt to exonerate himself in the eyes of more radical, provincial clerics who were angry over Mahrami's acquittal?

European human-rights organizations attempted to intervene. Since Europe traded with Iran and the US did not, Europe was in a stronger position to apply threats of damage to bilateral relations and trade if Iran continued to ignore basic human-rights standards. Thus early in 1997 as the Supreme Court was preparing to make its ruling, Ruprecht Polenz, an Iranian-affairs specialist and member of the ruling Christian Democrat Party in the German Parliament, condemned the Supreme Court verdict, insisted that it was in fact based on a charge of apostasy, and warned that Mahrami and Talibi were in imminent danger of being executed. He noted that as of early 1997, twelve Baha'is remained in custody as prisoners of conscience. The German government wrote letters of protest to the Iranian justice and foreign ministries and also to the Iranian Embassy in Bonn.[54] Polenz's and others' efforts notwithstanding, on 23 February 1997 a higher Revolutionary Court affirmed the sentence of death for Talibi and Mahrami. The Revolutionary Court chief, Ghulam Husayn Rahbarpur, announced the court's confirmation that the two would be executed for "spying for the Zionist" regime (i.e., working for the Israeli intelligence service, Mossad). Because Baha'is have their world headquarters in Israel, they are often falsely suspected in the Muslim world of being espionage agents for Israel.

Rahbarpur vehemently denied that the two had been condemned merely for their faith, calling such charges "false and fallacious." He added, "No one could be punished in Iran because of his beliefs or his religion."[55] The clerics in the judiciary had thumbed their noses at the world community, but the international outcry that ensued may have tied the hands of the executive branch, which was responsible for actually carrying out the sentence. One Baha'i was killed in a provincial prison in Iran in 1997, and another, a soldier, was shot with impunity by his commanding officer that summer. The major capital cases against Baha'is in the 1990s largely grew not out of simple adherence or even practice but out of an attempt to reverse a forced conversion to Islam by returning to the Baha'i fold. The ayatollahs clearly feel that strong sanctions against such reverse apostasies is called for to prevent thousands of reconversions, the death sentences against Talibi and Mahrami being a case in point. This use of judicial murder, however, is mainly a holding action and thus may well fail to intimidate those at whom it is aimed. Talibi and Mahrami have, at the risk of their own lives, already made the point that in the post-Khomeini era such reversals of the gains of the radical religious right are at least conceivable.

Rafsanjani's shift to a more nationalist discourse probably had some benefits for the Baha'is, who now had to be recognized as owed the basic rights of Iranian citizens. In contrast, the change appears to have benefited the Zoroastrians even more positively. The Zoroastrian minority was subject to certain constraints, mainly various forms of local discrimination, under the Khomeinist government. But its relations with the Rafsanjani government were favourable enough that it was permitted to hold the sixth Zoroastrian International Conference in Iran in 1996, a decision that one community representative said was made "after the fifth Majlis (Parliament) elections," probably a reference to the successive weakening of the radical Islamists.[56] The conference was addressed by President Rafsanjani, who stressed the need for harmony among the religions and cooperation in the face of Western materialism. He said of Zoroastrianism, "The canons of the Zoroastrian faith, including monotheism and the necessity of righteous ideas, speech, and behavior are also evident in Islam." He stressed "freedom of action and a peaceful and tranquil life for the religious minorities in Islamic Iran."[57] The president's speech was remarkable for its Iranian nativism, evoking a sort of nationalist pride in Iran's Zoroastrian heritage that was common in the Pahlevi era and against which the radical Khomeinists had strongly reacted. In a BBC interview, Zoroastrian leaders vehemently denied the implication voiced by the correspondent that "Zoroastrians in Iran are under pressure and being intimidated" and that the conference had been authorized only after years of putting pressure on the Iranian government.[58] A year later in a speech, the Zoroastrian member of Parliament, Parviz Ravani, commended the Iranian government for curtailing foreign influence in the country and confirmed that religious minorities in Iran enjoyed freedom of worship and were allowed to publish their community magazines. He added that "all religious minorities in Iran seriously confront any act of treason against the Islamic government and the nation."[59] Although, of course, all such official speeches and statements must be approached cautiously, it certainly appears to be the case that Zoroastrians enjoyed a warmth in their relations with the central Iranian government during Rafsanjani's second term that was missing with regard to Jews or non-Armenian Christians and that is quite different from the Islamic Republic's hostility to the Baha'is.

The second Rafsanjani term witnessed a renewed power struggle between the far right and the conservative pragmatists, in which the religious minorities often became pawns. Apostasy emerged as the primary issue seized upon by the reactionaries and the radical populists with which to menace the religious minorities. Radical frustration with the pragmatist status quo led to the assassination of prominent pastors and apostates by death squads. The radicals and reactionaries were reduced merely to defending the gains they had made in the 1990s and were unable to return to launching large-scale pogroms or judicial murders against the minorities. Moreover, after 1993 the Iranian electorate began shifting substantially to the left, leaving the radicals and reactionaries in the judiciary and high clerical office increasingly isolated and putting pragmatists and relative liberals in power in Parliament and the presidency from 1996 to 1997. The continued economic difficulties in Iran left it in greater than ever need of foreign investment and good relations with the European Community. Thus the international outcry over the persecution of the apostates from select religious minorities made it difficult for the executive branch to carry out the judicial murders occasionally ordered by the clerical judges, and it appears even to have in some instances dissuaded the Supreme Court from concurring in judgments passed on apostates by provincial courts.

THE KHATAMI PERIOD

In 1997, when the mood of the Iranian electorate unexpectedly swung to the liberal side, the dark-horse candidate Ayatollah Muhammad Khatami was elected with nearly 70 per cent of the vote. Khatami, a former minister of culture under Rafsanjani in the early 1990s who had been forced by reactionaries and radicals in Parliament to resign for being too liberal, was unexpectedly allowed to run for president by the Council of Guardians. He became a favourite candidate among youth, women, and the urban middle class. Having lived in Germany, where he had made a serious study of German philosopher Jürgen Habermas's work on civil society, Khatami incorporated the idea of the need for active citizens' organizations at the grass roots into his political ideology. Since both reactionaries and radicals favoured strong state control and regulation of such intermediate organizations, he was bound to come into conflict with them. Khatami also pursued an opening to the West and even called for dialogue and contact between the Iranian citizenry and Americans on a nongovernmental level.

The Khatami presidency provoked an extensive polarization of Iranian society and politics that was much more extreme than what had occurred early in Rafsanjani's second term. Liberals like 'Abdu'l-Karim Suroush were emboldened to speak to large crowds of students on subjects like freedom of speech and conscience and openly to question the whole idea of theocracy. Ayatollah Muntaziri openly challenged the idea of the Guardianship of the Jurisprudent and was threatened with jail time by Supreme Jurisprudent 'Ali Khamenei. In the summer of 1999, liberal students mounted large demonstrations in the capital. In response, radicals and reactionaries interrupted Suroush's speeches with heckling and violence, opponents of Khatami in the Ministry of Intelligence conducted a series of assassinations against prominent liberal and secular intellectuals in the fall of 1998 and the summer of 1999, and student demonstrations were infiltrated by agents provocateurs from the *basij*, who committed acts of violence in hopes of turning the public against the student activists.

Minorities of conscience have been among the chief victims of this new polarization. As mentioned, a string of secular-leaning and liberal intellectuals were assassinated in the fall of 1998. Some twenty members of the Baha'i faith were in jail in 1998. On 21 July 1998, a Baha'i, Ruhu'llah Rawhani, was executed in Mashhad on charges of converting a Muslim woman to the religion (a charge she denied). Rawhani, 52, a medical-supplies salesman and father of four, had been imprisoned in September 1997. He was never formally sentenced, was given no access to legal counsel, and was summarily executed.[60] It seems likely that provincial radicals acted in this hasty and arbitrary fashion precisely to avoid interference from the Khatami government in Tehran, which might have resulted in Rawhani being left for years on death row or even being released rather than executed. In late September 1998, Ministry of Information officials raided 500 private homes of Baha'is and arrested thirty-six Baha'is in a number of cities, charging them with teaching informally in the Baha'i "Open University," an institution set up by the community to circumvent the ban on Baha'i students attending university in Iran that had graduated some 140 students in the 1990s. The purge of Baha'i professors in the 1980s had left many with time on their hands and a willingness to teach their specialties in their own homes. The professors were eventually released, many only after they pledged to close the Open University.[61] Reza Afshari provides a useful summary of the situation in the late 1990s:

> Limitations on travel abroad were still in place, although some Baha'is succeeded in receiving limited exit permits. The problems faced by Baha'i physicians and lawyers continued unabated. No bank credit was made available to Baha'i applicants. Baha'i marriages and divorces were not legally recognized, nor was a right to inheritance, a situation Ann Mayer has aptly described as "civil death." The properties of a deceased Baha'i would go to the state if there were no Muslims in the family. The regime continued denying the Baha'is retirement pensions.[62]

Members of other religions suffered in the early Khatami period as well. Some twenty Muslim converts to Christianity disappeared between 1997 and 1998 when authorities learned of their baptisms. In May 1998 Jewish businessman Ruhu'llah Kadkhuda-Zadih was summarily executed, possibly for helping Iranian Jews flee the country. And in March 1999 thirteen Jews were arrested and charged with espionage, charges that human-rights analysts generally found implausible on the basis of the information released by the Iranian government. Even Shi'ites, such as members of Sufi orders, reported increasing persecution between 1998 and 1999.[63]

Although Khatami's election signalled the desire of a broad swathe of Iranian society for a certain amount of liberalization, the late 1990s were not noticeably better for religious minorities than before. Khatami's victory galvanized radicals and reactionaries into attacking him by scapegoating outspoken liberal intellectuals and members of religious minorities. Khatami, although president, did not control the armed forces, the police, the *basij*, or even some ministries, such as the Ministry of Intelligence, nor could he always count on the support of Parliament. He was therefore not in a position to push liberalization very far or very fast and was opposed by powerful enemies who often controlled substantial resources, including armed forces. If Iran really does move toward greater liberalization in the coming years, it is unlikely to be without a fight, and the religious minorities are likely to be in the crossfire. Baha'is continue to be branded national apostates by the radical populists and to be subjected to arbitrary arrest and punishment. They are excluded from national institutions and widely considered spies for foreign powers (despite the lack of any credible evidence for such charges). They are in an even more precarious situation than Iranian Jews, who have faced similar espionage charges on occasion.

CONCLUSION

The position of the Baha'is as members of the Iranian nation has been in dispute throughout the modern period. As early as the Constitutional Revolution, measures were enacted by a supposedly progressive and newly established Parliament to exclude them from political participation. Still, in the Pahlevis' secularizing form of Iranian nationalism, Baha'is had begun to find a precarious (and sometimes unsavoury) niche. The rise of Khomeinism knocked them off this perch rather decisively. Official Khomeinist discourse rejected the idea of the modern nation-state altogether and aimed at a Pan-Islamic union of the Muslim peoples across ethnic and linguistic, even across sectarian-Muslim, divides. In such a system, the only recognized position for non-Muslim religious minorities would be that of *dhimmis*, or protected communities. Such a status was accorded Jews, Christians, and Zoroastrians but was not available for a post-Islamic religion such as the Baha'i faith. Baha'is were denied any claim to belonging to a religion at all; instead, they were depicted as comprising a political party created and fostered by British colonialism and Israeli imperialism that had no specifically religious character. They were equated with organized atheism, and their adherents were defined as apostates from Islam (although significant portions of the community originated with conversions from Judaism and Zoroastrianism in the nineteenth century and thus had never apostatized). The Baha'is experienced civil death under Khomeinism, facing execution if prominent, imprisonment if vocal, and harassment in daily life. Baha'i marriages were redefined as prostitution, and those officers of the local spiritual assembly who conducted them were redefined as pimps. Parents were charged with endangerment of minors for bringing them up as Baha'is, and their children were sometimes confiscated and raised as Muslims. They were fired from government jobs and expelled from the universities and finally even from the cemeteries. No institution over which the Iranian Muslim state had direct control could tolerate Baha'is given that they were civilly dead.

Along with the official Khomeinist rhetoric of Muslims vs infidels, some Muslim fundamentalists gave a more central position to Iran and the Iranian nation but identified both with Islam. This Iranian nationalist form of Islamism became more appealing in the course of the Iran-Iraq war of 1980–88, when much of the Arab Muslim world supported secularist Iraq against Khomeini, profoundly disappointing Khomeini's ecumenical hopes. It has been argued that Rafsanjani, in power from 1989 to 1997, rehabilitated the discourse of Iranian nationalism. It was increasingly denied that Baha'is were persecuted because of their conscientious beliefs. It was alleged not only that they were spies for foreign powers, but also that they were national apostates, defectors from the Iranian Muslim nation. Still, the executions slowed dramatically, and the terms of imprisonment shrank to a few weeks, with hundreds of Baha'is being rotated in and out as a means of serial harassment rather than languishing behind bars for long periods of time. The key capital crime for which Baha'is were charged under positive law now became not abstract apostasy but the real thing. It was made clear that those Baha'is who converted under duress to Islam in the 1980s would not be allowed to revert to the Baha'i faith without facing the executioner. Nor would proselytizing other such "new-Muslims" to return them to the Baha'i faith be allowed.

Gulpaygani's document of the early 1990s laid out a plan for the extermination of the Baha'i faith in Iran not through a physical holocaust but through gradual attrition. Ordinary Baha'is would be granted some of the usual rights of Iranian citizenship. In some areas of life, their civil death was annulled, although it remained their lot in many other spheres. They could not be deprived of life and property arbitrarily – that is, just for being (inactive) Baha'is. They could again marry and have families without being unduly bothered. But they could not go to university or perhaps even finish high school. Even informal institutions of education inside the community were closed, forcing Baha'is into the ranks of the day labourers and the indigent. They could not hold government jobs or teaching positions. They were denied the respectability of holding professions. They could not even be properly buried. The icons of the nation – the bureaucracy, the university, the cemetery – were declared off limits to them. The areas of civil life that could in any way be seen as privileges bestowed by the state were denied to them. The hope was clearly that a dynamic middle-class community, finding such a fate intolerable, would convert to Islam to escape it. The Baha'is were to be akin to members of India's lowest castes in the old days – that is, permanently relegated to the status of low-ranking outsiders. Yet the Gulpaygani document recognized them as Iranians of a bizarre sort, not as Muslim Iranians or *dhimmi* Iranians, but still as Iranians. It made a place for them in the body public, however abject, that Khomeini's divide between Muslims and heretics could not have abided. As the Iranian nation reemerged in the 1990s within the discourse of Islamic republicanism, the Baha'is were at least somewhat renationalized. However, only in relation to the dire pogroms of the 1980s was their position much improved.

The two approaches – that of seeing the Baha'is as dangerous heretics who must be destroyed and that of seeing them as outcasts with Iranian citizenship who merely had to be curbed – coexisted into the late 1990s. Each of these views remained prominent in certain institutional settings. Because Rafsanjani and the pragmatic conservatives, along with Khatami's later reformers, wanted World Bank loans and international recognition, they had reason to put the Baha'i issue on the back burner. By comparison, the radical right-wing populists continued to seek political power within the country by scapegoating the Baha'is. Many of the specific legal cases initiated against Baha'is and members of other religious minorities appear to originate with local, provincial courts controlled by radical right-wing populists, who increasingly lost power in the realm of elective government and were therefore left with the judiciary as their primary means of influencing society. In some instances, the judgments of the provincial courts have been overturned by the Supreme Court despite its dominance by figures such as Yazdi, a radical right-wing populist himself. In other instances, the Supreme Court has called for the death sentence, but the executive branch, controlled first by conservative theocrats and after 1997 increasingly by liberal theocrats, has declined actually to implement it, leaving the accused (mainly those convicted of being apostates from Islam) on death row for long periods of time. Frustration over their frequent inability to secure actual executions of those charged in the provincial courts appears to have encouraged the radical theocrats to resort to death squads and vigilante tactics, resulting in the murders of several prominent evangelical pastors, Sunni activists, and Baha'is.

It is not unusual for nationalism to be construed so as to exclude some communities from the nation despite their long-standing residence on national territory. As Partha Chatterjee has noted, the more virulent forms of Hindu nationalism in India define Indian Muslims as foreign invaders – that is, essentially as illegal aliens – even though most are converts from Hinduism and their families have lived in what is now India for centuries if not millennia. White Protestant nationalism in the United States has sought to exclude Catholics and blacks and Jews from the American nation. The Nazis defined German Jews not as fellow Germans but as a pollution of German purity. The Iranian Muslim nationalism of Khomeini's successors can therefore be identified as a form of this sort of exclusionary nationalism. As Eliz Sanasarian notes, "This was the unique by-product of the theocratic system. The 'aqaliat' [religious minority] was 'the other,' 'the marginal,' 'the separate from us'; it was an institutionalized 'otherness' which was disturbing and different." She adds, "Before 1979, everyone was an 'Irani' albeit in pretense; after the Revolution, Irani was replaced by aqaliat, Bahai and Sunni."[64] All nations comprise such religious and ethnic communities, but, as Hobsbawm has argued,[65] civic nations make a place for them as constituents of the nation, whereas exclusionary nations achieve their unity precisely by singling out the unabsorbable minority within as a cultural and political fifth column. Islamically based nationalisms, as Ofra Bengio and Gabriel Ben-Dor argued after Bernard Lewis,[66] tend to be exclusionary in this way. Chatterjee has also shown that religious nationalisms, such as those of the Rashtrya Swayamsevak Sangh in India and Khomeinism in Iran, are no less "modern" than secular nationalism. Religious nationalism insists on a singular majoritarian source of identity, such that India must be Hindu and Iran Shi'ite. "Islam here is either the history of foreign conquest or a domesticated element of everyday popular life," Chatterjee observes. "None of these answers, however, can admit that the Indian nation as a whole might have a claim on the historical legacy of Islam." [67] A pluralist conception of the nation, which takes pride in its variegated strands and gives civil equality to all citizens, is the only sort of nationalism that can hope to avoid the virulent pathologies witnessed in the twentieth century. Iranians would have to admit that they might have a claim on the historical legacy of the Baha'i faith and vice versa. Khatami and his reforming supporters often speak as though they seek to make Iran a civic nation. Yet they or their successors cannot hope to do so as long as thousands of Iranians remain under the sentence of civil death.

NOTES

1. See Juan Cole, "The Modernity of Theocracy."
2. For a discussion of Baha'i theocrats, see Juan Cole, "Fundamentalism in the Contemporary U.S. Baha'i Community."
3. Eric Hobsbawm, *Nations and Nationalisms since 1780.*
4. Benedict Anderson, *Imagined Communities.*
5. Partha Chatterjee, *The Nation and its Fragments.*
6. Ofra Bengio and Gabriel Ben-Dor, *Minorities and the State in the Arab World,* 10–11, and on Sudan, chapter 4. On Sudan, see also Moshe Ma'oz, *Middle Eastern Minorities,* 91–100.
7. Neil MacMaster, *Racism in Europe: 1870–2000.*
8. Juan Cole, "Marking Boundaries, Marking Time: The Iranian Past and the Construction of the Self by Qajar Thinkers"; see also Mostafa Vaziri, *Iran as Imagined Nation,* although this source lays too much emphasis on Europeans and European influences and slights the contribution of Iranians themselves to their own nationalist thought.
9. Abbas Amanat, *Resurrection and Renewal: The Making of the Babi Movement in Iran, 1844–1850.*
10. Peter Smith, "A Note on Babi and Baha'i Numbers in Iran," suffers from simply repeating outsiders' guesses, and Smith was unaware of the 1921 census. He was also unaware that only 90,000 Baha'is were registered in Iran in the late 1970s.
11. Juan Cole, *Modernity and the Millennium: The Genesis of the Baha'i Faith in the 19th Century Middle East*; and "Millennialism in Modern Iranian History."
12. The results of the census, ordered by then leader Shoghi Effendi Rabbani, who headed the religion from 1921 to 1957, and carried out by his aunt Bahiyyih Khanum in the early 1920s, were never published presumably because they became an increasing embarrassment as the twentieth century progressed and the numbers of Iranian Baha'is shrank dramatically. A prominent US academic discovered the surprisingly large results in the Haifa Baha'i archives and reported them to a number of Baha'i academics, but I am constrained by considerations of confidentiality from divulging more at this point.
13. Baha'u'llah, *Majmu'ih-'i az alvah-i Jamal-i Aqdas-i Abha kih ba'd az Kitab-i Aqdas Nazil Shudih,* 46, 47–8; translation published as *Tablets of Baha'u'llah Revealed after the Kitab-i Aqdas,* 84, 85.
14. 'Abdu'l-Baha 'Abbas, *Risalih-'i Madaniyyih,* 8–9; translated by Marzieh Gail, *The Secret of Divine Civilization,* 6–7.
15. Ibid.

16 E.G. Browne, *The Persian Revolution of 1905–1909*, 424.
17 For the secular nationalist critique, see Ahmad Kasravi, *Bahayigari*; on anti-Baha'ism and the Islamists, see Mohamad Tavakoli-Targhi, "Baha'i sitizi va Islamgarayi dar Iran."
18 A.W. Samii, "Falsafi, Kashani and the Baha'is"; Shahrough Akhavi, *Religion and Politics in Contemporary Iran*, 77–80; and Tavakoli-Targhi, "Baha'i sitizi va Islamgarayi dar Iran."
19 Richard Cottam, *Nationalism in Iran*, 87–9.
20 On the Baha'is under Khomeini, see Eliz Sanasarian, *Religious Minorities in Iran*, 114–23; Firuz Kazemzadeh, "Baha'is in Iran: Twenty Years of Repression"; and the important memoir by Olya Roohizadegan, *Olya's Story: A Survivor's Dramatic Account of the Persecution of Baha'is in Revolutionary Iran*. For a general overview of jailings and torture in Khomeinist Iran, see Ervand Abrahamian, *Tortured Confessions: Prisons and Public Recantations in Modern Iran*.
21 Qaza'i, quoted in Sanasarian, *Religious Minorities in Iran*, 117.
22 Quoted in ibid., 121.
23 European Parliament, "Resolution on Iran," 4 April 1990.
24 US State Department, "Country Reports on Human Rights Practices for 1989," 1401.
25 See the Gulf2000 news archive at http://wwws/data/cu/sipa/GULF2000/chronology/data/90–03.html, which in part summarizes an article published in the *New York Times* on 19 November 1989. See also Amnesty International, *Country Reports for 1995: Iran*.
26 Mehri Samandari Jensen, "Religion and Family Planning in Contemporary Iran."
27 "U.S. Baha'is Ask Iran's President: Does His Call for Religion and Liberty Apply to Baha'is?" PR Newswire, 16 January 1998.
28 On the changes brought about during the early Rafsanjani presidency, see Bahman Bakhtiari, *Parliamentary Politics in Revolutionary Iran*, 184–216.
29 US State Department, "Country Reports on Human Rights Practices for 1989," 1400.
30 Amnesty International, *Country Reports for 1997: Iran*.
31 US State Department, "Country Reports on Human Rights Practices for 1988," 1349.
32 Amnesty International, *Country Reports for 1995: Iran*.
33 "Bahai Gets Death for Being Infidel," *Diplomat Recorder*, Arab Press Service Organization, 17 February 1996.
34 US State Department, "Country Reports on Human Rights Practices for 1996."

35 "Baha'is Pray for their Homeland," *Chicago Tribune*, 4 April 1997.
36 US State Department, "Country Reports on Human Rights Practices for 1993," 1180.
37 Galindo Pohl, quoted in Reza Afshari, *Human Rights in Iran*, 124.
38 See Thomas W. Laqueur, "Memory and Naming in the Great War"; and "Cemeteries, Religion, and the Culture of Capitalism."
39 Afshari, *Human Rights in Iran*, 122.
40 "1991 Memorandum from the Iranian Supreme Revolutionary Cultural Council on 'the Baha'i Question,'" in Baha'i International Community, *The Baha'i Question*, 38–9. On this issue, see also the Associated Press article of 23 February 1993, available in the Gulf2000 news archive at http://wwws/data/cu/sipa/GULF2000/chronology/data/90-03.html.
41 Houshang Amir Ahmadi, "Secular Nationalism."
42 "Rafsanjani Elected with Moderate Support," 13 June 1993, ABC-CLIO; "Middle East and North Africa: Iran, Country Risk Guide," IBC International, September 1994; "Regional Implications of Khatami Election Viewed," *al-Wasat* (London), 17 December 1997, trans. FBIS, insert date 19 December 1997, article ID drnes09081997001381.
43 On this period, see Bakhtiari, *Parliamentary Politics*, 217–34.
44 United Nations, "Situation of Human Rights in the Islamic Republic of Iran," 26.
45 Ibid., 25–6.
46 Amnesty International, *Country Reports for 1995: Iran*. The text says that these two were arrested in Gohardasht, but this is actually the name of the prison in which they were detained; other reports say that they were arrested in Karaj, a town near Tehran.
47 "Death Sentences for the Bahai," editorial, *New York Times*, 31 December 1993.
48 Amnesty International, "Dhabihullah Mahrami: Prisoner of Conscience," footnote 10.
49 Ibid., Appendix A.
50 Ibid.
51 Amnesty International, "AI Report 1997: Iran."
52 Amnesty International, "Worldwide Appeals: Iran."
53 "Bahai Faith Linked with Espionage," *Diplomatic Recorder*, Arab Press Service, 18 May 1996.
54 "German Deputy Urges Iran to Lift Death Sentences," Reuters, 3 February 1997.
55 "Iran Confirms Death Penalty on Two Bahai for Spying," Agence France Presse, 24 February 1997.

56 "Iran: BBC's 'Propaganda' on Zoroastrian Congress Criticized," Persian article from Mashad, Khurasan, dated 16 June 1996, FBIS, daily report, insert date 10 July 1996, Near East and South Asia, document number FBIS-NES-96–132.
57 "Rafsanjani Addresses Participants in Zoroastrian Conference," Tehran IRIB Television First Program Network in Persian, 0930 GMT, 22 June 1996, FBIS, daily report, South Asia, Iran, insert date 26 June 1996, article ID drnes123_s_96014.
58 "Iran: BBC's 'Propaganda' on Zoroastrian Congress Criticized."
59 "Iran: Zoroastrian Deputy: Minorities Free to Practice Rituals," Tehran IRNA in English, 1405 GMT, 3 February 1997, FBIS, daily report, South Asia, insert date 6 February 1997, article ID drnes024_s_97059, document number FBIS-NES-97–024.
60 "French Bahais Fear More Hangings in Iran," Reuters, Paris, 28 July 1998. See also the US Baha'i community's news release at http://www-personal.umich.edu/~jrcole/bahai/hrbh798.htm; and Afshari, *Human Rights in Iran*, 122.
61 See "Iran's Crimes at Home," *Washington Post*, 25 October 1998; Burton Bollag, "36 Professors Arrested in Iranian Crackdown on Underground Baha'i University," *The Chronicle of Higher Education*, 13 November 1998; and materials at http://www-personal.umich.edu/~jrcole/bahai/hrbh1098.htm.
62 Afshari, *Human Rights in Iran*, 125–6.
63 Radio Free Europe/Radio Liberty, "Iran Report," vol. 2, no. 25, 21 June 1999, http://www.rferl.org/bd/ir/index.html.
64 Sanasarian, *Religious Minorities in Iran*, 154.
65 Hobsbawm, *Nations and Nationalisms*.
66 Bengio and Ben-Dor, *Minorities and the State*.
67 Chatterjee, *The Nation and its Fragments*, 113.

7

Royal Interest in Local Culture: Amazigh Identity and the Moroccan State

DAVID CRAWFORD

INTRODUCTION

On 17 October 2001 King Mohammed VI of Morocco announced the creation of the Royal Institute of the Amazigh [Berber] Culture (l'Institut Royal de la culture amazighe, IRCAM), which had been promised in a speech in July. This royal edict, or *dahir*, indicates a dramatic reversal of legal discrimination against Imazighen (Berbers) and an attempt to reclaim Amazigh culture as part of the national community. Since Moroccan nationalist discourse has tended to emphasize links to the high culture of Arab Islamic civilization, particularly to the royal patriline leading back to the Prophet Muhammad, the IRCAM *dahir* indicates a shift in, or at least an amendment to, the officially imagined heritage of the nation. This new state-level embrace of the *volksgeist*, the local Amazigh/Berber culture,[1] provides a useful starting point for examining the much-debated status of Berbers in Moroccan society, particularly their potential for politicization as a corporate group. The *dahir* also brings into official Moroccan discourse an acknowledgment of Moroccan citizens who speak something other than the national language, perhaps suggesting a role for them in the national imagination.

Significantly, IRCAM has been empowered to pursue more than vague directives concerning the promotion of Amazigh art and culture.[2] The institute is charged with the important, concrete step of implementing the use of Tamazight (Berber language) in the classroom. Clearly, this education project necessitates lexical standardization of heretofore-oral Tamazight, the creation of dictionaries, and agreement over what script to use to teach an oral language in a formal classroom. Until now even Derija (Moroccan colloquial Arabic) was kept out of government schools in favour of a more standardized "correct" Modern Standard Arabic. Allowing Derija officially into the classroom presents a set of problems, but Tamazight stands to be even more difficult because of pronounced regional differences in the spoken language and because of the lack of a universally accepted way to write it. Standardizing the use and inscription of Moroccan Tamazight is a task that scholars and the Amazigh rights movement have been discussing for years,[3] but the king has now directly involved the state in the project. It is common for a state to promote its national language. It is far more unusual for a state to champion a minority language, especially one that it had previously all but banned.

Because we do not yet know how fully IRCAM will be implemented or what effects it will have, this chapter outlines some of the main issues involved rather than positing firm conclusions.[4] I begin with a review of four general points important for understanding the significance of the *dahir*. These include the deep historical roots of Berber politics in Morocco, regional diversity among Moroccan Imazighen, the way notions of Berberness (or Amazighness) fit with other idioms of affiliation in Morocco, and the political-economic conditions in which the *dahir* will be deployed. This background suggests four areas of contemporary Amazigh politics likely to be impacted by the changes promised in the *dahir*.

First, I contend that Imazighen need not understand themselves as a unified group in order for their linguistic particularity to have political potential at the national level. Second, I note that political-economic factors are likely to influence any nascent cultural or ethnic politics – a fairly obvious point but one that sometimes goes unappreciated by scholars writing on Amazigh culture. Third, I note that whatever happens with the IRCAM *dahir*, the general rise in Amazigh political consciousness in Morocco is part of a much larger, global florescence of identity politics; indeed, such cultural politics are not *inherently* progressive nor reactionary, neither politically liberating nor dangerously nativistic. Finally, I maintain that the *dahir* will have multiple uses for many different actors and that its significance will therefore be open to some manipulation. Changes promised by the *dahir* may on one level help some of Morocco's poorest and least educated people to better participate in the changing economy. At the same time, it may serve as a tool to manufacture political divisions useful to the central government for self-justification and political control.

AMAZIGH ROOTS AND MOROCCAN CULTURE

As others have pointed out, Berbers, or Imazighen, are significantly different from other "minorities" in the Middle East.[5] Unlike Copts or Kurds, Berbers represent the most ancient known inhabitants of all of North Africa – an overwhelming majority in a huge territory – who were never driven entirely from their land or fully absorbed into a large, colonizing population. Imazighen endured the Roman invasion 2,000 years ago, as they did the French invaders less than a century past, by fighting at times but also by co-opting the power of the invaders, by collaborating with or profiting from them, or simply by ignoring outsiders when possible. From a certain Berberist perspective, the Arabs who arrived in the far West in the eighth century were in many respects no different from the Phoenicians before them and the Portuguese afterward. The significant difference lies in the religious basis of Arab authority. Although the Arabs were relatively few in actual number, they had a profound impact through religious conversion and, arguably, through acculturation of the locals.[6] This grudging incorporation was a different style of rule from direct subjugation, indirect taxation, or genocidal extermination. The influence of the Arabs who settled in Morocco has far outweighed that of any other invading group, but Arabs arguably did not replace Imazighen so much as augment them, adding Arab overtones and some sense of Islamic unity to a diverse Amazigh country.

The main, obvious influence of the Arab invasion has been the Islamic faith, which has an important linguistic component. This is one reason so many Amazigh activists point to issues of language as vital to cultural survival. Unlike Iranians, Turks, or other distinct peoples Islamized by the expanding Arabs, the majority of Moroccans today – whether "originally" Berber or Arab – use Arabic as their everyday language. If many in the *mashreq* (Middle East) consider Arabic as spoken in Morocco to be fairly incomprehensible, Moroccans themselves are often adamant that it closely adheres to the Arabic of the Qur'an. This conflation of Arabic language, Islamic legitimacy, and Arab ethnicity is notable at the popular level of Moroccan society, especially in urban centres like Fez, making it a bone of contention for Amazigh activists. At various times since the arrival of Islam, Berber dynasties have controlled Morocco (and much of the rest of North Africa and Spain), but at least until the IRCAM *dahir* a notion of a sophisticated, culturally and historically rich Muslim civilization had been conceptually grafted to Arab ethnicity in the mainstream Moroccan national identity. Identity is born of consciousness. As Salem Chaker has noted, it is the Arab *consciousness* of most Moroccans that has relegated Berber language and cultural identity to "minority" status.[7]

This does not mean, of course, that this minority status is homogeneous or easily graspable or that there have been no historical transformations. Stephanie Saad has noted that for a period scholars launched "vehement arguments that the Berbers *were* an ethnic group, and later ... equally vehement arguments as to why they were not."[8] She concludes with the assertion that "Most ethnic identities are like that of the Berbers: nuanced, mutable, their boundaries and characteristics changing with time."[9] Ernest Gellner has argued a slightly different case, saying that in the "traditional situation," Berber socio-political "notions intermediate between tribal and Islamic were hazy and of doubtful social significance." He goes on to assert that "Where a notion of being Berber did exist, it was roughly co-extensive with the regional linguistic block. Historians have dug up signs of Berber consciousness, a mediaeval heresy with a Koran in Berber, or a religious movement of the seventeenth century, opposed to all 'who did not speak Berber.' But on the whole, the striking thing about these signs is not their occurrence, but their rarity."[10] Gellner's contention is that Berbers have been and were at the time of his fieldwork essentially "tribal" rather than broadly ethnic. By this he seems to mean that they reckon the social and political forms important to them through a genealogical framework (and little else) and that the variously sized groups formed this way do not extend to any Pan-Berber consciousness or even to a Morocco-wide sense of being "a" people. Gellner sometimes restricts his assertions to the area in which he did research, while at other times he seems to claim something broadly "Berber" about the segmentary political organization he outlines. Gellner's scheme suggests something solid and distinctive about being Berber even if in his view

Berbers themselves attach little significance to the wider ethnic category. However, not everyone agrees with Gellner's reading of the historical record or with Saad's emphasis on the fluidity of identity.

The Amazigh writer Kateb Yacine, for instance, says that "They want to depict us as a minority isolated within an Arab people, when in fact it is the Arabs who are a minute minority within us, but they dominate us through religion ... We are a majority which quickly becomes aware now of the Arab-Islamic affliction throughout the world, in Palestine, Iraq, Iran, wherever people are alienated, betrayed, drowned in blood in the name of race and religion." When Kateb Yacine uses the word "we," presumably this refers to all Berbers, not merely to Algerians. "We" certainly does not refer to a "tribe." It is tempting to attribute this sort of consciousness to a literate and thoroughly international perspective, particularly as Yacine's plea centres on "language which is the vehicle for history."[11] Clearly, such a consciousness of language, and for that matter of an abstracted notion of "history," is most commonly found among multilingual, educated observers. Gabriel Ben-Dor has asserted that "the most relevant axis separating minorities from others in modern society is the ethnic one."[12] Yacine would seem to agree, locating his ethnic identity in Tamazight, the Berber language, and that of his "other," the Arabs, in both the Arabic language and the Islamic faith through which Arabs have dominated. The language Yacine extols is Tamazight; the language he writes *in* is French. This is the fate of much explicitly Berber cultural production: It has necessarily been inscribed in languages that became lexically coherent and politically dominant through religion (such as Arabic) or through the linked processes of "print capitalism" by which national tongues such as French and English became consolidated.[13] The IRCAM project promises something different: an attempt to self-consciously standardize and promulgate a new national language in a long-standing, politically coherent state.

Still, there is evidence that forms of Amazigh consciousness have long existed and are not purely the result of contemporary cultural sensitivities projected onto the historical record. Maya Shatzmiller, for instance, has argued:

> The rise of the great Berber dynasties to political hegemony, beginning with the Almoravids in the 11th century, and continuing with the Almohads in the 12th and the Marinids in the 13th, enhanced the development of the

Berber-Islamic state, but also witnessed Berber alienation expressed by resistance to acculturation to Arabic and Islamic norms. The drive to bring the Berber populace into the mainstream of Islamic statehood, through intensified islamization, indoctrination in Islamic theology and expansion of the judicial system, deepened the awareness of Berber particularism, and refined and defined its expression vis-à-vis the Islamic state and its institutions.[14]

It is difficult to know what everyday people were thinking hundreds of years ago, and it is particularly tricky to determine their sense of identity. We do see, however, that when Imazighen have had political power, there have been indications of some scale of Berber identity in some official acts.

The rise of the Almohads in the twelfth century serves as one example of this. Inspired by a man named Ibn Tumart, the Almohads (from *al-muwahhidūn*, or unifiers) were the second great Berber Empire to rule North Africa and Spain. The first such empire was the Almoravid (*al-murābitūn*), which began as a tribe of Sanhaja Berbers from the desert beyond the Atlas who had controlled some part of the gold and salt trade with sub-Saharan Africa. They parlayed this position first into a small fiefdom and then into "the first Moroccan dynasty to achieve importance for Europe as well as North Africa."[15] The Almoravids did not merely conquer through military prowess and economic domination, but also rose through a potent, revisionist brand of Islam. They preached moral reform and asceticism but opposed "over-exclusive ideologies and aimed at a communitarian consensus."[16] One suspects, however, that their conservative "no new taxes" approach – a return to the fiscal policies of the original Islamic community – had as much to do with their success as anything else. As Abdallah Laroui puts it, "apart from legal alms (the *zakat*), to be spent for specified purposes, the state's only sources of income were the head tax (*jizya*), the territorial tax (*kharaj*) on nonconverts, and a fifth part of the spoils of war."[17] This must have seemed a dramatic improvement upon the excessive ("non-Islamic") taxation of the rulers they replaced and had the advantage of being divinely sanctioned. It was, however, a fiscal policy better suited to expansion than governance and to offensive rather than defensive wars, particularly in the North, where Christian princes harassed them. In the long term, religious ideology seems to have failed to sufficiently unite tribal warriors and urban bureaucrats, much less Andalusians and Maghrebis, and the fiscal policy seems to have been unable to fund the necessary armies of mercenaries. Tribesmen, after all, were keen to fight wars that would produce booty – not wars meant to defend state territory from others seeking booty. This ideologically potent, structurally shaky Almoravid Empire constituted the political environment that Ibn Tumart was eventually to transform.

A Tashelhit (Berber) speaker born in the Moroccan south sometime between 1076 and 1091, Ibn Tumart left home early for travels that took him to Cordoba, Tunisia, Alexandria, Baghdad, and perhaps Syria and Mecca.[18] These were more than mere wanderings, however, as the future *mahdi*, or "rightly guided one," sought out celebrated Islamic thinkers, including the scholar al-Ghazzali, whose works had been banned by the Almoravid elite.[19] Although he began as a sort of public moral critic – a role difficult to suppress in a state based on moral revisionism – Ibn Tumart nonetheless did not take long to draw the wrath of authorities. He seems, in fact, to have incurred the wrath of many people. One story has it that sailors impatient with his teachings keelhauled Ibn Tumart en route to Tangiers, and the future leader was only plucked from the water when his failure to die expeditiously was seen to be divinely ordained.[20] However, once he found his way back to his natal village in the Souss and later among the tribes south of Marrakech in the mountain stronghold of Tin Mal, Ibn Tumart had the opportunity to deploy his eloquence and education in his native language and on culturally familiar territory. What followed was a radical social upheaval, an attempt to return to the sort of Islamic community exemplified by the Prophet.

Ibn Tumart's political philosophy drew on diverse influences but emphasized personal moral reform and individual responsibility for communal standards – a notion that allegedly had him throwing the sultan's sister from her horse for appearing in public without a veil.[21] Perhaps more appealing to his mountain converts was Ibn Tumart's message of social justice. Half a century after the Almoravids established Marrakech, the political philosophy and ascetic teachings they had developed in the desert no longer accorded with their wealthy, urbane lifestyle.[22] Ibn Tumart seems to have convinced the mountain tribes that they – the poor, illiterate, non-Arabic-speaking "outsiders" – were destined to recapture and rejuvenate the vast House of Islam. How exactly he accomplished this remains a mystery, but the firebrand Ibn Tumart managed to galvanize the tribes of the Atlas and to turn the remote area around Tin Mal into the omphalos of Islam. As

Shatzmiller notes, the Almohads did not forget their Berber origins: "They were the first to implement Berber institutions in an Islamic garb and match them with a policy of accrediting the Berber language as equal to the Arabic, even in matters of worship. The Almohads appointed to the positions of preaching and leading the prayer, *khitaba* and *imama*, only individuals who could utter their unitarian credo, the *tawhid*, in the Berber language. To support this policy, they managed to get a *fatwa* which vouched that anyone who could not speak Arabic could say the prayer in Berber."[23]

Today, in the valleys around Tin Mal, the locals, who speak Tashelhit (Berber), still repeat tales of the coming of Ibn Tumart.[24] At least some families say that their ancestors came to the mountains with the *mahdi* and that those who had been Arabic speakers subsequently learned to speak Berber. Today Berber, specifically Tashelhit, is the only language that they speak. This suggests not only that many Berbers "became" Arab, as all scholars on the topic acknowledge, but also that *at least some Arabs became Berbers* through conversion, not just through marriage. This is evidence of the deep interrelatedness of Moroccans, whatever language they happen to speak today.[25]

Space does not allow for a complete accounting of the role of Berbers in Morocco's history or for discussion of the degree to which Amazigh culture is separable from, or capable of providing a base for, Moroccan national culture. Here I note that the discourse on Berbers has swung from a colonial-era perspective in which Berber issues took centre stage to a postcolonial period during which Berbers have had no place at all in Moroccan society.[26] The IRCAM *dahir* seems to suggest that the pendulum has now reversed direction again.

Despite the claims and counterclaims of historical, ideological engineering, it seems undeniable that as long as there has been an entity identifiable as Morocco, Tamazight-speaking people have been fundamental to it. At some historical junctures, Imazighen have been self-conscious of an ethnic or linguistic identity, and this has had some political significance; indeed, the politicization of Berber identity has at times been quite compatible with a powerful, political Islamic consciousness even if the present eruption is generally opposed to an affiliation with Islam. The perdurability of Berber language is indisputable, and manifestations of Berber identity in different guises at different places and times indicates something of the resilient character of at least some aspects of Amazigh culture. However, this should not cause us to ignore the many differences among Imazighen and the potential effects of these differences on contemporary cultural identity and on the Moroccan nationalist project.

REGIONAL DIVERSITY

To demand what have been defined as "human" rights, Amazigh activists in Morocco and elsewhere have necessarily asserted a unified cultural identity.[27] That is, to fight for much of what appears to have been granted in the IRCAM *dahir*, it has been necessary to aver that Imazighen have an essential culture that inheres in language and that members of this culture share certain disadvantageous social predicaments as a result of this culture. Part of this platform is irrefutable. Clearly, there is a unity to the language. The differences that exist within Tamazight are insignificant compared to the difference between all varieties of Tamazight and other languages, such as Arabic, French, or Spanish. It does not follow, however, that all Imazighen are equally discommoded by the oppression of their language and culture. Philosophers in Paris and Rabat experience their *amazighité*[28] differently than smugglers in the Rif, shepherds in the High Atlas, and shopkeepers in Fez and Casablanca. Such differences need careful attention. Regional historical differences bear on the contemporary subjective experience of being Amazigh, as do urban-rural variations and, perhaps most important, political-economic inequalities. The point I make in this section is that whatever Imazighen have in common, we cannot hope to understand the current social situation in Morocco, and the significance of the IRCAM *dahir*, without accounting for various forms of diversity that bear on linguistic affiliation, ethnic differentiation, and national consciousness.

It has long been understood that Moroccan Imazighen can be divided into three rough linguistic blocs centred in the Rif Mountains, the Middle Atlas, and the mountains of the South. While migration complicates the picture, large Berber-speaking communities remain a presence in rural Morocco today. Tarifit is spoken in the Rif Mountains of the North, Tamazight is the language of the Middle Atlas, and Tashelhit is spoken from the High Atlas south of Marrakech through the Anti Atlas. (In addition to its specific association with the Middle Atlas, Tamazight is also the general term for all of these language varieties.) There are sometimes sizable populations of Arabic speakers within these regions and sizable Berber-speaking migrant populations outside of them, and many people are now bilingual, but the preponderance of monolingual, or Berber-dominant, communities exist in these regional groupings. Linguists cite the close affiliation of these language varieties, but rural Imazighen only sometimes claim that they can understand other people from other regions. Imazighen are more likely to understand other language varieties if they have travelled extensively in other areas or lived in a city for some time, but occasionally villagers insist that they cannot, for instance, understand Tarifit if they have grown up speaking Tashelhit.

The spatial discontinuity of Moroccan Imazighen, and their association in regional linguistic subgroups, has resulted in some important differences, especially recently.[29] The Rif, for example, has had much closer involvement with Europe than some other areas. The Rif abuts the Mediterranean, which may be seen as a conduit of people, goods, and ideas rather than as a barrier. Rifis are in this sense wedged between Algerians (and Algerian Imazighen), Europeans (especially Spaniards), and the rest of Morocco. Spain rather than France colonized the Rif; there remain Spanish enclaves in the North, such as Ceuta and Melilla, and Spanish remains better understood than French. As Ninna Sørensen has noted, General Franco recruited tens of thousands of Moroccans – primarily from the Rif – for the Spanish Civil War and for his personal guard.[30] Not all Rifis are Berbers, but they do represent a majority in the region. Spain has its own contentious linguistic communities – Basques and Catalonians, to start with – and it seems unlikely that the political implications of linguistic nationalism in Spain could be completely lost on migrating Rifis.

The Rif was precocious in attempting to liberate itself from the Christians, as Abd al-Krim led the Rif to attempt independence in 1921, fully thirty years before the rest of Morocco. Educated in Arabic and motivated by the notion of *jihad*, Abd al-Krim drew the forces operating under his command mostly from Berber tribes, particularly the Aith Waryaghar.[31] Like the Almohads, Abd al-Krim found that Islamic discourse provided a better platform for political consolidation than Berber ethnic solidarity, but significantly the two seem to have worked together rather than to have opposed one another.

In short, when speaking of the colonial, or protectorate, period in Morocco, scholars generally refer implicitly to the experience of the French. Yet for the Berbers in the Rif, Spain is at least as important as France, and Spain remains but a relatively inexpensive boat ride away. Today the Rif supports the vast majority of Morocco's thriving drug production and transport industry. Hashish alone has been estimated to be worth US$2 billion a year,[32] with even more wealth generated as cocaine and heroin move from South America into Europe through northern Moroccan smuggling networks. Rifi Berbers hold no monopoly on the drug trade in Morocco, but they do live in an area where marijuana production is a major commercial force and where smuggling of various sorts has long been part of the *modus vivendi*. These brute economic facts have cultural repercussions.

A comparison of the Rif to other regions of the country is revealing. Accounts of the Middle Atlas note that the economy remains centred on pastoralism and subsistence agriculture rather than on marijuana production and smuggling. There remain areas that are many hours from paved roads, not to mention electricity. Middle Atlas Berbers are famous for their segmentary tribal organization, a putatively egalitarian means of governance that eschews central authority and that seems to have endured until very recently. Vanessa Maher notes that "French penetration ... disrupted the traditional segmentary organisation of the local tribes. It brought the imposition of strong and pervasive state control, and the creation of a labour market." However, this is seen as concerning men more than women, "whose relationship to the market and to the control of property barely changed. Their world is now still [as of 1974] structured largely according to the traditional criteria of status and segmentary alignments."[33] Wolfgang Kraus has gone further, suggesting that even for men the situation has not dramatically changed. He notes that "Hdidduland," an area in the Central High Atlas, "failed to attract modern agricultural or industrial exploitation, [and thus] traditional economic structures did not undergo radical changes during the protectorate period from 1933 until 1956 or the subsequent period of Moroccan national independence."[34] Surely, migration and the postindependence expansion of what Abdaslam Ben Kaddour calls the "neo-makhzen"[35] has had some effect on Tamazight-speaking people in the Middle Atlas, and Kraus does note that the expansion of the central government, or "neo-makhzen," has diminished genealogical "tribal" notions of political affinity while retaining other affective associations, something like "segmentary identities."[36] Bernhard Venema argues that local political institutions remain vital despite encroaching governmental structures.[37]

The upshot of these analyses is that the political-economic reality in the Middle Atlas seems quite unlike that in the Rif, especially insofar as "traditional" social forms that disappeared in the Rif at the time of Abd al-Krim have proven rather durable in the Middle Atlas, both among women in Maher's study and across a broader spectrum of the population according to Kraus and Venema.[38] Octave Marais states flatly, "At independence, the Berber world was even more divided than in 1912."[39]

This is not to say that in themselves "traditional forms" lacked regional differences. Settlements in the Rif, for instance, tended to comprise "widely dispersed" family compounds located "not less than 300 meters distant from the next."[40] In the Middle Atlas one might have seen this, but a concentrated village life is more likely, often combined with transhumance and, until recently, even pastoralists living in tents. The Berbers of the High Atlas most commonly live in very densely built villages of fewer than five hundred people located propitious distances from one another along rivers used for irrigation. Anti Atlas settlement also tended toward insular village construction, but defensible outcrops were favoured over riverside locations presumably because there are few reliable rivers in the region to use in irrigation and because the mountains themselves are not rugged enough to deter the depredations of outsiders.

Social and political organization also seems more variable than is sometimes assumed. Ernest Gellner wrote of the mountains east of Marrakech as a place where "equality and liberty go together" and argued that with the exception of religiously sanctioned arbiters, "saints," the tribes self-governed with a remarkable emphasis on equity.[41] The areas south of Marrakech, however, were anything but egalitarian. By the time the French arrived, the western High Atlas was in the hands of three all-powerful lords, some of whom had been in control from the middle of the nineteenth century. Robert Montagne has described the political organization of the region as having been divided between two maximal *lfuf,* or moieties, before the rise of *grand caids,* but by the time Montagne himself arrived on the scene, these had long been supplanted.[42] The three *grand caids,* or "Lords of the Atlas," remained in power until the departure of the French, with some family members playing active and important roles in the rule of the country during the colonial era and even still today. Gellner and David Hart have critiqued Montagne's model for traditional political organization, but here the point is that by the early twentieth century, different Berber regions looked very different politically.[43] At least for the hundred years preceding the French withdrawal from Morocco, political life in the western High Atlas had an extremely authoritarian flavour, in strong contrast to nearby areas to the east and northeast, as indicated by ethnographic reports.

Today the European appetite for illegal drugs has transformed the economy of the Rif. Subsistence farming continues, but marijuana's potential as a cash crop is evident and tempting. The High and Middle Atlas remain regions of desperately poor barley farmers with some pastoralism, arboculture, and seasonal wage labour. Villages here may still function as economic units, particularly in terms of irrigation organization,[44] but they are insinuated into the larger economy through circular labour migration. The far South, on the other hand, has been utterly transformed by the more-or-less permanent emigration of men to the cities, particularly to work in the dry goods industry.[45] Today many parts of the Anti Atlas are almost totally supported rather than merely subsidized by remittances, and the permanent local population consists disproportionately of women, the very old, and the very young. Many Anti Atlas communities are nowhere close to being economically self-supporting, but this should not be taken to mean that they are any less culturally or affectively vital. Migrants in the cities wait all year to return to the Anti Atlas during Ramadan or at the 'Aid al-Adha. Migrants maintain village ties for emotional and cultural reasons; they hope to expose children to village mores and even to find brides appropriately uncorrupted by urban life. Some men invest significant sums in building overwrought versions of traditional village houses, including vast stables for sheep that quite evidently could not live on the meager herbage of the dry mountains. The women and relatively few men who remain in these villages still farm, tending almond trees or sowing fields of rain-fed barley when the weather cooperates, but they rely on the migrants' returns. The absence of these migrants from the Anti Atlas may in fact increase the self-conscious value of village life and with it Amazigh consciousness.

In sum, rural Berber communities take various forms, comprising relatively isolated homesteads in the North, densely populated and irrigation-dependent villages in the High Atlas, and economically enervated southern villages that subsist partially as consciously maintained cultural icons. Some of these differences have been exacerbated or even caused by recent political economic changes, but the huge area inhabited by Morocco's Imazighen virtually ensures significant regional variation even in the "traditional" context. Important, too, is that large populations of Imazighen are now urban, with especially significant communities in Casablanca and Agadir. The interactions of urban Imazighen with their complexly different homelands evinces the rich tapestry of contemporary Amazigh society, which cannot be easily sketched or simply amalgamated and set in opposition to "Arab" or national culture. A discussion of Amazigh identity formation cannot ignore internal diversity. The policies of the IRCAM *dahir* are likely to be carried out differently in different regions and will certainly take different forms in cities than in the countryside. The effects on Imazighen, and their expressions of and interest in being Imazighen, are likely to be similarly diverse.

IDIOMS OF AFFILIATION AND PARADIGMS OF INCLUSION

Above I touched on the differences between an Amazigh activist vision of a unified Berber culture and nationalist, tribal, and other interpretations of who Berbers are and what matters to them. Some of these differences in interpretation surely have to do with the varying conditions in which contemporary Imazighen live – from urban Paris to suburban Rabat and from isolated Rif homesteads to dense, mud-walled High Atlas villages – and with the varying employment status of the Imazighen, from overworked subsistence farmers to unemployed college graduates. As real – and important – as these differences are, the *perception* of affiliation and difference constitutes the core of identity, whether local or national. The idioms and discursive frameworks deployed in the construction of social identity bear on the shape that such identity takes, and in Morocco there seems remarkably little scholarly agreement on which idioms and frameworks are regnant. The IRCAM *dahir* is meant in part to promote Amazigh culture. What exactly comprises this culture is an enduring and particularly fraught question in Moroccan social science.

Berber speakers are estimated to make up 40 per cent of the Moroccan population, so the question of their place in Moroccan society is of real concern, especially as Berber speakers are increasingly educated in Arabic and migrate to urban areas.[46] In urban conditions, notions of "tradition" and "culture" assume new, and newly meaningful, forms. As I have noted elsewhere, literate Amazigh scholars and activists are now disseminating strikingly modern notions of their identity.[47] These notions are modern in their expression (websites, cultural organizations, Internet discussion groups, radio programs), in their location (cyberspace and urban centres rather than villages and small towns), and in their forms. The modern, activist form of Amazigh identity is explicitly culturalist, involving a meaningful essence seen to infuse Imazighen everywhere and to stretch back to the very origins of North African history.[48] Such activists forcefully argue not only that there is salience to the notion of a distinct, enduring Berber culture, but also that this culture is under threat. Salem Chaker states the position eloquently: "To be a Berber today, and to want to stay one, is to necessarily commit an act that is at once military, cultural, possibly scientific, and always political."[49] Simply being Berber in North Africa is a political act – at least for some.

What has made Berberness political has been Arab resistance to seeing Berbers as a valid part of North African culture and society, but the Maghreb states and their Arabist ideologues have not been the only problem. Some Western scholars, most famously Ernest Gellner, seem to contradict the claims made by Chaker. Gellner writes that "Arab and Berber are not corporate groups; they are simply linguistic classifications."[50] It is hard to see how a mere "linguistic classification" evokes the political passion Chaker describes. Gellner's work on Berber tribal life does provide a view of Berbers as culturally inclined toward equality and liberty – a positive cultural valuation that contradicts some urban depictions of Berbers as ignorant bumpkins – but Gellner also portrays Berber society as "segmentary" and premodern and thus isolated from the Moroccan state and nation. This interpretation complicates activist efforts to develop a broad Berber/Amazigh consciousness necessary to fight for cultural and linguistic rights and a place in the national imagination. As Gellner's main interest is theoretical – the potential for "segmentary" stateless governance – the question of the nature of Berber identity couples arcane debates in social theory to real political concerns.[51]

I need not review all of what Gellner and his interlocutors have said about the "segmentary hypothesis," but it is useful to touch on the issue at least insofar as much contemporary scholarship in Morocco reacts to Gellner's vision. In Gellner's work on Berbers, the important entity is the tribe rather than the language (as it would be for activist Imazighen) or the state (as it is for most scholars today).

His main theoretical thrust is that tribes contain – or did contain – nested, isomorphic segments balanced against each other. Tribes themselves can combine to form larger entities that mirror the organization of the component units. Such a notion builds explicitly on Emile Durkheim's notion of "mechanical solidarity," such that, as Gellner puts it, "similarity is not merely lateral but also vertical: it is not simply that groups resemble their neighbors at the same level of size, but it is also the case that groups resemble, organizationally, the sub-groups of which they are composed, and the larger groups of which they are members. This is totally unlike the organisational principle on which our own society is based."[52]

Durkheim himself initially drew from the early ethnography on Algerian Berbers, especially Kabyles, to develop the thesis of mechanical solidarity. In *De la division de travail social*, Durkheim defines the ideal terms of mechanical solidarity among extinct societies, citing Berbers as a living example of such a social type. He writes, "Thus, among the Kabyles the political unity is the clan, constituted in the form of a village (djemmaa or thaddart); several djemmaa form a tribe (arch'), and several tribes form the confederation (thak'ebilt), the highest political society that the Kabyles know. The same is true among the Hebrews … These societies are such typical examples of mechanical solidarity that their principal physiological characteristics come from it."[53] This theory, and Gellner's elaboration of it, have been exhaustively debated and roundly criticized,[54] although some scholars continue to find segmentary theory illuminating of Moroccan social reality. In recent work Kraus, for instance, writes that "political relations are described by informants as a rather stable structural disposition of segmented groups."[55] According to Kraus, the "groups" are preeminently Berber and imbued with an "egalitarianism which (gender inequalities apart) is an important value in relations among tribespeople."[56] The implication of this perspective is that such "tribespeople" are not Moroccan in any very significant way. Rather, their principle locus of affiliation lies in their "contestable identities."[57] Kraus discusses a small part of the Moroccan population, but even so his is a minority viewpoint among scholars today.

In fact, most contemporary academics do not seem interested in *Berber* politics at all but in "power" as it is broadly understood and actualized in Morocco. "Power" was perhaps the most popular term in social theory for most of the 1990s. Interestingly, however, the type of power preferred (at least by anthropologists) has tended to be actorless, dislocated "discourse" rather than anything vested in the historically situated social configurations that Michel Foucault, who inspired much of this work, might have wished to see. Interest in the power of culture has evolved into a fascination with the mostly elite, mostly state-centred concentration of power.

In Morocco this is exemplified by Abdellah Hammoudi's work on the "master and disciple" *diagramme*, or cultural model, which is thought to lock Moroccans into a ramifying field of "dominating/dominated" dyads that ultimately serve the dominance of the state.[58] This work builds on the Geertzian "interpretivist" approach but assumes asymmetrical power relations not as easily "negotiated" as scholars such as Lawrence Rosen imply.[59] In fact, Hammoudi seems to draw on Anthony Giddens's version of practice theory when he examines the "structuration of power relations."[60] Hammoudi is concerned not merely with culture, but with the "the exact ways in which ... abstract principles of legitimation are vested with an emotional impact sufficient to foster action" and the means by which "unfolding configurations ... [come] into existence through a dynamic of confrontation, efforts, disputes, compromises, and mere chance."[61] Whether they accept Hammoudi's cultural explanation of power operations, most scholars agree that the state is the preeminent level of analysis. Rahma Bourqia and Susan Gilson Miller write, "What do we mean by power in Morocco? Where is it located, how does it work its way through society, bending people to its will? A conceptualization of power begins with the state."[62] Here the issue of power is clearly Moroccan rather than Berber or Arab and thus hierarchically organized rather than diffuse. This is the most prevalent viewpoint today concerning power and politics in Morocco.

It is difficult to disagree with much of this perspective. Certainly, the Moroccan monarchy has successfully maintained itself through many crises, and today state power seems at least as important as at any time since independence. This partly has to do with fairly old-fashioned methods – censorship, patronage, secret police, and not-so-secret prisons – but governance is rarely accomplished only through force.[63] Hammoudi is almost certainly right that a cultural model exists that supports the legitimacy of the regime. The problem is that other cultural models also exist in Morocco – for instance, genealogically ordered segments (in some areas, as noted by some scholars)[64] and a general notion of Amazigh affinity preferred by many Berber activists. Even if Hammoudi is right, his *diagramme* is far from unitary, and it can be called "hegemonic" only if we ignore the visceral technologies that allow Morocco's masters to assert control over their putative disciples. As Elaine Combs-Schilling has shown, the existence of a particular cultural frame (in her example, the notion of segmentarity) does not preclude the simultaneous existence of other frameworks for meaning.[65] Culture is not a zero sum game. Anyone is capable of holding logically and substantively contradictory notions without any subjective sense of incongruity whatsoever. The question is why one idiom or framework for meaning takes precedence or how particular discourses are vested with power. At present there is no entirely convincing model for the murky relationship between culture and action, much less for the relation between action and the panoply of cultural models available for deployment in any given place and time. In terms of the Imazighen, this means that actual, historically relevant manifestations of Berber or Amazigh consciousness must rely on more than the existence of people who happen to speak Tamazight. What else "more" varies through time and across space.

Finally, in discussing the power of the Moroccan state, the salience of national culture, and the role of Berbers in both, we cannot ignore religion.[66] Islam has provided a consistent idiom of affiliation for Moroccans for over a millennium, and its significance does not appear to be declining with any evident rapidity. Without delving into the complex bases for, or the many forms of, political Islam, it is worth mentioning that the message of equality before God resonates powerfully among politically oppressed and economically dispossessed people. If the universalistic discourse of some Islamic activists has opposed the particularistic vision of some Amazigh activists, it is worth remembering that this need not be so. Historically, it has not been *despite* but *through* Islam that Imazighen have achieved significant political power. The Qur'an has been enduringly useful for men (far more than women) bent on forging isolated individuals into cohesive social bodies – and on inspiring these bodies to action.

This success is undoubtedly due in part both to the poetic force of the Holy Book and to historical happenstance. Many have suggested, however, that some portion of the current surge of political Islam in Morocco and elsewhere must come from its position as one of the few alternatives to a "new world order" in which the poor are assured yet more time at the bottom of the social ladder. Even in Latin America some are crying "seamos moros!" ("let us be Moors!"),[67] declaring solidarity with the Muslim world in the face of "a new imperial age" and the so-called "war" on terror.[68] Promises that the global tide of structural adjustment will lift all boats are no longer credible, as the standard of living continues to decline for many who already endure pitiable conditions. As Azzadine Layachi writes, in Morocco "it is feared that as the social and economic exclusion touches more people, the ensuing situation may mobilize greater numbers, under the religious banner, to press for a radical change."[69] The Qur'an pronounces all believers equal before God, which means that Bill Gates, King Mohammed VI, and both George Bushes will stand in judgment alongside unemployable young men from the *bidonvilles* of Casablanca and shepherds from the High Atlas too poor to buy shoes. For the pious and materially impoverished of the world, this has to be a satisfying vision.

Some ethnographers have asserted that there is a specifically Berber cultural emphasis on equality that seems to complement the Islamic ideal. Of the High Atlas, Gellner writes that "Here, at least, equality and liberty go together."[70] Hart has noted of some Rif Berbers that "Aith Waryaghar society is characterized by a fierce and highly competitive egalitarianism ... hence the only workable political system or arrangement is that of superimposed representative councils – a system of organized acephaly. Egalitarianism is the keynote."[71] Elsewhere Hart writes that "a constant preoccupation of all Berbers is never to let one head rise above the rest."[72] John Chiapuris notes that in the Middle Atlas, "Berber tribal organization stressed equality of male members and open recruitment, both of which served to maintain flexible and viable social entities in an environment of political and ecological hazards."[73] I have already noted Kraus's assertion of a certain Berber "egalitarianism which (gender inequalities apart) is an important value in relations among tribespeople."[74]

Not everyone entirely agrees with this assessment. Early last century Robert Montagne noted that "The egalitarianism which exists within a council of notables in a Berber republic is purely nominal. Despite the respect paid to egalitarian institutions – to such an extent that the rich have houses that are no finer than those of the poor – one finds that it is the rich who exercise power behind the scenes."[75] This recalls Amartya Sen's observation that "The central question in the analysis and assessment of equality is ... 'equality of what?'"[76] Based on my own work among villagers in the High Atlas, I make the case that culturally elaborated norms of deference and domination coexist with the value placed on some kinds of egalitarianism. In concert with these cultural frameworks, local social organization mitigates inequality in some respects but exacerbates differences in others.[77] Still, most observers agree that at least the notional value placed on some forms of equality is a notable feature of Berber culture. This notion seems consonant with the rhetoric of much of political Islam today and suggests that in some ways Islamic paradigms of affiliation and inclusion are (or have become) compatible with "traditional" Amazigh culture.

RURAL POVERTY AND AMAZIGH IDENTITY

The role of economic factors in shaping social identity in Morocco should be taken seriously. This is not to reduce eruptions of self-conscious cultural identity to a straightforward case of ideology, but it is not possible to understand manifestations of cultural consciousness without reference to the material contexts in which they happen. For instance, if the IRCAM *dahir* is primarily aimed at issues of cultural identity, the changes the *dahir* demands of the education system will affect variously positioned Moroccans differently. I have already discussed significant variation in the economic organization of different regions; there are also differences that cut across regions.

The classic, preeminent trope is that of a rural-urban cleavage mapped on to a Berber-Arab divide. This is wrong in at least one important sense: Morocco's cities are full of Imazighen, and the countryside has large areas where Arabic is the dominant language. Frustration over the too-easy equation "rural = Berber" has caused some scholars to disavow or disregard any rural connection for Berber culture. However, this seems as wrong as treating all Berbers as rural and all Arabs as urban. Surely, the experience of being Berber in urban Arabic-, French-, and Spanish-speaking society is as important to "the" Amazigh culture as the experience of being Amazigh in a monolingual, Tamazight-speaking milieu. Of course, neither condition is more or less authentically Berber; both are part of the contemporary Amazigh social reality. To discuss differences within Amazigh culture and political economy does not undercut the notion that a general *amazighité* exists.

Despite these caveats, it remains the case that many parts of the Moroccan mountains are nearly exclusively Amazigh, with all socio-economic indicators in these areas being significantly worse than the national average. I have argued elsewhere that the failure to address the overlap between Berber-speaking areas and impoverished areas threatens to inject a material urgency into questions of linguistic distinctiveness.[78] I have also noted that the assignment of monolingual, Arabic-speaking teachers to rural Tamazight-speaking areas virtually ensures frustration on the part of teachers and students alike.[79] The IRCAM *dahir* seems to address the latter issue, but the former remains intractable.

In fact, the economic situation of the poorest Moroccans is bad and seems to be getting worse. Quoting a 1989 publication by David Seddon, Mark Tessler writes, "the structural adjustment policies being pursued by the government hurt the poorest categories of the population while benefiting others."[80] Abdeslam Maghraoui writes, "Four decades after independence more than half of Morocco's 29 million people are illiterate. Nineteen percent of Moroccans live in abject poverty and 21 percent of the working-age urban population is unemployed, including some 100,000 university graduates."[81] He goes on to note that a woman dies every six hours giving birth in Morocco and that "in Casablanca, a city of three million people, some 10,000 homeless children fall prey to drug and prostitution rings. By comparison, Sao Paulo, Brazil, a city of more than 10 million people, has 5,000 homeless children."[82] World Bank data show that the number of Moroccans living on less than a dollar a day, what the Bank calls "below the absolute poverty line," has *increased 50 percent since 1991*.[83] Remy Leveau writes that "in 1998 [Morocco] ranked 125th in the world on the United Nations Human Development Index. It comes a long way behind Algeria and Tunisia, and even behind Egypt and Syria, looking at the statistics for schooling, health care and per capita GDP."[84] There have been some improvements in some aspects of the Moroccan infrastructure and economy over the past decade. Unfortunately, these have not percolated down to the most vulnerable strata of society. As Layachi writes, "Morocco was the first country in North Africa to engage in structural adjustment. The program, which began in 1983, is credited with a major overhaul of the national economy. At the aggregate level, Morocco succeeded in stabilizing a deteriorating situation and in restructuring its economy, notably through privatization and stringent fiscal policies.

However, success at the macro-level did not improve the lot of most people."[85]

If the situation in Morocco is bad overall, it is worse in the countryside. Maghraoui states flatly that "Women and rural populations are the most afflicted by poverty in Morocco ... Eighty percent of villages have no access to paved roads, running water or electricity, and 93 percent have yet to obtain basic health care facilities."[86] A World Bank report on Moroccan education estimates that while 52 per cent of the country live in rural areas, only 10 per cent of the education budget was spent in those rural areas during the 1980s.[87] It is impossible to get data on Berber-speaking areas specifically, but to the degree that the Moroccan mountains remain significantly Amazigh, rural Imazighen are significantly disadvantaged vis-à-vis their urban cousins, whether these are Arab or Berber. As Layachi points out, "Disparities between rural and urban incomes and living standards are critical. Among the rural population, 63 per cent have no water, 87 per cent are without electricity, 93 per cent have no access to health services and 65 per cent are illiterate. The health system, which receives only one per cent of the GDP, is deteriorating and corruption has become an institution."[88]

For the purposes of this chapter, what is significant about material inequality and regional differences in Morocco is the implications for the politicization of Morocco's Amazigh population. My contention is that material inequality has been underappreciated as a factor in Moroccan social and cultural life. This is not to say that class consciousness lurks beneath Amazigh consciousness but that material factors work in tandem with social and cultural forces to amplify politicized forms of identity. Hugh Roberts has written convincingly of the material basis of the "Kabyle question" among Algerian Berbers.[89] Without transmuting cultural activism into political-economic equations, we still must deal with the impact of political and economic inequality on ethnic and national consciousness. We must attend to the social predicaments of variously situated Berbers in order to understand what being Berber means today. This is too rarely done in my own discipline of anthropology, where the pursuit of "culture" blinds us to the multivalent significance of poverty and political disenfranchisement.

In Morocco it is the rural poor in particular who are likely to be affected by the education changes promised in the IRCAM *dahir*. Since much of the Moroccan countryside remains Berber-speaking and since the countryside is far worse off economically than the cities, the poorest Imazighen are likely the first to be educated in the new Tamazight language curriculum. In the countryside, poverty suffuses daily life. This is the context in which discourse – whether nationalist, socialist, Islamist, Amazigh, or some combination – will be deployed. These discourses are not mutually exclusive, and the way they articulate the urgent material concerns of Morocco's masses will determine the saliency of the discourse itself – and part of Morocco's political future.

CONCLUSIONS AND POSSIBILITIES

Clearly Berber speakers have existed in North Africa since time immemorial; they have reproduced their language, and arguably their culture, across a long period of time against what would seem fairly daunting odds. I have tried to suggest that the political significance of the linguistic fact of Berber particularity has varied across time and space. The IRCAM *dahir* is but one act in this long history, and its relevance will depend on how it interacts with other cultural, social, and political forces. Despite much progress since this chapter was originally drafted in 2001, there is not yet a full sense of how the *dahir* will be implemented, what sorts of changes it will really make in the education system, or what sorts of actors it will empower and/or inspire. I can, however, make some preliminary observations of how it is likely to affect both the enduring Berber/Amazigh question in Morocco and Morocco's national identity.

First, it has been shown that "the" Berber issue in Algeria is far more complicated than a binary ethnic cleavage.[90] Other ideological factors play a role – for instance, the socialist or Islamist inclinations of particular Berbers – as do the differing material conditions of Imazighen coming of age in different generations and living in different regions of the country. The same is true in Morocco, except that unlike its neighbour, Morocco has no Kabylia, no single, dominant subgroup of Berbers that have come to be taken as a synecdoche. Still, I would argue that there need not be a single, concentrated, overarching or even widely shared sense of Amazigh consciousness for Amazighness to prove politically salient in some ways. Amazigh distinctiveness can merge with other social affiliations to play a role in a variety of social groups and movements, from Islamists and socialists to royalists and secular liberal democrats. In the complex social and political geography of Morocco, convergences matter.

Interest groups are temporally fluid and strategically reconstituted. If we look for a homogeneous Amazigh perspective, we are bound to be disappointed. This does not preclude "being Amazigh" as an important *part* of the perspective of the many millions of Moroccans who speak some version of Tamazight as their first or only language. If it cannot be said a priori what influence *amazighité* will have on a particular issue, group, or action, neither should one assume that it will have no influence.

Second, political-economic factors should not be underestimated. Morocco's poor have always suffered, but the combination of rising expectations with disintegrating conditions can prove explosive. Scholars and government officials have worried over the plight and political potential of unemployed college graduates. In searching for an idiom of protest, these literate urbanites have articulated their grievances in many ways but rarely ethnically as Berbers or Arabs. Now, however, the rural poor are coming to share some of the expectations that have left urban Moroccans disgruntled, and many thousands – perhaps millions – of these rural poor are Tamazight speakers. The promise of a new king, and the expanding ambit of World Bank and other development projects, have injected more hope into rural communities than can be met by the pace of change. The slow spread of literacy and the more rapid proliferation of radios, cassette decks, and satellite television have meant that rural Berbers are coming to understand the larger world more immediately. The juxtaposition of hopeful (Arabic and French) words and images from "outside" with the daily drudgery of rural poverty leads, at least in the mountains, to a consciousness of being both poor and Berber. Whatever the statistical reality, if rural Berbers come to see themselves as a group that is disproportionately impoverished, there will emerge real potential for a distinctly radical Berber politics.[91] The IRCAM *dahir* seems aimed at eliminating some of the main forms of linguistic discrimination in Morocco – in the legal and education systems. This is an important step, but if the expanding younger generation finds it impossible to work, marry, and raise families as their parents did, they are likely to organize resistance. The government clearly hopes that this will take some form other than Islamic radicalism, but Islam's message of equality and justice resonates powerfully among disaffected Berbers as well as Arabs.

Third, it is worth remembering that the general issues raised by IRCAM are not restricted to Morocco or even North Africa more generally. Scholars around the world have noted the political saliency of "culture" of late, particularly the use of culture in national projects and even the conceptualization of nations as cultural projects. Culture has become political material,[92] whether employed by indigenous people in Brazil pressing their demands at the United Nations or by the far right in France excoriating "Arabs" for their inassimilable, non-French "culture" – rather than their non-French "race."[93] There is no guarantee that Berber culture will become a significant idiom of political expression in Morocco, but it would hardly be out of line with a worldwide explosion in identity politics and projects.

Finally, the IRCAM *dahir* stands to have many uses for many different actors. To start with, the establishment of IRCAM seems intended to please Amazigh rights activists and will serve as a visible symbol of an emerging civil society. Some groups are already contesting such measures, which they regard as cultural cooptation by the state, while others embrace the potential to gain at least some education in the native tongue of rural children and to see Amazigh art and culture openly produced in the cities. This will satisfy some international observers, too, but there would seem to be more to the story. What does the handling of Amazigh demands in Morocco have to do with the upheaval in Algeria, particularly the huge protests by Kabyle-based Amazigh political parties in May 2001? What does it have to do with the emerging Islamist challenge within Morocco, such as the March 2000 demonstrations in Casablanca, which are estimated to have drawn 200,000 people into the streets? Critics will note that the IRCAM *dahir* seems to value Berber particularity in a way that is reminiscent of the ill-fated, French-sponsored "Berber *dahir*" that inflamed Moroccan nationalist passion in 1930. While the new *dahir* does not outline separate Islamic laws for urban people (understood to be Arabs) and customary, "tribal" laws for rural people (understood to be Berbers), it does pave the way for different educational formats in different parts of the Kingdom. The areas where Berber is to be the language of instruction are likely to be in the countryside rather than in the city, which could easily beget a situation in which rural and urban education become even more separate – and even less equal.

Many have noted that the Moroccan monarchy bases its practical relevance partly on its ability to manipulate sectarian politics. Hammoudi states that "the authoritarian government must have diversity in order to appear as the mediator,"[94] while Edward Thomas notes that the present king's father "proved himself to be remarkably skillful in playing different factions off against one another, thereby gathering decisive power into his own hands."[95]

The point seems to be that the Moroccan monarchy requires sectarian politics in order to function and thus that there will be those who view IRCAM as a tool to turn the political energies of activist Imazighen against Islamists – on university campuses and in the streets. This is conjectural, of course, and is complicated by the strong Muslim faith of many Imazighen and their overrepresentation in Morocco's religious schools.

The promotion of Amazigh culture seems laudable to anyone who believes that cultural and linguistic expression is a fundamental human right; the *dahir* is sure to please most Western observers. However, what IRCAM will mean in Morocco, how the edict will be implemented, and a full sense of why it is being promulgated is not yet clear. The promotion of Amazigh culture in the IRCAM *dahir* may be simultaneously the product of a genuine desire to improve the plight of Morocco's linguistic minorities *and* a means of extending royal control over a diverse nation. It may be at once co-optation and a kind of liberation. From a scholarly perspective, the IRCAM *dahir* represents an experiment in constituting a multicultural national identity that includes Imazighen – a first for North Africa and a project worthy of continued attention.

NOTES

1 Herein I use "Berber" and "Amazigh" interchangeably. While some activists object to the use of the non-Amazigh term "Berber," many activists and scholars do use it. I do not believe Berber carries any negative connotation in English, as pointed out by Fatima Sadiqi, "The Place of Berbers in Morocco."
2 See the many publications and activities sponsored by the Centre Tarik Ibn Zyad at http://www.centretarik.org.ma.
3 A. Allouche, "Arabization and Linguistic Politics in Maghreb"; Ahmed Boukous, "La langue berbere: Maintien et changement," and "L'amazighe dans l'éducation et la formation"; Salem Chaker, *Berbéres aujourd'hui*; David Crawford and Katherine Hoffman, "Essentially Amazigh: Urban Berbers and the Global Village"; Lahcen Oulhaj, "Possibilité et nécessité d'intégrer Tamazight à l'université marocaine"; Fatima Sadiqi, "The Place

of Berbers in Morocco"; and Jilali Saib, "Pour une integration effective de l'enseignement de l'amazighe à l'université marocaine."
4 Since the original drafting of this chapter just after the IRCAM *dahir* was announced, there has been a flurry of intellectual activity on the topic. See, for instance, Aziz Kich, ed., *L'Amazighité*; and Moha Enanji, "Reflections on Arabization and Education in Morocco."
5 Bruce Maddy-Weitzman, "The Berber Question in Algeria."
6 While actual treatment of Berbers by Arabs continued Roman discrimination, converts were within the bounds of faith; thus "North Africa in its entirety was for the first time embraced by the philosophy of the dominant culture and brought within its scope." Michael Brett and Elizabeth Fentress, "The Berbers," 83.
7 Chaker, *Berbéres aujourd'hui*, 11.
8 Stephanie S. Saad, "Interpreting Ethnic Quiescence: A Brief History of the Berbers of Morocco," 167, emphasis in the original.
9 Ibid., 177.
10 Ernest Gellner, *Saints of the Atlas*, 15.
11 Maya Shatzmiller, *The Berbers and the Islamic State*, xi.
12 Gabriel Ben-Dor, "Minorities in the Middle East," 1. This is not to say that I necessarily agree with Ben-Dor on the centrality of ethnic distinctions. Jack Goody, "Bitter Icons," 8, has written that "The term 'ethnic' has become a cant word in the social sciences and often in everyday speech, where it is frequently used in a blanket fashion to refer to any collective grouping with a semblance of homogeneity, in situations of conflict or positions of subordination. The concept of ethnicity has been so widely taken up because it gets around the problem of defining what it is that makes a people – that is, an ethnos – distinctive. Is the unity it possesses based on language, faith, descent, or culture in some vague sense? Ethnicity covers all as well as covering up all."
13 Benedict Anderson, *Imagined Communities*.
14 Shatzmiller, *The Berbers and the Islamic State*, xii.
15 (al 'Arawi) Abdallah Laroui, *The History of the Maghreb*, 157.
16 Ibid., 164–5.
17 Ibid., 165.
18 Rachid Bourouiba, *Ibn Tumart*, 11–13.
19 Laroui, *The History of the Maghreb*, 175.
20 See H.T. Norris, *The Berbers in Arabic Literature*, 161, for one version of this tale.
21 See Vincent I. Cornell, "Understanding is the Mother of Ability: Responsibility and Action in the Doctrine of Ibn Tumart," for a review of Ibn Tumart's "doctrine of responsibility."

22 This represents exactly the sort of dynastic cycle that Ibn Khaldun outlines in his classic works of political sociology.
23 Shatzmiller, *The Berbers and the Islamic State*, 10.
24 See David Crawford, *Work and Identity in the Moroccan High Atlas*, 179.
25 Of course, it may also be a purely ideological claim to Arab ancestry and the associated prestige.
26 See David Crawford, "Morocco's Invisible Imazighen."
27 For instance, see Paul Silverstein, "Of Rooting and Uprooting: Kabyle Habitus, Domesticity, and Structural Nostalgia," for an account of how social theory and social activism conspired to produce a sense of precolonial Amazigh cultural unity in Kabylia.
28 See Kich, ed., *L'Amazighité*.
29 See David A. McMurray, *In and Out of Morocco*.
30 Ninna Nyberg Sørensen, "Crossing the Spanish-Moroccan Border with Migrants, New Islamists, and Riff-Raff," 89.
31 David Hart, *The Aith Waryaghar of the Moroccan Rif*.
32 James Ketterer, "Networks of Discontent in Northern Morocco," 31.
33 Vanessa Maher, *Women and Property in Morocco*, 31.
34 Wolfgang Kraus, "Contestable Identities: Tribal Structures in the Moroccan High Atlas," 6.
35 Abdaslam Ben Kaddour, "The Neo-Makhzen and the Berbers."
36 Kraus, "Contestable Identities."
37 Bernhard Venema, "The Vitality of Local Political Institutions in the Middle Atlas, Morocco."
38 Kraus, "Contestable Identities"; Venema, "The Vitality."
39 Octave Marais, "The Political Evolution of the Berbers in Independent Morocco," 277.
40 Hart, *The Aith Waryaghar of the Moroccan Rif*, 29.
41 Gellner, *Saints of the Atlas*, 64.
42 Robert Montagne, *The Berbers*.
43 See Gellner, *Saints of the Atlas*, 65–7; and Hart, *The Aith Waryaghar of the Moroccan Rif*.
44 David Crawford, "Arranging the Bones: Culture, Time and In/equality in Berber Labor Organization," 465.
45 John Waterbury, *North for the Trade: The Life and Times of a Berber Merchant*.
46 See Chaker, *Berbéres aujourd'hui*, 9, for statistics on estimated numbers of Berber speakers in North Africa. See also Brett and Fentress, "The Berbers," 276; Boukous, "La langue berbere," and *Société, langues et cultures au Maroc*; and Sadiqi, "The Place of Berbers in Morocco."
47 Crawford, *Work and Identity*; and "Morocco's Invisible Imazighen."

48 See Crawford and Hoffman, "Essentially Amazigh," for a discussion of this rhetoric and the communicative practices associated with the movement. See Hugh Roberts, "The Economics of Berberism: The Material Basis of the Kabyle Question in Contemporary Algeria," for a historical account of Berber-consciousness groups and activism; see Chaker, *Berbéres aujourd'hui*, for a scholarly account of the cultural-historical significance of Berbers and for resources on contemporary journals and organizations interested in Berber cultural and linguistic rights. Brett and Fentress, "The Berbers," offers a combined archeological and historical account of Berber history.

49 Chaker, *Berbéres aujourd'hui*, 7, my translation. Chaker begins his account with a quote from Ibn Khaldun: "The Berbers have always been a powerful, formidable, brave, and numerous people; a real people like so many others in this world, like the Arabs, Persians, Greeks, and Romans" (my translation). This explains Chaker's position in a nutshell: Berbers are *a* people in the same sense as the Persians, the Greeks, and the Romans. For other activist views on Amazigh identity, see any issue in the list of activist newsletters and publications that Professor Chaker lists (143–4) or websites such as www.mondeberbere.com, www.waac.org, and www.tinghir.org. For more history of the rise of Berber-identity activism, see Hugh Roberts, "The Unforeseen Development of the Kabyle Question in Contemporary Algeria," and "The Economics of Berberism"; and Brett and Fentress, "The Berbers," chapter 8.

50 Gellner, *Saints of the Atlas*, 73.

51 Again, see Silverstein, "Of Rooting and Uprooting," for more on the confluence of social theory and social activism.

52 Ernest Gellner, *Culture, Identity, and Politics*, 31.

53 Émile Durkheim, *The Division of Labor in Society*, 178.

54 See M.E. Combs-Schilling, "Family and Friend in a Moroccan Boom Town"; Abdellah Hammoudi, "Segmentarity, Social Stratification, Political Power, and Sainthood"; David Hart, *Dadda 'Atta and his Forty Grandsons*, and "Rejoinder to Henry Munson Jr"; Henry Munson, Jr, "On the Irrelevance of the Segmentary Lineage Model in the Moroccan Rif," "The Segmentary Lineage Model in the Jebalan Highlands of Morocco," and *Religion and Power in Morocco*; Hugh Roberts, "Perspectives on Berber Politics"; and John Waterbury, "Bargaining for Segmentarity."

55 Kraus, "Contestable Identities," 10.

56 Ibid., 17.

57 See Crawford, "Arranging the Bones," for a very different analysis of how genealogical ties are used in the High Atlas and for an account of how complicated the notion of "equality" can be in a rural context.

58 Abdellah Hammoudi, *Master and Disciple: The Cultural Foundations of Moroccan Authoritarianism.*
59 Lawrence Rosen, *Bargaining for Reality: The Construction of Social Relations in a Muslim Community.*
60 Anthony Giddens, *The Constitution of Society;* and Hammoudi, *Master and Disciple,* 3.
61 Hammoudi, *Master and Disciple,* 2, 3.
62 Rahma Bourqia and Susan Gilson Miller, eds, *In the Shadow of the Sultan: Culture, Power and Politics in Morocco,* 5.
63 See Susan Slyomovics, "A Truth Commission for Morocco," and "No Buying Off the Past: Moroccan Indemnities and the Opposition"; for a candid appraisal of political repression in Morocco, see Abdeslam Maghraoui, "Political Authority in Crisis."
64 See Gellner, *Saints of the Atlas.*
65 Combs-Schilling, "Family and Friend in a Moroccan Boom Town."
66 Goody, "Bitter Icons," 15, argues that "European historians, sociologists and political scientists reared in skeptical traditions dismiss the power of religion in the modern world at their peril," but arguably, religion is if anything overemphasized in North Africa and the Middle East, serving as a default explanation for nearly everything people do.
67 According to Hisham Aidi, "Let Us Be Moors," 43, this was uttered by the Cuban poet José Martí in 1893 "in support of the Berber uprising against Spanish rule in Northern Morocco."
68 Ibid.
69 Azzadine Layachi, "Reform and the Politics of Inclusion in the Maghrib," 31.
70 Gellner, *Saints of the Atlas,* 64.
71 Hart, *The Aith Waryaghar of the Moroccan Rif,* 279.
72 Hart, *Dadda 'Atta and his Forty Grandsons,* 77.
73 John Chiapuris, *The Ait Ayash of the High Moulouya Plain,* 161.
74 Kraus, "Contestable Identities," 17.
75 Montagne, *The Berbers,* 59.
76 Amartya Sen, *Inequality Reexamined,* viii.
77 Crawford, *Work and Identity,* 358; and "Arranging the Bones."
78 Crawford, "Morocco's Invisible Imazighen."
79 Crawford and Hoffman, "Essentially Amazigh."
80 Mark Tessler, "Morocco's Next Political Generation," 8.
81 Maghraoui, "Political Authority in Crisis," 14.
82 Ibid., 16.
83 This statistic was found on the World Bank website in a report entitled "Morocco in Brief," http://wbln0018.worldbank.org/mna/mena.nsf/

5d1f9bb6c6c4c660852567d60065a6a0/
   a3c12c72a8890b3b8525680c00024df1.
84 Remy Leveau, "A Democratic Transition in Morocco?"
85 Layachi, "Reform and the Politics of Inclusion in the Maghrib," 25–6.
86 Maghraoui, "Political Authority in Crisis," 14.
87 This information is quoted in Crawford, "Morocco's Invisible Imazighen," 64–6. The statistics come from the World Bank website, World Bank Discussion Paper No. 264, Shahidur R. Khandker, Victor Lavy, and Deon Filmer, "Schooling and Cognitive Achievements of Children in Morocco: Can the Government Improve Outcomes?" http://www.worldbank.org/html/extpb/abshtml/13046.htm, 1 November 1994.
88 Layachi, "Reform and the Politics of Inclusion in the Maghrib," 27.
89 Roberts, "The Economics of Berberism."
90 Roberts, "The Unforeseen Development," "The Economics of Berberism," and "Perspectives on Berber Politics"; Heba Saleh, "Algerian Insurrection"; and Azzadine Layachi, chapter 8 herein.
91 Azzadine Layachi, *The United States and North Africa,* among others, has made the point that in this context what is true is sometimes less important than what is perceived to be true.
92 Marshall Sahlins, "Two or Three Things That I Know about Culture."
93 Kevin Dwyer, "The Uses and Misuses of 'Culture.'"
94 Hammoudi, *Master and Disciple,* 154.
95 Edward H. Thomas, "The Politics of Language in Former Colonial Lands," 26–7.

8

The Berbers in Algeria: Politicized Ethnicity and Ethnicized Politics

AZZEDINE LAYACHI

INTRODUCTION

Throughout the 1990s Algeria was torn by violent fighting between religious groups and the state that left around 150,000 people dead. As this conflict started to subside, another one began to take shape in the early 2000s that has been pitting Berber militants against the state over economics and politics as well as over language and culture. Even though this conflict is not new, since 2001 it has acquired a firm and sustained articulation. While the confrontation has been relatively peaceful, occasional clashes with security forces have caused the deaths of more than eighty demonstrators and the arrests of several others.

This chapter examines the Berber "minority" question in Algeria, a country that is officially Arab and Muslim. It analyses the genesis and nature of the Berber (Amazigh) identity in Algeria and its inspiration of a political movement in a country that has been driven by strong Arab and Muslim identifiers. In the past, these identifiers served as central features of an Algerian nationalism opposed to colonial France and today constitute two key themes in Algerian patriotism.[1] For several reasons, both Algerian nationalism and patriotism have downplayed or ignored the Amazigh component of the country's identity. However, in recent years, a relentless social movement for a radical change in the official definition of the Algerian nation and its attributes gained momentum at a time when the state faced serious discredit and exhaustion from a long fight against an Islamist guerrilla movement.

The questions tackled here include: Is the Berber movement in Algeria an ethnicity in search of recognition and self-determination (ethno-nationalism) or a civic movement in search of the fulfilment of citizenship in a modern Algerian state (civility)? Can Arabs and Berbers be distinguished from one another in today's Algeria, and what role does this distinction play in the current clash between Amazigh militants and the state? Is it possible to speak of an "imagined" Berber community in an Algerian society characterized by a complex web of interwoven cultures, languages, and histories? Furthermore, and more important, if there is a Berber political community, what factors have stimulated its mobilization as an ethnicity?

To answer these questions, this chapter's analysis focuses on the empirical interplay between notions of ethnicity, nationalism, and nationhood in Algeria's current political and economic climate.

At the outset, it can be said that there exists today an "imagined" Berber community concentrated in a small geographical area east of Algiers known as the Kabylie region (see Maps 8.1 and 8.2). However, it does not have all of the characteristics attributed by Benedict Anderson to the "imagined community."[2] Although it is limited both geographically and ideologically, it is not sovereign since the centralized Algerian state exercises full control over the area identified by the movement as being the land of the Kabylie region's Berbers, known as the Qbayil (Kabyles). Moreover, political consciousness and mobilization remain limited to the Kabylie region, and not all people living there have heeded the calls for political action. The other limitation resides in the fact that the movement is in a pre-national stage, commonly referred to as "ethnicity."

The politicization of the Berber ethnicity resulted from a host of factors, including old linguistic demands that became more pressing in response to a reinforcement of the state's control over the country's culture and language, the repression of cultural and linguistic pursuits not sanctioned by the state, and an exacerbation of the political and economic crises that have beset the country since the early 1980s. Beginning in 1989, a relative political opening allowed the birth of a movement that became openly mobilized for the realization of Berber cultural and linguistic demands and for substantial economic and political change. To this politicization of the Berber ethnicity, the ruling elite reacted with a tactical ethnicization of politics, which will be discussed below.[3]

The Berbers in Algeria

The Kabylie region lies between Algiers and Setif
Source: http://ph.infoplease.com/ipa/A0748517.html

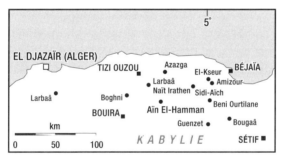

The Kabylie region
Source: http://www.internationalist.org/kabylie0601a.html

The outcome of the current showdown between Berberist militants and the state will greatly depend not only on how the general question of Algerian identity is treated in the near future, but also on political dynamics taking place in other arenas of interaction and confrontation, notably in the areas of state-society relations and the distribution of power between central institutions and local communities.

Thus this chapter analyzes the domestic context, the genesis, and the content of the Berber identity and its politicization; it also deals with how this identity relates to Algeria's Arabo-Islamic nationalism and patriotism and to the political institutions and dynamics of the country. Finally, it looks into the potential evolution of the current conflict, in which a politicized Berber ethnicity opposes the state. To tackle the issue of Berber identity in Algeria and the many questions it begs, it is necessary first to look at how the post-Cold War international system and globalization have affected ethnicity and nationalism.

THE POST-COLD WAR ERA AND ETHNIC AND NATIONAL REVIVAL

When the Cold War ended and the Soviet Union collapsed in 1991, many people thought that the world might finally be heading toward peace, security, and prosperity for all. The optimistic – and maybe the naive – expected the great powers to cooperate in reducing international tensions and to help end most conflicts around the world. However, and contrary to this expectation, the planet witnessed a rash of ethnic and nationalist tensions, skirmishes, and even full-fledged wars. Most of the conflicts were directly caused by changes in the surrounding circumstances, both internal and external. With the demise of authoritarian and totalitarian states in the former USSR and Eastern Europe, many domestic, regional, and international orders were suddenly open to challenge and overhaul.

In its various forms, globalization contributed to weakening the state and its authority in many parts of the world, especially in the developing areas where internal economic disparities and inequalities were made worse by an authoritarian rule that kept most avenues for political expression and participation closed. While weakening the state and threatening the unique identities of its ethnic, cultural, and religious communities, globalization also provided rebellious groups with the means to appeal for support and sympathy and to establish networks of solidarity beyond the state's borders.

As the international order entered a period of restructuring, the domestic orders of many countries also began to be questioned; societies, or parts of them, began to challenge long-established systems that had kept individuals and groups at the mercy of arbitrary state authorities. Many ruling groups resisted cultural, religious, and political pluralism for ideological reasons or for the sake of retaining power; they tried to maintain order and uniformity through repression, cooptation, and deception.

A few countries managed to begin a comprehensive process of transition to a new domestic order characterized by liberal economics and relative political, cultural, and religious tolerance. Others, however, have not been able to tackle the internal and external challenges they faced; their rulers continue to resist change even when faced with serious societal challenges driven by a host of claims and demands, some of which are ethno-cultural, ethno-linguistic, and ethno-nationalist. In fact, many of the conflicts that have erupted around the world since the end of the Cold War are attributed to particularism-driven mobilization.

Some ethnic movements have been seeking economic and political inclusion (e.g., the Chiapas in Mexico); others have been demanding recognition for their group's culture or language and their incorporation within the identity of the larger national entity of which the group is a part (e.g., the Berbers); and others have been demanding either relative autonomy within the state or total political control of their destiny through independence, as in Chechnya, Kosovo, and East Timor.

Even though many of the particularism-driven movements may have existed for decades, albeit in a dormant state, their recent revival and upsurge resulted directly from the combination of internal and external factors.

The end of the Cold War reduced tensions but also revived old conflicts and stimulated new ones within and between states; some of these tensions stemmed from economic, political, or territorial claims that coincided with ethno-cultural distinctions. The collapse of the Soviet Union unleashed drives for liberal democracy and self determination in the former USSR republics, in Eastern Europe, and elsewhere in the world. In some cases, this encouraged demands for a reconfiguration of the national identity.

Economic crises and globalization sharpened internal divisions along ethnic and cultural lines, as people made demands for the prosperity of their particular groups. When the fault line between the haves and the have-nots coincided with ethnic lines, some minorities chose "to opt out of a state that is seen as failing or failing them."[4]

Tensions within states over minority questions were also affected by internal political fragmentation, weak elite cohesiveness, and a resilient authoritarianism that was incapable of solving problems. Finally, the legacy of colonialism, which is mostly reflected in artificial states and ethnicities, has made "nation building" difficult for many postcolonial states.

In many countries where potential ethnic mobilization was ignored or inhibited for many years by a given domestic order (repressive authoritarianism and/or equitable distribution of goods and services), a sudden change of circumstances allowed ethnicity as an identifier to come to the fore. Democratization facilitated this development, and, when it failed, various groups came to a head in bitter disputes.

Ethnicity-based tensions tend to increase whenever democratization starts and then fails, especially after a political and economic opening does not bring about an all-inclusive political change; in other words, liberalization stimulates political mobilization and raises expectations without inclusion. Tensions also tend to increase when the elite of a dominant ethnic group continue to control a multiethnic state plagued by a multitude of problems (i.e., Pakistan, India, China, Burma, Thailand, Malaysia, Indonesia, and Iraq). In these states, tensions based on primordial distinctions (e.g., blood ties, religion, language, etc.) tend to increase as some ethnic groups resist, protest, and/or seek secession.

The current Berber crisis in Algeria must be analyzed in the context of similar developments. Furthermore, in the case of former colonies, such as Algeria, the roots of ethnic conflict quite often go back to colonial times. The Berber question was in fact born under the French occupation, which lasted from 1830 to 1962.

THE BERBERS AND ANTICOLONIAL NATIONALISM

During Algeria's independence war, which began in earnest in November 1954, conflict over the national character of the struggle erupted among the nationalists and threatened the unity of the armed anticolonial rebellion. Between 1930 and 1954, the Algerian nationalists were faced with a crucial identity question: Should the Algerians fight French colonialism as a united front under the banner of an Algerian nationalism that is part of Arab nationalism, or should the Berber component of Algeria be explicitly identified as part of this nationalist effort or even stand apart as a distinct Amazigh nationalism against French occupation?

In 1945 a meeting of Berber nationalists organized by high school students in Algiers and the publication of the first nationalist songs in Berber – which evoked historical Berber figures such as Massinissa, Jugurtha, the Kahina, and Messali[5] – augured a potential clash with the rest of the Algerian nationalists, who feared divisive ethnic distinctions at a moment when unity was of essence in the face of harsh and unrelenting colonial rule. The language question was raised within the underground nationalist Party of the Algerian People (PPA, revolutionary) and the Movement for the Triumph of Democratic Liberties (MTLD, reformist). Two nationalist tendencies opposed each other: one favouring an "Algerian nationalism" that explicitly identified the Berber component and one favouring an "Arabo-Islamic" nationalism that dismissed the ethnic element. In 1949 a major crisis exploded within the nationalist movement over this issue. As a result of the predominance of the Arabist tendency, many Berber militants in the PPA and MTLD ended up either leaving the movement or being thrown out. Others were assassinated.[6]

In July of the same year, under the pseudonym Idir el-Watani (Idir the nationalist), a group of three university students, members of the editorial committee of *el-Maghrab el-Arabi* (the Arab Maghrib), published a pamphlet with the PPA and MTLD entitled "Free Algeria Will Live," declaring that "the nation does not necessarily require a common race, or a common religion, or a common language." For the authors of the pamphlet, the nation was based on four requirements: "the territory; the economy; the national character, which is reflected in a way of life, a psychological make-up, and a culture; the cult of a common past; and the desire for a common future." They praised multilingualism in Algeria as a source of wealth and noted that Algeria's history "predates Islam by thousands of years."[7] This declaration did not end the conflict within the nationalist movement, but later developments put the question aside for the sake of a united front against French colonialism.

This manifestation of the Berber sentiment focused only on the issues of opposing colonialism and recovering Algeria's independence. However, it was inspired by a history of resistance that predated not only the French presence in Algeria, but also the Arabo-Islamic invasion of the seventh century.

Algerian Nationalism: Essentially Arab and Muslim

As noted above, during the struggle for independence, Algerian nationalism identified itself as essentially Arab and Muslim. This distinction from the French forces and European settlers, who were mostly Christians, helped to mobilize a united population behind the National Liberation Front (FLN) and helped to attract material and moral support from people and governments across the Arab and Muslim worlds.

Once independent, Algeria was declared officially an Arab and Muslim country, thereby pushing aside for the following forty years the Berbers' cultural and linguistic claims. However, the grassroots drive to keep the Berber culture and language alive continued even under the threat of state repression. From the 1960s on, and especially after 1980, there was a marked proliferation of Berber literary, linguistic, and artistic production, which helped to solidify the ethnic identity of the younger generation of Berberophones. This cultural output also helped to improve the status among the young of the Berber language in relationship to the formal Arabic language and the national dialect.[8] The role of writers, poets, singers, and political dissidents living in France was crucial to keeping alive the ethnic culture and language. It was also going to be very instrumental in articulating the Berber cause and in mobilizing support for it both domestically and internationally.

Independent Algeria continued to identify itself with Arab nationalism and patriotism based on geographical contiguity, shared history and culture, a common Arabic language, shared suffering under colonialism and opposition to it, and a shared wish to establish a single, united Arab nation-state. The Islamic component was also strongly embedded in the Algerian society well before independence, having become fundamental to the Algerian nation so defined.

After an initial resistance to the Muslim invader from the east, who came to North Africa in two successive waves in the seventh and ninth centuries, the indigenous Berber populations accepted Islam more than they did the Arabic element. There are of course different views on this, one of them being "the myth of Arab origin of the Berbers."[9] According to this myth, the Amazigh descended from the Arab Middle East (either Palestine or Yemen); thus espousing the Arab culture and Islam came naturally to them. Another view avers that the acceptance of Islam and of the Arab identity by the Berbers of North Africa was either a survival strategy (in the face of the overwhelming Arabo-Islamic invasion and control) or a simple acceptance of an admired culture and civilization.

Today the overwhelming majority of people claiming to be Berbers are Muslims, most of whom are devout observers of the faith. An insignificant number of Berbers have espoused Christianity across the centuries. The Islamized Berbers were very instrumental in the invasion and Islamization of Spain, which lasted 400 years and left an important historical legacy there.

While the majority of people believed to be of Berber descent have remained fundamentally Muslim, the militant movement for the Berber language and identity has taken on a secular character and downplayed the Islamic component of today's Berber identity – probably because of the mental association of Islam with the Arabs and vice versa. This development, however, has not prevented the Kabylie region from producing some of the most radical Islamist militants, as it did during the crisis of the 1980s and 1990s.

THE ISLAMISTS, THE STATE, AND THE BERBER MOVEMENT

For over a decade, Algeria has been experiencing a severe multidimensional crisis characterized by economic decline, social dislocations, weakening state and leadership legitimacy, and an internal war waged by Islamist groups against both state and society. It is in this context that a previously constrained and latent Berber movement came to the fore in the early 2000s and entered into an open clash with the state.

Beginning in the late 1980s, an economic decline caused by both internal and external factors contributed to social dislocations that were already underway because of the combined effect of inadequate economic reforms, social mutation, and rural migration. Unable adequately to deal with the economic crisis, and incapable of alleviating its social effects, the state and its leadership lost a substantial degree of legitimacy and, by 1992, faced a violent rebellion from a society that vowed to destroy the existing one-party system and establish an Islamic state governed by Islamic law, the *shari'a*. The challenge to state authority and legitimacy was facilitated by the sudden and substantial political opening that emerged in the wake of major riots in October 1988. These riots were a spontaneous expression of frustration and anger over difficult living conditions, worsening unemployment among the young, grim overall prospects for the future, and unresponsive public authorities. After an initial repressive response to the uprising, which left hundreds of people dead, the state allowed a sudden political liberalization that permitted the birth of scores of new parties and civic associations covering a wide spectrum of interests, fields of activities, and ideological orientations. Among the most prominent formations to appear were religious organizations and Berber parties and associations. Both kinds of organizations took advantage of the new 1989 law on the freedom of association to quickly mobilize substantial support for their claims, demands, and programs.

The Islamist organizations were by far the most active and the most successful. They dominated the political field from the start, displaced the old party (the National Liberation Front), and under the leadership of the Islamic Front of Salvation (FIS), mobilized millions of people behind a new social and political project based on faith and on a national identity centred mainly on Islam. To this Islamic identity was automatically attached a strong commitment to the Arab culture and language. As a new social and political phenomenon that was totally opposed to the existing system of government, the Islamist movement rallied a large segment of the population, which was yearning for change and for urgent solutions to its problems. This mobilization helped the FIS to win a sweeping victory in the first multiparty municipal elections of 1990 and in the first round of parliamentary elections in 1991. However, the military intervened in January 1992 to cancel the second round of the parliamentary elections and to ban the FIS. This encouraged the Islamist movement to resort to open, armed rebellion as the only means to reclaim the power it had won through the ballot box. From then on, Algeria descended into an abyss of political violence that caused over 150,000 deaths, the destruction of economic infrastructures, the unsettling of society, and isolation of the country at the international level.

Islamism in the Berber Movement of Kabylie

The relationship between the citizenry of the predominantly Berber region of Kabylie and the adherents of militant Islam has not been a simple one of a clash of perspectives, with the predominantly secular militant movement opposing the Islamists. Rather, the relationship is complicated by at least three factors:

1 The Kabylie region produced many members of the radical Islamist movement in general and of the radical faction in particular. The main reason for this is that living hardships and authoritarian rule extended to the entire country, including Kabylie. Berber-speaking populations had as

many reasons as other groups to rise up against the system, and Islamism became the appropriate conduit for such an undertaking. When it failed, it was later replaced by ethnic mobilization.
2 The Berber region of Kabylie has also produced a fierce resistance to Islamism, which is perceived as a mortal enemy to the Amazigh cultural and linguistic cause, notably since the religious movement appears intent on denying the cultural diversity of Algeria by imposing Arab culture and language in the new order it seeks to establish.
3 Some of the Berber militants perceive the Islamist movement as a social rebellion against an authoritarian state and unjust socio-economic order. They favour civic actions and an end to the repression of all opposition forces, including the Islamists.

Whatever the attitude within the Berber movement regarding Islamism, it is undeniable that the Islamist rebellion has had a strong and direct impact on the ethnic and civic demands being expressed today by people in the Kabylie region; both movements share grievances and a strong opposition to the existing regime. Nevertheless, they push in opposite directions: The Islamists favour a quasi-hegemonic order characterized by strict Islamic rule and the Arab identity, while the Berber movement seeks an essentially secular order in which the Berber language shares preeminence with Arabic.

THE BERBER POLITICAL MOVEMENT OF KABYLIE

In the context of the crisis and developments outlined above, the Berber movement attempted through two parties and one association to impose itself by putting forth two main demands: (1) effective democratization of the state and (2) official recognition of the Berber language (Tamazight) and culture as fundamental elements of Algerian national identity. These demands were articulated by the Front of Socialist Forces (FFS, formed in the 1960s but illegal until 1989), the Rally for Culture and Democracy (RCD, formed in 1989), and the Berber Cultural Movement (MCB, an association formed in 1980).

Some elements of the Berber movement – especially the RCD – formed a tactical alliance with the state in the struggle against the Islamist groups. The RCD pressed for recognition of the Berber ethnic and cultural tenets of Algeria's identity, applauded the cancellation of the parliamentary elections and the banning of the FIS, and aligned itself with the state in the fight against the radical religious movement, which it perceived as a grave threat to the secular Berber cause. Led by Said Saadi, this party had several representatives elected to parliaments, some of whom held ministerial posts.

Upon its recognition as a legal party, the FFS openly pushed for democracy, condemning the cancellation of the parliamentary elections and demanding the reinstatement of the banned Islamist party and the resumption of the 1992 parliamentary elections. Led by Hocine Ait Ahmed, a national-liberation leader, the FFS maintained a steadfast opposition to the regime, with which it refused to ally itself. For this party, the main enemy was the ruling regime and its intolerance of any viable opposition. Despite its attempt to gain national appeal, the FFS remained a party based mainly in Kabylie.

Represented by these two parties and the Movement for Berber Culture, the Berbers' political mobilization was divided from the start, and their political strategy was incoherent. It was also substantially weakened by the Islamist rebellion and its political implications and by manipulations by the ruling elite. Nevertheless, a symbolic tradition that had started in 1981 acquired more strength in the 1990s and early 2000s, bringing together all Berber militants every April of each year for the commemoration what became known as the "the Berber Spring." In the spring of 1980 the Berber movement had been harshly repressed by the government following a series of mass actions undertaken to promote the Berber language and culture. Since then, the event's yearly commemoration has served as the main occasion for public articulation of the movements' grievances and demands. By this and other means, the Berber militants kept pressure on the government, albeit in a moderate fashion, during the terror years of the 1990s. In 1995 they managed to get the government to create a High Commission for Amazighity (Berberity), which, among other things, was to oversee the introduction of Tamazight courses in schools. Of course, this action progressed extremely slowly and without the support of the necessary educational and political instruments. In this decade, the Berber movement attempted to extract other concessions from the regime in exchange for support in the anti-Islamist war. As the Islamist rebellion began to weaken by 1998, the movement increased its public pressure on the government.

The killing of a popular singer, Maatoub Lounes – a radical militant of the Berber cause – in the summer of 1998 marked the beginning of new and relentless efforts to promote the Berber culture and language. Furthermore, the killing in 2001 of an eighteen-year-old man, Massinissa Guermah, in the custody of the Gendarmerie (paramilitary police in rural areas) further enflamed the push for the Berber cause and mobilized more people across a wider geographical area than the usual confines of the main city of Kabylie, Tizi Ouzou, and its immediate vicinity. The state responded to the challenge with a crackdown on demonstrations that left around eighty people dead. However, this did not prevent street protests from becoming a daily event that threatened the precarious stability established after the exhaustion of the armed Islamist rebellion.

The death of Massinissa Guermah prompted people to take matters into their own hands, leaving no role for the established parties and associations. As a result, these representative structures (FFS, RCD, MCB) ceased pressing the Berber cause. Instead, it was taken over by old village structures known as the *aârouch* (sing. *aârch*), which were revived for the occasion. These structures suddenly became the main instruments by which to aggregate and articulate popular demands because of the failure of established parties and associations to do so. The latter seemed to suffer from exhaustion, internal divisions, and cooptation by the state and were thus unable to mount the kind of political offensive for which the Berber militants were calling.

It is important to note that the demands put forward by the *aârch* representatives of several provinces of the Kabylie region (which includes the Greater Kabylie and the Lesser Kabylie) were not confined to cultural and linguistic issues; these leaders also sought a new civil order based on social justice, democracy, accountability of office holders, and economic opportunities. The demands were articulated in the fifteen-point el-Kseur Platform (see Appendix), adopted on 11 June 2001 in the town of el-Kseur by a conclave of *aârch* representatives. In this platform, only point eight refers to the Berber language. Even after President Abdelaziz Bouteflika pledged in the spring of 2002 to make the Berber language official and national, the grassroots protest movement did not stop.

Following Bouteflika's pledge, the focus of the Berber movement shifted to the remaining fourteen points of the el-Kseur Platform. However, the ethnic overtone still plagued the showdown between what became known as the "Citizen Movement" (Mouvement Citoyen) and the state. This is an indication that ethnicity tends to become a rallying point mostly when there are other unresolved problems; in this case, the problems include authoritarianism, injustice, unemployment, corruption, and political violence. These and other issues exacerbated the cultural and linguistic divide, prompting a direct confrontation between people in Kabylie and the state.

Whereas the mainstream leaders of the Citizen Movement tried to present their demands and claims as being those of the widest possible range of people across the entire country, the government attempted to portray the movement's actions as being divisive and orchestrated essentially by radical Berber militants driven by a dangerous ambition for autonomy and secession as well as by personal political motives. France has also been accused of playing a major role in the Berber challenge in Algeria, having been perceived as encouraging the Berber dissidents to thrive on French soil with the hope of increasing France's own influence in Algeria through an autonomous or independent Kabylie region. France has allowed the formation of numerous Amazigh associations in its territory and the creation of Berber radio and television stations, and in 2001 it permitted the introduction of Berber language courses in its schools. For the opponents of the Berber movement, these developments in France prove that the movement is not only antipatriotic and anti-Algerian, but also an instrument of French neocolonialism.

BERBER PARTICULARISM: A COMPLEX PHENOMENON

As in many other cases involving an "ethnic minority," the Berber question in Algeria is complex. The Berbers do not constitute a clear-cut ethnic minority dominated and repressed by an ethnic majority that controls the state. The notion of minority status does not easily apply here even though many Berber militants and some outside observers think differently. Two important factors need to be noted at the outset.

First, there is no general agreement – even among the Berber militants themselves – on whether the Berbers constitute a minority within Algeria or the majority of the Algerian population. In fact, because of the mixing of original ethnicities through marriages and internal migration, it has become very difficult to know who is truly of Berber origin and who is not. As French historian Charles-André Julien notes in his 1956 book, *Histoire de l'Afrique du Nord*:

Nothing is more erroneous than to believe, as is often done, that the division between Arabophones and Berberophones corresponds to an ethnic division between Arabs and Berbers. This only means that Berber dialects have survived in mountainous regions, which are less accessible to conquerors, while giving way elsewhere to a language that was better adapted to social needs.[10]

Today only a few families may rightly claim to be of pure Berber descent. The same can be said about those claiming to be pure Arabs.

The only tangible and meaningful distinction that can safely be made is between those who speak Berber and those who do not. Moreover, because of the Arabization policy pursued by Algeria after independence, many young descendants of Berberophone families do not speak or understand Berber well.

Second, there is no explicit social or economic discrimination in Algeria against those who are self-defined or other-defined as Berbers. In fact, many people of Berber origin – especially from Kabylie – are among the country's top political leaders,[11] among the most successful business people, and among the best literary authors and artists. Well-to-do people of Berber origin are part of a socioeconomic minority of successful individuals whose Berber heritage is coupled to a variety of cultural backgrounds. The majority of the population of Algeria – which is worse off economically – includes people claiming either Berber or Arab descent or no ethnic identity at all. In other words, social and economic stratification does not generally follow ethnic or linguistic lines. Thus the Berber issue in Algeria is more complex than it would be if the matter were one of a simple distinction between Berbers and Arabs.

It is almost impossible to claim that the Berbers in all parts of the country are discriminated against by the state or society because of ethnicity. This explains, in part, why most of the demands of the current Berber movement deal not with ethnicity and language but with general issues of justice, economic opportunity, corruption, and state arbitrariness, which affect most people in the entire country, not just those living in Kabylie or in other predominantly Berber areas. There is no tangible basis for claiming that that a Berber ethnic group is specifically more disadvantaged than the rest of the population. Nevertheless, given the successful political mobilization of the mostly Berberophone population of Kabylie, ethnicity remains a central theme. Ethnicity – as a subjective element rather than as a sociological phenomenon – has helped to mobilize and organize dissent in Kabylie better than elsewhere in the country. The Islamists are the only other force to have achieved a larger and more effective mobilization of political dissent in independent Algeria. Their springboard was wide-scale opposition to the ruling regime, and their common identity was their Islamic faith. It is known from the study of ethnicity that the primordial identity of groups often serves as an effective rallying point for mobilization and for the articulation of diverse demands on the state (e.g., Mexico's Chiapas).

POLITICIZATION OF ETHNICITY AND ETHNICIZATION OF THE CIVIC STRUGGLE

People claiming Berber descent are spread across many regions of Algeria. The four main groups are the Qbayil (of Kabylie) in the north, the Shawiyya in the east, the Mzab in the northern Sahara, and the Tuareg in the far south. Each of these groups speaks a variant of the Berber language. However, militant actions in favour of the Berber language and identity in general have always been led by the Qbayil (living either in Kabylie or in France). Indeed, this mountainous region has a tradition of resistance to the central government, especially in the areas of culture and language, that predates even the Ottoman rule in Algeria. In more recent times, such resistance was encouraged by colonial France's policy of creating and reinforcing a distinction between the Qbayil of Greater Kabylie (the main and central part of Kabylie) and the rest of the population in order to gain better control of Algeria.[12] This policy included: favouring the Berber language over Arabic, which was a potent instrument of nationalist mobilization, and encouraging its teaching; offering the Qbayil more educational and professional opportunities than the rest of the population, including the Berbers of other regions; favouring them for migration to France as labourers; and trying to instil in them the belief that they had descended from the Europeans. Even though this policy succeeded in creating a serious and lasting schism between the people of the Greater Kabylie and the rest of the population, it did not prevent this region from providing the fiercest resistance to French colonialism and some of the bravest nationalists.

After Algeria gained independence from France in 1962, and in the face of an intensifying Arabization process, Berber militants unsuccessfully challenged the government's linguistic and cultural policies.

Not until the 1990s was such a challenge able to extract substantial concessions, this relative success being partly due to the weakness and vulnerability of a state besieged by a host of internal and external challenges, to the intensification of Berber demonstrations, and to the incorporation of the Berbers' cultural and linguistic demands within a comprehensive framework of civility, democracy, and citizenship initiatives.

This shift brought the Berber question to the fore with much greater force than in the past. This happened at a time of social upheaval across much of the country as people protested the state's inaction in the face of a host of problems (housing and water shortages, high unemployment, corruption, insecurity, etc.). In the Kabylie region, however, social upheaval took the form of ethnic mobilization, the traditional linguistic demand being combined with the demands expressed throughout the country for justice, economic reforms, security, and even regime change. In other words, in Kabylie the civic struggle took on an ethnic overtone, a fact subsequently used by the state leadership to present this social movement as purely ethno-secessionist.

Whereas in the past, political action in Kabylie was limited to cultural demands and mobilized only a few militants on a regular basis, since 2001 the movement has extended to a much larger number of people and to a much wider geographical area than Tizi Ouzou, the region's main city, and Greater Kabylie. This evolution constitutes an effective politicization of ethnicity. That is, people united by a sense of belonging to the same ethnic group and by common claims and grievances against the state became mobilized en masse for political action.

The government reacted by accusing the social movement in Kabylie of being divisive and of threatening national unity and territorial integrity. It placed the focus on the ethnic components of the demands emanating from the Qbayil while downplaying the wider political, economic, and cultural questions raised by the movement. This ethnicization characterized the Qbayil's political challenge as radical Berberism seeking the destabilization and break-up of Algeria. However, the government's ethnicization of this civic struggle in Kabylie played into the hands of the ethnicist (radical) faction within the movement and thus risked contributing to the development of a Berber nationalist drive. In fact, one radical faction, the Movement for the Autonomy of Kabylie (MAK), has already openly started to push for the autonomy of Kabylie. For some prominent Berber intellectuals, autonomy or independence, which were not an option years ago, are now being considered as favoured outcomes. Among many others, Salim Chaker, a teacher of the Berber language in France and a fervent spokesperson for the Berber cause, has changed his mind over the years. In his 1990 book, *Imazighen Ass-A*, he emphasizes the Berbers' degree of integration in Algerian society while dismissing their particularism and potential nationalism:

The degree of historical, cultural, economic, and political fusion of Berberophone populations throughout Algeria (and probably also Morocco) is such that it is not possible to foresee a nationalist type of evolution. I do not believe much in the reality or the possibility of a "Berber national idea" in Algeria (or in Morocco) because it has no historical root and because the Berbers have been integrated for centuries in the general history of the Maghrib. There are undeniable cultural elements that are specifically Berber, regional particularisms, but there is no Berber national or historical consciousness.[13]

In a 1995 article published in an Algerian newspaper, Chaker seems to have changed his mind when he exalts Berber particularism in a call for autonomy, which he qualifies as "a necessity":

To call a spade a spade, there is no doubt that there is a Kabyle people, with its collective identity, its culture, its language, and its territory. It is time to acknowledge this evidence, this reality lived daily but always repressed and taboo in the fields of political debate and projects. The idea of autonomy is based on an entire cluster of objective data, which are self-sufficient in themselves. It is also legitimized, even if on the surface it appears secondary, by the absolute defeat of the centralized Algerian nation-state, founded in 1962.[14]

ETHNICITY AND CIVILITY

The example of Salim Chaker's evolving stand on the question of Berber autonomy is one of many reflecting not only the hardening of positions within the Berber movement, but also the tensions that exist therein between ethnicity and civility. It leaves one to wonder whether the Berber movement is an ethnicity in search of recognition and self-determination (ethno-nationalism) or a civic movement in search of the fulfilment of citizenship in a modern Algerian state (civility). This question is prompted by the fact that this heterogeneous movement has simultaneously been making ethnic (linguistic and cultural), political, and economic demands. It exhibits both elements – an ethnic basis and the desire for civility – which are inseparable for some of its militants and mutually exclusive for others. These two elements can be mutually supportive rather than exclusive, but their interaction depends on how they are articulated and on how their objectives are fulfilled.

Ethnicity and Nationhood

Ethnicity refers to a bond between members of a group of people sharing primordial loyalties and affinities based on one or more of the following elements: territorial contiguity, kin relationship, a common religion, a common language or dialect, and common social practices. According to Clifford Geertz, ethnicity is "the commitment to 'primordial' loyalties which give people a distinct identity ... [and] a desire to be recognized and publicly acknowledged as responsible agents whose wishes, acts, and hopes 'matter.'"[15] For Anthony Smith, ethnicity, as the basis for a cultural community with some solidarity among members, is rooted in a myth of common origins, in shared memories and cultural characteristics, and in a link to an identified homeland.[16] Michael Ignatieff suggests that ethnic mobilization originated among the German Romantics due to their *volkish* conception of a linguistic, religious, or cultural commonality.[17] This type of mobilization is not rational and tends to be authoritarian.

The Berbers ethnicity in Algeria is based on a set of beliefs, myths, and cultural traits – including language and customs – that combine to establish a unique connectedness between people who identify themselves as Berbers (Imazighen). Geographical contiguity seems to be an important factor to only a segment of the ethnic Berbers in Algeria, those of the Kabylie. Many other population segments across the country are believed to have Berber ancestry even though they are not contiguous. Contiguity is not always a necessary condition for the birth and development of an ethnic and national consciousness and cohesion, notably since ethnic and national communities are mostly imagined and not always the result of direct social interaction.[18] A feeling of natural connectedness plays a more significant role than social interaction in stimulating the formation of primordial affinities and attachments.

There has long been awareness of a Berber particularity opposed to the official Arab identity of the Maghrib states and the desire to institutionalize this particularity by incorporating it into the cultural and linguistic definition of the entire Maghrib region. Some historians date this desire back to the days of the Arabo-Islamic Empire, or civilization, which began in the seventh century. Others date it to the period of French colonization, which created the Arab-Berber schism for the sake of dividing the colonized.

The desire to institutionalize the Berber identity was reinvigorated by the policies of independent Algeria, such as the Arabization policy, which sought to generalize the use of formal Arabic and to strengthen Algeria's Arab identity. Berber particularism was viewed as divisive and, most important, as being encouraged by the former colonizer in order to maintain its influence in Algeria through the Berbers of Kabylie.

In recent years, the interactions of four main protagonists – the Berber militants, the state, the Islamist militants, and France – have stimulated ethnic awareness and a desire that it be institutionalized in one of two ways: (1) by fully and officially integrating the Berber ethnicity within the Algerian identity, with tangible cultural and political implications; and (2) by granting the Kabylie region autonomy or independence.

The Berber movement remains essentially an ethnic movement, but if its adherents start expressing a desire for self-determination, it will have evolved into a movement for nationhood. While ethnicity does not comprise nationhood, several factors and conditions may lead to it. For Walter Connor, an ethnic group turns into a nation when its members become aware of their uniqueness. While an ethnic group is "otherdefined," a nation is selfdefined. The main distinction is the degree of selfconsciousness.[19]

Many definitions of a nation focus on the aspiration for self-government as a determinant of national consciousness. That is, a nation exists only when it has a political project such as achieving statehood for itself. Ethnic groups turn into nations when they aspire to, or demand, self-government.[20] A nation is based on "a psychological bond [such as blood ties and a unique common past] that joins a people and differentiates it, in the subconscious conviction of its members, from all other people in a most vital way." This determination is less rational than emotional, less factual than intuitive.[21]

The Berber movement has not evolved into a quest for nationhood; indeed, the nation that most Berber militants claim as their own is Algeria. However, these militants believe that Algeria should be identified primarily as a Berber nation. This contention is not new but goes back to the period of the struggle to liberate the nation from French colonialism. In fact, the struggle to redefine the Algerian nation and to make its governing system more inclusive and just is a struggle for a civic order (or civility) that has eluded Algeria since its independence.

Civility

Civility is defined by Clifford Geertz as the desire for citizenship in a modern state. This desire manifests itself as the wish to create an efficient and dynamic modern state characterized by an effective political order, social justice, and a role in world politics.[22] For Michael Ignatieff, a civic order is based on rationality and "sociological realism." It is "inclusive, democratic, and patriotic, a political association drawn from Enlightenment principles of individual equality."[23]

A civic movement wishes to see the primordial characteristics of the group it represents – mainly language in the Berber case – officially acknowledged and respected in the context of a modern, democratic state in which individuals enjoy justice and full citizenship. Today most Berber militants do not call for a separate national entity distinct from an overarching Algerian nationhood. Instead, they seek to enjoy full citizenship rights and duties in an Algerian state and society that officially acknowledge and incorporate the Berber component into the country's identity.

With regard to both ethnic mobilization and nationalism, one of the dilemmas particularly faced by countries with a history of colonialism has been a tension between ethnicity and civility. People's sense of self remains strongly based on blood, race, language, locality, religion, or tradition, while the modern sovereign state calls for a collective identity.[24] This collective identity is ideally embodied in the civic state, which is normally all-inclusive. One is expected to be loyal to the civic state and order rather than to a particular ethnicity. However, in a multiethnic and multilingual country, some people believe that to subordinate their primordial identities to a "generalized commitment to an over-arching and somewhat alien civil order is to risk a loss of definition" and autonomy through absorption into a "culturally undifferentiated mass" or into a larger group whose identifiers do not explicitly include theirs.[25] The dilemma becomes even more acute when civic political structures are inherently weak

– as is the case in Algeria – and thus cannot guarantee the protection and security that primordial attachments are believed to offer. This situation generates tensions between the push for civility and the pull of primordialism. In the Berber movement, this tension is reflected in the opposition of two views that dominate the debate: the ethnicist and the civic. However, these views are not necessarily mutually exclusive but can complement each other.

The Ethnicist View According to this view, the Berbers constitute a markedly distinct social group held together by blood ties, history, culture, and language. As such, this group should be afforded a destiny separate from that of Algeria's non-Berber population. From this perspective, the Berbers in Algeria are a "minority" persecuted by an Arab majority and by a hegemonic and authoritarian Arab-controlled state.

Those who hold this view, which caters mostly to international institutions and international public opinion, seek support for the defence of a Berber "minority" and its culture. They call for international protection for this "minority" or for an end to the central state's control over the Kabylie region, which they believe should be granted independence or, at least in the short term, autonomy. Harbouring xenophobic ideas, many proponents of this view have taken a radical stand against those they refer to as Arabs; they do not wish to be associated with a state dominated by Arabists – that is, people inspired by an Arabist ideology and pursuing an Arabist foreign policy.[26] This essentially ethnicist perspective borders on Berber nationalism (i.e., the desire for a Berber nation) and is strongly anti-Arab. However, at this moment there is little support in Algeria and elsewhere for such a perspective and the actions it advocates. But this may change due to further politicization of the Berber ethnicity and to ethnicization of the civic struggle in the Kabylie region – especially if the state remains unresponsive to noncultural demands.

Both the ethnicist view and the state's intransigence have increasingly radicalized the Berber movement since the spring of 2001. The violent interference of Berber militants with the legislative elections of 30 May 2002, which prevented voting in Kabylie, constituted a marked escalation in their use of force and a step toward the total rejection of the central state and its authority in this region. This radicalization was further reflected in the movement's disavowal of some of its self-proclaimed delegates, who had decided to enter into negotiations with the government in 2002 over the movement's fifteen demands; the delegates were branded "traitors of the Berber cause," and their names were posted in public places. The faction of the movement behind such actions holds an unyielding ethnicist view and thus does not believe that the central government's achievement of a civic order would do justice to their cause.

It is advisable here to specifically refute the argument emanating from "democratic" circles, according to whom the Amazigh question is nothing more than a problem of democracy that would naturally find its solution within the framework of a national democratic alternative and that need not be isolated from the democratic struggle. The Kabyles should, as a consequence, mobilize only for democracy in Algeria. There is here staggering naiveté or crude political manipulation.[27]

The Civic View Proponents of this view can be subdivided into those who see the Algerian Berbers as a minority in a predominantly Arab state and those who view them as the majority in a country controlled by a hegemonic, authoritarian, and intolerant Arab or Arabist component of Algerian society. For the latter, the Amazigh constitute *the* majority of the population of Algeria and the entire Maghrib region. Algeria in particular and the Maghrib in general are ruled by a minority of Arabs or by pro-Arab Berbers driven by a hegemonic Arabist ideology and by an Arab nationalism that inhibits the Berber language and the Berber elements of the national cultures while promoting solely the Arab culture and the Arabic language.

Whether they see their ethnic group as a minority or a majority, those who hold the civic view agree that their struggle is to turn Algeria into a genuine civic state that is all-inclusive, equitable, secular, and based on the rule of law. For them, Algeria's political system must substantially change, becoming truly civic and democratic. They reject stopgap or half measures. Besides an urgent overhaul of the entire system, they also call for reinstatement of the inherently Berber essence of Algeria by: (1) officially acknowledging the predominance of Algeria's Berber heritage, (2) making the Berber language a national and official language, and (3) enabling the Tamazight language to reclaim its rightful place in the national educational and cultural spheres.

On the basis of its own logic, this view, which is expressed more in domestic than in international discourse, rejects international intervention in favour of the Berbers and seeks support only for what it presents as a set of civic demands (the el-Kseur Platform) aimed at achieving a genuine democratization of Algeria. Through these demands, which are not limited to cultural and linguistic issues, the civic component of the Berber movement seeks to mobilize all Algerians – particularly those beyond the Kabylie region – for a new societal and political project. In other words, its linguistic and cultural demands are coupled to a general plea for democratization and the establishment of justice, equity, accountability, and security. It accepts the Arabic component of the Algerian nation and state as long as the Berber component is granted equal status.

However, the proponents of this view, which has gained the support and sympathy of Berber- and non-Berber-based parties and associations throughout the country, faces the resistance of the ethnicist faction and the intransigence of the political regime, which has generally not been responsive to calls for genuine reforms.

ESCALATION, DIVISION, AND DEADLOCK

The Berber question in Algeria remains inadequately addressed by all sides – dissidents and government alike. Also, like other major issues that Algeria has faced in recent years, the Berber crisis has stimulated important divisions in the ranks of all of the protagonists. These divisions have contributed to the escalation of the almost daily showdown between Berber militants and state security personnel in the streets of many towns and villages of the Kabylie region. They have also made it extremely difficult even to begin to search of a solution to the conflict.

The Berber movement itself is divided into at least two factions: the radical ethnicist and the civil activist. Furthermore, and despite the legitimacy of its demands on language and democracy, the Citizen Movement of Kabylie has not been able to generate a wide popular mobilization – either beyond the relatively small Berber-speaking region of Kabylie or within the region itself. In fact, by the spring of 2004, the movement had lost some steam, as more and more people had grown indifferent to the cause because of the public display of sharp differences among the leadership and because of the degradation of the quality of life in the cities and towns where street protests were being held almost daily without many results. More important, the movement proved incapable of unanimously articulating a winning discourse and a clear strategy for the realization of its objectives.

The revived *aârouch*, which serve as the legitimizing backbone of the movement, are led by individuals bitterly divided on how to deal with the state's offer of formal negotiations. As mentioned above, the small group of delegates that entered into negotiations with the Prime Minister's Office in 2002 was chastised and harassed by the radical faction. When President Bouteflika, on the eve of the 2002 parliamentary elections, pledged to make Tamazight a national and official language, the movement did not disband but continued to demand the "unconditional and immediate" implementation of the remaining fourteen points of the el-Kseur Platform. Since some of these points are not acceptable to the state (especially point four, which insists on the immediate departure of the Gendarmerie brigades and of all police support from Kabylie), the deadlock is understandable.

This deadlock may last if neither the state nor the Kabylie movement exhibits the minimum flexibility required for a fruitful "dialogue." Without formal representation in the political system, and without a clear, coherent, and unified strategy for attaining its objectives, the protest movement risks being completely taken over by its radical ethnicist faction, which would push to the fore the particularism of the Berberophones of Kabylie and of the region itself. In other words, autonomy or independence will become its only demand.

As for the established Berber-based political parties (RCD and FFS) and associations (MCB), they seem to have lost much of their popular appeal in recent years, a development to which the Kabylie crisis greatly contributed. Each became mired in the dilemma of how to achieve national stature while remaining particularly responsive to its main constituency, the Berberophones of Kabylie. The RCD in particular was discredited for having cooperated with the regime and for not having been at the forefront of the Berber political struggle. As for the FFS, given that its political platform was essentially civic in nature, it was unable to lend tangible support to the Kabylie movement. Furthermore, these two parties and the MCB have become internally divided on how to deal with the Citizen Movement, which, in shunning these organizations, makes them even more irrelevant than they already are in the overall societal struggle for change.

With the crisis continuing to escalate in 2002, and fearing a massive loss of constituents, the RCD and FFS finally decided to pull their elected representatives from Parliament and to boycott the 2002 legislative elections. As these measures do not seem to have affected the Kabylie region's grassroots movement, the two parties have lost both constituent support and representation in state institutions.

As for the state and its leaders, the Berber issue has become a thorny one since the spring of 2001. Government officials have divergent views on a solution to the stand-off. Some do not mind negotiating with the Berber movement's proponents in the interest of accommodation and appeasement. Others believe that, like the Islamist rebellion, the Berber movement must be crushed to prevent it from inspiring other groups in the country and, thereby, threatening national unity.[28] After an initial state crackdown characterized by a violent repression in the spring and summer of 2001, the government decided to minimize direct confrontation with the protesters in Tizi Ouzou and other Kabylie towns.

A series of attempts in the fall of 2001 failed to engage the leadership of the movement in what became known as "dialogue." One of the reasons for this failure was the radical opposition that developed within the movement against those who accepted the government's invitation to dialogue (the "dialoguists") and met with officials.[29] Another reason for the failure was the government's refusal to agree to a key demand before any serious talks could begin: that of the immediate and total removal of the Gendarmerie forces from the Kabylie region. As the movement and the state resisted making any preliminary concessions, the situation in Kabylie worsened. Daily events included street clashes with security forces, violent attacks against garrisons of the Gendarmerie, sit-ins, general strikes, and road blocks with burning tires.

By the end of 2001, the government had arrested scores of protesters, including a large number of the leaders of the Berber movement, most of whom remained in jail for almost a year. They were finally released in the wake of a crisis that had developed between President Bouteflika and his prime minister, Ali Benflis. The latter, a committed reformer whose party, the National Liberation Front, controlled Parliament, ended up being replaced in early May 2003 for reasons of divergences with the president over economic-reform issues and over the possibility that he might challenge Bouteflika in the presidential elections of April 2004. After replacing Benflis with Ahmed Ouyahia (former prime minister and leader of the second most dominant party in Parliament, the National Democratic Rally, RND), the president appeared eager to deal head on with the Kabylie crisis, which, if unresolved, might constitute a serious impediment to his reelection bid. After the release of most Berber militants from jail, Ouyahia and Bouteflika were able to open negotiations with twenty-four *aârch* delegates who formally met with the prime minister on 20 January 2004 to begin looking for a way out of the crisis. However, this first attempt to resolve the crisis failed after just one week of negotiations because the government indicated that the language demands would ultimately have to be settled by way of a national referendum, which the Berber delegates rejected. They wanted the "fulfilment of the Amazigh demand in all its dimensions (as an identity, a civilization, a language, and a culture) without referendum and without conditions, as well as the consecration of Tamazight as a national and official language."[30] Since President Bouteflika is not likely to agree to several points in the el-Kseur Platform, it is difficult to expect a ground-breaking compromise in the near future. However, if he does agree to all points for electoral or other reasons, except for the one related to removing the Gendarmerie, their implementation will not necessarily be automatic, especially if he is removed from office.

CONCLUSION

The Berber movement in Algeria – as in Morocco – is the manifestation of two equally important sets of problems: (1) the suppression of ethnic identifiers and an ethnic language in the definition of an overarching national identity, which remains officially Arab and Islamic; and (2) the combination of economic hardship, authoritarian rule, corruption, and injustice. Regarding the second set of problems, Algerian society has been waging a struggle for many years, as the state has proved incapable of affecting positive change in the lives of most people. At one point, this struggle was mobilized by Islamist forces wishing to overthrow the existing order, to establish an Islamic state, and to consolidate the Arabo-Islamic identity of Algeria. Even though this rebellion failed to attain its objectives, it prompted many changes, the most important being people's realization that they can challenge the existing system and at least extract concessions from it when radical change is not possible.

Today's Berber movement constitutes a continuation of this societal challenge to the existing order but with ethnicity and language as its main instruments of mobilization. Even though this mobilization remains limited to a small area of the country, it nevertheless addresses the two sets of problems mentioned above. As long as the issues of ethnic identity and language are not satisfactorily addressed by the state, they will continue to be potent catalysts for mobilization in response to other persistent problems (e.g., economic disparity, authoritarian rule, corruption, injustice, etc.). When these problems are not addressed and resolved, they continue to stimulate a societal mobilization based on a number of meaningful identifiers (i.e., religion, language, ethnicity, or social class). Throughout the 1990s, Islam was the mobilizing identifier; today it is Tamazight.

The Amazigh language and identity are likely to remain the source of contention between the state and the Berber militants, as they have been for decades, even during times of relative economic prosperity.

Based on other ethno-linguistic movements in recent history, some final observations can be made concerning the Berber movement in Algeria.

First, in a country where the politically and culturally dominant group – which can be ethnically mixed – establishes and maintains national cohesion based on its own cultural dominance, national unity is promoted with the help of an official ideology calling for allegiance to a real or imagined civic state, and this allegiance is enforced with the use of ideological exhortation and force. This has been the policy pursued by Algeria's governing elite since independence. This elite has always included people claiming both Arab and Berber descent. Yet from a cultural and linguist point of view, the official ideology has essentially been Arabist, with the acquiescence of most people.[31]

Second, when an overarching – or hegemonic – definition of nationhood dismisses or ignores important and distinct ethnic and linguistic groups within the country, national unity may be challenged by one or more of these groups as soon as problems arise in areas such as the distribution of economic resources, the configuration of political power, and the determination of cultural and linguistic identifiers for the whole country. The challenge can also occur in the wake of political liberalization, which can make it possible for previously repressed ethnic groups to mobilize and openly articulate cultural and political demands. In Algeria the Kabylie Berbers have been the most important ethnic and linguistic group formally ignored and even repressed by the ruling elite for fear of national disintegration. When there were no major problems or disputes over other issues, the state and its Arabo-Berber elite exercised a hegemonic determination of national identity without major challenge. Berber militants were few, and most of them resided in France. However, when serious problems arose in the distribution of economic resources, in the configuration of power, and in personal security, some elements of society used primordial identifiers to mobilize people behind cultural and civic demands and even behind the push for a comprehensive regime change. For the Islamists this primordial identifier was Islam; for the Berbers it is ethnicity.

Third, when an emerging modern state tries to create a new collective identity that is above primordial attachments and identifiers, it may face the resistance of social and cultural subgroups that fear either losing their particular identity within a larger, culturally undifferentiated group or being dominated by another group.[32] Members of subgroups can also resist becoming subjects of a political system that they neither accept nor identify with. In the worst-case scenario, this resistance may degenerate into a nationalist drive aimed at achieving autonomy or secession, for ethnic groups tend to be persistent, challenging, and capable of a degree of political mobilization that can undermine the state.[33] The Algerian political system, which does not have a tradition of civic politics and has been unable to respond adequately to secular, religious, and ethnic challenges, may experience a new crisis that is likely to be destabilizing for the whole country. Because the Kabylie crisis is about more than ethnic and linguistic issues, its solution lies in addressing most of the points of the el-Kseur Platform and more.

If Algeria's ruling elite wishes to go beyond a survival strategy in dealing with the crisis prompted by the Berber challenge, it must pave the way for a new social contract between state and society that honours the ethnic and linguistic diversity of the country as well as people's yearning for justice, fairness, economic opportunities, and genuine representation in institutions empowered to make public policy. If this happens, it will usher in a democratic transition, but no one expects the process to be easy.

However, if the regime opts for a full-scale repression of the challengers, it may push the protest movement underground and encourage its radical faction to turn a relatively peaceful struggle into an armed rebellion, as happened with the Islamist opposition in 1992. The Berber movement will then be able to strengthen its case at the international level by presenting itself as a persecuted minority pushed into an armed struggle for autonomous status within Algeria or for a state of its own.

Because Algeria's rulers are aware of the possibility of this dreadful scenario, they may try to continue to isolate the Berber movement while allowing it to vent its grievances and demands in a limited number of towns in the Kabylie region. At the same time, they may continue to discredit the movement, portraying it as a divisive ethnic campaign seeking the disintegration of Algeria. This policy will fail to end the Berber challenge, especially if the problems with the regime, the economy, and injustice remain unresolved. What today appears to be an overwhelmingly social movement for inclusion and substantial change in state-society relations may turn into a nationalist movement whereby one part of Algeria chooses to opt out of a state that it perceives as unresponsive to its needs and as a failed institution altogether.

In situations characterized by ethnic or nationalist mobilization, denial and repression may lead to the hardening of positions and a worsening of the conflict. Since there is no explicit demand from the ethnic movement for a separate destiny, a solution to the conflict may be found in genuine processes of political liberalization and democratization. However, democratization can stimulate further ethnic mobilization and nationalism; thus the overall political system must first be readied to accommodate the demands occasioned by people's freedom to organize, to express themselves, and to seek accountability from their leaders. "Uncontrolled conflict is more likely when mass participation increases before civic institutions have been extensively developed."[34] In a country experiencing newly found political liberalization – albeit limited and imperfect – the rising demand for participation must be met with the institutionalization required to channel it peacefully. In Algeria, which lacks both a civic tradition and a functioning institutional framework, conflict can become endemic if the demands for institutionalization and inclusion are not seriously and immediately addressed.

APPENDIX: SUMMARY OF THE EL-KSEUR
PLATFORM OF JUNE 2001

1 State assistance for all those injured in the repression and for the families of those martyred.
2 Trial by civil courts of all individuals who ordered and committed crimes against civilians and their expulsion from the ranks of the security forces and from public-service functions.
3 Bestowal of the status of martyr on every victim and the protection of witnesses.
4 The immediate departure of the Gendarmerie brigades and of all police support from the Kabylie region.
5 The cancellation of judicial proceedings against all demonstrators.
6 The immediate end of all punitive expeditions against the population.
7 The dissolution of the investigation commissions created by the state.
8 The unconditional proclamation, without referendum, of Tamazight as a national and official language.
9 State guarantees of all socio-economic rights and all democratic liberties.
10 Opposition to the politics of underdevelopment, which have lead to the impoverishment of the Algerian people.
11 The placement of all executive state functions, as well as the security corps, under the effective control of democratically elected institutions.
12 An urgent program of socio-economic development for the Kabylie region.
13 Actions against *hogra* (i.e., the abuse of power and disdain for the people).
14 An unemployment compensation equal to 50 per cent of the guaranteed national minimum wage for all individuals seeking employment.
15 Reform of the examination system used in schools.

NOTES

1 "Nationalism," or nationalist sentiment, is generally understood as the spirit of belonging together as a nation and the desire to institutionalize

this nation as a nation-state. "Patriotism" involves affection for one's country, loyalty to its institutions, and a zeal and readiness to defend them.
2 Benedict Anderson, *Imagined Communities*. Anderson defines a nation as "an imagined community which is inherently limited and sovereign" (5). This definition is adapted here to the Berber ethnicity, which is imagined and limited but not sovereign.
3 The expressions "politicization of ethnicity" and "ethnicization of politics" are borrowed from Ralph D. Grillo, ed., *"Nation" and "State" in Europe*, 7, and adapted for this study. In Grillo's writing, the two expressions deal with nation and nationalism, while the Berber case study is limited to ethnicity (a pre-national stage). For Grillo, nationalism can result from two processes: (1) the "politicization of ethnicity," whereby an ethnic group becomes politically mobilized and seeks statehood; and (2) the "ethnicization of the polity," whereby the state creates a nation from heterogeneous elements and attributes to it a specific ethnic identity.
4 Graham E. Fuller, "Redrawing the World's Borders," 15.
5 Ali Guenoun, *Chronology du movement berber*, 10.
6 For more on the 1949 crisis and the birth of Berber culturalism in the nationalist movement, see Mohammed Harbi, *L'Algérie et son destin*.
7 Guenoun, *Chronology du movement berber*, 23, my translations.
8 The Algerian dialect is the product of the fermentation over many centuries of a combination of words and expressions borrowed from the many cultures that affected the region throughout history (i.e., the Berber, Arabic, Turkish, French, Spanish, Portuguese, Italian, and African languages).
9 Maya Shatzmiller, *The Berbers and the Islamic State*, 15–27.
10 Charles-André Julien, *Histoire de l'Afrique du Nord: Tunisie, Algérie, Maroc: Des Origines à la Conquête Arabe*, 647 ap. J.-C., 50, my translation.
11 These include the current prime minister, Ahmed Ouyahia, and his predecessor, Mohamed Benflis, as well as the top military leader, Mohamed Lamari.
12 The French policy of "divide and rule" was also reflected in the Berber *dahir* (edict) of 1930, through which colonial France tried to exempt Berberophone Moroccans from Islamic jurisprudence in order to set them apart from the Arabophones. However, the Berberophones rejected this decree and continued to resist the colonizer.
13 Salim Chaker, *Imazighen Ass-A*, 104, my translation.
14 Salim Chaker, "More Than A Suggestion, A Necessity!" *Le Matin* (Algiers), 14 October 2001, www.AmazighWorld.org, translated by the World Amazigh Action Coalition (WAAC) with my modifications.

15 Clifford Geertz, "Primordial and Civic Ties," 31; for the full text, see Geertz, "The Integrative Revolution," 107–13.
16 Anthony D. Smith, "The Formation of National Identity," 133.
17 Michael Ignatieff, *Blood and Belonging: Journeys into the New Nationalism*, 4, cited in Eric Garcetti, "Civic and Ethnic Allegiances: Competing Visions of Nationalist Discourse in the Horn of Africa."
18 Ignatieff, *Blood and Belonging*, 6.
19 Walter Connor, "A Nation is a Nation, is a State, is an Ethnic Group, is a …"
20 Anthony D., Smith, *The Ethnic Origins of Nations,* 91, 207, 216.
21 Ibid.
22 Geertz, "Primordial and Civic Ties," 30.
23 Ignatieff, *Blood and Belonging*, 6.
24 Geertz, "Primordial and Civic Ties," 30.
25 Ibid.
26 "Arabism," which is referred to in the popular political language as "Islamo-Baâthism," names an ideology that is both Muslim conservative and Arab nationalist. This ideology and the people who hold it are thought to be opposed to secular and ethnically distinct groups within the Arab world. Arabists include individuals of both Arab and Berber descent. The Arabist elite is attached to the Arab identity and language and to Algeria's historical and cultural ties with the Arab world.
27 Chaker, "More Than A Suggestion, A Necessity!" translated by WAAC with my modifications.
28 This view was also shared by Mahfoud Nahnah, the former leader of the moderate Islamist party, the Movement of Society for Peace (MSP), which was part of the governing coalition in Parliament. He died in 2003.
29 The antidialogue faction within the Berber movement is known as the Mechtras group. In January 2004 it accused the "dialoguists" of capitulating to and compromising with a state authority that has killed innocent civilians.
30 Point 8 of the el-Kseur Platform, my translation.
31 For example, in the early 1970s the Arabization movement, which supported the generalized use of the Arabic language, included many people from the Kabylie region whose first language was Berber but who believed that the national language should be Arabic and that the national culture should be Arab. These individuals were then actively involved in recruiting others to the Arabization cause.
32 Geertz, "Primordial and Civic Ties," 30.

33 Michael Freeman, "Theories of Ethnicity, Tribalism and Nationalism," 18.
34 Jack Snyder, *From Voting to Violence: Democratization and Nationalist Conflict*, 310.

9

Kurdish Nationalism in Turkey[1]

M. HAKAN YAVUZ

The construction and politicization of Kurdish ethno-nationalism in Turkey evolved in five stages,[2] with state policies, intra-Kurdish dynamics, and international factors (i.e., institutions) playing a determinant role. The major reason for the initial politicization of Kurdish cultural identity was a shift from the multiethnic, multicultural realities of the Ottoman Empire to the nation-state model, which occurred in the nineteenth century when the empire decided to *govern* rather than simply *rule*.[3]

The Ottoman Empire's attempts at centralization introduced the question of governance, creating a conflict between local power structures and the state. Modernization's expansion of the Turkish state's capacity to govern facilitated the politicization of Kurdish ethnicity. I refer here to what Michael Mann defines as "the capacity of the state actually to penetrate civil society, and to implement logistically political decisions throughout the realm."[4] This expansion of state power was accompanied by a series of reforms intended to modernize society while creating a new national identity and sense of loyalty to the state. In particular, these reforms favoured a Turkish nationalism since the reformist state elite aligned themselves with Turkism and with Turkish nationalist groups. The reformist project included mandatory military service; a uniform legal system, which likely undermined the traditional power structure; primary education; a new communication infrastructure; and efforts to homogenize national culture and identity. Under the Ottoman system, some Kurdish tribes paid their taxes, sent their sons to the army, and in turn maintained a degree of autonomy in governing their own domestic affairs. The centralized state sought to demolish these arrangements by building a new system that would exert state authority and free ordinary Kurds from the pressures of tribal chiefs. In multiethnic states, state building often accompanies the nation-building process, which is based on policies that tend to exclude those groups that resist assimilation. This tendency, in turn, deepens the grievances of a state's ethnic groups, causing them eventually to evolve into ethno-political movements. In short, the assimilation policies of the Turkish state both molded the Kurdish conception of "self" and prompted strategies to protect this Kurdish "self" from the dominant Turkish "other."

Geographic conditions and traditional tribal loyalties helped Kurdish people to maintain and reproduce their culture. The rural villages dispersed throughout the Kurdish region comprised separate, small communities, preventing the Kurds from developing a wider sense of ethnicity. With centralization and economic development, the Kurds were forced into closer contact with the Turks and the state, resulting in their acculturation and assimilation, which in turn politicized the Kurdish identity. In the early days of the republic, many people expected the emergence of a new Turk, or a "modified Kurd," within the Turkish-centric culture. However, rather than bringing about the death of Kurdish identity and culture, modernization led to the Kurds' adaptation of Turkish culture through imitation and acculturation. That is, the Kurds mimicked Turkish identity but did not internalize it.

The relatively successful modernization project of President Mustafa Kemal Atatük (1923–38), which affected education, urbanization, and communication, not only created regional differences, but also helped to create a conscious Kurdish ethnic elite – two outcomes that directly motivated the mobilization of a Kurdish nationalist movement in Turkey.[5] In the context of regional economic disparity, loyalty to Kurdish ethnic identity gave rise to Kurdish nationalism. The Kemalist reforms, which aimed to "civilize" the people of Turkey in order to create a secular nation-state, resulted in the construction of Kurdish ethno-nationalism. The introduction of modern communication technology and political liberalization in the 1980s served as catalysts for the political articulation of Kurdish identity. Ethnically politicized Kurdish intellectuals functioned as "ethnic entrepreneurs" in Turkey by interpreting all present and past events in a manner intended to historicize and legitimize Kurdish nationalism.[6]

This chapter identifies the dominant factors in the evolution of Kurdish identity during five historical stages. The first stage (1878–1924) is marked by the centralization policies of the Ottoman state in the nineteenth century. In response to these policies and to the penetration of European capitalism, local Islamic networks were politicized and mobilized. Of particular significance during this stage were the roles of the Nakşibendi and Kadiri Sufi orders in organizing resistance against the centralization of the Ottoman Empire and in encouraging Kurdish identity formation.[7] The second stage (1925–61) is characterized by the socio-political consequences of the transformation of the multiethnic Ottoman entity into a new "nation-state" and by the reaction of the Kurdish tribes to the nation-building project of Mustafa Kemal.[8] These anticentralization rebels demanded the maintenance of autonomous tribal structures, a stand that helped in the articulation of Kurdish proto-nationalism. The discourse of the new republican ideology of Mustafa Kemal either denied the existence of the Kurds or reconstructed political language in order to talk about the issue without using the term "Kurds." As a part of the radical nation-building reforms, traditional Kurdish identity and culture were constructed as "reactionary," "tribal," and an outcome of regional "backwardness." The third stage (1962–83) is defined by the secularization of Kurdish identity within the framework of the broader leftist movement in Turkey between the 1960s and 1970s. The fourth stage (1983–98) spans the period of violent insurgency lead by the Kurdistan Workers' Party (PKK). The arrest of Abdullah Öcalan, the head of the PKK in 1999, represents the cusp of a still emerging fifth stage, in which some accommodation is possible between divergent Turkish and Kurdish aspirations. (It should be noted that the divisions among Turks on the roles of culture and identity are as serious as the divisions among the Kurds in Turkey.) This final stage started with the question of Turkey's candidacy for admission to the European Union (EU) and the Europeanization of the Kurdish issue in Turkey. As long as the Kurdish problems exist, Turkey will be crippled both inside and outside – doomed to live with the wear and tear of constant international criticism.

THE FRAGMENTATION OF KURDISH IDENTITY

There is a growing tendency to analyze Kurdish nationalism as a "natural" force.[9] One needs to remind policy makers that nationalism, whether Turkish or Kurdish, is always constructed by "identity entrepreneurs" and shaped by political context. The major difference between Turkish and Kurdish nationalism derives from the state's role in the formation of each. Whereas the modernizing nation-state formed the Turkish nation and nationalism, stressing the nation's civic aspect, Kurdish nationalism in Turkey, Iraq, and Iran evolved in response to modernizing nation-states, constantly stressing its ethnic "difference" and sometimes even evoking racism to historicize itself. According to Anthony D. Smith, a group must qualify as an *ethnie* (i.e., share a collective name, a myth of descent, a history and culture, a specific territory, and a sense of solidarity) if it is to form a nation.[10] The Kurdish *ethnie* gave rise to modern Kurdish nationalism, which is based on common ethnic roots, shared myths, and collective memories and values. Kurdish nationalism is an outcome of the tension between the state's efforts to achieve national homogenization and the Kurds' struggle to maintain their cultural and local autonomy. This tension is at the core of the politicization of the Kurdish culture.

Although Kurdish "ethnic entrepreneurs" tend to identify Turks as their "other" in the construction of Kurdish nationalism, there are major tribal, linguistic, religious, alphabetical,[11] and regional fissures within Kurdish identity itself. The sources of these divisions are socio-historical and prevent the emergence of a full-fledged Kurdish identity. Kurdish life was tribally structured and based on tightly knit rural communities under a tribal or religious leader, known as an *ağa, şeyh, seyyid,* or *molla*.[12] The tribes, also known as *asiret*s in Turkish, are kinship-based, territorially oriented, and religiously shaped solidarity groups. The Nakşibendi and Kadiri Sufi orders, which are led by a *şeyh,* have been utilized to integrate different Turkish or Arab groups into larger *asiret*s. In many cases, since the *ağa* is also the head of the Sufi order, he exercises a dual authority over his tribe. This tribal structure served two purposes: It prevented the formation of Kurdish unity by keeping the Kurds fragmented, and it preserved a heightened Kurdish particularism vis-à-vis the Turks, Persians, and Arabs. Tribal structure constituted the core repository of Kurdish identity and facilitated mobilization against centralizing governments. Moreover, it prevented the formation of a modern conception of nationalism until the mid-twentieth century. In other words, allegiances among the Kurdish tribes are fluid, and their separation is a constant feature. The Turkish state pursued three competing policies: (1) a policy of assimilation by breaking down tribal structure, which usually resulted in armed rebellion; (2) a policy of cooptating tribal leaders with the aim of controlling these unruly regions; and (3) a policy of "divide and rule," using one tribe against another.

In addition to tribal structure, geography is also a source of the fragmentation of Kurdish identity. Although the Kurds are a "nation" in formation at the crossroads of the Persian, Arab, and Turkish worlds, natural boundaries have afforded the Kurdish tribes a high degree of autonomy. In the borderland between the Persian and Ottoman Empires, there was a loose connection among the Kurdish tribes as well as between the centre and the subregions. But most Kurds live in extremely rugged, mountainous terrain, which not only isolates them from the Arabs, Persians, and Turks, but also separates each community from the others. These rugged geographic conditions have been a major impediment to the formation of Kurdish unity. Due to tribal structure and geographic conditions, diverse Kurdish dialects dominate the region, and subethnic identities are more powerful than Kurdish consciousness. No clan has ever wanted to see a rival clan succeed in leading Kurdish movements, and the central governments have never hesitated to use one tribe against another. Even Saddam Hussein's campaign against the Kurds in northern Iraq, for instance, could not overcome this fragmentation.[13] Due to the centralization policies of the Ottoman state and the reforms of Mustafa Kemal, the least tribal and most politicized Kurds are those living in Turkey. However, even in Turkey, conflicting religious (Sunni vs. Alevi), linguistic (Kirmanji vs. Zaza), regional (west vs. east), and class identities compete with a larger Kurdish identity.[14]

In the formation of modern Kurdish identity in Turkey, the confrontation between religious and secular forces plays an important role. Religious loyalties used to be more powerful among the Sunni Kurds.[15] For instance, some tribal chiefs claim to be *seyyids*, whose genealogy can be traced to the family of the Prophet Muhammad, in order to justify their worldly power with religious qualifications. Islam has been both a unifying and dividing force among the Kurds. The religious divide between Sunni and Alevi Kurds has played a key role in preventing Kurdish unity, forming the basis for different political trends within the Kurdish movement. For instance, Alevi Kurds strongly supported the reforms of Mustafa Kemal and became the incubator of leftist ideology in Turkey, whereas the Sunni Kurds supported the anti-Kemalist Islamic movement of Necmettin Erbakan.[16] The gradual emancipation of the Alevis became a reality as a result of the reforms of Mustafa Kemal. In examining the evolution and politicization of Kurdish ethno-nationalism in Turkey, one must stress the socio-political process of uncoupling Islam and Kurdish nationalism as well as the social forces that simultaneously unify and fragment Kurdish identity.[17]

STAGE ONE: ANTICENTRALIZATION REVOLTS AND THE POLITICIZATION OF ISLAMIC IDENTITY, 1878–1924

During the Ottoman period, ethnic identity had very little political significance. Religious identity shaped political loyalty. Attempts at centralization during the nineteenth century politicized peripheral ethnic and religious identities. Most of the Kurdish tribal revolts against the central government resulted from tribal reactions to the intrusive and centralizing modernization policies of the Ottoman state and the Republic of Turkey. By monopolizing the use of violence and education, these policies threatened tribal autonomy and the interests of the *ağa* or *seyyid*. Some of these tribes resisted the extension of the rule of law in this region because it aimed at ending their feudal tyranny over the local people. Thus one should be extremely cautious when attributing Kurdish nationalist motives to these tribes' anticentralizing revolts. Indeed, to carry out the centralization policies, the Ottoman imperial order of 1846 created the first Kurdish province, granting it special status and autonomy. This province existed until 1867, when it was replaced by Diyarbakır Province. The geographic boundaries of the first Kurdish province were used in the 1919 Paris Peace Conference to make a case for a Kurdish homeland.[18]

The centralization of the Ottoman Empire was intended to destroy tribal ties and coalitions. This threat, in turn, reactivated the Nakşibendi and Kadiri Sufi orders and led to the emergence of the *şeyh* as an intermediary in the conflicts between diverse Kurdish tribes and even between the centralizing state and the tribal networks. In other words, the erosion of tribal ties enhanced Sufi networks and politicized Islamic identity. Kurdish ethnic awareness evolved within the framework of Islamic consciousness. In the anticentralization movements, Nakşibendi Sufi networks played a pivotal role, replacing the more aristocratic Kadiri orders. The first proto-religio-ethnic rebellion took place in 1880 under şeyh Ubeydullah (d. 1883), a local religious leader, in reaction to the centralizing policies of Sultan Abdulhamid II (1878–1909). After putting this religio-tribal rebellion down, Sultan Abdulhamid II formed the Hamidiye Regiments from various Kurdish tribes to counter Russian-backed Armenian nationalism in eastern Anatolia. The officers and recruits of the Hamidiye Regiments played an unforseen role in the constitution of Kurdish nationalism. For instance, some of the officers of the Hamidiye units "helped Mustafa Kemal to regain independence for modern Turkey, and ... the Kurdish nationalist party, Azadi [Freedom; established in 1923], also drew its membership" from these units.[19]

In the nineteenth century, the centralization policies of the Ottoman regime succeeded in weakening tribal structures but did not eliminate them. Moreover, these policies resulted in the politicization of Islamic networks. However, the close ties between Islam and Kurdish nationalism did not continue to develop. By comparison, Islam has always played an important role in the vernacularization of Turkish nationalism, which is essentially based on the cosmology of Islam and its conception of community. Although Turkey is a national and secular state, religion lies at the core of its identity debate and political landscape. The patterns of collective action, the meaning of justice, and the organizational networks in Turkey are very much informed by Islamic practices and organizations.

STAGE TWO: NATIONAL SECULARIZATION, 1925–61

Ethno-linguistic groups in the Ottoman state were classified on the basis not of ethnicity but of religion. Within the religious groups, diverse ethno-linguistic communities existed. The loss of this cosmopolitan character of the empire, together with vast chunks of territory in the Balkans and the Middle East, left its imprint on Turkish political culture. The weakening and partitioning of the Ottoman Empire by the European colonial powers left deep scars on the collective memory of Turks. During and after the First World War,

Kurdish cultural committees were formed in major Kurdish cities.[20] As a result of this political mobilization and British support for an independent Kurdish state, Şerif Paşa presented the Kurdish case at subsequent international conferences. The 1920 Sevres Treaty, which constitutes the Kemalist state discourse on identifying internal and external enemies, created "local autonomy for the land where the Kurd element predominates" (Arts. 62–4). Although never put into practice, the Sevres Treaty remains part of the collective memory of the Turkish state. Fear of partition still haunts Turkish society and breeds continuing suspicion of foreigners and their "sinister" domestic collaborators.

Before the First World War, many European powers became the defenders of certain minorities and used "minority rights" to get more concessions from the state. During the First World War, the Ottoman Empire was partitioned, and the heartland of the empire, Anatolia and Rumelia, was occupied. As a result of the First World War and the Turko-Greek War, which lasted from 1919 to 1922, there were few non-Muslim peoples left in Anatolia. The majority of Turkey's Armenians were deported to Syria and Mesopotamia in 1915 so that they would not side with advancing Russian troops and declare independence in the eastern part of the empire. The remaining Orthodox Greek population, who had not fled after the Turko-Greek War, was exchanged for Muslims in Greece according to the Lausanne Treaty of 1923. The Ottoman Empire's transformation from a multicultural, cosmopolitan entity into the Republic of Turkey resulted in the promotion of a homogenous, secular nationalism that did not tolerate diversity but required all inhabitants to become Turks.

Due to the Ottoman legacy, the Republic of Turkey has embodied an irresolvable paradox since its founding in the 1920s. On the one hand, the state defined its "progressive" civilizing ideology, known as Kemalism, in opposition to Islam, calling upon the men and women of Turkey to participate in a *jihad* against the occupying European armies in order to liberate their homeland and caliphate. On the other hand, the state was formed through demographic Islamization of the country, with Islam being used to unify diverse ethno-linguistic groups. In the Treaty of Lausanne, the state stressed the common religious identity of Turks as Muslims and referred to non-Muslims as a "minority."[21] Instead of accepting ethnicity as the basis for its nationalism, Turkey favoured religio-territorial identity. The cohesive force in the establishment of the Republic of Turkey was Islamic identity, which consists of religious devotion and ritual practices as well as a set of historically based socio-political roles and schematic means of demarcating the significance of events, experiences, and objects. Turkish national identity was modelled on the Islamic conception of community and disseminated through Islamic terms. Incorporating religious vocabulary into the nationalist vocabulary in order to vernacularize and disseminate national identity – such as *millet* (which refers to a religious community in the Ottoman Empire and was appropriated by the republic to mean "nation"), *vatan* (homeland), *gazi* (which refers to those who fought in the name of Islam and became the title of Mustafa Kemal), and *şehid* (those who die for the protection and dissemination of Islam) – also had the effect of nationalizing Islamic identity. Islam remained imbedded both in the definition of the Turkish identity and in the construction of the external boundaries of the Turkish national identity and continued, for the most part, to form the hidden identity of the Turkish state.

After the 1925 Sheik Said Rebellion against the new republic, the nation-building process was intensified.[22] Once again the caliphate, which had been abolished in 1924, came to represent an Islam-sanctioned union of multiethnic groups. The caliphate recognized ethnic diversity without assigning ethnicity any political role. In other words, it symbolized a multiethnic polity and authority and the unity of Muslims as a faith-based community, allowing space for diverse loyalties and permitting local autonomy for the periphery. The aim of the 1925 rebellion was to preserve the region's religiously sanctioned religio-tribal structure. The rebellion used Islamic networks and identity to expand its social base and thereby gain the support of other antisecularist Sunni Turks.

Sheik Said (1865–1925), of the Nakşibendi Sufi order, was initially successful and even controlled the areas surrounding Diyarbakır and Elazığ. However, tribal rivalries and religious divisions prevented full Kurdish participation. Although the Turkish army captured Sheik Said and hanged him in Diyarbakır, his rebellion, the first ethno-religious uprising, made the Turkish republic very suspicious of any form of Kurdish activity. In October 1927 a group of Kurdish tribal leaders and intellectuals formed the Kurdish National League (Hoyboun) under the leadership of İhsan Nuri Paşa of Bitlis, a successful Ottoman general. This group organized the revolt of Ağrı (Ararat)

Mountain between 1930 and 1931. The Turkish army had difficulty putting the rebellion down in its early stages due to the superior arms the rebels had received from outside. Eventually, however, the Kurdish rebellion was defeated, and İhsan Paşa took refuge in Iran. In order to establish law and order in the region, the 1934 Law organized a selective deportation, exiling some Kurdish tribal chiefs to western Turkey. The state's assimilationist policies triggered a new revolt in and around the mountainous areas of Dersim, which are inhabited mostly by the Alevi Kurds, known as Zazas, in 1937-38.[23] After suppressing the rebellion, during which several key military posts were attacked and hundreds of soldiers were killed, the Turkish state erased Dersim from the map, renaming it Tunceli.

These three rebellions against the young and inexperienced republic created a cumulative image of the people of the region as socially tribal, religiously fanatic, economically backward, and most important, a threat to the national integrity of the Republic of Turkey. The state's framing of Kurdish resistance sought to legitimize these claims and to justify state domination of the Kurdish community. In other words, Kemalist state discourse on the Kurdish issue evolved in response to these rebellions. The state became more committed to its policies of creating a secular Turkish nation. Thus one needs to take these rebellions into account in explaining the state's representation of the Kurdish question. The republic did not deny the existence of the Kurds but rather developed a new discourse to speak about them without using the term "Kurd" in the ethno-national sense. By constructing the Kurdish tribal structure as "reactionary, backward, and dangerous," the Turkish republic constructed itself as modern, secular, and progressive. After the rebellions, politicized Sunni Islam evolved as a surrogate Kurdish identity in southeastern Anatolia. For instance, the Islamist National Outlook Movement of Necmettin Erbakan remained a powerful force among the Sunni Kurds until the 1995 elections.[24]

After 1925 the multiple identities that had prevailed during the Ottoman period officially coalesced into a secular ethnic Turkish nationalism. The historians of the Kemalist period and the official Turkish Historical and Language Society redefined identity in terms of ethnicity and language. The state used the army, education, media, and art to consolidate Turkish national identity and attempted to diminish the role of Islam and its Ottoman legacy. Nevertheless, during the formative Kemalist period (1922-50), two versions of nationalism actually competed: secular linguistic nationalism and ethno-religious communal nationalism.

Nationalism and secularism constituted the core of the Kemalist ideology in Turkey. The Kemalist project of secularism aimed to "civilize" the cultural and social domains of the nation. Although nationalism presupposes the creation of an ethnically homogenous society at the expense of other identities, "race" never became a factor in one's being a Turk; rather, being a citizen of the Republic of Turkey (i.e., civicness) was the foundation of the Kemalist nationalism. The 1924 Constitution provides: "Without religious and ethnic difference, every person of the people of Turkey who is a citizen is regarded as a Turk."[25] Being a Turk is defined in terms of legal ties with the state. This definition reflects the legacy of the Ottoman Empire – everyone with Ottoman citizenship was considered Ottoman. One sees the gradual ethnification of the term "Turk" in the 1961 and 1982 Constitutions. The 1961 Constitution removes "the people of Turkey" (*Türkiye ahalisi*) and provides that every citizen is "accepted as a Turk regardless of ethnic and religious identity." Under Article 66 of the 1982 Constitution, everyone related to the Republic of Turkey through citizenship is a Turk. In modern Turkey the term "Turkish nation" includes all Turkish citizens whatever their ethnic roots. Turkish citizens of Kurdish origin represent a new conceptualization that has been put into use in response to European pressures.

STAGE THREE: SECULARIZATION OF THE KURDISH QUESTION THROUGH SOCIALISM, 1961–83

The secularization and transformation of Kurdish identity took place within the broader leftist movement in Turkey in the 1960s and 1970s. This secularization of Kurdish identity took place as a result of interactions with socialist ideology. Alevi Kurds played a critical role in this process of secularization. With the spread of universal education and the socio-political liberalization that resulted from the 1961 Constitution, new modern intellectuals rather than tribal and religious leaders started to shape Kurdish identity. Under the 1961 Constitution, Kurdish intellectuals expressed Kurdish concerns and grievances in socialist idioms to promote the self-determination of the Kurds. The Kurds, particularly the Alevi Kurds, dominated Turkey's left-wing movement in the 1970s. Between 1965 and 1968, the bilingual Turkish-Kurdish *Dicle-Firat* and *Deng* magazines were published. In the late 1960s the Kurdish identity question was expressed in terms of regional economic inequalities, and a socialist solution was suggested.[26] At its Fourth National Congress, the Labour Party of Turkey passed a resolution acknowledging that "there is a Kurdish people in the East of Turkey." The goal of this statement was to carve a socialist base for the Labour Party by using the ethnic card. In the 1970s leftist groups and identities were used to challenge the "central political authority" in Ankara. Criticism of the centre was the major unifying force of the leftist movement.

Another major development was the establishment of the Revolutionary Cultural Society of the East (DDKO) in 1969, the first organizational attempt to raise the consciousness of the Kurdish population by stressing the uneven economic development within regions of the country. The leftist movement in Turkey always tried to expand its base by stressing Alevi and Kurdish issues. Between 1969 and 1971, the DDKO organized regular teach-ins to raise Kurdish consciousness throughout Turkey. Abdullah Öcalan took part in DDKO activities and established connections with other students when he was in Istanbul in 1970.[27] The DDKO blended Marxism and Kurdish nationalism to mobilize youth in the name of social justice and identity.[28] Some leaders of the DDKO were active members of the Turkish Labour Party. With the 1971 coup – in which the army seized power from Prime Minister Süleyman Demirel, leaving the country under the leadership of a supraparty Cabinet until the elections of 1973 – the Labour Party and the DDKO were outlawed. Although ex-members of the DDKO tried to revive the organization in 1974 under the Revolutionary Democratic Cultural Association (DDKD), they were unable to create a unified Kurdish body due to ideological, regional, and personal rivalries. In the 1970s the Kurdish nationalists started to challenge the Kemalist view. In 1979 a Cabinet minister, Serafettin Elçi, caused a scandal by openly declaring himself a Kurd. After the 1980 coup – in which the generals again removed Prime Minister Demirel from power, directly ruling the country until 1983 – the state identified Kurdish nationalism, along with radical Islam and the left, as a divisive force and banned all forms of Kurdish cultural expression.

One of the key goals of the 1980 coup was control of the centrifugal forces of Kurdish and religious movements.[29] The coup used oppressive measures to destroy the organizational power of Kurdish networks within Turkey. It jailed many Kurdish activists, some of whom took refuge in Europe, where they formed the core of a transnational Kurdish activism. But the oppression of the 1980 coup had the opposite impact from that intended: It further politicized and strengthened the Kurdish sense of identity, an outcome exploited by the PKK. The policies of the Turkish military and regional developments in Iraq and Iran further consolidated Kurdish separatism, and the PKK launched an armed uprising to defeat the Turkish state in 1984.[30] No Kurdish organization captured the minds and resources of the Kurds as successfully as the PKK. Yet there is no single sociological study of this organization.[31] Peasant tribes and religious Kurds were the least ethnic-conscious sector of the population, reflecting a view of state-society relations rooted instead in the idea of an *umma* (Islamic community). They established a sense of *difference* from Ankara by utilizing the Islamic idiom associated with Shafi'i (one of the four jurisprudence schools of Sunni Islam). Tribes stress Islam because it does not negate tribal identities and offers a common space for communication and interaction. By comparison, the newly created suburbs of Diyarbakır, Istanbul, and Ankara, where peasants are cut off from traditional ties, became centres of a nationalist, rather than Islamic, Kurdish identity.

In the late 1990s, Kurdish nationalism was still "in formation" and composed of different heterogeneous groups. In the formation of this new politicized Kurdish identity, class questions have been perceived in national (Kurdish) terms. Kurdish nationalism offered a space within which class and regional differences could be suppressed. In short, it was the PKK that ended the mutually constitutive relationship between Islam, tribe, and nationalism in favour of the latter.

STAGE FOUR:
THE EMERGENCE OF THE KURDISTAN
WORKERS' PARTY (PKK), 1983–99

Kurdish nationalists have employed "repertoires of violence" ranging from the PKK-led terror campaign to the establishment of mainly Kurdish parties and the struggle for cultural and political rights. Many Turks feel that exclusion and racism are problems of individual bigotry and hatred, while the Kurds often understand it as an intricate web of individual attitudes and cultural messages about marginalized Kurds. The Kurdish perception of Turkey's socio-political realities is filtered through this new Kurdish nationalism.

The PKK played a critical role in raising Kurdish political consciousness by establishing a web of networks inside and outside Turkey to recruit militants and by undermining the religio-tribal structure of the region via new opportunities for the middle class and urbanized Kurdish youth. At the same time, one of the most important unexpected outcomes of the PKK terror campaign was the deepening politicization of Turkish nationalism.[32] As a result of the PKK's campaign against all walks of Turkish life, the issue of Turkish nationalism became popularized among Turks and was articulated at almost all Turkish public gatherings. In response to this assertive Turkish nationalism, the PKK's activities encouraged Kurds to criticize not the "political authority" in Ankara but Turkish nationalism as a construct in order to legitimize their own separatist nationalism. This shift from being critical of the state power to being critical of Turkish nationalism marked a turning point in the separation of Kurdish nationalism and the leftist movement of Turkey.

As a result of a centralized education system, urbanization, and population displacement, a new wave of Kurdish youth came to major cities to study or work. This became the movement of first-generation Kurdish university students, who had doubts about finding jobs and encountered a new socio-economic life in the cities with very few opportunities to share the benefits of the cities' expanding urban life. The PKK targeted these "displaced" and "semi-intellectual university students," offering them identity (Kurdish nationalism) and commitment to justice (a socialist economic order). During this disintegration of the social fabric as a result of major social transformation in the 1970s, the PKK presented itself as a "liberation movement" and voiced the desire to restore Kurdish identity and justice by violent means. The 1980 coup and its oppressiveness helped to create a siege mentality among the Kurds, compelling them to think that their future was constrained by the Turkish state. They had two options: (1) move to Europe as political refugees and search for a new life or (2) join the PKK to fight against the Turkish state. The PKK became more popular as the oppression of the military coup increased.

The PKK remained under the autocratic leadership of Abdullah Öcalan, who was born the son of an impoverished Kurdish farmer in 1948 in a village in Urfa. Öcalan studied political science in the prestigious Faculty of Political Science at Ankara University in 1971. Due to his involvement in an underground leftist movement, he was arrested in 1972 and spent seven months in a military prison in

Ankara. He did not graduate from the university. By 1973 he had organized a Marxist group, which initially included Kurdish as well as Turkish militants and whose goal was socialist revolution in Turkey. After years of recruiting and indoctrinating followers, the PKK was established on 27 November 1978. Öcalan's personality was strongly shaped by his childhood experiences and by the socio-political conditions of southeastern Turkey. He developed a deep animosity for the traditional structure of Kurdish society, in which his family had no standing. This aversion extended to the Turkish state. His main goal was to destroy the traditional Kurdish societal structure and create a socialist Pan-Kurdish state.

Öcalan's PKK engaged in campaigns of terror against the officials of the Turkish state. Its main goal was to destabilize Turkey and create an independent Kurdish state with the support of some foreign countries, such as Syria, Greece, and Russia. For more than two decades, Öcalan operated from Syria and Syrian-occupied Lebanon. The PKK is responsible for the indiscriminate killing of moderate Turkish Kurds both in Turkey and in Europe. It consistently targeted the educational infrastructure in the region, branding the public schools "instruments of Ankara's assimilation policy." The PKK reportedly killed 200 teachers and destroyed 150 schools to "stop assimilation," blew up bridges and hospitals, and slaughtered "collaborators." It killed Kurds and Turks alike so long as the victims were perceived as pro-state. The PKK and its leadership never tolerated dissent from the party line and considered assimilated Kurds to be the "biggest enemy." In his interview with M. Ali Birand, Öcalan gave a number of examples of how he punished perceived disloyal acts.[33] The PKK failed to generate popular support among many Kurds yet politicized their consciousness. The PKK also forced families to give up a son or daughter for PKK service.

Turkey was a successful case of national integration in the 1930s and 1940s. The politicization of the Kurdish identity has been gradual. The Kurdish movement was partly stimulated by international events and by interactions between Turkish and Iraqi Kurds, but this new ethnic consciousness is also descended from local socio-political conditions. The revolutionary leftist Kurdish movement played a critical role in the politicization of Kurdish identity. Those intellectuals and politicians involved in the revolutionary movement were later converted to ethnic entrepreneurism. The lack of democratization and worsening economic conditions consolidated ethnic and regional loyalties. People gradually became more aware of their "Kurdish-being," which in turn translated into political activism. As Kurds became modern, they obtained the skills to better define and protect their culture and identity. With the birth of Kurdish political consciousness, Turkey has become a nation divided by ethno-cultural pluralism.

The Transnational Public Sphere and Kurdish Nationalism

After the 1980 coup, many Kurdish intellectuals and activists emigrated to Germany, France, and Sweden, where they formed the most powerful and effective Kurdish network in Europe. Not only did this network raise the political consciousness of the Kurdish migrants, but it also shaped the Kurdish political debate in Turkey and provided political and economic aid for the PKK. Political freedoms and economic resources empowered the small number of Kurdish intellectuals and political entrepreneurs to bypass Turkey's state institutions in Europe in constructing and disseminating the Kurdish language and culture. The Kurdish diaspora provides a constituency, political skills, and financial resources, enabling the Kurdish entrepreneurs to politicize the Kurdish identity and shape the debate in Turkey. There are at least twenty-five Kurdish publishing houses centred in Sweden, France, Germany, and other European countries. In Sweden a new Kurdish library was established with funds from the Swedish Ministry of Culture, and forty-five to fifty books in Kurdish are published every year. According to van Bruinessen, in Sweden 268 books in Kurdish have been published since 1974.[34] Moreover, the Institut Kurde de Paris, founded in 1983, and the Kurdish library in Sweden play very important roles in the standardization of the Kurdish language.[35]

Those Kurds forced out of Turkey due to their leftist activism during the 1980 coup played a formative role in the constitution of transnational Kurdish spaces in terms of establishing printing houses, newspapers, and associations in Europe. These transnational spaces were very much facilitated by an increased flow of ideas, skills, and financial means between Turkey and the countries within the European Union (EU). These activists skillfully linked the Kurdish national agenda with the global discourses of human rights and democratization. They utilized transnational norms and institutions to articulate and generate support for the Kurdish agenda. Although the Kurdish activists utilized international norms against the Turkish state, they were also inadvertently forced to internalize their conduct and claims. Various Kurdish organizations, networks, and hometown loyalties were mobilized in order to articulate and solidify Kurdish identity. These networks also developed close ties with European institutions by creating a common ground on human-rights causes. In Europe human-rights discourse has given rise to a powerful Kurdish ethno-nationalism. The Kurdish diaspora has formed well-functioning institutions and networks to mobilize large numbers of Kurds and human-rights-oriented Europeans. By framing their ethno-nationalism in terms of human-rights discourse, the European Kurds created a number of political and legal opportunities to challenge the policies of the Turkish state. This use of human-rights discourse also conditioned the Kurds not to push too hard for particularistic claims of self-determination but rather for universal claims of human rights, such as equality and political participation. For instance, some Kurdish groups, such as the London-based legal-advocacy organization the Kurdish Human Rights Project (KHRP), utilize the European Commission and Court of Human Rights to pressure Turkey to update its legal and administrative system in accordance with international human-rights conventions.[36]

Turkey's westernization project, which has involved seeking to become a member of the EU and signing a number of EU conventions, makes the Turkish government more vulnerable to international pressures. The transnational public sphere has empowered the domestically weak Kurdish groups to shape Turkey's relations with the EU by diplomatic means.

Most of these cultural, political, and social associations and networks either were established or are controlled by the PKK. Since the 1980s the PKK-oriented, Turkey-based Democratic People's Party (DEHAP), the European-based Kurdistan Liberation Front (ERNK), the daily newspaper *Ozgur Politika*, and the newly established Federation of Kurdish Organizations in Germany (YEM-KOM) have consolidated material, intellectual, and political resources to mobilize advocates of Kurdish identity against the policies of the Turkish state. In many European cities, the PKK collects money in the form of either "donations" or "taxes" to fund its activities both inside and outside Turkey. In short, the PKK, as a nonstate actor, politicized and managed the Kurdish diaspora in order to implement its political vision of creating Kurdish spaces and empowering Kurdish enthno-nationalists against Turkey.

The PKK, according to German intelligence sources, has 10,000 supporters among the half million Kurds in Germany. It has also managed to mobilize 20,000 Kurds for political campaigns. Although PKK militants form a small minority, they are well organized and violent.[37] It has also been reported that the PKK is involved in trafficking heroin (and illegal aliens) throughout western Europe, these lucrative investments serving to fund such activities as the London-based television station MED-TV, an extensive Internet presence, and various Kurdish organizations in Europe and North America. The PKK has carried out its political activities in Europe via ERNK, and ex-PKK activists who were part of the Kurdistan Parliament in Exile recently formed the Kurdish National Congress (KNK).

To contain and repress PKK-led activities, the Turkish state pursued a number of policies. Under the leadership of Turgut Özal (as prime minister, 1983–89, and as president, 1989–93), Turkey implemented the village-guard militia system, hiring Kurdish villagers for the militia at wages well above southeastern Anatolian standards in 1985. In addition, a special legal system was introduced in Kurdish-populated provinces, which were appointed a regional governor in 1987. One of the major social costs of the conflict between the PKK and the state was the securement of normal life in these heavily Kurdish-populated provinces. The Kurdish-inhabited zones of southeastern Anatolia were under the Regional State of Emergency Governorate (OHAL) for almost twenty years. The fight against the PKK was carried out under martial law until OHAL was introduced in 1987. The OHAL region contained the Provinces of Bingöl, Diyarbakır, Elazığ, Hakkari, Mardin, Siirt, Tunceli, and Van and was subsequently expanded to include Adıyaman, Bitlis, and Muş. In 1990 the OHAL region also included Batman and Sirnak. Elazığ and Adıyaman were the first provinces removed from the OHAL region. The OHAL's provinces are subject to special government decrees that do not require the Constitutional Court's supervision; thus they are governed according to different legal and administrative rules from those applied in the rest of the country – a factor that has further consolidated Kurdish nationalism.

According to state statistics, since 1984 as many as 4,302 civil servants, 5,018 soldiers, 4,400 civilians, and 23,279 PKK terrorists have been killed in the region and thousands wounded. Many Kurdish families have lost their sons. Recruited by the PKK between the ages of fifteen and forty to fight for a separate state, many Kurdish young men were wounded on the front lines of the separatist war. All neighbourhoods carry scars of the war.[38] An entire generation of youth was born and socialized into this bloody and violent culture. Thousands of Kurds left the country in search of security and peace. The social and political milieus were torn apart, and socio-cultural fault lines were politicized, which in turn politicized the Kurdish consciousness and radicalized ethnic nationalism. The human cost of the PKK terror campaign also includes a new generation whose self-image has been shaped by OHAL conditions. Stockbreeding and agriculture, the main sources of livelihood in the region, were destroyed. During the conflict, the government vacated a total of 4,000 villages and other hamlets, and approximately 1 million people were relocated to cities for security reasons.[39] Those people forced out of their villages constitute a major source of the problems in large cities, where crime has increased and most of the criminals are purportedly jobless Kurdish youth who have little hope in the future. These new urban settlers are less likely to return to their villages, which are in ruin. As the OHAL region is practically no longer a part of Turkey, it is clear that the government must end its emergency rule in Kurdish-populated provinces if it is to unify the country.

The conflict has eroded the rule of law, and the state has used ultra-rightist gangsters and religious fanatics to fight Kurdish nationalists. For instance, Hizbullah, a fundamentalist religious organization, has used weapons imported by the governor of Batman.[40] Salih Salman, the governor of Batman in the mid-1990s, was instrumental in the formation of Hizbullah, a terrorist group believed to have killed suspected members of the PKK. Young Hizbullah assassins operated in broad daylight in mainly Kurdish provinces, targeting anyone who opposed the Islamic Republic of Kurdistan. The Turkish state was involved in a no-holds-barred war against the PKK militants and remained deaf to allegations that its security services were working with Hizbullah assassins. Hizbullah members are usually first-generation Kurds from major urban centres, and it is mainly an urban organization. Its aim was to establish an Islamic Republic of Kurdistan by overthrowing the secular system in Turkey. Most of Hizbullah's targets were people with a history of being harassed and detained by the police. Hizbullah never targeted Turkish officials but rather directed its campaign against secular PKK members and moderate Kurdish Nurcus, the followers of Said Nursi.

STAGE FIVE:
THE KURDISH PROBLEM AS A EUROPEAN
PROBLEM: THE POST-HELSINKI SITUATION

Despite the PKK's attacks on civilian targets, the majority of Turks trust the military officials and have not given in to the fear sown by the PKK, which has targeted teachers, doctors, journalists, businessmen, the police, and the army. Since the 1983 insurrection, the Kurds have grown accustomed to being despised and rejected. Even in some urban cities, the conflict has turned into a Kurdish-Turkish one. In order to prevent the further polarization of society along ethnic lines, the military decided to use all means to stop PKK activities.

On 16 September 1998, while on an inspection tour of the Syrian border, the commander of the Turkish army, General Atilla Ateş, issued the following statement: "Some of our neighbors, especially Syria, are misinterpreting our efforts and goodwill for having good ties. By supporting the bandit Abdullah [Öcalan] they have helped plunge Turkey into the trouble of terrorism ... Our patience is exhausted."[41] After this statement, Süleyman Demirel, then president of Turkey, issued a sharper statement condemning Syria and indicated Turkey's readines to "retaliate." With Egypt mediating, Turkey and Syria signed the Adana Memorandum on 20 October 1998, in which Syria agreed to stop supporting PKK terror. Subsequently, it worked closely with Turkey to remove Öcalan from Lebanon. The key reason Syria caved into Turkish pressures was the isolation it had experienced since the collapse of the Soviet Union. Deprived of the Soviet Union's military support, its army could not even find spare parts for its Soviet-made weaponry. The reason Turkey pursued a confrontational policy against Syria in 1998 was Turkey's close ties with Israel and the United States. The Turkish army had come to the conclusion that Syria's ability to wage war was limited. Moreover, between 1983 and 1994 the Turkish army had abandoned its traditional and confused strategy. Previously, Turkish military doctrine had been based on "force protection" and "shock and awe" in the region. In practice, these strategies meant killing any PKK member or sympathizer who appeared to pose any threat to Turkish forces and overcoming the enemy through the use of overwhelming firepower and constant control of the specified territories. Although effective in the early stages of the war, when the PKK was well armed and mobile in large numbers, this policy became deeply counterproductive when the PKK's popularity among much of the population started to increase. This policy came to an end with the initiation of a more socially oriented policy intended to win over the people. Low-intensity conflict entails an integrated political-economic-military approach supplemented by psychological, social, and diplomatic devices in order to limit the use of military force. The Turkish armed forces retrained and equipped itself to carry out such a conflict over the long term, reorganizing itself from division into brigade lines in order to be more flexible and mobile. It evolved from being an overgrown and sluggish giant into an organization with an effective system of command, control, and communications. The delegation of power to local command played an important role in defeating the PKK terror campaign.

In response to Turkey's determined position, the Syrian government forced Öcalan to leave for Moscow. Then he took refuge in Rome, and eventually the Turkish military brought him to Turkey from Nairobi, Kenya, on 16 February 1999.[42] After his arrest Öcalan told journalists, "I really love Turkey and the Turkish people. My mother is Turkish. Sincerely, I will do all I can to be of service to the Turkish state."[43] His brother Osman Öcalan, who was second in command, called on all Kurds to attack the Turkish state. He said that the Kurds throughout the world should "extract a heavy price from the Turkish state for the conspiracy it has engaged in against our leadership."[44] The Sixth PKK Congress authorized its military arm, the Peoples Liberation Army of Kurdistan (ARGK), "to wage a war that will make the Turkish state tremble" and called for a *serhildan* (Kurdish *intifadah*).[45]

The PKK tried every means to defeat the Turkish state, but their call for mass violence did not materialize. The worst attack took place in Istanbul, when a group calling itself the Revenge Hawks of Apo (Öcalan) attacked a shopping mall, killing thirteen people in the suburb of Kadiköy. The arrest of Öcalan and the defeat of the PKK shattered the common myth of its image as a "heroic and undefeatable" nationalist organization among the Kurds. However, Öcalan's arrest, despite helping to erode the appeal of the PKK, did not curb the Kurds' violence-ridden culture and its reliance on force to solve social conflicts.

The PKK-led protracted insurgency was ended by the Turkish military. After his arrest, Öcalan revealed PKK ties with Greece and Russia. Öcalan was tried at the State Security Court between 31 May and 29 June 1999. During his trial, Öcalan offered "to serve the Turkish state" and declared that "the democratic option ... is the only alternative in solving the Kurdish question. Separation is neither possible nor necessary." During his statements, Öcalan praised Mustafa Kemal's attempt to create a secular and European state and sharply criticized "the Seyh Said uprising of 1925 and traditional tribal system which promoted landlords – *ağas*."[46]

The State Security Court found him guilty of separatist treason and sentenced him to death. The Court of Appeals upheld his sentence on 25 November 1999. His lawyers took the case to the European Court of Human Rights (ECHR), to which Turkey belongs. As an interim measure, the ECHR asked the Turkish government to suspend the execution until it could rule on the appeal, and the officials in Ankara agreed.[47] After the arrest of Öcalan, the People's Democratic Party (HADEP) emerged as the centre of Kurdish politics in Turkey. In January 1999 the public prosecutor asked the Constitutional Court to ban the party on the basis of organic links with the PKK. Nevertheless, Kurds in the southeast voted heavily for HADEP, which stressed the value of constitutional citizenship, the recognition of Kurdish cultural rights, the consolidation of local governments, land reform for landless peasants, and a regional economic-development plan that included a number of free-trade zones with Iran, Iraq, and Syria. However, HADEP failed to obtain any seats in Parliament because it did not get 10 per cent of the total national vote, the threshold required for parliamentary representation in the April 1999 elections. This 10 per cent threshold defeats proportional representation's purpose of ensuring the inclusion of all viable political entities in government. The people of this region are therefore denied national representation. The Turkish government imposes taxes in the region and expects loyalty without representation. HADEP secured key mayoral posts in the southeastern Cities of Batman, Bingöl, Hakkari, Siirt, and rnak and in the regional capital, Diyarbakır.

At the Helsinki Summit of 10–11 December 1999, the European Union declared Turkey "a candidate state destined to join the Union on the basis of the same criteria as applied to the other candidate states."[48] The European Copenhagen political criteria require full implementation of democracy, human rights, the rule of law, and the protection of minorities.⁴⁹ On the basis of the Copenhagen criteria, the EU asked the Turkish government to reform its legal system and to solve the Kurdish problem by peaceful means. This represents a turning point in Turco-EU ties and has created optimism about ending the tragic conflict, which has resulted in 30,000 deaths and has cost more than $100 billion. Reflecting on the EU's requirements for resolving the Kurdish problem, Mesut Yılmaz of the Motherland Party has said, "The road to the EU passes through Diyarbakır ... Democracy is the right of both the Turk and the Kurd."⁵⁰ Internationalization of the Kurdish question is a result of the activities of the Kurdish diaspora in Europe. With millions of Kurds living in a number of European cities, especially in Germany, Turkey's Kurdish question has become a European Kurdish problem.

Turkey's struggle to join the EU is the critical factor in explaining the legal and political "silent revolution" in Turkey. The Turkish Parliament has accepted seven major harmonization packages designed to update Turkey's legal and political system in accordance with EU criteria. These reforms, unlike those previously undertaken in Turkey, are intended to consolidate Turkish society, rather than the state, and to expand the role of civil society vis-à-vis the state. Thus the EU has arguably been the major force stimulating Turkey's internal transformation, including changes to how it handles the Kurdish question.⁵¹ The current dynamics of Kurdish nationalism are rooted in: (1) the neoliberal economic policies of Özal and the state's failure to deal with Kurdish identity claims; (2) the increasing significance of human-rights discourse and its utilization by Kurdish intellectuals; (3) the visibility of the Kurds after the Gulf War in 1991; and (4) the increased role of the European diaspora in asserting Kurdish identity claims. The Kurds have employed various political means at different times to promote their ethnic consciousness, appealing to the Islamic religion, Marxist ideology, and most recently, respect for human rights.

HOW TO MANAGE TURKEY'S KURDISH PROBLEM: DECENTRALIZATION AND THE RECOGNITION OF CULTURAL RIGHTS

Turkey needs to recognize the cultural rights of the Kurds by lifting the bans on Kurdish broadcasting, allowing education in the Kurdish language, and forming a pro-Kurdish political party. The EU might function as an intermediary between the Kurds and the Turkish state, but Turkish Kurds are divided on the question of Europe's role. The extreme nationalists regard Turkey's integration in the EU as an obstacle to achieving their goal of a united Pan-Kurdish state. By contrast, Serafettin Elci and other moderates have enthusiastically supported the notion of a Europe of Regions capable of providing the context for political accommodation between the Republic of Turkey and the Kurds.

The Kurdish question has injected an abrupt and perhaps lethal issue into Turkish-European relations. Those Europeans who would like to build a cultural boundary between Turkey and the EU present the Kurdish question as a minority problem, knowing that Turkey cannot treat the Kurds as a "minority." Given the impact of the Ottoman collapse and the utilization of minority rights against the Ottoman state, Turkey will not grant "minority status" to the Kurds, which would give them collective group rights.[52] The best hope for lasting peace in Turkey is to divorce ethnic identity from political access. As a result of EU pressures, Turkey is likely to devolve central power to municipalities and recognize the individual cultural and political rights of the Kurds within the territorial boundaries of Turkey.

On 19 March 2001 the Government of Turkey introduced its National Program (NP). On the Kurdish issue, which has been a major source of contention in Turkish-EU dialogue, the program did not commit itself to allowing education in the Kurdish language. The NP stressed that "the official language and the formal education language of the Republic of Turkey is Turkish. This, however, does not prohibit the free usage of different languages, dialects and tongues by Turkish citizens in their daily lives. This freedom may not be abused for the purposes of separatism and division."[53] The terms "Kurdish" or "education in mother tongue" do not appear in the program's wording. It was clear from the NP that the military commanders and an ultra-nationalistic Nationalistic Action Party (MHP) were resisting many of the conditions on which the EU had been insisting. The EU wanted to see full civilian control over the military, a requirement intended to weaken the military-dominated National Security Council.

In addition to implementing legal and political changes, Turkey is also seeking to address the region's economic problems. Nationalist Kurds regard the relative deprivation of the Kurdish regions as evidence of state "discrimination," making economic disparity is a contributing factor in the emergence of Kurdish radicalism. Indeed, Ted Gurr's seminal study indicates that relative deprivation politicizes ethnic identities.[54] In Turkey, where regional inequalities are interpreted along ethnic lines and the Kurdish regions are among the country's poorest, the Kurdish left has actively presented regional inequality as the manifestation of Turkish "discrimination" against the Kurds. In response, the Turkish state has introduced a number of economic initiatives to tackle the Kurdish question. Destruction, however, is the price of progress in southeast Anatolia. Turkey is involved in the $32 billion Southeastern Anatolian Project (GAP), a network of twenty-two dams and nineteen hydroelectric plants, which is the key to the economic development of Upper Mesopotamia. It will irrigate 2,500 square miles of land and affect the lives of 6.5 million people in this region. The government of Turkey sees this project as a way of addressing the Kurdish problem, but the Kurds' grievances extend beyond poverty to issues of cultural and political rights. Bülent Ecevit, a leading leftist politician and former prime minister, believes that "there is no Kurdish problem in Turkey but the problem of feudalism and economic backwardness."[55] Indeed, the socio-economic structure of the region has played an important role in the formation of Kurdish ethno-nationalism. However, one needs to take political and cultural factors into account as well.

At the core of the contemporary crisis in Turkey lie three sociopolitical features of Kemalism: (1) Its uncritical modernization ideology prevents open discussion that would lead to a new and inclusive social contract recognizing the cultural diversity of Turkey; (2) it does not tolerate the articulation of different identities and lifestyles in the public sphere since they undermine the Kemalist vision of an ideal society; and (3) it treats politics as a means of controlling political developments and engineering a new society.[56] Thus Kemalism does not see social, cultural, and political difference as an integral part of democracy but rather treats socio-political "difference" as a source of instability and a threat to national unity. The current ethnic (Kurdish) and religious (Sunni Islamic and Alevi) movements seek to redefine themselves as "Muslims," "Kurds," and "Alevis" through the means provided by globalization. These identity- and justice-seeking social movements are in direct conflict with the Kemalist project. Turkey needs a new social contract. The founding principles of this contract should include an Anglo-Saxon (as opposed to a rigid

French laicism-based) conception of secularism, the rule of law, and recognition of the multicultural nature of Turkey. Both Kurds and Turks need to be involved in this search for a new social contract. Turkey needs to accommodate the demands of the Kurdish nationalist movement.[57]

THE KURDISH SEARCH FOR A SOLUTION

There are a number of initiatives in Turkey to find a just and durable solution to the Kurdish problem. None of the civil Kurdish movements have managed to build a broad coalition of nonstate actors to pressure the Turkish state for resolution of contentious problems. Thus the Kurdish movement's contribution to the process of political change is now limited. The movement helped to expand the boundaries of public debate over identity and state-society relations. But its use of terrorist tactics promoted the securement of daily life and forced large sectors of Turkish society to support the state. Moreover, its separatist language and constant attempt to link itself with outside forces, even with some hostile countries, delegitimized Kurdish demands in the eyes of many Turks. Instead of trying to develop a societywide language of politics, the Kurdish movements always stressed their "difference." For instance, neither the PKK nor HADEP have managed to combine identity, modernity, and democracy to construct a new social contract.

The Initiative Commission for Unity, a group formed by the Democracy and Peace Party (DBP), and the Initiative Commission for a New Political Formation, representing the Free Democrats, have decided to act together to lay the groundwork for a new political platform. A meeting held at Genel-İş labour-union headquarters on 26 August 2000 was attended by many Kurdish intellectuals and politicians, including Abdulmelik Fırat of the Free Democrats, who is the grandson of Seyh Said, the leader of the largest rebel movement during the 1920s; former deputy of the Province of Muş Mehmet Emin Sever; Ferda Cemiloğlu of the People's Republican Party (CHP); Kasım Fırat; former Bingöl mayor Selahattin Kaya; Ibrahim Güçlü; and the DBP chairman, Yılmaz Camlıbel, and deputy chairman, Fehmi Demir. Although Şerafettin Elçi was part of this initiative, he quit the meetings due to his disagreements with Abdulmelik Fırat. The new initiative is critical of both the "democratic-republic" strategy of Öcalan and the "submissive and unimaginative" strategy of HADEP.

In addition to these domestic initiatives, the PKK has been trying to internationalize itself by forming the Kurdish National Congress (KNK) as a Pan-Kurdish movement. At the second meeting of its Regular General Council, which took place in August 2000 in the Belgian village of Bilzen, forty new members were accepted into the KNK. Its main goal is to organize and coordinate anti-Turkish activities in different parts of Europe. Although the KNK's membership has expanded from 176 to 216 since it was formed in Holland on 24 May 1999, the new members are picked by PKK representative Rıza Erdoğan, who spoke at the meeting, calling on the congress to be more active against the policies of the Turkish state. Due to PKK control over the congress, the Iraqi Kurdish leadership, Jalal Talabani and Masud Barzani, refused to join the KNK.[58] The PKK has tried to transform itself not only outside, but also inside, Turkey by seeking to become a part of mainstream politics. There are close and organic ties between the PKK and HADEP.

In the 2002 election, Islamic identity was not a "space between identities" or a "shared worldview" that blended ethnic identities under the leadership of Necmettin Erbakan of the Felicity Party (SP) and Recep Tayyip Erdoğan of the reformist Justice and Development Party (AKP), which came to power with 34.4 per cent of ballot and 363 seats. Although the Kurdish ethnic party – the Democratic People's Party (DEHAP) – emerged the number one party in the twelve Kurdish provinces, indicating Kurdish nationalism's increasing autonomy from Islamism, it failed to win the national threshold of 10 per cent of the votes required to enter Parliament, receiving only 6.23 per cent. Nevertheless, because of the electoral structure, Kurds will still be represented in Parliament by a Kurdish member of the AKP (Abdulkadir Aksu, a prominent Kurdish politician from Diyarbakır, appointed minister of the interior) and by members of the People's Republican Party (CHP), although these are not the parties for which Kurds overwhelmingly voted. Due to new policies of the AKP government to recognize the cultural rights of the Kurds, the Kurdish population voted for the AKP candidates in local elections held on 28 March 2004. DEHAP participated in the local elections under the Social Democrat People's Party (SHP). This could have major repercussions in the future depending on how the AKP capitalizes on its electoral victory and how Kurds are represented within the new government.

CONCLUSION

The collapse of the multiethnic Ottoman Empire and the formation of ethnically based nationalist regimes are the root causes of the politicization and radicalization of Kurdish identity. Successful Turkish modernization, increased communication, and greater mobility heightened ethnic Kurdish consciousness and mobilized the Kurdish movements. In turn, this radicalized Kurdish nationalism politicized and popularized Turkish nationalism. Today, there is a heightened Kurdish consciousness but very little unity due to competing subethnic loyalties. The Kurds need to recognize that there is no territorial or political room in the Middle East for an independent Kurdish state, while Turkey must recognize the cultural rights of the Kurds and search for a new social contract by which the cultural mosaic of Turkey can flourish. The Kurdish problem impedes necessary legal reforms and the implementation of democratic and human rights in Turkey. Moreover, the Kurdish problem has seriously constrained Turkey's foreign policy by giving foreign states a powerful issue on which to pressure the Turkish government and has become the main obstacle in Turkey's drive for full membership in the European Union.

NOTES

1 An earlier version of this chapter was published as "Five Stages of the Construction of Kurdish Nationalism in Turkey." I thank William Safran for allowing me to use a substantial part of that essay. I also thank Yasin Aktay, Hamit Bozarslan, Cemalettin Hasimi, Nihat Ali Özcan, Saleha Abedin, and Michael M. Gunter for their comments as well as the Institute of Muslim Minority Affairs (London) and the Department of Education and the Center for Middle East Studies at the University of Utah for their financial support.

2 There are different ways of ascribing periods to the evolution of Kurdish nationalism; see Hamit Bozarslan, "Some Remarks on Kurdish Historiographical Discourse in Turkey, 1919–1980." For background on Kurdish ethno-nationalism in Turkey, see Hakan Özoğlu, *Kurdish Notables and the Ottoman State*; M. Hakan Yavuz, ed., *The Kurdish Question in Turkey*, and

"Turkey's Fault Lines and the Crisis of Kemalism"; M. Hakan Yavuz and Michael M. Gunter, "The Kurdish Nation"; David McDowall, *A Modern History of the Kurds;* Henri J. Barkey and Graham E. Fuller, *Turkey's Kurdish Question;* Michael M. Gunter, *The Kurds and the Future of Turkey;* and Kemal Kirişci and Gareth M. Winrow, *The Kurdish Question and Turkey.* See also İsmet G. Imset, *The PKK: A Report on Separatist Violence in Turkey, 1973–1992,* and "The PKK: Terrorists or Freedom Fighters?"; Nicole F. Watts, "Allies and Enemies: Pro-Kurdish Parties in Turkish Politics, 1990–1994"; and S. Mutlu, "Ethnic Kurds in Turkey."

3 For more on the differences between the imperial and modern state, see David Held, "The Development of the Modern State."
4 Michael Mann, "The Autonomous Power of the State," 113.
5 Tom Nairn, *The Break-up of Britain,* explains the formation and diffusion of nationalism in terms of a country's uneven economic development. In the case of Kurdish nationalism, a particular ethnic identity served to translate regional economic disparities into a nationalist movement.
6 For more on the role of "ethnic entrepreneurs," see Crawford Young, *The Politics of Cultural Pluralism,* 28, 45–6.
7 There is no doubt that Kurdish cultural identity existed before the modern era. One finds evidence of an "ethnic core" – a prerequisite for ethnic status from Anthony D. Smith's perspective (see *The Ethnic Origin of Nations*) – in the premodern tribal structure of the Kurds. However, this "ethnic core" was politicized and turned into nationalism in reaction to the invasive inroads that Turkish, Iranian, and Iraqi nationalist movements made against the Kurdish communities after the collapse of the Ottoman Empire by imposing direct rule and facilitating the penetration of capitalism. Nevertheless, Kurdish nationalism remains heavily influenced by the premodern tribal social structure. As Michael Hecter suggests, nationalism is very much an outcome of state policies favouring centralization. For more on the theoretical approach to nationalism, see Hecter, *Containing Nationalism.*
8 Soner Cağaptay, "Reconfiguring the Turkish Nation in the 1930s," and "Population Resettlement and Immigration Policies of Interwar Turkey."
9 For instance, Mesut Yeğen assumes that there was a full-fledged Kurdish nationalism and focuses on the state strategies for confronting it rather then problematizing Kurdish nationalism. See Yeğen, "The Kurdish Question in Turkish State Discourse."
10 Anthony D. Smith, *The Ethnic Origin of Nations;* and *National Identity.*
11 The Kurds of Iraq, Iran, and Syria use the Arabic alphabet, whereas the Kurds of Turkey use the Latin alphabet.

12 *Ağa* means "landlord" and usually refers to the head of the tribe, a *şeyh* is the leader of a Sufi order, and a *seyyid* is one believed to be descended from the Prophet Muhammad. Each has a different role, but they are the integrating personalities of the Kurdish society. See Necdet Subaşı, "Şeyh, Seyyid ve Molla."
13 Middle East Watch, *Genocide in Iraq*. This book details Saddam Hussein's attacks against the Kurds.
14 For more on the Alevi identity, see M. Hakan Yavuz, "Değişim Sürecindeki Alevi Kimliği; and Krisztina Kehl-Bodrogi, "Kurds, Turks, or a people in Their Own Right?"
15 Müfid Yüksel, *Kürdistan'da Değişim Süreci*, 50–70; Ismail Kara, "Kürt Medreseleri Gündeme Gelecek mi?"; Martin van Bruinessen, *Mullas, Sufis and Heretics*.
16 Burhanettin Duran, "Approaching the Kurdish Question via Adil Düzen."
17 "Nationalism" should be understood in this context as referring to a quest for self-determination.
18 Hakan Özoğlu, *Unimaginable Community*, 65–8.
19 van Bruinessen, *Agha, Shaikh and State*, 189.
20 Ismail Göldaş, *Kürdistan Teali Cemiyeti*; Naci Kutlay, *Ittihat Terakki ve Kürtler*, 218–27.
21 Ismail Göldaş, *Lozan: "Biz Türkler ve Kürtler."*
22 Halil Şimşek, *Şeyh Sa'id Isyanı ve* PKK. This book is written by an active duty general. He examines the Seyh Said Rebellion as an ethnic movement. According to Şimşek, although Seyh Said used Islam to consolidate support, his real goal was to "carve an independent Kurdish state" (31). For more on the changing views of the Turkish military, see Genel Kurmay Başkanlığı, *100 Soru ve Cevapta Türk Silahlı Kuvvetleri ve Terörle Mücadele*, 1–45.
23 Robert Olson, "Their Impact on the Development of the Turkish Air Force and on Kurdish and Turkish Nationalism."
24 Umit Cizre Sakallioğlu, "Kurdish Nationalism from an Islamic Perspective."
25 "Türkiye ahalisine din ve ırk farkı olmaksızın vatandaşlık itibariyle Türk itlak olunur" (translation mine).
26 Ismail Besikci, *Doğu Mitingleri'nin Analizi, 1967*.
27 M. Ali Birand, *Apo ve* PKK, 83.
28 *Devrimci Doğu Kültür Ocakları Dava Dosyası*, 25–9. Along with the DDKO's publications, this book provides the best picture of the Turkish state's discourse on the Kurdish question in the late 1960s and early 1970s. The

DDKO played an important role in the construction of Kurdish political consciousness.

29 During the government of Prime Minister Bülent Ecevit (1978–79), many pro-Nationalistic Action Party (MHP) teachers and schools were forced into different parts of the country. One of my sisters, who was a student at the Nenehatun Teachers' School in Erzurum, was forced to continue her education in Van. Her new school in Van was under the control of a group of Kurdish leftists, known as the Rizgari (Liberationists). The school was the centre of ideological struggle between the Rizgari and the Kawa (Maoists). In late 1978, the Rizgari controlled the schools and subjected all students and teachers to ideological training. Every morning the Rizgari forced the students and teachers to attend propaganda meetings and never allowed the national anthem to be aired. In other words, contrary to the claims of some journalists and scholars, there was a separatist movement before the military coup in 1980. The coup oppressed this aggressive and separatist movement. There is a new trend in Turkey to explain separatist nationalism and Islamic radicalism in terms of the policies of the 1980 coup. For instance, see Ömer Laciner, *Kürt Sorunu: Henüz Vakit Varken*. According to Laciner, the repressive policies of the 1980 coup were the source of the radicalization of the Kurdish identity. Öcalan's interview with M. Ali Birand, *Apo ve PKK*, indicates that Kurdish separatism was a powerful force in southeastern Anatolia before the 1980 coup. In Birand's book, Öcalan explains his journey from his village to the head of the PKK.

30 Nihat Ali Özcan, *PKK: Tarihi, Ideolojisi ve Yöntemi*, 222–349.

31 The studies usually focus on Öcalan and the leadership. They ignored the sociological issues of "framing" identity claims, of economic divisions, and most important, of the urban, rural, and transnational networks of the organization.

32 Hakan M. Yavuz, "The Politics of Fear."

33 Birand, *Apo ve PKK*, 36, 121. Öcalan explains how he punished his bird and dog because he perceived their acts as disloyal. There is a fine analysis of Öcalan's mindset by Vamik Volkan, *Bloodlines: From Ethnic Pride to Ethnic Terrorism*, 168–80.

34 Martin van Bruinessen, "Shifting National and Ethnic Identities: The Kurds in Turkey and the European Diaspora."

35 Osten Wahlbeck, *Kurdish Diaspora*, 152–78.

36 The KHRP was founded in 1992 by Kerim Yıldız, a Turkish Kurd, who is still the executive director of the organization; see the organization's

website at www.khrp.org. The KHRP works closely with the Human Rights Association in Turkey, which has a number of offices.

37 PKK Terrorism, 13. This booklet was prepared in order to inform the public of the PKK's activities.

38 See Naki Özkan's interview with Yasin Aktay, "Ölüm estetize ediliyor," Milliyet (Istanbul), 31 October 2000. In "Güneydoğu'da Intihar: Kalan Sağlar Bizimdir," Aktay examines the reasons for the high suicide rate in Batman. He identifies the weakening of traditional ties and the new culture of violence, which celebrates death as a way of "purifying the self." He makes implicit links between the conflict and the new culture.

39 Zeynep Gökçe Akgür, Türkiye'de Kırsal Kesimden Kente Göç ve Bölgeler Arası Dengesizlik, 1970–1993, 67–9; Mert Gözde, "Parliamentary Commission Reports on Migration: 4,000 Villages Evacuated, 1 Million People Displaced," Turkish Daily News (Ankara), 30 January 2001: "During a 14-year process in the course of which the security forces fought with the militants of the outlawed Kurdistan Workers' Party (PKK) some 4,000 villages and hamlets were evacuated in the East and the Southeast and 1 million people migrated from the region."

40 Human Rights Watch, "What is Turkey's Hizbullah," 16 February 2000.

41 Hürriyet (Ankara), 17 September 1998, translation mine.

42 For details, see the statement by Dylan Semsi Kılıç (under the byline of Cemal Ucar) – a close associate of Öcalan's and an eyewitness to his capture – broadcast by the PKK's MED-TV and accessed on the Internet, 21 February 1999, www.ozgurpolitika.org/1999/02/21/index.html; Tim Weiner, "U.S. Helped Turkey Find and Capture Kurd Rebel," New York Times, 20 February 1999; Marcus Gee, "The Odyssey of a Kurdish Hot Potato," Globe and Mail (Toronto), 24 February 1999; Helena Smith, Chris Morris, and Ed Vulliamy, "Global Plot that Lured Kurds' Hero into Trap," Observer (London), 21 February 1999; and Ismet Berkan, "The Story of Apo's Capture," Radikal (Istanbul), 17 February 1999. Turkey's prime minister, Bülent Ecevit, declined to elaborate on any of the details, merely citing a Turkish proverb: "Let us eat the grape and not ask where it came from."

43 "Turks vs. Kurds: Turning Point," New York Times, 21 February 1999, 8.

44 Cited in Michael M. Gunter, "The Continuing Kurdish Problem in Turkey after Öcalan's Capture," 851.

45 "MED-TV Reports More on PKK Statement on Congress Result," Foreign Broadcast Information Service-Near East/South Asia, FBIS-WEU-1999-0304, 4 March 1999.

46 Abdullah Öcalan, Declaration on the Democratic Solution of the Kurdish Question, 18, translated by the Kurdistan Information Centre.

47 The European Court of Human Rights has passed twenty-six successful judgments in cases brought by the London-based Kurdish Human Rights Project, headed by Kerim Yıldız, the majority of which have centred on the right to life (Art. 2), prohibition of torture (Art. 3), right to a fair trial (Art. 6), right to an effective remedy (Art. 13) and freedom of expression (Art. 10). The European Court of Human Rights was set up in Strasbourg in 1959 to deal with alleged violations of the 1950 European Convention on Human Rights. On 1 November 1998 a full-time court was established, replacing the original two-tier system of both a part-time commission and a part-time court.

48 For the full text, see Presidency Conclusions Helsinki European Council, 10–11 December 1999, http://presidency.finland.fi/doc/summit/summit.html.

49 Most Kurdish intellectuals and politicians support Turkey's membership in the EU. See "Serafettin Elci Discusses Kurd Party with Swedish Foreign Minister," *Turkish Daily News* (Ankara), 22 February 2000.

50 "Yılmaz: Road to EU Passes through Diyarbakır," *Turkish Daily News* (Ankara), 17 December 1999. Diyarbakır is the largest city in southeast Anatolia, and the majority of its population is comprised of Kurds.

51 Nevertheless, most of these changes have not been implemented due to (1) a powerful nationalist bureaucracy characterized by the dominance in Ankara of the conservative Sunni culture of central and eastern Anatolia and (2) the fact that these changes were agreed to without public debate. The only legitimacy of the proposed changes derives from their role in meeting the demands of the EU and in facilitating Mustafa Kemal's ultimate goal: the creation of a European state and society.

52 For more on the reaction to "minority rights," see Onur Öymen, "Bu Sevr korkusu yersizdir," *Radikal* (Istanbul), 11 September 2000.

53 For the full text see, http://www.mersina.com/special/article.asp?cid=39#1.2.9.

54 Ted Robert Gurr, *Why Men Rebel*.

55 See the program of the Bülent Ecevit government at www.tbmm.gov.tr/ambar/kp57.htm-20k.

56 Yavuz, "Turkey's Fault Lines," 34.

57 There are three institutional solutions to the challenges posed by the Kurdish ethnic movements: consociationalism, electoral systems, and federalism. The most likely outcome in the case of Turkey is an electoral system allowing Kurds to vote for any party, including an ethnic party, with representation perhaps based on the proportion of votes that candidates receive. Turkey has to realize that too much centralization causes

rebellion and that too little centralization would also cause fragmentation. Turkey needs to develop a balance between centralization and decentralization, between imposing direct rule and allowing indirect rule. OHAL has been the major force motivating Kurdish nationalism.

58 Talabani has been critical of the KNK as a "front organization" of the PKK; see FBIS-translated text in Washington Kurdish Institute, *News Bulletin*, 7 September 2000, www.kurd.org/kurd.

10

The Kurdish Minority Identity in Iraq

MICHAEL M. GUNTER

SELF-IDENTITY

Although there is great academic disagreement over the definition of the terms "nation" and "nationalism,"[1] as well as over what constitutes a minority,[2] there can be no doubt that the Kurds are a nation in the theoretical sense more than any other minority in the Middle East. Indeed, within their historical homeland, Kurdistan, the Kurds constitute a huge majority. They are a minority only because Kurdistan has been divided among other nation-states. Thus the Kurds hold the dubious distinction of being the largest nation on earth without their own independent state.

The Kurds share a common history,[3] language,[4] territory (Kurdistan), religion (largely Sunni Islam), and culture,[5] which lead to their being both self- and other-defined as a nation. Indeed, Amir Hassanpour has concluded that "Kurdish nationalism is probably the oldest nationalist ideology in the Muslim world."[6] A century ago the Wigrams (Christian missionaries who chronicled their travels through Kurdistan) simply stated that the Kurds "are a very ancient people."[7] C.J. Edmonds (a British military officer who served in Iraqi Kurdistan during the 1920s and became one of the foremost scholars studying the Kurds) added that "the Kurds constitute a single nation … They have their own history, language, and culture."[8] Despite their famous divisions, fostered by their mountainous homeland and the divide-and-rule tactics of the states that have governed them, Mehrdad Izady has concluded that the "Kurds are a multi-lingual, multi-religious, multi-racial nation, but with a unified, independent, and identifiable national history and culture."[9]

As do other nations, the Kurds share a number of myths to help trace their origins. One tale explains that in the dim past, King Solomon exiled 500 magical spirits, or *jinn*, to the Zagros Mountains, where – with 500 beautiful virgins captured on a foray into Europe – these *jinn* sired the Kurdish nation.[10] Another myth relates how the Kurds descended from children who had escaped the child-eating tyrant Zahhak. The Kurdish New Year's celebration, Newroz, at the beginning of the spring is related to Zoroastrian fire worship and stories of a legendary blacksmith who rebelled against an evil tyrant. Most Kurds also claim to be descendants of the Medes, who helped overthrow the Assyrian Empire in 612 B.C.E.[11] In addition, many believe that the Kardouchoi, who gave Xenophon and his 10,000 such a mauling as they retreated from Persia in 401 B.C.E., were the ancestors of the Kurds. In the seventh century of the present era, the conquering Arabs applied the name Kurds to the mountainous people they Islamicized in the region, while history records that the famous Saladin, who fought so successfully against Richard the Lionheart and the Christian Crusaders in the twelfth century, was a Kurd.[12]

Two important literary works testifying to the Kurds being both self- and other-defined hundreds of years ago are Sharaf Khan Bidlisi's *Sharafname* and Evliya Chelebi's *Seyahatname* (Book of travels). The former was written at the end of the sixteenth century by the ruler of the Kurdish Emirate of Bitlis. It is an erudite history of the ruling families of a number of Kurdish emirates, some of which continued to hold sway over various parts of Kurdistan into the nineteenth century. The latter is a travelogue written in the middle of the 1600s by an Ottoman sophisticate. It is an important account of the social, political, economic, and cultural life prevalent in the Ottoman Empire at this time. Evliya Chelebi's detailed observations of Kurdistan constitute a rich source of data concerning the Kurds.

In addition, a century before the French Revolution heralded the beginning of the modern European nation and nationalism, the Kurdish poet Ahmad Khani adumbrated the idea of a Kurdish nation distinct from those of its fellow Muslim neighbours, the Arabs, Turks, and Persians, when he lamented in *Mem u Zin* (the Kurdish national epic): "If only there were harmony among us, if we were to obey a single one of us, he would reduce to vassalage Turks, Arabs and Persians, all of them. We would perfect our religion, our state, and would educate ourselves in learning and wisdom."[13]

Between the sixteenth and nineteenth centuries, a type of feudal[14] Kurdish nationalism began to emerge as a reaction to the Ottoman and Persian Empires' destruction of the numerous semi-independent Kurdish emirates that had previously prevailed. This campaign against the emirates, however, strongly stunted the development of Kurdistan and inhibited Kurdish unity. The treaty signed between the Ottoman and Persian Empires in 1639 established a frontier that divided Kurdistan and still separates modern Turkey and Iran. As the seventeenth century Kurdish poet Ahmad Khani lamented: "Whenever the Ottoman Sea and the Tajik Sea [the Persians] flow out and agitate, the Kurds get soaked in blood."[15]

A famous Kurdish proverb claims that "the Kurds have no friends but the mountains." This means, of course, that their mountainous homeland has isolated and protected the Kurds enough to preserve them as a separate nation. As Izady has concluded: "Their history and culture are so intertwined with the mountains that the ethnic identity of a Kurd on the plain becomes a contradiction in terms."[16] However, as Izady has also observed, the mountains have contributed to such divisive differences as to call into doubt the very notion of a Kurdish nation: "The mountains have broken down the language of the Kurds to a babble of dialects, their religions to a case study in diversity, and their art and costumes to a zoo of colorful variety."[17]

Despite these divisions, Kendal Nezan, the director of the Institut Kurde de Paris, notes that a strong sense of Kurdish identity still remains. While attending a Pan-Kurdish conference in Moscow in 1990, he met other Kurds from Turkey, Syria, Kirhizstan, Kazakhstan, and Caucasia. Despite their geographical separation, "these people were laughing at the same jokes and mentioning the same proverbs ... and were moved by the same songs."[18] Nezan concluded that "maybe being a Kurd means ... to share, despite [separate] borders and geographical distances, the same basic cultural identity forged by centuries of history."[19]

The division of Kurdistan into five separate states following the First World War helped to maintain Kurdish disunity, which was in turn exacerbated by traditional elements such as tribalism, the feudalistic relationships maintained by the *ağas* (landlords), and the political power wielded by religious sheiks.[20] In reaction, however, *Kurdayeti* gradually developed – that is, a modern sense of a unified Kurdish nationalism that would free the Kurds from social and national oppression within a united Kurdistan. Sedentarization of the rural population, increased urbanization, the rise of a middle and intellectual class, the development of a modern leadership, and the unique international attention that the Kurds received following the Gulf War in 1991 all contributed to *Kurdayeti*.

Interestingly, religion played only a minor role in this process. Although the Kurds mostly belong to the dominant religious persuasion prevalent in the Middle East, Sunni Islam, Islam has largely failed to unify the Kurds and Arabs in Iraq. In addition, although Saddam Hussein attempted to play on the theme of Islamic unity during his final years in power, he was clearly a secularist, and his appeal to Islam largely failed.

Furthermore, as another Kurdish adage explains: "Compared to a non-believer, a Kurd is a good Muslim." In other words, despite their share of religious extremists, most Kurds disdain religious fanaticism. Thus, although almost all Kurds dream of a united Kurdistan, *Kurdayeti* remains only a vision. Given the harsh lessons of the twentieth century, most Kurds accept the political realities of the existing international boundaries. "Democracy for Iraq (Turkey, Iran, etc.), autonomy for Kurdistan" became the slogan of most Kurdish organizations in the twentieth century. More extremist demands for independence have been repeatedly and brutally crushed, and even the modest goal of democracy and autonomy has often seemed unattainable. Because of Saddam Hussein's egregious brutality toward the Kurds and his profound miscalculations in invading Kuwait, however, a de facto Kurdish state and government began to develop in northern Iraq after the Gulf War in 1991. With these facts in mind, the purpose of this chapter is to analyze the Kurdish minority identity in Iraq.

OVERVIEW[21]

During the First World War, the Sykes-Picot Agreement (1916) largely divided the postwar Middle East between Britain and France.[22] After more haggling, Britain eventually created Iraq out of the former Ottoman Vilayets (provinces) of Mosul in the Kurdish north, Baghdad (home to most of the new state's Sunnis), and Basra in the Shi'ite south.²³ Since this new ersatz state had less legitimacy than Turkey and Iran – two states that had existed in one form or another for many centuries despite their large Kurdish minorities – revolt probably came easier to the Iraqi Kurds.²⁴

Iraq's division between its ruling but minority Sunni Arabs and its suppressed but majority Shi'ite Arabs has facilitated the Iraqi Kurds' rebelliousness. By comparison, although the Kurds in Iran are largely Sunni, such a religious divide does not exist in Iran, which is otherwise Shi'ite and where the Indo-European-speaking Kurds are ethnically related to the Persians. Similarly, although as much as 20 per cent or more of Turkey's Muslim population may be Alevi, the resulting split with the majority Sunnis in Turkey is much less important than the divisions that exist in Iraq. Finally, the approximately 3.4 million Kurds now in Iraq have long constituted a greater, more concentrated proportion of their country's population (20 to 23 per cent) than even the much larger in absolute numbers but increasingly dispersed 12 million Kurds do in Turkey (18 to 21 per cent) or the 6 million Kurds do in Iran (11 per cent).

With good reason the Iraqi state also feared that Kurdish separatism might set a dangerous precedent for its Shi'ites, who numbered at least 55 per cent of Iraq's population.²⁵ In addition, since virtually all of the fresh water originated in the Kurdish north, along with approximately two-thirds of the oil reserves and much of the fertile land, the Iraqi government felt that Kurdish secession would strike at its economic heart.

To facilitate their rule, the British originally invited Sheik Mahmud Barzinji of Sulaymaniya to serve as their governor in Mosul. The gambit failed, as Sheik Mahmud almost immediately revolted, proclaimed himself "king of Kurdistan," and commenced secret dealings with the Turks, who still claimed the area. Employing its air force with maximum results, the British easily defeated these early Kurdish efforts. With Sheik Mahmud's final defeat in 1931, Mulla Mustafa Barzani (1903–79) began to emerge as the Kurds' leader, becoming almost synonymous with the Kurdish movement in Iraq.²⁶

Although their power was originally founded in the nineteenth century on their religious authority as Naqshbandi sheiks, the Barzanis also became noted for their martial prowess.²⁷ For more than half a century, Mulla Mustafa Barzani fought the then relatively weak Iraqi government in one way or another. Despite his inherent conservatism and even tribal mentality, Barzani was the guiding spirit of the Kurdistan Democratic Party (KDP), founded on 16 August 1946, and one of the generals in the short-lived Mahabad Republic of Kurdistan[28] in Iran immediately following the Second World War. After the collapse of this failed Kurdish state, Barzani fled to the Soviet Union, where he spent a decade in exile until the Iraqi monarchy was overthrown in July 1958. Iraq's new leader, General Abdul Karim Kassem – erring mightily in judgment – invited Barzani home as a balance against his many other potential domestic foes. By 1961, however, Barzani's *peshmergas* (guerrillas) were again in full-scale revolt.

At the height of his power, Barzani negotiated the March Manifesto of 1970, which theoretically provided for Kurdish autonomy under his rule. However, some Kurds – derisively referred to as *josh* (little donkeys) – supported the Iraqi government. Endemic Kurdish infighting with other leaders, such as Ibrahim Ahmad (1914–2000) and his son-in-law Jalal Talabani (b. 1933), and a more powerful Iraqi government now headed in practice by Saddam Hussein finally helped to precipitate Barzani's ultimate defeat in 1975. This debacle mainly occurred, however, because Iran and the United States withdrew their support from Barzani in return for Iraqi border concessions, an action that the US national security advisor, Henry Kissinger, cynically explained as necessary covert action not to be confused with missionary work.[29]

Following Barzani's defeat in March 1975, his son Massoud Barzani eventually emerged as the new leader of the KDP, while Talabani established his Patriotic Union of Kurdistan (PUK) on 1 June 1975. Divided by philosophy, dialect, geography, and ultimately ambition, Barzani's KDP and Talabani's PUK have alternated between cooperation and bloody conflict ever since. They have also suffered grievously from horrific repression, such as Saddam Hussein's genocidal *Anfal* campaigns of 1987–88 and his chemical attack on Halabja in March 1988, which were meant as retribution for the Kurds' support of Iran in the murderous Iran-Iraq War of 1980–88.[30]

After the Gulf War of 1991 and the failure of the ensuing Kurdish uprising in March 1991, the mass flight of Kurdish refugees to the mountains reluctantly forced the United States to launch Operation Provide Comfort (OPC). OPC created a safe haven and maintained a no-fly zone in which a de facto Kurdish state began to develop in northern Iraq.[31] In addition, the unprecedented United Nations Security Council Resolution 688, of 5 April 1991, condemned "the repression of the Iraqi civilian population ... in Kurdish populated areas" and demanded "that Iraq ... immediately end this repression." As symbolic as it may have been, never before had the Kurds received such official international mention and protection.

Despite the abject failure of Iraqi nationalism to satisfy and encompass Kurdish nationalism, Barzani still maintained that "our goal is not to set up an independent state."[32] Talabani shared this sentiment, declaring at the same time that "We do not want to break away from Iraq; we want a democratic Iraq."[33] Shortly after returning from a trip to Turkey and Europe in February and March 1992, Barzani explained his reasoning: "The situation in the world today is such that it will not permit any changes in regional borders. Nor will it stand for any partitioning." Therefore, argued the leader of the KDP, the Iraqi Kurds should "not swim against the international tide. We should act with wisdom ... [and] bear in mind that there is a wide gap between our wishes and our rights on the one hand, and what we can achieve on the other."[34]

Thus the Iraqi Kurds opted instead for some type of federalism, and on 4 October 1992 the fledgling Kurdish state sought to fortify its position by declaring itself a federated state within a post-Saddam Iraq. Queried about the meaning of what had been declared, Barzani argued that a federation "is a more advanced concept than autonomy but is not outside the framework of Iraq."[35] When asked if federation would not amount to secession from Iraq, he responded that "what leads to partitioning Iraq is the use of chemical weapons, genocide campaigns, racial discrimination and similar racist and chauvinistic (blind ethnic bigotry) measures."[36] Elaborating, the Iraqi Kurdish leader declared that "if Kurdish self-determination is contingent on our not seceding from Iraq, the nature of the regime that rules Baghdad will have to be radically different from what it is now. Iraq should become a democratic, pluralistic, and parliamentarian country."[37]

Talabani seemingly concurred: "We will not set up an [independent] state in northern Iraq ... This will be a new federal state ... For example, Germany is a federal state. Canada is ... a federation."[38] In another interview, Talabani again denied that "this decision [should] be considered as a first step towards a new and independent state. 'No, never. This is not a step in that direction. On the contrary, this decision will be a step, jointly with Iraq, towards ... Iraqi territorial integrity.'" He added that "the federal state will be like the State of

California in the United States."³⁹ Alluding to the continuing dream of Kurdish independence, however, Talabani told a Turkish reporter one month later that "we are a state ... We have a parliament, judges, prosecutors, and independent courts."⁴⁰

On 27 October 1992 some 234 delegates representing most of the Iraqi opposition groups began to gather for the first time on Iraqi soil in the town of Salahaddin near Irbil under the auspices of the fledgling Iraqi Kurdish state. This unprecedented conference resulted in a decision to make Iraq into a democratic and federal state once Saddam Hussein was overthrown.⁴¹

Reflecting upon the conference's achievements, both Barzani and Talabani maintained that the Kurds wanted to remain within a federal Iraq. The KDP leader declared that "the federated Kurdish state will exist within the territorial integrity of Iraq," while the PUK head asserted that "we want a federation within Iraq's territorial integrity."⁴² Claiming that he was speaking for the Kurds, Shi'ites, Sunnis, Turkomans, and Assyrians, Barzani concluded that "we wish to maintain the unity of the state and build a democratic, parliamentary, and multiparty federation capable of strengthening rather than splitting Iraq." He added that "the decision is to stay in Iraq and keep it united." The KDP leader maintained, however, that "they must allow us the right to decide what sort of relationship we want between us and the central government,"⁴³ thus implying that otherwise the Kurds might still opt for independence. And, of course, until the proposed new government succeeded in somehow coming to power, the fledgling Kurdish state in northern Iraq would remain.

Indispensable to the Iraqi Kurdish movement were Turkey's permission and logistical support for these proposed actions as well as OPC (since 1 January 1997, Operation Northern Watch), particularly its no-fly zone to protect the Iraqi Kurds. Without Turkey's cooperation, it would have been almost impossible for the United States to maintain the no-fly zone because there was nowhere else but Turkey to base its operations. Furthermore, given the double economic blockade placed on the Kurds by the United Nations – Iraqi Kurdistan was still legally part of Iraq, which remained under UN sanctions – and by Baghdad itself, Turkey became the Kurds' lifeline to the outside world.

Many Turks, however, believed that OPC was facilitating the vacuum of authority in northern Iraq that was enabling the Kurdistan Workers Party (PKK) to enjoy sanctuary there, from which it could launch attacks against Turkey.⁴⁴ Some even argued that OPC was the opening salvo of a new Treaty of Sevres (1920) that would lead to the creation of a Kurdish state in northern Iraq, as almost happened after the First World War. Thus, went the argument, Turkey was facilitating its own demise by housing OPC.

For Turkey to abandon OPC, however, would alienate the United States and strip the Turkish government in Ankara of important influence over the course of events. OPC, for example, has enabled Turkey to launch military strikes into Iraqi Kurdistan against the PKK at almost any time. If the United States refused to allow such Turkish incursions, Turkey could threaten to withdraw its permission for OPC. Ironically, an operation that was supposed to protect the Iraqi Kurds has allowed Turkey to attack the PKK as well as to inflict collateral damage on the host Iraqi Kurds. Turkey's interventions in northern Iraq have also implicitly challenged the very authority of the de facto Kurdish state.

Moreover, in May 1994 Barzani's KDP and Talabani's PUK fell into a civil war that further complicated the overall situation, leading to two rump Kurdish governments that continue today.⁴⁵ (How could the United States continue to protect the Iraqi Kurds when they were busy killing themselves?) Ultimately, their conflict derived from the old struggle for power between the more conservative, nationalist KDP, associated with the Kurmanji- or Bahdinani-speaking areas in the montainous northwest of northern Iraq, and the more leftist, socialist PUK, largely based in the Sorani-speaking areas of Sulaymaniya in the southeast. The hostility of Turkey, Iran, and Iraq to any Kurdish state, in addition to the desperate economic situation in the de facto state, also helped to fuel Kurdish infighting.

Further Kurdish infighting erupted in August 1995 when the PKK suddenly attacked the KDP for having agreed to police the border with Turkey as part of a deal the United States was trying to broker in order to prevent PKK raids against Turkey from northern Iraq. Both Syria and Iran covertly supported the PKK as a means to prevent Turkey and the United States from gaining further influence in the area, while the PUK supported the PKK as a means to reduce the influence of the KDP. Northern Iraq seemed to be falling into chaos.⁴⁶

In August 1996 the situation further degenerated when the PUK began to use arms received from Iran to threaten the KDP's very future. Desperate, Barzani did the unthinkable and invited Saddam Hussein to help beat back Talabani. (How could the United States enforce the no-fly zone against Saddam Hussein when some of the very people it was supposed to protect had invited him into northern Iraq?) Halfheartedly, the United States responded by bombing a few meaningless targets south of Baghdad. Saddam used the few hours he had to capture and execute some ninety-six Iraqis who had defected to the US-financed opposition, the Iraqi National Congress (INC). After Saddam withdrew, the conflict between the KDP and the PUK virtually returned to the status quo that had existed before his entry, except that the KDP now held the city of Irbil.

Following still more bloody Kurdish infighting, the United States finally helped to broker a tenuous ceasefire and invited Barzani and Talabani to Washington in September 1998 in an attempt to reach a permanent settlement. Although it has helped to end the KDP-PUK fighting, to date the resulting Washington Accord has failed to achieve a single, unified Kurdish government.

In addition, Turkey remains very suspicious of and adamantly opposed to the emergence of a Kurdish state in northern Iraq that would be able to act as an unwanted magnet for its own restless Kurds. Indeed, Turkey has gone so far as to declare that the creation of such a Kurdish state would be a *casus belli*. In late 2000 Turkey also encouraged the PUK to attack the PKK, which had been sheltering some of its units in the territory controlled by the PUK since 1992, when the earlier infighting had ended between the two Iraqi Kurdish parties, both of which were supported by Turkey against the PKK. Due to this past fighting, to Iraqi expulsions of Kurds from Kirkuk and other areas it controls, and to continuing economic and social problems, there are presently hundreds of thousands of internally displaced persons in Iraqi Kurdistan.

CONTINUING DEVELOPMENTS

The two most important but conflicting developments that the de facto state of Kurdistan in northern Iraq has experienced in its tenuous ten years of existence are (1) the debilitating KDP-PUK civil war that raged intermittently from 1994 to 1998 and (2) the much more encouraging fact that an entire generation is being raised under a Kurdish-run administration and will not be easily or willingly returned to dictatorial rule by Baghdad.[47] Economic conditions have also improved, with the Kurds receiving 13 per cent of Iraq's allotted funds from the oil that the UN now allows Iraq to sell under United

Nations Security Council Resolution 986, of 14 April 1995 – a percentage that was dramatically increased by Resolution 1153, of 20 February 1998. Over the past four years, the UN oil-for-food program has pumped some $4.6 billion into the de facto state, making it to some extent a UN welfare state.

Indeed, the Kurds get an even larger portion of the funds because some money is taken from the Iraqi government's share to cover war reparations and administrative costs. As a result, the Kurds get approximately 50 per cent more of these funds per capita than the rest of Iraq and are now considerably better off than their Iraqi counterparts. New roads are being built, refugees are being resettled, food supplies are adequate, water and electricity are available, and shops are full of refrigerators from Turkey, soaps from Syria, and even potato chips from Europe.[48] Nongovernmental organizations (NGOs) contribute maybe an additional $20 million via literacy and community-building initiatives not addressed by the United Nations.

A civil society is also emerging, characterized by dozens of newspapers, magazines, and television and radio stations representing a broad spectrum of opinions. People enjoy freedoms impossible to imagine in the rest of Iraq: In additon to the KDP and PUK, there are several smaller political parties in northern Iraq, and criticism of both the KDP and PUK administrations is tolerated. During the past year, municipal elections were successfully held in both the KDP and PUK areas. Islamists control Halabja within the PUK area and recently won almost 20 per cent of the seats on several student councils. Islamists also control the Ministry of Justice in both Kurdish administrations.

On 18 February 2001, however, Tawhid, an Islamic extremist group that had split off from the more moderate Islamic Movement of Kurdistan, assassinated Francis Hariri, a member of the KDP politburo and also a Christian. Several months later Tawhid joined other Islamic extremists to form the Jund al-Islam (Soldiers of Islam), now renamed the Ansar al-Islam (Supporters of Islam), an extremist Islamic group reputedly linked to elements of Osama bin Laden's al-Qa'ida network. Heavy fighting took place around Halabja in September 2001 between the PUK and the Jund al-Islam before the Islamic extremists were defeated and pushed back to the border with Iran. Although Turkey belittled the supposed connection to bin Laden, the threat of further Islamist violence clearly persists.

Some 3.4 million people live in the de facto state, including maybe 100,000 to 200,000 Turkomans and 50,000 Assyrians. Given recent developments, approximately 75 per cent of the population is now urban, and only 25 per cent is rural. Irbil has some 750,000 people, and Sulaymaniya has maybe a few less. The KDP administation controls about two-thirds of the de facto state's territory, its jurisdiction including maybe 2.2 million people, while the PUK administration controls the remaining one-third, which is inhabited by 1.2 million people. As many as 900,000 people are internally displaced, while each month about 200 people are maimed or killed by landmines strewn over the landscape during generations of past wars. The honour killing of women remains a problem, but attempts are being made to curtail it.

Since it controls the border trade with Turkey through the Ibrahim al-Khalil (Habur) gate, the KDP region is much more prosperous than its PUK counterpart. Indeed, the KDP area makes as much as $100 million a year from the oil it smuggles out of Iraq and from the consumer goods entering its territory via trade between Iraq and Turkey. At times the tanker trucks create traffic jams at the border stretching as far as six miles. Continuing disputes over the allocation of these border-trade funds are one of the main points of dispute between the two rump Kurdish administrations. There have also been charges of corruption and drug dealing involving leading personalities.

Nevertheless, shoppers fill the main boulevards of the PUK's capital, Sulaymaniya, where there is also a water park complete with toy motor boats, refreshment stands, and a functioning zoo that attracts crowds of people. A few miles outside the city stands the de facto state's only oil refinery.[49] The entire de facto state uses Iraqi currency printed before the Gulf War, called "Swiss dinars." These dinars now trade at a rate of nineteen per US dollar, a much better rate than that applied to the dinars currently used by Baghdad. The Kurdish region also has telecommunication systems and converts to daylight-saving time in the summer, making it one hour ahead of Baghdad time.

The entire Kurdish region has ten hospitals. Better medical training, however, is needed, and some medical specialities, such as neurosurgery and plastic surgery, are lacking. The electricity is often turned off, but hospitals have their own generators. The incidence of cancer is high, probably because of the use of chemical warfare in the past, and its treatment is hindered by the current lack of chemotherapy. Most sevices require only a nominal fee.

There are three separate universities (Salahaddin in Irbil, Sulaymaniya, and Dohuk), each with a medical school. "We have absolute academic freedom," declared Sarteed Karkai, the vice chancellor at Salahaddin University (named for Saladin, the famous Muslim leader who, as noted above, so chivalrously battled the Crusaders and was arguably the most famous of all Kurds).[50] At Salahaddin University approximately 5,000 students study at twelve colleges, their courses including education, agriculture, arts, sciences, economics, law, pharmacology, and dentistry. The universities have cell phones, and there is even Internet access on some computers.

The creation of an increasingly influential and in part highly educated diaspora of more than 500,000 Kurds in the West has provided an additional reservoir of support for the de facto state. This new diaspora already plays an important lobbying role both in the West and in the de facto state itself. The Kurdish diaspora also increasingly facilitates the return of needed human and technical resources to the homeland. When I originally met several current Kurdish leaders, for example, they were living in Europe or the United States. Hopefully, the democratically socialized diaspora will also begin to further the democratization process in Kurdistan.

US PROTECTION

The future of the de facto state of Kurdistan, of course, is very uncertain. Protection from the Iraqi government in Baghdad is the ultimate concern, and this security must continue to be provided by the United States. Given the withdrawal of US support in 1975 and the lack of support during the uprising in 1991, continuing US protection cannot be assumed. While brokering the accord between Barzani and Talabani in 1998, however, US Secretary of State Madeleine Albright did make general promises of US support for the Kurds contingent upon their continuing unity: "The United States will decide how and when to respond to Baghdad's actions based on the threat they pose to Iraq's neighbors, to regional security, to vital U.S. interests and to the Iraqi people, including those in the north."[51] President Clinton repeated Albright's tepid assurances in letters to Congress on 6 November 1998 and again on 19 May 1999.[52]

While announcing a halt to the four-day bombing of Iraq on 19 December 1998, however, Clinton seemed to make a much stronger guarantee by declaring, "we will maintain a strong military presence in the area, and we will remain ready to use it if Saddam ... moves against the Kurds. We also will continue to enforce no-fly zones in the North [and the South]."⁵³ In addition, on 22 April 1999, Martin Indyk, the assistant secretary of state for Near Eastern affairs, declared in a speech to the Council on Foreign Relations in New York, "we maintain a robust force in the region, which we have made clear we are prepared to use should Saddam cross our well-established red lines. Those red lines include ... should he move against his own people, especially in the north, or should he challenge us in the no-fly zone."⁵⁴ In August 2001 Colin Powell, the secretary of state in the new George W. Bush administation, assured Barzani and Talabani of continuing US support.⁵⁵

Although these pronouncements did not constitute an ironclad agreement of protection, they were – in contrast to Nixon's and Kissinger's covert and unkept promises of a quarter of a century earlier⁵⁶ – public declarations. Thus they could not be so cavalierly ignored. At best, however, these guarantees applied only against Saddam Hussein. They did not apply to Turkey or Iran, both of which continued militarily to intervene at will in the de facto state, especially Turkey in pursuit of the PKK.

As Talabani tellingly observed, "the [US] international protection is ... against alleged or possible Iraqi aggression and is not for protection against Turkish or Iranian interference ... We believe that the Turkish military interference can sometimes be more dangerous than the Iraqi military interference."⁵⁷ Finally, the US guarantees did not necessarily apply against a post-Saddam Iraqi government hostile to the de facto state. The US concern for the Iraqi Kurds was motivated by its continuing animus toward Saddam Hussein. Once the Iraqi dictator disappeared from the scene, continuing US support seemed problematic.

The US war that removed Saddam Hussein from power in 2003, however, has largely created a new situation. During the events leading up to the war, the Kurds renewed their commitment to remaining in a post-Saddam democratic and federal Iraq.⁵⁸ During the war itself, the Kurds, at the expense of Turkey, became an even closer US ally than anyone could ever have expected. This ironic situation was brought about by Turkey refusing to allow the United States to use its territory as a base for a northern front to attack Iraq in March 2003. Courtesy of Turkey, the Iraqi Kurds suddenly were thrust into the role of US ally, a novel position they eagerly and successfully assumed. Quickly, the Iraqi Kurds occupied the oil-rich Kirkuk and Mosul areas, which would have been unthinkable encroachments upon Turkish "red lines" had Turkey anchored the northern front. Moreover, Turkey has no choice but to acquiesce to the Kurdish moves.

The new situation was further illustrated in July 2003 when the United States apprehended eleven Turkish commandos in the Iraqi Kurdish city of Sulaymaniya who were apparently seeking to carry out acts that would destabilize the de facto Kurdish governments and state in northern Iraq. Previously, as the strategic ally of the United States, Turkey had been granted carte blanche to do practically anything it wanted to in northern Iraq. This is no longer true. The "Sulaymaniya incident" caused what one high-ranking Turkish general called the "worst crisis of confidence"[59] in US-Turkish relations since the creation of the NATO alliance. It also illustrated how the United States was willing to protect the Iraqi Kurds from unwanted Turkish interference. In addition, powerful Iraqi Kurdish opposition to the proposed deployment of 10,000 Turkish troops to areas in Iraq south of the Kurdish region – a decision the Turkish Parliament made in October 2003 in an effort to revive its failing fortunes with the United States and to regain control over evolving events in Iraq – helped to force Turkey to rescind its offer shortly after it was issued.

Of course, Turkey still possesses an important geographical location and tremendous military superiority over the Iraqi Kurds. Given time, therefore, it is likely that Turkey will partially reassert its strategic relationship with the United States even if the Iraqi Kurds offer the United States ready military bases to replace those no longer as available in Turkey. For the time being, however, there is a historic opportunity for the Iraqi Kurds to achieve (with US support) what Turkey has always opposed (with US support): a Kurdish federal state within Iraq or even some kind of an independent Iraqi Kurdish state.

The Iraqi Kurds, however, would be well advised to proceed with the consent of Turkey because, when the United States leaves Iraq, the Kurds will have to live with the Turks, who will always be next door. Thus the Iraqi Kurds should be rather modest in their demands and from their newfound position of relative strength try to cut the best deal possible with Turkey in order to show the Turkish government in Ankara that the Kurds are not the enemies of Turkey and that the two can cooperate to the mutual advantage of both. This will take extraordinary skill and imagination on the part of both parties, but given the past tragedies that failed earlier policies have engendered, both the Kurds and Turkey deserve better in the post-Saddam world.

In addition, of course, the increasing difficulties with anti-US insurgents that the United States was experiencing in Iraq at the end of 2003 may prove to be the mere tip of the iceberg among factors impeding the US's attempts to create a democratic federal Iraq that will satisfy the Kurdish fears of renewed, oppressive Arab-majority rule. Clearly, the Shi'a Arabs in Iraq seek to implement a unitary state based on their majority status, while the Sunni Arabs in Iraq seek to maintain their privileged position despite forming a minority. Where is the basis in these opposed agendas for recognizing Kurdish rights? For democracy and federalism to work, all groups must recognize the legitimacy of the state, trust in one's fellow citizens, and have faith in majority rule. Since there is no tradition of any of this in Iraq, the Kurdish future in post-Saddam Iraq remains problematic.

NOTES

1 For an excellent survey of the various theories involved, see John Hutchinson and Anthony D. Smith, eds, *Nationalism*.
2 For a discussion of numerous theoretical approaches, see Gabriel Ben-Dor, "Minorities in the Middle East."
3 For an excellent recent history of the Kurds, see David McDowall, *A Modern History of the Kurds*.
4 Philip G. Kreyenbroek, "On the Kurdish Language."
5 Philip G. Kreyenbroek and Christine Allison, eds, *Kurdish Culture and Identity*.
6 Amir Hassanpour, *Nationalism and Language in Kurdistan, 1918–1985*, xxiv. Hassanpour's erudite study is an excellent source on the state of the Kurdish language.
7 Edgar T.A. Wigram and W.A. Wigram, *The Cradle of Mankind: Life in Eastern Kurdistan*, 39 n.
8 C.J. Edmonds, "Kurdish Nationalism," 88.
9 Mehrdad R. Izady, *The Kurds: A Concise Handbook*, 185.
10 Margaret Kahn, *Children of the Jinn*, xi.
11 C.J. Edmonds, *Kurds, Turks and Arabs*, 4.
12 For a detailed analysis of the Kurds' complicated and heterogeneous ethnic make-up, see Vladimir Minorsky, "Kurds."

13 Cited in Martin van Bruinessen, *Agha, Shaikh and State*, 267.
14 Kurdish society during this period may be termed "feudal" because loyalties were mainly to primordial entities such as families, tribes (with their *ağas*, or landlords), and religious sheiks.
15 Cited in Hassanpour, *Nationalism and Language in Kurdistan*, 55.
16 Izady, *The Kurds*, 188.
17 Ibid. Although fascinating, Izady's discussion of Kurdish religions greatly exaggerates their current diverstiy. Most Kurds today are Sunni Muslim.
18 Kendal Nezan, "The Kurds," 18.
19 Ibid.
20 For an excellent analysis of this situation, see van Bruinessen, *Agha, Shaikh and State*, 50–264.
21 I originally published portions of the following section in M. Hakan Yavuz and Michael M. Gunter, "The Kurdish Nation."
22 See David Fromkin, *A Peace to End All Peace: Creating the Modern Middle East, 1914–1922*.
23 See Stephen H. Longrigg, *Iraq, 1900 to 1950*.
24 For background, see Toby Dodge, *Inventing Iraq*; Edmonds, *Kurds, Turks and Arabs*; Edmund Ghareeb, *The Kurdish Question in Iraq*; and Ismet Sheriff Vanly, "Kurdistan in Iraq."
25 For insights into the dynamics involved, see Kanan Makiya, *Cruelty and Silence: War, Tyranny, Uprising and the Arab World*.
26 For further analysis of Barzani, see Massoud Barzani, *Mustafa Barzani and the Kurdish Liberation Movement*; and Dana Adams Schmidt, *Journey Among Brave Men*.
27 Mark Sykes, *The Caliph's Last Heritage. A Short History of the Turkish Empire*, 561.
28 On the Mahabad Republic, see *The Republic of Kurdistan: Fifty Years Later*; and William Eagleton, Jr, *The Kurdish Republic of 1946*.
29 "The CIA Report the President Doesn't Want You to Read," *The Village Voice* (New York), 16 February 1976, 87–8. This report is commonly referred to as the US House Pike Committee Report, which, like its more famous counterpart, known as the US Senate Church Committee Report, detailed the US Congress's investigation of the CIA in the mid-1970s.
30 Human Rights Watch/Middle East, *Iraq's Crime of Genocide*.
31 For more background, see Michael M. Gunter, *The Kurds of Iraq*, 87–95, and "A De Facto Kurdish State in Northern Iraq."
32 "Turkish Paper Interviews Barzani," as cited in *Foreign Broadcast Information Service: Near East and South Asia* (hereafter FBIS-NES), 9 June 1992, 26.

33 "PUK Leader Talabani Interviewed," *2000 Ikibin'e Dogru* (Istanbul), 31 May 1992, 1012; as cited in FBIS-NES, 9 June 1992, 27.

34 "Kurds' Barzani Discusses Peace Efforts, Autonomy," (Clandestine) Voice of Iraqi Kurdistan in Arabic, 1653 GMT, 13 April 1992; as cited in FBIS-NES, 15 April 1992, 41.

35 Cited in "KDP's Barzani Interviewed on Federation Plans," *Al-Akbar* (Cairo), 22 November 1992, 4; as cited in FBISNES, 1 December 1992, 25. Since the 1960s "autonomy" had been the official goal of most Iraqi Kurdish parties, and since 1975 the Kurdish region in northern Iraq had been referred to by the Baghdad government as the "Autonomous Region." Most Iraqi Kurds now felt, however, that this experience with autonomy had been a terrible failure.

36 Ibid., 25.

37 Ibid., 24.

38 Cited in "Explains Intentions in North," *Tercuman* (Istanbul), 11 November 1992, 10; as cited in FBIS-NES, 18 November 1992.

39 Cited in "Kurdish Officials Interviewed," Ankara Kanal6 Television Network in Turkish, 1730 GMT, 19 October 1992; as cited in *Foreign Broadcast Information Service: West Europe* (hereafter FBIS-WEU), 22 October 1992, 72.

40 Cited in "Report Views Relations between Ankara, Peshmergas," *Tercuman* (Istanbul), 3 December 1992, 11; as cited in FBIS-WEU, 9 December 1992, 40. Talabani was taking a tough stance against the Turkish request that the PKK fighters who had surrendered to the Iraqi Kurds be handed over to the Turks. They were not.

41 "First Successful Opposition Meeting Concludes," Ankara Anatolia in Turkish, 1500 GMT, 31 October 1992; as cited in FBIS-NES, 2 November 1992, 24.

42 Cited in "Temporary Government Planned," Ankara Anatolia in Turkish, 1630 GMT, 28 October 1992; as cited in FBIS-NES, 29 October 1992, 28.

43 "Barzani Interviewed on Planned 'Government in Exile,'" *Avanti!* (Rome), 3 November 1992, 14; as cited in FBIS-NES, 6 November 1992, 22.

44 On the PKK, see Michael M. Gunter, *The Kurds and the Future of Turkey*; and Paul White, *Primitive Rebels or Revolutionary Modernizers?*

45 For background, see Michael M. Gunter, *The Kurdish Predicament in Iraq*, 67–109, and "The KDP-PUK Conflict in Northern Iraq."

46 For background, see Michael M. Gunter, "Turkey and Iran Face Off in Kurdistan."

47 The following data were largely gathered from interviews with, among others, Nechirvan Idris Barzani, the prime minister of the KDP administration in Irbil, Washington, DC, 17 April 2000; Barham Salih, the prime

minister of the PUK administration in Sulaymaniya since January 2001, Washington, DC, 21 November 1999; Hoshyar Zebari, a leading KDP official and subsequently the first foreign minister in the post-Saddam Iraqi government, Washington, DC, 17 April 2000; Noshirwan Mustafa Amin, a leading PUK official, London, UK, 21 December 1997; Kamal Fuad, a leading PUK official, Berlin, Germany, 10 April 1999; and Mahmud Uthman, an important Kurdish activist and subsequently a member of the post-Saddam Iraqi Governing Council, London, UK, 18 December 1997. Earlier, in August 1993, I travelled extensively through the de facto state of Kurdistan at the invitation of both the KDP and the PUK. At this time I had the opportunity to interview, among others, Massoud Barzani; Jalal Talabani; Fuad Masum, the first prime minister of the unified Kurdish administration, 1992–93; his successor, Kosrat Abdallah Rasul, who continued in this role in the PUK administration until January 2001; and Sami Abdurrahman, currently the deputy prime minister in the KDP administration. See also the excellent new study by Gareth R.V. Stansfield, *Iraqi Kurdistan: Political Development and Emergent Democracy.*

48 For further background, see Louis Meixler, "Kurds Still Dependent on Outsiders," Associated Press, 15 January 2001; David Hirst, "Kurds Reap Sanctions' Rewards," *Washington Times*, 15 August 2001; and Jeffrey Goldberg, "The Great Terror," *The New Yorker*, 25 March 2002, 52–75.

49 For further background, see David Aquila Lawrence, "A Shaky De Facto Kurdistan," www.merip.org/mer/mer215/215_lawrence.html; and Kendal Nezan, "A Renaissance in Iraq: The Kurds, a Fragile Spring," *Le Monde Diplomatique* (Paris), August 2001, www.monde-diplomatique.fr.

50 This citation and the following discussion were taken from David Aquila Lawrence, "In Their Own Universities, Kurds Taste Academic Freedom," A55.

51 Cited in Harun Kazaz, "Ambiguity Surrounds N. Iraq Kurdish Agreement," *Turkish Probe* (Ankara), 11 October 1998, www.turkishdailynews.com/past_probe/10_11_98/foreign.htm#f1.

52 Both letters were entitled "Text of a Letter from the President to the Speaker of the House of Representatives and the President Pro Tempore of the Senate" and dated respectively 6 November 1998 and 19 May 1999, www.globalsecurity.org/wmd/library/news/iraq/1998/98110601_nlt.html; www.globalsecurity.org/wmd/library/news/iraq/1998/990519_iraq-usia02.htm.

53 Cited in "Remarks of the President on Iraq," 19 December 1998, www.globalsecurity.org/wmd/library/news/iraq/1998/98121913_tlt.html.

54 Cited in "Amb. Martin S. Indyk Assistant Secretary of State for Near Eastern Affairs Remarks to the Council on Foreign Relations, NYC, 22 April 1999," www.state.gov/www/policy_remarks/1999/990422_indyk_mepolicy.html.
55 "U.S. to Protect the Democratic Experiment in Iraqi Kurdistan," *Kurdistan Observer* (London), 21 August 2001, *http://mywebpage.netscape.com/kurdistanobserve/21-8-01-ko-us-assures-kurds.html*.
56 In 1975 the United States and Iran withdrew their support from the Iraqi Kurds, thus allowing Baghdad to defeat the long-running rebellion of Mulla Mustafa Barzani, Massoud Barzani's famous father. For Kissinger's recent reappraisal of these events, see his *Years of Renewal*, 576–96.
57 Cited in Salah Awwad, "Interview with Jalal Talabani," *Al-Quds al-Arabi* (London), 22 September 1998, 3, www.alquds.co.uk/.
58 For details, see Michael M. Gunter, "Kurdish Future in a Post-Saddam Iraq."
59 "Ozkok: Biggest Crisis of Trust with US," *Turkish Daily News* (Ankara), 8 July 2003, www.turkishdailynews.com/old_editions/07_08_03/for.htm.

CONCLUSION

The term "identity formation" began its scholarly journey in psychology, where it originally referred to formation of the individual ego rather than to formation of a collective conscience. Erik Erikson provided the interdisciplinary link in 1946, when he criticized Freud for dismissing the influences of one's ethnicity, historical era, and economic pursuit in the process of ego formation.[1] Erikson argued that the individual ego is shaped at a younger age by the "masses" (a sociological multitude without definitive structures), by images of good and evil, and by historical change, the latter often being difficult to clearly discern. These influences, rather than the fact that all children go through the "oedipal-complex" phase or that sexuality begins at birth, were in his view the qualifiers of ego formation.[2] Although his conclusions were based on the study of North American Indians, the historical analysis of how minority identities in general developed has benefitted from Erikson's observations. He pointed out that given the appropriate definition, anyone can be described as belonging to one minority group or another and that minority and majority identities are interlinked. This is the element of Erikson's work that people in other disciplines, whether historical, social, or political, have found rewarding when analyzing group behaviour.

For instance, historians of minorities in medieval Europe have used minority identities to measure and analyze how they were collectively perceived by the majorities that persecuted them. In studying the persecution of Muslims, Jews, and lepers in the Crown of Aragon in the fourteenth century, David Nirenberg referred to minority identities as the "majority's collective anxieties."[3] Norman Cohn has shown how the stereotypes of medieval sects made their way into Nazi Germany's race mythology.[4] To his mind, when minority stereotypes are used in establishing the image of the "other," they become so persistent that they prevent any major shifts in perception and thus predict future persecutions.

For their part, when minorities come under attack, they show intellectual creativity. Melkite, Jacobite, and Nestorian Christians in the Middle East responded to Islam by composing a rich Christian apologetic literature and, when facing a rise in the number of conversions to Islam in the ninth century, by translating the gospels into Arabic.[5] The Berbers in North Africa, suffering from their image as apostates who repeatedly renounced Islam, replied by inventing for themselves a myth of origin claiming that their conversion to Islam took place in the seventh century as the result of a mission they sent to the Prophet in Medina.[6] Whether historical or mythical, primordial ties based on blood, kinship, religion, clan, and/or presumed historical affinities, have continued to surface in the collective psyche of both minority and majority communities, persisting as powerful factors in violence toward minorities as recently as the early 1990s.[7]

The case of the Bosnian war of 1992–95, a conflict involving an Islamic minority, the Bosnian Muslims, within a Christian-majority state, connects us to the cases studied in this volume by highlighting the role of the modern nation-state.[8] Case after case has shown that a state's authoritarian rule, uncompromising attitude toward expressions of particularism, and inability to offer tools for inclusion, whether institutional or otherwise, have been responsible for the politicization and radicalization of minority identities. While still preserving their classical and historical qualifiers, minority and majority peoples have reinvented themselves in the modern nation-state through an antagonistic process of mutual exclusion. The authoritarian nature of the state, with which Islamic societies acquiesce, together with antidemocratic political processes have highlighted its role in the exclusion of minorities and contributed to civil unrest.

Economic hardships, including poverty and deprivation, a lack of economic progress, and inadequate access to economic resources and opportunities, certainly define grievances against the modern nation-state in general, but when a minority is identified with being poor, its economic plight becomes an element in its minority identity formation. Language and culture play similar roles as qualifiers of minority identities. The Islamic nation-state purposely forbids cultural diversity as nationally divisive. However, the cases discussed in this book show that because there were so many local dialects, language could hardly be called a unifying factor in the formation of minority identities, but neither was it a divisive element. Minority groups voiced their political agendas in the state's majority language but still used the language issue as an instrument for mobilization.

The place of Islam in this process is complex. Early Islamic dogma famously recognized and accepted, although in a somewhat qualified manner, religious pluralism in Islamic societies by giving Jews and Christians freedom to practice. Islam also provided the rationale for crossing ethnic lines. Arabs, Kurds, Berbers, and Turks were fused together within a global and universal Islamic community *(umma)* and acted as its political leaders. The implementation of the modern nation-state changed all this, intitially by denying religion as a qualifier of national unity in favour of secular nationalist qualifiers and later by making Islam a qualifier for unity. In both cases the authoritarian nation-state established the exclusion of minority identities by adopting Western-style political tools, such as parliamentary elections, laws, and political parties, in a complete reversal of the Islamic traditions of political inclusion. Also part of the Islamic factor is the significant role that the majority society's Islamic radicalization has played in radicalizing and politicizing minority identities. For their part, minorities have conceptualized the struggle to equate the Islamic identity with national identity as an additional inhibition of their own "cultural" and "religious" identifiers.

In general, universalist secular ideologies such as nationalism, socialism, and communism had made some inroads into the formation of minority identities before their influence subsided in tandem with their decline across the world. As the central ideology of the modern nation-state, however, secular nationalism had the effect not of facilitating minority identity formation but of excluding minorities, whose identities were deemed incompatible with state ideology. The state's later recourse to international social ideologies as an alternative to secular nationalism proved unsuitable for Islamic societies, giving rise to the supreme leader, intellectual or otherwise, whose fascist-like call for blind obedience has been a feature of Islamic extremism – a development not seen among minority identities.

The growing effect of ethnic migration in reaction to persecution or economic hardships is another factor present in the formation of minority identities. Diaspora groups exercise their influence through expatriate organizations and through the international media, a clear example being the case of the Copts. However, whether "cultural" or "religious," any demands for autonomy presented to the state via expatriate activities are represented to the majority society as evidence of the minority's disloyalty to the nation and of its call for outside intervention. While the local Egyptian Coptic community, led by the church, is eager to stress the essentially "national Egyptian" nature of their "minorityness," diaspora Coptic communities claim that their religion is being sacrificed in order to ingratiate Copts in the eyes of a Muslim state that continues to harass them. Egyptian Copts, whose identity defines them as Egyptians, rightly fear the majority's wrath against them when expatriates protest Egypt's handling of their community from their safety in a pluralistic society.

But globalization and outside intervention have energized minority identities in other cases, such as among the Kurds in Iraq, by facilitating a hitherto nonexistent measure of political independence. However, the transitory nature of such an intervention should be seen as playing only a minor and temporary role that will not eliminate the minority's need to interact with their nation state. Thus the ideas of separation or autonomy are rarely voiced even though they may still reside in the historical consciousness of minority identities. Having said this, what distinguishes "cultural" from "religious" minorities are their future opportunities. "Cultural" minorities have a greater ability to pressure the state and force it into dialogue with them. This capacity, which results from a combination of a less threatening identity and limited numerical power, is favourable to their status in the modern nation-state. Minorities claiming autonomy for identities based on language and culture are more likely to be accommodated by the state than are "religious" minorities with a political agenda. With the global decline in secularism, "religious" minorities, although smaller in numbers and stigmatized, remain no less vulnerable than were their medieval predecessors.

Maya Shatzmiller

NOTES

1 Erik H. Erikson, "Ego Development and Historical Change."
2 "Analysis of the ego should include that of the individual's ego identity in relation to the historical changes which dominated his childhood milieu ... For the individual's mastery over his neurosis begins where he is put in a position to accept the historical necessity which made him what he is ... only thus he can derive ego strength from the coincidence of his own and only life cycle with a particular segment of human history" (ibid., 49).
3 David Nirenberg, *Communities of Violence: Persecution of Minorities in the Middle Ages*, 13–14.
4 Norman Cohn, *The Pursuit of the Millenium*, and *Warrant for Genocide*.
5 Sidney H. Griffith, *Arabic Christianity in the Monasteries of Ninth-Century Palestine*.
6 Maya Shatzmiller, *The Berbers and the Islamic State*, 5–27.
7 Michael A. Sells, "The Construction of Islam in Serbian Religious Mythology and Its Consequences."
8 This theme is dealt with in one way or another by all the essays in Maya Shatzmiller, ed., *Islam and Bosnia*.

Bibliographies

CHAPTER ONE

Bengio, Ofra, and Gabriel Ben-Dor, eds. *Minorities and the State in the Arab World*. Boulder, CO: Lynne Reinner, 1999.
Bulliet, Richard W. *Conversion to Islam in the Medieval Period: Essay in Quantitative History.* Cambridge, MA: Harvard University Press, 1979.
Cahen, Claude. "Dhimma." In H.A.R. Gibb et al., eds, *Encyclopaedia of Islam*, 2nd ed. Leiden: E.J. Brill, 1960.
de Planhol, Xavier. *Minorités en Islam: Géographie politique et sociale*. Paris: Flammarion, 1997.
El Fadl, Khaled Abou. "Islamic Law and Muslim Minorities: The Juristic Discourse on Muslim Minorties from the Second/Eighth to the Eleventh/Seventeenth Centuries." *Islamic Law and Society* 1, no. 1 (1994): 141–87.
– "Legal Debates on Muslim Minorities: Between Rejection and Accommodation." *Journal of Religious Ethics* 22, no. 1 (1994): 127–62.
– "Striking a Balance: Islamic Legal Discourse on Minorities." In Yvonne Yazbeck Haddad and John L. Esposito, eds, *Muslims on the Americanization Path?* 47–63. Oxford and New York: Oxford University Press, 1998.
Enderwitz, Susanne. "Shu'ubiyya." In H.A.R. Gibb et al., eds, *Encyclopaedia of Islam*, 2nd ed. Leiden: E.J. Brill, 1960.
Esack, Farid. *Qur'an, Liberation and Pluralism: An Islamic Perspective of Interreligious Solidarity Against Oppression*. Oxford: Oneworld, 1997.

Geertz, Clifford. "The Integrative Revolution." In *Old Societies and New States: The Quest for Modernity in Asia and Africa*, 105–57. New York: Free Press, 1963.

Gibb, Hamilton A.R. *Studies on the Civilization of Islam*. Edited by Stanford J. Shaw and William R. Polk. Boston: Beacon Press, 1962.

– et al., eds. *Encyclopaedia of Islam*. 2nd ed. Leiden: E.J. Brill, 1960.

Hodgson, Marshall G.S. *The Venture of Islam: Conscience and History in a World Civilization*. 3 volumes. Chicago and London: The University of Chicago Press, 1974.

Hourani, Albert H. *Minorities in the Arab World*. London, New York, and Toronto: Oxford University Press, 1947.

Kettani, M. Ali. *Muslim Minorities in the World Today*. London and New York: Mansell Publishing, 1986.

Lawrence, Bruce B. *Defenders of God: The Fundamentalist Revolt Against the Modern Age*. San Francisco: Harper and Row, 1989.

Lewis, Bernard. *Race and Color in Islam*. New York: Harper and Row, 1970.

Madelung, Wilferd. "The Murji'a and Sunnite Traditionalism." In *Religious Trends in Early Islamic Iran*, 13–25. Albany, NY: Persian Heritage Foundation, 1988.

Marty, Martin E., and Scott Appleby, eds. *Fundamentalisms Observed*. Chicago: Universty of Chicago Press, 1991.

an-Na'im, Abdullahi Ahmed. *Human Rights in Cross-Cultural Perspectives: A Quest for Consensus*. Philadelphia: University of Pennsylvania Press, 1992.

– "Toward an Islamic Hermeneutics of Human Rights." In Abdullahi A. an-Na'im et al., eds, *Human Rights and Religious Values: An Uneasy Relationship?* Grand Rapids, MI: W.B. Eerdmans, 1994.

Rose, Arnold M. "Minorities." In Neil J. Smelzer and Paul B. Baltes, eds, *International Encyclopedia of the Social and Behavioral Sciences*, vol. 14, 9894–901. Amsterdam and New York: Elsevier, 2001.

Tritton, A.S. *The Caliphs and their Non-Muslim Subjects: A Critical Study of the Covenant of 'Umar*. 1930. Reprint, London: Frank Cass and Company, 1970.

Ye'or, Bat. *Islam and Dhimmitude: Where Civilizations Collide*. Translated by Miriam Kochan and David Littman. Madison and Teaneck, NJ: Fairleigh Dickinson University, 2002.

CHAPTER TWO

'Abd Allah, Isma'il Sabri, William Sulaiman Qilada, and Muhammad Salim al-'Awa. *Al-Muwatina*. Cairo: The Coptic Centre for Social Studies, 1998.

'Abd el-Fattah, Nabil, and Diaa Rashwan. *The State of Religion in Egypt Report 1995: Summary.* Cairo: Al-Ahram Centre for Political and Strategic Studies, 1997.

Assad, Maurice. "Prägung der koptischen Identität." In Paul Verghese, ed., *Koptischen Christentum.* Stuttgart: Evangelisches Verlagswerk, 1973.

[Athanasius, Anba] Bishopric of Beni Suef, ed. *Bustan al-Ruhban* [The garden of the monks]. Beni Suef: 1968.

Atiya, Aziz Souriyal, ed. *The Coptic Encyclopedia.* Volume 1. New York: Macmillan, 1991.

Barth, Fredrik. "Ethnic Groups and Boundaries." In John Hutchinson and Anthony D. Smith, eds, *Ethnicity,* 75–83. Oxford and New York: Oxford University Press, 1996.

Cannuyer, Christian. *Coptic Egypt: The Christians of the Nile.* New York: Harry N. Abrams, 2001.

Carter, R.B.L. *The Copts in Egyptian Politics, 1918–1952.* London: Croom Helm, 1986.

Castells, Manuel. *The Information Age: Economy, Society, and Culture.* Vol. 2, *The Power of Identity.* Malden, MA: Blackwell Publishers, 1997.

Chitham, E.J. *The Coptic Community in Egypt: Spatial and Social Change.* Durham: Centre for Middle Eastern and Islamic Studies, 1986.

Country Reports on Human Rights Practices 2002: Egypt. Washington DC: Bureau of Democracy, Human Rights and Labor, 31 March 2003.

Esman, Milton J., and Itamar Rabinovich, eds. *Ethnicity, Pluralism, and the State in the Middle East.* Ithaca and London: Cornell University Press, 1988.

Farah, Nadia Ramsis. *Religious Strife in Egypt: Crisis and Ideological Conflict in the Seventies.* New York and London: Gordon and Breach Science Publishers, 1986.

General Census of Population and Housing, all Egypt. Cairo: Central Agency for Public Mobilization and Statistics, 1986.

Hasan, S.S. *Christians versus Muslims in Modern Egypt: The Century-Long Struggle for Coptic Equality.* Oxford and New York: Oxford University Press, 2003.

Hutchinson, John, and Anthony D. Smith, eds, *Ethnicity.* Oxford and New York: Oxford University Press, 1996.

Ibrahim, Saad Eddin, et al. *The Copts of Egypt.* London: Minority Rights Group, 1996.

– Letter on the Occasion of the Visit to Egypt by the US Commission on International Religious Freedom. *Copts Digest,* 20–23 March 2001, Coptsdigest.com.

Kater, Nathan. "On the Arabhood of the Copts." *Copts Digest*, 20 September 2001, Coptsdigest.com.

Kepel, Gilles. *The Prophet and the Pharaoh: Muslim Extremism in Egypt*. London: Al-Saqi Books, 1985.

Khalidi, Tarif. "Religion and Citizenship in Islam." In Jorgen S. Nielsen, ed., *Religion and Citizenship in Europe and the Arab World*. London: Grey Seal Books, 1992.

Markos, His Grace Bishop Antonius. *Come Across ... and Help Us: The Story of the Coptic Orthodox Church in Africa and Our Present Time*. Vols 1 and 2. Cairo: Coptic Bishopric of African Affairs, 1993.

Martin, Maurice S.J. "The Coptic-Muslim Conflict in Egypt: Modernization of Society and Religious Renovation." In CEMAM *Reports 1: Tensions in the Middle East*. Beirut: Dar el-Mashreq, 1973.

el-Masri, Iris Habib. *The Story of the Copts*. Cairo: The Middle East Council of Churches, 1978.

Nasr, Amir. *Al-Musharika al-Wataniya lil-Aqbat fi al-'Asr al-Hadith*. Vol. 1. Cairo: The Coptic Centre for Social Studies, 1998.

Nielsen, Jorgen S., ed. *Religion and Citizenship in Europe and the Arab World*. London: Grey Seal Books, 1992.

Qilada, William Sulaiman. *Mabda'u-l-Muwatina*. Cairo: The Coptic Centre for Social Studies, 1999.

Reiss, Wolfram. *Erneuerung in der Koptisch-Orthodoxen Kirche: Die Geschichte der Koptisch-Orthodoxen Sontagsschulbewegung und die Aufnahme ihrer Reformansätze in den Erneuerungsbewegungen der Koptisch-Orthodoxen Kirche der Gegenwart*. Hamburg: Lit, 1998.

Smith, Anthony D. *Myths and Memories of the Nation*. Oxford and New York: Oxford University Press, 1999.

– *National Identity*. Reno, Las Vegas, and London: University of Nevada Press, 1991.

Stene, Nora. "Becoming a Copt: The Integration of Coptic Children into the Church Community." In Pieternella van Doorn-Harder and Kari Vogt, eds, *Between Desert and City: The Coptic Orthodox Church Today*. Oslo: Novus Forlag, 1997.

– "Multiple Choice? Language-usage and the Transmission of Religious Tradition in the Coptic Orthodox Community in London." *British Journal of Religious Education* 20, no. 2 (1998): 90–101.

van Doorn-Harder, Pieternella. *Contemporary Coptic Nuns*. Columbia, SC: University of South Carolina Press, 1995.

– and Kari Vogt, eds. *Between Desert and City: The Coptic Orthodox Church Today*. Oslo: Novus Forlag, 1997.

van Nispen tot Sevenaer, Christiaan. "Changes in Relations between Copts and Muslims." In Pieternella van Doorn-Harder and Kari Vogt, eds, *Between Desert and City: The Coptic Orthodox Church Today.* Oslo: Novus Forlag, 1997.
Vatikiotis, P.J. "Non-Muslims in Muslim Society: A Preliminary Consideration of the Problem on the Basis of Recent Published Works by Muslim Authors." In Milton J. Esman and Itamar Rabinovich, eds, *Ethnicity, Pluralism, and the State in the Middle East*, 54–70. Ithaca and London: Cornell University Press, 1988.
Verghese, Paul, ed. *Koptischen Christentum.* Stuttgart: Evangelisches Verlagswerk, 1973.
Zeidan, David. "The Copts: Equal, Protected or Persecuted? The Impact of Islamization on Muslim-Christian Relations in Modern Egypt." *Islam and Christian-Muslim Relations* 10, no. 1 (1999): 53–67.

CHAPTER THREE

Afifi, Mohamed. "Reflections on the Personal Laws of Egyptian Copts." In Amira El Azhary Sonbol, ed., *Women, the Family, and Divorce Laws in Islamic History.* Syracuse: Syracuse University Press, 1996.
Anderson, Benedict. *Imagined Communities: Reflections on the Origins and Spread of Nationalism.* 2nd ed. New York: Verso, 1991.
Atiya, Aziz Suryal, ed. *The Coptic Encyclopedia.* 8 volumes. New York: Macmillan International, 1991.
Ayalon, Ami. "Egypt's Coptic Pandora's Box." In Ofra Bengio and Gabriel Ben-Dor, *Minorities and the State in the Arab World.* Boulder, CO: Lynne Rienner, 1999.
al-Banna, Rajab. *al-Aqbat fi misr and al-mahjar: hiwarat ma' al-baba shanuda* [The Copts in Egypt and abroad: Conversations with Patriarch Shenuda]. Cairo: Dar al-Ma'arif, 1997.
Bayly, C.A. "Representing Copts and Muhammadans: Empire, Nation, and Community in Egypt and India, 1800–1914." In Leila Tarazi Fawaz and C.A. Bayly, eds, *Modernity and Culture: From the Mediterranean to the Indian Ocean*, 158–203. New York: Columbia University Press, 2002.
Beinin, Joel, and Joe Stork, eds. *Political Islam: Essays from Middle East Report.* Berkely: University of California Press, 1997.
Bengio, Ofra, and Gabriel Ben-Dor, eds. *Minorities and the State in the Arab World.* Boulder, CO: Lynne Rienner, 1999.
Berdun, Gubernau i, and Maria Montserrat. *Nations without States: Political Communities in a Global Age.* Malden, MA: Blackwell, 1999.

Botiveau, Bernard. "The Law of the Nation-State and the Status of non-Muslims in Egypt and Syria." In Andrea Pacini, ed., *Christian Communities in the Arab Middle East: The Challenge of the Future*, 111–26. London: Oxford University Press, 1999.

– "National Law and Non-Muslim States." In Andrea Pacini, ed., *Christian Communities in the Arab Middle East: The Challenge of the Future*. London: Oxford University Press, 1999.

Brown, H. Scott Kent. "The Coptic Church in Egypt: A Comment on Protecting Religious Minorities from Nonstate Discrimination." *Brigham Young University Education and Law Journal* 2000, no. 3 (September 2000): 1049–99.

Carter, B.L. *The Copts in Egyptian Politics*. London: Croom Helm, 1986.

Chatterjee, Partha. "Whose Imagined Community?" In Gopal Balakrishnan, ed, *Mapping the Nation*. New York: Verso, 1996.

Collins, Jeffery G. *The Egyptian Elite under Cromer, 1882–1907*. Berlin: K. Schwarz, 1984.

Courbage, Youssef, and Philippe Fargues. *Christians and Jews under Islam*. Translated by Judy Mabro. New York: I.B. Tauris, 1998.

Eickelman, Dale, and James Piscatori. *Muslim Politics*. Princeton: Princeton University Press, 1996.

Eriksen, Thomas Hyland. *Ethnicity and Nationalism: Anthropological Perspectives*. Boulder, CO: Pluto Press, 1993.

Everard, Jerry. *Virtual States: The Internet and the Boundaries of the Nation State*. New York: Routledge, 2000.

Fargues, Philippe. "The Arab Christians of the Middle East: A Demographic Perspective." In Andrea Pacini, ed., *Christian Communities in the Arab Middle East: The Challenge of the Future*. London: Oxford University Press, 1999.

al-Fattah, Nabil 'Abd, ed. *Taqrir al-hala al-diniyya fi Misr, 1995* [Report on the religious situation in Egypt, 1995]. Cairo: Al-Ahram Centre for Strategic and Political Studies, 1996.

Fox, Jonathan. "The Copts in Egypt: A Christian Minority in an Islamic Society." In Ted Robert Gurr, ed., *Peoples vs States: Minorities at Risk in the New Century*. Washington, DC: United States Institute of Peace Press, 2000.

– "Religious Causes of Discrimination against Ethno-Religious Minorities." *International Studies Quarterly* 44 (2000): 423–50.

Gelvin, James. "Modernity and Its Discontents: On the Durability of Nationalism in the Arab Middle East." *Nations and Nationalism* 5, no. 1 (January 1999): 71–90.

Gershoni, Israel, and James Jankowski. *Redefining the Egyptian Nation, 1930–1945*. New York: Columbia University Press, 1995.

Goldschmidt, Arthur, Jr. "The Egyptian Nationalist Party, 1892–1919." In P.M. Holt, ed., *Political and Social Change in Modern Egypt*, 308–33. London: Oxford University Press, 1968.

Hanna, Nelly. "Marriage among Merchant Families in Seventeenth-Century Cairo." In Amira El Azhary Sonbol, ed., *Women, the Family, and Divorce Laws in Islamic History.* Syracuse: Syracuse University Press, 1996.

Haynes, Jeff, ed. *Religion, Globalization, and Political Culture in the Third World.* New York: St Martin's, 1999.

Hosking, Geoffery, and George Schopflin, eds. *Myths and Nationhood.* New York: Routledge, 1997.

Hunter, F. Robert. *Egypt under the Khedives, 1805–1879: From Household Government to Modern Bureaucracy.* Cairo: American University in Cairo Press, 1999.

Husayn, Taha. *Fi al-Shi'r al-Jahili* [On pre-Islamic poetry]. 1st ed. Cairo: n.p., 1926.

Hutchinson, John, and Anthony D. Smith, eds. *Ethnicity.* New York: Oxford University Press, 1996.

Ibrahim, Saad Eddin, et al. *The Copts of Egypt.* London: Minority Rights Group, 1996.

Iklé, Fred. "Stopping the Next Sept. 11: Intelligence Is One Element, Offense and Defense Are the Others." *Wall Street Journal,* 2 June 2002, www.opinionjournal.com/?id=110001790.

Jackson Preece, Jennifer. *National Minorities and the European State System.* New York: Oxford University Press, 1998.

Jankowski, James. "Arab Nationalism in 'Nasserism' and Egyptian State Policy, 1952–1958." In Israel Gershoni and James Jankowski, eds, *Rethinking Nationalism in the Arab Middle East,* 150–67. New York: Columbia University Press, 1997.

– and Israel Gershoni. *Egypt, Islam, and the Arabs: The Search for Egyptian Nationhood, 1900–1930.* Oxford: Oxford University Press, 1986.

Keating, Michael. *Nations against the State: The New Politics of Nationalism in Quebec, Catalonia, and Scotland.* 2nd ed. New York: Palgrave, 2001.

el-Khawaga, Dina. "The Political Dynamics of the Copts: Giving the Community an Active Role." In Andrea Pacini, ed., *Christian Communities in the Arab Middle East: The Challenge of the Future,* 172–90. London: Oxford University Press, 1999.

– *Le renouveau copte: La communaute comme acteur politique.* PhD thesis, Institut d'Etudes Politique, Paris, May 1993.

Kramer, Martin. *Ivory Towers on Sand: The Failure of Middle Eastern Studies in America.* Washington, DC: Washington Institute for Near East Policy, 2001.

Larson, Warren Frederick. *Islamic Ideology and Fundamentalism in Pakistan: Climate for Conversion to Christianity?* Lanham, MD: University Press of America, 1998.

Leeder, S.H. *Modern Sons of the Pharaohs: A Study of the Manners and Customs of the Copts of Egypt.* New York: C. Scribner and Sons, 1913.

Marshall, Paul. *Their Blood Cries Out: The Growing Worldwide Persecution of Christians.* Nashville: W. Publishing Company, 1997.

Meinardus, Otto. *Christian Egypt, Faith and Life.* Cairo: American University in Cairo Press, 1970.

– *Two Thousand Years of Coptic Christianity.* Cairo: American University in Cairo Press, 1999.

Mellini, Peter. *Sir Eldon Gorst: The Overshadowed Proconsul.* Stanford, CA: Hoover Institution Press, 1977.

Mikhail, Kyriakos. *Copts and Moslems under British Control: A Collection of Facts and a Resume of Authoritative Opinions on the Coptic Question.* 1911. Reprint, Port Washington, NY: Kennikat Press, 1971.

Mortimer, Edward, ed. *People, Nation, and State: The Meaning of Ethnicity and Nationalism.* New York: I.B. Tauris, 1999.

Oommen, T.K. *Citizenship, Nationality, and Ethnicity: Reconciling Competing Identities.* Cambridge, MA: Blackwell, 1997.

Pacini, Andrea, ed. *Christian Communities in the Arab Middle East: The Challenge of the Future.* London: Oxford University Press, 1999.

Pickett, Terry H. *Inventing Nations: Justifications of Authority in the Modern Age.* Westport, CT: Greenwood, 1996.

Piterberg, Gabriel. "The Tropes of Stagnation and Awakening in Nationalist Historical Consciousness: The Egyptian Case." In Israel Gershoni and James Jankowski, eds, *Rethinking Nationalism in the Arab Middle East*, 42–62. New York: Columbia University Press, 1997.

al-Raziq, 'Ali 'Abd. *al-Islam wa Usual al-Hukm* [Islam and the principles of government]. 1st ed. Cairo: n.p., 1925.

Rowe, Paul S. "Four Guys and a Fax Machine? Diasporas, New Information Technologies, and the Internationalization of Religion in Egypt." *Journal of Church and State* 43, no. 1 (2001): 81–93.

Schopflin, George. *Nations, Identity, Power: The New Politics of Europe.* London: Hurst, 2000.

Scott, James C. *Domination and the Arts of Resistance: Hidden Transcripts.* New Haven: Yale University Press, 1990.

Seikaly, Samir. "Coptic Communal Reform, 1860–1914." *Middle Eastern Studies* 6 (1970): 247–75.

– "The Copts under British Rule, 1882–1914." PhD thesis, University of London, 1967.
– "Prime Minister and Assassin: Butrus Ghali and Wardani." *Middle Eastern Studies* 13, no. 1 (1997): 112–23.
Siebers, Tobin. *The Subject and Other Subjects: On Ethical, Aesthetic, and Political Identity*. Ann Arbor: University of Michigan Press, 1998.
Smith, Anthony D. *The Ethnic Origin of Nations*. Oxford: Blackwell, 1986.
Smith, Charles D. "Imagined Identities, Imagined Nationalisms: Print Culture and Egyptian Nationalism in Light of Recent Scholarship." *International Journal of Middle East Studies* 29 (1997): 607–22.
– *Islam and the Search for Social Order in Modern Egypt: A Biography of Muhammad Husayn Haykal*. Albany: State University of New York Press, 1983.
Wakin, Edward. *A Lonely Minority: The Modern Story of Egypt's Copts*. New York: Morrow, 1963.
Winter, Michael. *Egyptian Society under Ottoman Rule, 1517–1798*. New York: Routledge, 1992.

CHAPTER FOUR

Ansari, Hamied. "Sectarian Conflict in Egypt and the Political Expediency of Religion." *Middle East Journal* 38, no. 3 (Summer 1984): 397–418.
Bengio, Ofra, and Gabriel Ben-Dor, eds. *Minorities and the State in the Arab World*. Boulder, CO: Lynne Rienner, 1999.
Betts, Robert Brenton. *Christians in the Arab East*. Revised edition. Atlanta: John Knox Press, 1977.
"Bkirki's Blast Could Spark Unity Dialogue." *The Daily Star* (Beirut), 21 September 2000.
Chayban, Badih. "March to Damascus Draws Thousands." *The Daily Star* (Beirut), 10 March 2003.
Cofsky, Warren. "Copts Bear the Brunt of Islamic Extremism." *Christianity Today* 8 March 1993, 47.
Cox, Robert. "Civil Society at the Turn of the Millenium: Prospects for an Alternative World Order." *Review of International Studies* 25 (1999): 13–15.
Cragg, Kenneth. *The Arab Christian: A History in the Middle East*. London: Mowbray, 1991.
Dalrymple, William. *From the Holy Mountain*. New York: Owl Books, 1997.
Dawoud, Khaled. "Precarious Politics." *Al-Ahram Weekly*, 25–31 May 2000.
Entelis, John P. *Pluralism and Party Transformation in Lebanon, Al-Kataib, 1936–1970*. Leiden: Brill, 1974.

Esposito, John. *Islam and Politics*. 3rd ed. Syracuse: Syracuse University Press, 1991.
– *Unholy War: Terror in the Name of Islam*. Oxford: Oxford University Press, 2002.
Harris, William. *Faces of Lebanon*. Princeton: Markus Wiener, 1996.
Hudson, Michael. *The Precarious Republic: Political Modernization in Lebanon*. New York: Random House, 1968.
– "The Problem of Authoritative Power in Lebanese Politics: Why Consociationalism Failed." In Nadim Shehadi and Dana Hoffar Mills, eds, *Lebanon: A History of Conflict and Consensus*, 224–39. London: I.B. Tauris, 1988.
Ibrahim, Saad Eddin, et al. *The Copts of Egypt*. London: Minority Rights Group, 1996.
"Interview with Patriarch Shenouda III: Marriage, Politics, and Jerusalem." *Al-Ahram Weekly*, 1–7 April 1999.
Irani, George Emile. *The Papacy and the Middle East*. Notre Dame, ID: University of Notre Dame Press, 1986.
Kaufman, Asher. "Phoenicianism: The Formation of an Identity in Lebanon in 1920." *Middle Eastern Studies* 37, no. 1 (January 2001): 173–94.
Khashan, Hilal. *Inside the Lebanese Confessional Mind*. Lanham, MD: University Press of America, 1992.
el-Khawaga, Dina. *Le renouveau copte: La communaute comme acteur politique*. PhD thesis, Institut d'Etudes Politique, Paris, May 1993.
Kienle, Eberhard. "More Than a Response to Islamism: The Political Deliberalization of Egypt in the 1990s." *Middle East Journal* 52, no. 2 (Spring 1998): 219–35.
Kurtz, Lester R. *Gods in the Global Village*. Thousand Oaks, CF: Pine Forge Press, 1995.
Laurent, Annie. "A War Between Brothers: The Army-Lebanese Forces Showdown in East Beirut." *Beirut Review* 1 (Spring 1991): 88–101.
Madan, T.N. *Modern Myths, Locked Minds*. Oxford: Oxford University Press, 1998.
Malik, Habib C. "Review of *The Arab Christian: A History in the Middle East*." *Beirut Review* 3 (Spring 1992): 109–22.
Moosa, Matti. *The Maronites in History*. Syracuse: Syracuse University Press, 1986.
Norton, Augustus Richard. "Lebanon After Ta'if: Is the Civil War Over?" *Middle East Journal* 45, no. 3 (Summer 1991): 457–73.
Sadowski, Yahya. "The New Orientalism and the Democracy Debate." *Middle East Report* 23, no. 4 (July-August 1993): 14–21, 40.
Said, Edward. *Orientalism*. New York: Vintage Books, 1978.

Salamé, Ghassan. *Lebanon's Injured Identities*. Oxford: Centre for Lebanese Studies, 1986.

Salibi, Kamal. "Community, State, and Nation in the Arab Mashriq." *The Beirut Review* 3 (Spring 1992): 39–52.

Shehab, Shaden. "Tabloid's Outrageous Toll." *Al-Ahram Weekly*, 21–27 June 2001.

Snider, Lewis W. "The Lebanese Forces: Their Origins and Role in Lebanon's Politics." *Middle East Journal* 38, no. 1 (Winter 1984): 13–26.

van Doorn-Harder, Pieternella. *Contemporary Coptic Nuns*. Columbia, SC: University of South Carolina Press, 1995.

US Department of State. "Country Reports on Human Rights Practice for 1999." *Country Reports on Human Rights Practice for 1999*. Washington DC: US Department of State, February 2000, www.state.gov/www/global/human_rights/1999_hrp_report/egypt.html.

Warren, Kay B., ed. *The Violence Within: Cultural and Political Opposition in Divided Nations*. Boulder, CO: Westview Press, 1993.

Zahar, Marie-Joelle. *Fanatics, Mercenaries, Brigands ... and Politicians: Militia Decision-making and Civil Conflict Resolution*. PhD thesis, McGill University, Montreal, 1999.

CHAPTER FIVE

Afzal, Iqbal. *Islamisation of Pakistan*. Lahore: Vanguard Books, 1986.

Ahmed, Feroz. *Ethnicity and Politics in Pakistan*. Karachi: Oxford University Press, 2000.

Akbar, S. Ahmed. *Jinnah, Pakistan and Islamic Identity: The Search for Saladin*. London. Routledge, 1997.

Anderson, Benedict. *Imagined Communities: Reflections on the Origin and Spread of Nationalism*. 2nd ed. London: Verso, 1991.

Bjorkman, James Warner, ed. *Fundamentalism, Revivalists and Violence in South Asia*. Riverdale, MD: The Riverdale Company, 1988.

Blondeel. *A Short History of the Catholic Diocese of Lahore*. Lahore: St Mary's Church, n.d.

Blood, Peter R., ed. *Pakistan: A Country Study*. 6th ed. Washington, DC: Federal Research Division, 1995.

De Long, Edmund Lucas, and F. Das Thakur. *The Rural Church in the Punjab*. Lahore: Northern India Printing and Publishing Co., 1938.

Deliege, Robert. "At the Threshold of Untouchability: Pallars and Valaiyars in a Tamil Village." In C.J. Filler, ed., *Caste Today*. New Delhi: Oxford University Press, 1997.

Dharmarja, Jacob E. *Colonialism and Christian Mission: Postcolonial Reflections.* Delhi: Indian Society for Promoting Christian Knowledge, 1993.

Forrester, Duncan. *Caste and Christianity.* London and Dublin: Curzon, 1980.

Geertz, Clifford. "The Integrative Revolution." In Vincent P. Pecora, ed., *Nations and Identities.* Malden, MA: Blackwell, 2001.

Haward, Raffat Khan. "An Urban Minority: The Goan Christian Community in Karachi." In Kenneth Ballhatchet and John Harrison, eds, *The City in South Asia: Pre-Modern and Modern,* 299–323. London: Curzon, 1980.

Huntington, Samuel P. *The Clash of Civilizations and the Remaking of World Order.* New York: Simon and Schuster, 1996.

Ibbetson, Denzil. *Punjab Castes.* Lahore: Sang-e-Meel, 1994.

Iqbal, Afzal. *Islamization of Pakistan.* Lahore: Vanguard Books, 1986.

Jalalzai, Musa Khan. *Sectarianism and Ethnic Violence in Pakistan.* Lahore: Izharsons, 1996.

– *Sectarian Violence in Pakistan and Afghanistan.* Lahore: System Books, 1999.

Lawton, David. *Blasphemy.* Philadelphia: University of Pennsylvania Press, 1993.

Levy, Leonard W. *Blasphemy.* Chapel Hill: The University of North Carolina Press, 1993.

Oddie, G.A. "Christian Conversion among Non-Brahmans in Adhra Pradesh, with Special Reference to Anglican Missions and Dornaka Diocese, c. 1900–1936." In G.A. Oddie, ed., *Religion in South Asia: Religious Conversion and Revival Movements in South Asia in Medieval and Modern Times,* 67–100. Delhi: Manohar, 1977.

Rushdie, Salman. *The Satanic Verses.* London: Viking Penguin, 1988.

Seyyed, Vali Reza Nasr. *The Vanguard of the Islamic Revolution: The Jama'at-Islimi of Pakistan.* London: I.B. Tauris, 1994.

Stock, Frederick, and Margaret Stock. *People Movements in the Punjab.* South Pasadena, CA: William Carey Library, 1975.

Streefland, Pieter. *The Sweepers of Slaughterhouse: Conflict and Survival in a Karachi Neighbourhood.* Van Gorcum, Assen, the Netherlands: Van Gorcum, 1979.

CHAPTER SIX

'Abbas, 'Abdu'l-Baha. *Risalih-'i Madaniyyih.* Hofheim-Langenhain: Baha'i-Verlag, 1984. Translated by Marzieh Gail, *The Secret of Divine Civilization.* Wilmette, IL: Baha'i Publishing Trust, 1970.

Abrahamian, Ervand. *Tortured Confessions: Prisons and Public Recantations in Modern Iran.* Berkeley and Los Angeles: University of California Press, 1999.

Afshari, Reza. *Human Rights in Iran: The Abuse of Cultural Relativism*. Philadelphia: University of Pennsylvania Press, 2001.

Ahmadi, Houshang Amir. "Secular Nationalism." 1996. http://www.iranian.com/Jan96/Opinion/SecularNationalism.html.

Akhavi, Shahrough. *Religion and Politics in Contemporary Iran: Clergy-State Relations in the Pahlavi Period*. Albany: State University of New York Press, 1980.

Amanat, Abbas. *Resurrection and Renewal: The Making of the Babi Movement in Iran, 1844–1850*. Ithaca, NY: Cornell University Press, 1989.

Amnesty International. "AI Report 1997: Iran." http://www.amnesty.org/ailib/aireport/ar97/MDE13.htm.

– *Country Reports for 1995: Iran*. http://www.amnesty.org/ailib/aipub/1995/MDE/130295.MDE.txt.

– *Country Reports for 1997: Iran*. http://www.amnesty.org/ailib/aireport/ar97/MDE13.htm.

– "Dhabihullah Mahrami: Prisoner of Conscience." October 1996. http://www.amnesty.org/ailib/aipub/1996/MDE/51303496.htm.

– "Worldwide Appeals: Iran." April 1997. http://www.amnesty.org//news/1997/N2200297.htm.

Anderson, Benedict. *Imagined Communities: Reflections on the Origin and Spread of Nationalism*. 2nd ed. London: Verso, 1991.

Baha'u'llah. *Majmu'ih-'i az alvah-i Jamal-i Aqdas-i Abha kih ba'd az Kitab-i Aqdas Nazil Shudih*. Hofheim-Langenhain: Baha'i-Verlag, 1980. Translation published as *Tablets of Baha'u'llah Revealed after the Kitab-i Aqdas*. Wilmette, IL: Baha'i Publishing Trust, 1988.

Baha'i International Community. *The Baha'i Question: Iran's Secret Blueprint for the Destruction of a Religious Community*. New York: Baha'i International Community Publications, 1993.

Bakhtiari, Bahman. *Parliamentary Politics in Revolutionary Iran: The Institutionalization of Factional Politics*. Gainesville: University of Florida Press, 1996.

Bengio, Ofra, and Gabriel Ben-Dor. *Minorities and the State in the Arab World*. Boulder, CO: Lynne Rienner, 1999.

Browne, E.G. *The Persian Revolution of 1905–1909*. Cambridge: Cambridge University Press, 1910.

Chatterjee, Partha. *The Nation and its Fragments*. Princeton, NJ: Princeton University Press, 1993.

Cole, Juan. "Fundamentalism in the Contemporary U.S. Baha'i Community." *Religious Studies Review* 43, no. 3 (March 2002): 195–217.

– "Marking Boundaries, Marking Time: The Iranian Past and the Construction of the Self by Qajar Thinkers." *Iranian Studies* 29, nos 1–2 (Winter/Spring 1996/97): 35–56.

- "Millennialism in Modern Iranian History." In Abbas Amanat and Magnus Bernhardsson, eds, *Imagining the End: Visions of Apocalypse from the Ancient Middle East to Modern America*, 282–311. London: I.B. Tauris, 2002.
- *Modernity and the Millennium: The Genesis of the Baha'i Faith in the 19th Century Middle East*. New York: Columbia University Press, 1998.
- "The Modernity of Theocracy." In *Sacred Space and Holy War*. London: I.B. Tauris, 2002.
- *Sacred Space and Holy War*. London: I.B. Tauris, 2002.

Cottam, Richard. *Nationalism in Iran*. 1963. Reprint, Pittsburgh: University of Pittsburgh Press, 1979.

Hobsbawm, Eric. *Nations and Nationalisms since 1780*. Cambridge: Cambridge University Press, 1990.

Jensen, Mehri Samandari. "Religion and Family Planning in Contemporary Iran." In Peter Smith, ed., *In Iran: Studies in Babi and Baha'i History*, vol. 3, 213–37. Los Angeles: Kalimat Press, 1986.

Kasravi, Ahmad. *Bahayigari*. 1335. Reprint, Tehran: Mard-i Imruz, [1956 or 1957].

Kazemzadeh, Firuz. "Baha'is in Iran: Twenty Years of Repression." *Social Research: An International Quarterly of Social Science* 67, no. 2 (Summer 2000): 537–58.

Laqueur, Thomas W. "Cemeteries, Religion, and the Culture of Capitalism." In Colin Mathews and Jane Garnett, eds, *Revival and Religion since 1700*. London: Hambledon Press, 1993.

- "Memory and Naming in the Great War." In John Gillis, ed., *Memory and Commemoration*. Princeton: Princeton University Press, 1993.

MacMaster, Neil. *Racism in Europe: 1870–2000*. New York: Palgrave Macmillan, 2001.

Ma'oz, Moshe. *Middle Eastern Minorities: Between Integration and Conflict*. Washington, DC: Washington Institute for Near East Policy, 1999.

Roohizadegan, Olya. *Olya's Story: A Survivor's Dramatic Account of the Persecution of Baha'is in Revolutionary Iran*. Oxford: Oneworld Publications, 1993.

Samii, A.W. "Falsafi, Kashani and the Baha'is." *Research Notes in Shaykhi, Babi and Baha'i Studies* 2, no. 5 (August 1998): http://h-net2.msu.edu/~bahai/notes/vol2/falsafi.htm.

Sanasarian, Eliz. *Religious Minorities in Iran*. Cambridge: Cambridge University Press, 2000.

Smith, Peter. "A Note on Babi and Baha'i Numbers in Iran." *Iranian Studies* 15, nos 2–3 (1984): 295–301.

Tavakoli-Targhi, Mohamad. "Baha'i sitizi va Islamgarayi dar Iran" [Anti-Bahaism and Islamism in Iran, 1941–1955]. *Iran Nameh* 19, nos 1–2 (Winter/Spring 2001): 79–124.

United Nations. "Situation of Human Rights in the Islamic Republic of Iran: Note by the Secretary-General." Transmitting interim report of Maurice Copithorne, A/52/472, 15 October 1997.

US State Department. "Country Reports on Human Rights Practices for 1988." Washington, DC: Committee on Foreign Affairs, House of Representatives, and US Senate Committee on Foreign Relations, 1989.

– "Country Reports on Human Rights Practices for 1989." Washington, DC: Committee on Foreign Affairs, House of Representatives, and US Senate Committee on Foreign Relations, 1990.

– "Country Reports on Human Rights Practices for 1993." Washington, DC: Committee on Foreign Affairs, House of Representatives, and US Senate Committee on Foreign Relations, 1994.

– "Country Reports on Human Rights Practices for 1996." Washington, DC: Committee on Foreign Affairs, House of Representatives, and US Senate Committee on Foreign Relations, 1997.

Vaziri, Mostafa. *Iran as Imagined Nation: The Construction of National Identity.* New York: Paragon House, 1993.

CHAPTER SEVEN

Aidi, Hisham. "Let Us Be Moors: Islam, Race and 'Connected Histories.'" *Middle East Report* 33, no. 4 (2003): 42–53.

Allouche, A. "Arabization and Linguistic Politics in the Maghreb." *Language In Society* 18, no. 3 (1989): 411–14.

Anderson, Benedict. *Imagined Communities: Reflections on the Origin and Spread of Nationalism.* 1st ed. New York: Verso, 1983.

Ben-Dor, Gabriel. "Minorities in the Middle East: Theory and Practice." In O. Bengio and G. Ben-Dor, eds, *Minorities and the State in the Arab World.* Boulder, CO: Lynne Rienner, 1999.

Ben Kaddour, Abdaslam. "The Neo-Makhzen and the Berbers." In E. Gellner and C. Michaud, eds, *Arabs and Berbers.* London: D.C. Heath, 1972.

Boukous, Ahmed. "L'amazighe dans l'éducation et la formation: Pour un enseignement intégrateur et émancipateur." In A. Kich, ed., *L'Amazighité.* Rabat: Centre Tarik Ibn Zyad, 2003.

– "La langue berbere: Maintien et changement." *International Journal of the Sociology of Language,* no. 112 (1995): 9–28.

– *Société, langues et cultures au Maroc: Enjeux symboliques.* 1st ed. Rabat: Université Mohamed V, Faculté des lettres et des sciences humaines, 1995.

Bourouiba, Rachid. *Ibn Tumart.* Alger: SNED, 1974.

Bourqia, R., and Susan Gilson Miller, eds. *In the Shadow of the Sultan: Culture, Power and Politics in Morocco*. Harvard Middle Eastern monographs 31. Cambridge, MA: Distributed for the Center for Middle Eastern Studies of Harvard University by Harvard University Press, 1999.

Brett, Michael, and Elizabeth Fentress. "The Berbers." In P. Shipton, ed., *The Peoples of Africa*. Oxford: Blackwell, 1996.

Chaker, Salem. *Berbéres aujourd'hui*. Paris: Editions l'Harmattan, 1989.

Chiapuris, John. *The Ait Ayash of the High Moulouya Plain: Rural Social Organization in Morocco*. Ann Arbor: University of Michigan, 1979.

Combs-Schilling, M.E. "Family and Friend in a Moroccan Boom Town: The Segmentary Debate Reconsidered." *American Ethnologist* 12 (1985): 659–75.

Cornell, Vincent I. "Understanding is the Mother of Ability: Responsibility and Action in the Doctrine of Ibn Tumart." *Studia Islamica* 66 (1987): 71–103.

Crawford, David. "Arranging the Bones: Culture, Time and In/equality in Berber Labor Organization." *Ethnos* 68, no. 4 (2003): 463–86.

– "Morocco's Invisible Imazighen." *The Journal of North African Studies* 7, no. 1 (2002): 53–70.

– *Work and Identity in the Moroccan High Atlas*. PhD thesis, Department of Anthropology, University of California, Santa Barbara, 2001.

– and Katherine Hoffman. "Essentially Amazigh: Urban Berbers and the Global Village." In R.K. Lacey and R.M. Coury, eds, *The Arab-African and Islamic Worlds: Interdisciplinary Studies*. New York: Peter Lang, 2000.

Durkheim, Émile. *The Division of Labor in Society*. 1893. Translated by G. Simpson, New York: Free Press, 1964.

Dwyer, Kevin. "The Uses and Misuses of 'Culture': A Comment." *The Journal of North African Studies* 3, no. 2 (1998): 130–7.

Enanji, Moha. "Reflections on Arabization and Education in Morocco." In A. Youssi, M. Dahbi, and L. Haddad, eds, *The Moroccan Character*. Rabat: AMPATRIL, 2003.

Gellner, Ernest. "Culture, Identity, and Politics." Cambridge, MA: Cambridge University Press, 1987.

– *Saints of the Atlas*. London: Weidenfeld and Nicholson, 1969.

Giddens, Anthony. *The Constitution of Society: Outline of the Theory of Structuration*. Cambridge, MA: Polity Press, 1984.

Goody, Jack. "Bitter Icons." *New Left Review* 7 (Jan/Feb 2001): 5–16.

Hammoudi, Abdellah. *Master and Disciple: The Cultural Foundations of Moroccan Authoritarianism*. Chicago: University of Chicago Press, 1980.

– "Segmentarity, Social Stratification, Political Power, and Sainthood: Reflections on Gellner's Thesis." *Economy and Society* 9, no. 3 (1980): 279–303.

Hart, David. *The Aith Waryaghar of the Moroccan Rif: An Ethnography and History.* Tucson: University of Arizona Press, 1976.
- "Berber Tribal Alliance Networks in Pre-Colonial North Africa: The Algerian Saff, the Moroccan Liff and the Chessboard Model of Robert Montagne." *The Journal of North African Studies* 1, no. 2 (1996): 192–205.
- *Dadda 'Atta and his Forty Grandsons: The Socio-Political Organization of the Ait Atta of Southern Morocco.* Boulder, CO: Middle East and North African Studies Press, 1981.
- "Rejoinder to Henry Munson Jr." *American Anthropologist* 91 (1989): 765–9.
Ketterer, James. "Networks of Discontent in Northern Morocco." *Middle East Report* 218 (2001): 30–45.
Khandker, Shahidur R., Victor Lavy, and Deon Filmer. "Schooling and Cognitive Achievements of Children in Morocco: Can the Government Improve Outcomes?" World Bank Discussion Paper No. 264, http://www.worldbank.org/html/extpb/abshtml/13046.htm, 1 November 1994.
Kich, Aziz, ed. *L'Amazighité.* Rabat: Centre Tarik Ibn Zyad, 2003.
Kraus, Wolfgang. "Contestable Identities: Tribal Structures in the Moroccan High Atlas." *Journal of the Royal Anthropological Institute* 4, no. 1 (1998): 1–22.
Laroui, (al 'Arawi) Abdallah. *The History of the Maghreb.* Princeton: Princeton University Press, 1977.
Layachi, Azzadine. "Reform and the Politics of Inclusion in the Maghrib." *The Journal of North African Studies* 5, no. 3 (2000): 15–42.
- *The United States and North Africa.* New York: Praeger, 1990.
Leveau, Remy. "A Democratic Transition in Morocco?" *Le Monde diplomatique online,* http://www.monde-diplomatique.fr/en/1998/12/06maroc, 1998.
Maddy-Weitzman, Bruce. "The Berber Question in Algeria: Nationalism in the Making?" In O. Bengio and G. Ben-Dor, eds, *Minorities and the State in the Arab World.* Boulder, CO: Lynne Rienner, 1999.
Maghraoui, Abdeslam. "Political Authority in Crisis." *Middle East Report* 218 (2001): 12–17.
Maher, Vanessa. *Women and Property in Morocco: Their Changing Relation to the Process of Social Stratification in the Middle Atlas.* Edited by M. Fortes, J.R. Goody, E.R. Leach, and S.J. Tambiah, Cambridge Studies in Social Anthropology. Cambridge, MA: Cambridge University Press, 1974.
Marais, Octave. "The Political Evolution of the Berbers in Independent Morocco." In E. Gellner and C. Michaud, eds, *Arabs and Berbers.* London: D.C. Heath, 1972.
McMurray, David A. *In and Out of Morocco.* Minneapolis: University of Minnesota Press, 2001.

Montagne, Robert. *The Berbers*. 1930. Translated by D. Seddon, London: Frank Cass, 1973.
Munson, Henry, Jr. "On the Irrelevance of the Segmentary Lineage Model in the Moroccan Rif." *American Anthropologist* 91 (1989): 386–400.
– *Religion and Power in Morocco*. New Haven: Yale University Press, 1993.
– "The Segmentary Lineage Model in the Jebalan Highlands of Morocco." In E.G.H. Joffé and C.R. Pennell, eds, *Tribe and State: Essays in Honour of David Montgomery Hart*. Cambridgeshire: Middle East and North African Studies Press, 1991.
Norris, H.T. *The Berbers in Arabic Literature*. London: Longman, 1982.
Oulhaj, Lahcen. "Possibilité et nécessité d'intégrer Tamazight à l'université marocaine." In A. Kich, ed., *L'Amazighité*. Rabat: Centre Tarik Ibn Zyad, 2003.
Roberts, Hugh "The Economics of Berberism: The Material Basis of the Kabyle Question in Contemporary Algeria." *Government and Opposition* 18, no. 2 (1983): 218–34.
– "Perspectives on Berber Politics: On Gellner and Masqueray, or Durkheim's Mistake." *Journal of the Royal Anthropological Institute* 8, no. 1 (2002): 107–26.
– "The Unforeseen Development of the Kabyle Question in Contemporary Algeria." *Government and Opposition* 17, no. 3 (1982): 312–34.
Rosen, Lawrence. *Bargaining for Reality: The Construction of Social Relations in a Muslim Community*. Chicago: University of Chicago Press, 1984.
Saad, Stephanie S. "Interpreting Ethnic Quiescence: A Brief History of the Berbers of Morocco." In R.M. Coury and R.K. Lacey, eds, *The Arab-African and Islamic Worlds*. New York: Peter Lang, 2000.
Sadiqi, Fatima. "The Place of Berbers in Morocco." *International Journal of the Sociology of Language*, no. 123 (1997): 7–21.
Sahlins, Marshall. "Two or Three Things That I Know about Culture." *Journal of Royal Anthropological Institute* 5, no. 3 (1999): 399–421.
Saib, Jilali. "Pour une integration effective de l'enseignement de l'amazighe à l'université marocaine." In A. Kich, ed., *L'Amazighité*. Rabat: Centre Tarik Ibn Zyad, 2003.
Saleh, Heba. "Algerian Insurrection." *Middle East Report* 31, no. 3 (2001): 8–10.
Sen, Amartya. *Inequality Reexamined*. 6th ed. Cambridge, MA: Harvard University Press, 1992.
Shatzmiller, Maya. *The Berbers and the Islamic State*. Princeton: Markus Wiener, 2000.
Silverstein, Paul. "Of Rooting and Uprooting: Kabyle Habitus, Domesticity, and Structural Nostalgia." *Ethnography* 5 (forthcoming).

Slyomovics, Susan. "No Buying Off the Past: Moroccan Indemnities and the Opposition." *Middle East Report* 33, no. 4 (2003): 34–7.
- "A Truth Commission for Morocco." *Middle East Report* 218 (2001): 18–21.
Sørensen, Ninna Nyberg. "Crossing the Spanish-Moroccan Border with Migrants, New Islamists, and Riff-Raff." *Ethnologia Europaea* 30, no. 2 (2000): 87–100.
Tessler, Mark. "Morocco's Next Political Generation." *The Journal of North African Studies* 5, no. 1 (2000): 1–26.
Thomas, Edward H. "The Politics of Language in Former Colonial Lands: A Comparative Look at North Africa and Central Asia." *The Journal of North African Studies* 4, no. 1 (1999): 1–44.
Venema, Bernhard. "The Vitality of Local Political Institutions in the Middle Atlas, Morocco." *Ethnology* 4, no. 2 (2002): 103–17.
Waterbury, John. "Bargaining for Segmentarity." In E.G.H. Joffé and C.R. Pennell, eds, *Tribe and State: Essays in Honour of David Montgomery Hart*. Cambridgeshire: Middle East and North African Studies Press, 1991.
- *North for the Trade: The Life and Times of a Berber Merchant*. Berkeley: University of California Press, 1972.

CHAPTER EIGHT

Anderson, Benedict. *Imagined Communities: Reflections on the Origin and Spread of Nationalism*. 2nd ed. New York: Verso, 1991.
Andrau, René. *Ladérive multiculturaliste*. France: Bruno Leprince, 2000.
Assous, Omar. "Arabization and Cultural Conflicts in Algeria." PhD thesis, Northwestern University, 1985; Ann Arbor, MI. University Microfilms International, 1998.
Chaker, Salim. *Imazighen Ass-A*. Algiers: Editions Bouchene, 1990.
- "More Than A Suggestion, A Necessity!" *Le Matin* (Algiers), 14 October 2001, www.AmazighWorld.org.
Connor, Walter. "A Nation is a Nation, is a State, is an Ethnic Group, is a ..." *Ethnic and Racial Studies* 1, no. 4 (1978): 377–99.
Christie, Kenneth, ed. *Ethnic Conflict and Tribal Politics: A Global Perspective*. Richmond and Surrey, UK: Curzon Press, 1998.
Freeman, Michael. "Theories of Ethnicity, Tribalism and Nationalism." In Kenneth Christie, ed., *Ethnic Conflict and Tribal Politics: A Global Perspective*. Richmond and Surrey, UK: Curzon Press, 1998.
Fuller, Graham E. "Redrawing the World's Borders." *World Policy Journal* (Spring 1997): 11–21.

Ganguly, Rajat, and Raymond C. Taras. *Understanding Ethnic Conflict: The International Dimension.* New York: Longman, 1998.

Garcetti, Eric. "Civic and Ethnic Allegiances: Competing Visions of Nationalist Discourse in the Horn of Africa." Paper presented at the 40th Annual Meeting of the International Studies Association, Washington, DC, 16–20 February 1999.

Guenoun, Ali. *Chronology du movement berber: Un combat et des hommes.* Algiers: Casbah Editions, 1999.

Geertz, Clifford. "The Integrative Revolution: Primordial Sentiments and Civil Politics in the New States." In Clifford Geertz, ed., *Old Societies and New States: The Quest for Modernity in Asia and Africa.* New York: Free Press, 1963.

– "Primordial and Civic Ties." In John Hutchinson and Anthony D. Smith, eds, *Nationalism.* New York: Oxford University Press, 1994.

Grillo, Ralph D., ed. *"Nation" and "State" in Europe: An Anthropological Perspective.* New York: Academic Press, 1980.

Harbi, Mohammed. *L'Algérie et son destin.* Paris: Arcantère, 1992.

Ignatieff, Michael. *Blood and Belonging: Journeys into the New Nationalism.* London: BBC Books, 1993.

Julien, Charles-André. *Histoire de l'Afrique du Nord: Tunisie, Algérie, Maroc: Des Origines à la Conquête Arabe, 647 ap. J.-C.* Paris: Payot, 1956.

– *Histoire de l'Afrique du Nord: Tunisie, Algérie, Maroc: De la Conquête Arabe à 1830.* Paris: Payot, 1961.

Kellas, James. *The Politics of Nationalism and Ethnicity.* London: MacMillan, 1991.

Layachi, Azzedine. *Economic Crisis and Political Change in North Africa.* New York: Praeger, 1998.

Migdal, Joel. *Strong Societies and Weak States.* Princeton: Princeton University Press, 1988.

Shatzmiller, Maya. *The Berbers and the Islamic State: The Marinid Experience in Pre-Protectorate Morocco.* Princeton: Markus Wiener, 2000.

Smith, Anthony D. *The Ethnic Origins of Nations.* Oxford: Basil Blackwell, 1986.

– "The Formation of National Identity." In Henry Harris, ed., *Identity: Essays Based on Herbert Spencer Lectures Given in the University of Oxford.* Oxford: Clarendon Press, 1995.

Snyder, Jack. *From Voting to Violence: Democratization and Nationalist Conflict.* New York: Norton, 2000.

CHAPTER NINE

Akgür, Zeynep Gökçe. *Türkiye'de Kırsal Kesimden Kente Göç ve Bölgeler Arası Dengesizlik, 1970–1993.* Ankara: Kültür Başkanlığı, 1997.

Aktay, Yasin. "Güneydoğu'da Intihar: Kalan Sağlar Bizimdir." *Tezkire*, no. 18 (2001): 33–48.
Barkey, Henri J., and Graham E. Fuller. *Turkey's Kurdish Question*. New York: Rowman and Littlefield, 1998.
Başkanlığı, Genel Kurmay. *100 Soru ve Cevapta Türk Silahli Kuvvetleri ve Terörle Mücadele*. Ankara: Genel Kurmay IGHD Başkanlığı, 1998.
Berkan, Ismet. "The Story of Apo's Capture." *Radikal* (Istanbul), 17 February 1999.
Besikci, Ismail. *Doğu Mitingleri'nin Analizi, 1967*. Ankara: Yurt, 1992.
Birand, M. Ali. *Apo ve PKK*. Istanbul: Milliyet, 1992.
Bozarslan, Hamit. "Some Remarks on Kurdish Historiographical Discourse in Turkey, 1919–1980." In Abbas Vali, ed., *Essays on the Origins of Kurdish Nationalism*, 14–40. Costa Mesa: Mazda, 2003.
Cağaptay, Soner. "Population Resettlement and Immigration Policies of Interwar Turkey: A Study of Turkish Nationalism." *Turkish Studies Association Bulletin* 26, no. 2 (Fall 2002): 1–24.
– "Reconfiguring the Turkish Nation in the 1930s." *Nationalism and Ethnic Politics* 8, no. 2 (Summer 2002): 67–82.
Devrimci Doğu Kültür Ocakları Dava Dosyası. Ankara: Komal, 1975.
Duran, Burhanettin. "Approaching the Kurdish Question via Adil Düzen: An Islamist Formula of the Welfare Party for Ethnic Coexistence." *Journal of Muslim Minority Affairs* 18, no. 1 (1998): 111–28.
Gee, Marcus. "The Odyssey of a Kurdish Hot Potato." *Globe and Mail* (Toronto), 24 February 1999.
Göldaş, Ismail. *Kürdistan Teali Cemiyeti*. Istanbul: Doz, 1991.
– *Lozan: "Biz Türkler ve Kürtler."* Istanbul: Avesta, 2000.
Gözde, Mert. "Parliamentary Commission Reports on Migration: 4,000 Villages Evacuated, 1 Million People Displaced." *Turkish Daily News* (Ankara), 30 January 2001.
Gunter, Michael M. "The Continuing Kurdish Problem in Turkey after Öcalan's Capture," *Third World Quarterly* 21, no. 5 (2000): 849–69.
– *The Kurds and the Future of Turkey*. New York: St Martin's Press, 1997.
Gurr, Ted Robert. *Why Men Rebel*. Princeton: Princeton University Press, 1970.
Hecter, Michael. *Containing Nationalism*. New York: Oxford University Press, 2000.
Held, David. "The Development of the Modern State." In Stuart Hall et al., eds, *Modernity*, 55–69. Cambridge: Polity Press, 1995.
Human Rights Watch. "What is Turkey's Hizbullah." 16 February 2000.
Imset, İsmet G. *The PKK: A Report on Separatist Violence in Turkey, 1973–1992*. Istanbul: Turkish Daily News Publications, 1992.

- "The PKK: Terrorists or Freedom Fighters?" *International Journal of Kurdish Studies* 10, nos 1–2 (1996): 45–100.
Kara, Ismail. "Kürt Medreseleri Gündeme Gelecek mi?" In Ismail Kara, ed., *Seyhefendinin Rüyasındaki Türkiye*, 69–72. Istanbul: Kitab, 1998.
Kehl-Bodrogi, Krisztina. "Kurds, Turks, or a People in Their Own Right? Competing Collective Identities among the Zazas." *Muslim World* 89, nos 3–4 (1999): 439–454.
Kirişci, Kemal, and Gareth M. Winrow. *The Kurdish Question and Turkey: An Example of a Trans-state Ethnic Conflict*. London: Frank Cass, 1997.
Kutlay, Naci. *Ittihat Terakki ve Kürtler*. Ankara: Beybun, 1992.
Laciner, Ömer. *Kürt Sorunu: Henüz Vakit Varken*. Istanbul: Birikim, 1991.
Mann, Michael. "The Autonomous Power of the State: Its Origins, Mechanisms and Results." In John A. Hall, ed., *States in History*. Oxford: Blackwell, 1986.
McDowall, David. *A Modern History of the Kurds*. New York: St Martin's Press, 1996.
Middle East Watch. *Genocide in Iraq: The Anfal Campaign Against the Kurds*. New York: Human Rights Watch, 1993.
Mutlu, S. "Ethnic Kurds in Turkey: A Demographc Study." *International Journal of Middle Eastern Studies* 28 (1997): 517–44.
Nairn, Tom. *The Break-up of Britain: Crisis and Neo-Nationalism*. London: New Left Books, 1977.
Öcalan, Abdullah. *Declaration on the Democratic Solution of the Kurdish Question*. Translated by the Kurdistan Information Centre. London: Mesopotamian Publishers, 1999.
Olson, Robert. "The Impact on the Development of the Turkish Air Force and on Kurdish and Turkish Nationalism." *Die Welt des Islams* 40 (2000): 67–94.
Öymen, Onur. "Bu Sevr korkusu yersizdir." *Radikal* (Istanbul), 11 September 2000.
Özcan, Nihat Ali. *PKK: Tarihi, Ideolojisi ve Yöntemi*. Ankara: ASAM, 1999.
Özkan, Naki. "Ölüm estetize ediliyor." *Milliyet* (Istanbul), 31 October 2000.
Özoğlu, Hakan. *Kurdish Notables and the Ottoman State: Evolving Identities, Competing Loyalties, and Shifting Boundaries*. New York: State University of New York Press, 2004.
- *Unimaginable Community: Nationalism and Kurdish Notables in the Late Ottoman Era*. PhD thesis, Ohio State University, 1997.
PKK *Terrorism*. Booklet. Ankara: Ministry of Foreign Affairs, 1998.
Sakallioğlu, Umit Cizre. "Kurdish Nationalism from an Islamic Perspective." *Journal of Muslim Minority Affairs* 18, no. 1 (1998): 73–90.

"Serafettin Elci Discusses Kurd Party with Swedish Foreign Minister." *Turkish Daily News* (Ankara), 22 February 2000.
Şimşek, Halil. *Şeyh Sa'id Isyanı ve PKK*. Istanbul: Harp Akademileri, 2000.
Smith, Anthony D. *The Ethnic Origin of Nations*. Oxford: Blackwell, 1986.
– *National Identity*. Reno, Las Vegas, and London: University of Nevada Press, 1991.
Smith, Helena, Chris Morris, and Ed Vulliamy. "Global Plot that Lured Kurds' Hero into Trap." *Observer* (London), 21 February 1999.
Subaşı, Necdet. "Şeyh, Seyyid ve Molla: Güneydoğu Anadolu Örneğinde Dinsel Itibarın Kategorileri." *Islamiyat* 2, no. 3 (1999): 121–40.
"Turks vs. Kurds: Turning Point." *New York Times*, 21 February 1999, 8.
van Bruinessen, Martin. *Agha, Shaikh and State: The Social and Political Structures of Kurdistan*. London: Zed Books, 1992.
– *Mullas, Sufis and Heretics: The Role of Religion in Kurdish Society*. Istanbul: ISIS, 2000.
– "Shifting National and Ethnic Identities: The Kurds in Turkey and the European Diaspora." *Journal of Muslim Minority Affairs* 18, no. 1 (April 1998): 46, 51–2.
Volkan, Vamik. *Bloodlines: From Ethnic Pride to Ethnic Terrorism*. New York: Farrar, Straus, and Giroux, 1997.
Wahlbeck, Osten. *Kurdish Diaspora: A Comparative Study of Kurdish Refugee Communities*. New York: St Martin's Press, 1999.
Washington Kurdish Institute. *News Bulletin*, 7 September 2000, www.kurd.org/kurd.
Watts, Nicole F. "Allies and Enemies: Pro-Kurdish Parties in Turkish Politics, 1990–1994." *International Journal of Middle East Studies* 31 (November 1999): 631 56.
Weiner, Tim. "U.S. Helped Turkey Find and Capture Kurd Rebel." *New York Times*, 20 February 1999.
Yavuz, M. Hakan. "Değişim Sürecindeki Alevi Kimliği: Die alewitische Identitat in VeranderungsprozeB." *Aleviler: Identitat und Geschichte* 1 (Hamburg: Deutsche-Orient Institut, 2000): 75–95.
– "Five Stages of the Construction of Kurdish Nationalism in Turkey." *Nationalism and Ethnic Politics* 7, no. 3 (Autumn 2001): 1–24.
– "Turkey's Fault Lines and the Crisis of Kemalism." *Current History* 99 (January 2000): 33–9.
– "The Politics of Fear: The Rise of the Nationalistic Action Party (MHP) in Turkey." *Middle East Journal* 56, no. 2 (2002): 200–21.
– ed. *The Kurdish Question in Turkey*. Special issue of *Journal of Muslim Minority Affairs* 18, no. 1 (1998).

– and Michael Gunter. "The Kurdish Nation." *Current History* 100 (January 2001): 33–9.
Yeğen, Mesut. "The Kurdish Question in Turkish State Discourse." *Journal of Contemporary History* 34, no. 4 (1999): 555–68.
"Yılmaz: Road to EU Passes through Diyarbakır." *Turkish Daily News* (Ankara), 17 December 1999.
Young, Crawford. *The Politics of Cultural Pluralism*. Madison: The University of Wisconsin Press, 1976.
Yüksel, Müfid. *Kürdistan'da Değişim Süreci*. Ankara: Sor, 1993.

CHAPTER TEN

Awwad, Salah. "Interview with Jalal Talabani." *Al-Quds al-Arabi* (London), 22 September, 1998, 3.
Barzani, Massoud. *Mustafa Barzani and the Kurdish Liberation Movement*. New York: Palgrave, 2002.
Ben-Dor, Gabriel. "Minorities in the Middle East: Theory and Practice." In Ofra Bengio and Gabriel Ben-Dor, eds, *Minorities and the State in the Arab World*, 1–28. Boulder, CO: Lynne Rienner, 1999.
"The CIA Report the President Doesn't Want You to Read." *The Village Voice* (New York), 16 February 1976, 87–8.
Dodge, Toby. *Inventing Iraq: The Failure of Nation Building and a History Denied*. New York: Columbia University Press, 2003.
Eagleton, William, Jr. *The Kurdish Republic of 1946*. London: Oxford University Press, 1963.
Edmonds, C.J. "Kurdish Nationalism." *Journal of Contemporary History* 6, no. 1 (1971): 87–107.
– *Kurds, Turks and Arabs: Politics, Travel and Research in North-Eastern Iraq, 1919–1925*. London: Oxford University Press, 1957.
"Explains Intentions in North." *Tercuman* (Istanbul), 11 November 1992, 10; as cited in *FBISNES*, 18 November 1992.
"First Successful Opposition Meeting Concludes." Ankara Anatolia in Turkish, 1500 GMT, 31 October 1992; as cited in *FBISNES*, 2 November 1992, 24.
Fromkin, David. *A Peace to End All Peace: Creating the Modern Middle East, 1914–1922*. New York: Henry Holt, 1989.
Ghareeb, Edmund. *The Kurdish Question in Iraq*. Syracuse: Syracuse University Press, 1981.
Goldberg, Jeffrey. "The Great Terror." *The New Yorker*, 25 March 2002, 52–75.
Gunter, Michael M. "A De Facto Kurdish State in Northern Iraq." *Third World Quarterly* 14, no. 2 (1993): 295–319.

- "The KDP-PUK Conflict in Northern Iraq." *Middle East Journal* 50 (Spring 1996): 225–41.
- "Kurdish Future in a Post-Saddam Iraq." *Journal of Muslim Minority Affairs* 23 (April 2003): 9–23.
- *The Kurdish Predicament in Iraq: A Political Analysis*. New York: St Martin's Press, 1999.
- *The Kurds and the Future of Turkey*. New York: St Martin's Press, 1997.
- *The Kurds of Iraq: Tragedy and Hope*. New York: St. Martin's Press, 1992.
- "Turkey and Iran Face Off in Kurdistan." *Middle East Quarterly* 5 (March 1998): 33–40.

Hassanpour, Amir. *Nationalism and Language in Kurdistan, 1918–1985*. San Francisco: Mellen Research University Press, 1992.

Hirst, David. "Kurds Reap Sanctions' Rewards." *Washington Times*, 15 August 2001.

Human Rights Watch/Middle East. *Iraq's Crime of Genocide: The Anfal Campaign Against the Kurds*. New York: Human Rights Watch/Middle East, 1995.

Hutchinson, John, and Anthony D. Smith, eds. *Nationalism*. Oxford and New York: Oxford University Press, 1994.

Izady, Mehrdad R. *The Kurds: A Concise Handbook*. Washington, DC: Crane Russak, 1992.

Kahn, Margaret. *Children of the Jinn: In Search of the Kurds and Their Country*. New York: Seaview Books, 1980.

Kazaz, Harun. "Ambiguity Surrounds N. Iraq Kurdish Agreement." *Turkish Probe* (Ankara), 11 October 1998.

"KDP's Barzani Interviewed on Federation Plans." *AlAkbar* (Cairo), 22 November 1992, 4; as cited in *FBISNES*, 1 December 1992, 25.

Kissinger, Henry. *Years of Renewal*. New York: Simon and Schuster, 1999.

Kreyenbroek, Philip G. "On the Kurdish Language." In Philip G. Kreyenbroek and Stefan Sperl, eds, *The Kurds: A Contemporary Overview*, 68–83. London and New York: Routledge, 1992.

- and Christine Allison, eds. *Kurdish Culture and Identity*. London and New Jersey: Zed Books, 1996.

"Kurdish Officials Interviewed." Ankara Kanal6 Television Network in Turkish, 1730 GMT, 19 October 1992; as cited in *FBIS-WEU*, 22 October 1992, 72.

"Kurds' Barzani Discusses Peace Efforts, Autonomy," (Clandestine) Voice of Iraqi Kurdistan in Arabic, 1653 GMT, 13 April 1992; as cited in *FBIS-NES*, 15 April 1992, 41.

Lawrence, David Aquila. "In Their Own Universities, Kurds Taste Academic Freedom." *Chronicle of Higher Education*, 6 October 2000, A55.

- "A Shaky De Facto Kurdistan." *Middle East Report*, no. 215 (Summer 2000): 24–6.
Longrigg, Stephen H. *Iraq, 1900 to 1950: A Political, Social, and Economic History.* London: Oxford University Press, 1953.
Makiya, Kanan. *Cruelty and Silence: War, Tyranny, Uprising and the Arab World.* New York: Norton, 1993.
McDowall, David. *A Modern History of the Kurds.* London and New York: I.B. Tauris, 1996.
Meixler, Louis. "Kurds Still Dependent on Outsiders." Associated Press, 15 January 2001.
Minorsky, Vladimir. "Kurds." In *The Encyclopaedia of Islam*, vol. 2, 1132–55. Leiden: E.J. Brill, 1927.
Nezan, Kendal. "The Kurds: Current Position and Historical Background." In Philip G. Kreyenbroek and Christine Allison, eds, *Kurdish Culture and Identity*, 7–19. London and New Jersey: Zed Books, 1996.
- "A Renaissance in Iraq: The Kurds, a Fragile Spring." *Le Monde Diplomatique* (Paris), August 2001, www.monde-diplomatique.fr.
"Ozkok: Biggest Crisis of Trust with US." *Turkish Daily News*, (Ankara), 7 July 2003.
"PUK Leader Talabani Interviewed." *2000 Ikibin'e Dogru* (Istanbul), 31 May 1992, 1012; as cited in FBISNES, 9 June 1992, 27.
"Report Views Relations between Ankara, Peshmergas." *Tercuman* (Istanbul), 3 December 1992, 11; as cited in FBIS-WEU, 9 December 1992, 40.
The Republic of Kurdistan: Fifty Years Later. Special issue of *International Journal of Kurdish Studies* 11, nos 1–2 (1997).
Schmidt, Dana Adams. *Journey Among Brave Men.* Boston: Little, Brown, and Co., 1964.
Stansfield, Gareth R.V. *Iraqi Kurdistan: Political Development and Emergent Democracy.* London and New York: Routledge Curzon, 2003.
Sykes, Mark. *The Caliph's Last Heritage: A Short History of the Turkish Empire.* London: Macmillan, 1915.
"Temporary Government Planned." Ankara Anatolia in Turkish, 1630 GMT, 28 October 1992; as cited in FBISNES, 29 October 1992, 28.
"Turkish Paper Interviews Barzani." Cited in FBISNES, 9 June 1992, 26.
"U.S. to Protect the Democratic Experiment in Iraqi Kurdistan." *Kurdistan Observer* (London), 28 August 2001.
van Bruinessen, Martin. *Agha, Shaikh and State: The Social and Political Structures of Kurdistan.* London: Zed Books, 1992.
Vanly, Ismet Sheriff. "Kurdistan in Iraq." In Gerard Chaliand, ed., *People without a Country: The Kurds and Kurdistan*, 153–210. London: Zed Press, 1980.

White, Paul. *Primitive Rebels or Revolutionary Modernizers? The Kurdish National Movement in Turkey.* London: Zed Books, 2000.
Wigram, Edgar T.A., and W.A. Wigram. *The Cradle of Mankind: Life in Eastern Kurdistan.* 2nd ed. London: A. & C. Black, 1922.
Yavuz, M. Hakan, and Michael M. Gunter. "The Kurdish Nation." *Current History* 100 (January 2001): 33–9.

CONCLUSION

Cohn, Norman. *The Pursuit of the Millenium: Revolutionary Messianism in Medieval and Reformation Europe and Its Bearing on Modern Totalitarian Movements.* New York: Harper and Row, 1961.
– *Warrant for Genocide: The Myth of the Jewish World-Conspiracy and the Protocols of the Elders of Zion.* London: Eyre and Spottiswoode, 1967.
Erikson, Erik H. "Ego Development and Historical Change." *Identity and the Life Cycle: Psychological Issues* 1 (1959): 18–49.
Griffith, Sidney H. *Arabic Christianity in the Monasteries of Ninth-Century Palestine.* Aldershot and Brookfield: Ashgate Publishing, 1992.
Nirenberg, David. *Communities of Violence: Persecution of Minorities in the Middle Ages.* Princeton: Princeton University Press, 1996.
Sells, Michael A. "The Construction of Islam in Serbian Religious Mythology and Its Consequences." In Maya Shatzmiller, ed., *Islam and Bosnia: Conflict Resolution and Foreign Policy in Multi-Ethnic States,* 56–86. Montreal and Kingston: McGill-Queen's University Press, 2002.
Shatzmiller, Maya. *The Berbers and the Islamic State: The Marinid Experience in Pre-Protectorate Morocco.* Princeton: Markus Wiener, 2000.
– ed. *Islam and Bosnia: Conflict Resolution and Foreign Policy in Multi-Ethnic States.* Montreal and Kingston: McGill-Queen's University Press, 2002.

Contributors

Professor JUAN R.I. COLE
Department of History
University of Michigan

Professor DAVID L. CRAWFORD
Department of Sociology and Anthropology
Fairfield University

Professor MICHAEL GUNTER
Department of Political Science
Tennessee Technological University

Professor AZZEDINE LAYACHI
Department of Government and Politics
St John's University

Professor RICHARD C. MARTIN
Department of Religion
Emory University

Professor PAUL S. ROWE
Department of Political Science
The University of Western Ontario

Professor MAYA SHATZMILLER
Department of History
The University of Western Ontario

Professor CHARLES D. SMITH
Department of Near Eastern Studies
The University of Arizona

Professor PIETERNELLA VAN DOORN-HARDER
Department of Theology
Valparaiso University

The late Professor LINDA S. WALBRIDGE
Department of Anthropology
The University of Oklahoma

Professor M. HAKAN YAVUZ
Department of Political Science
The University of Utah

Index

Abbas Hilmi, Khedive, 69
Abbasids, 13
Abd al-Krim, 173, 175
'Abd al-Malik b. Marwan, 13
'Abd al-Raziq, 'Ali, 73
'abd el-Fattah, Nabil, 23
'Abdu'l-Baha, 132, 133, 134
Abdulhamid II, Sultan, 235
Abou El Fadl, Khaled, 15, 16
Abu Arz, 98
Abu Hanifa, 16
Abu l-Walid ibn Rush, 17
Achaemenids, 131
Adana Memorandum, 248
Adıyaman, 246
Afghanistan: refugees in Iran, 130; Soviet Union in, 110; Taliban in, 110
Afifi, Mohamed, 65
Africa: Coptic churches in, 47; Muslims in, 18
Afshari, Reza, 155
Agadir, 177

Ağrı Mountain, 237–8
Ahl al-Kitab, 5
Ahl-i Haqq sect, 127, 130
Ahmad, Ibrahim, 268
Ahmadi, Houshang Amir, 144–5
Ait Ahmed, Hocine, 206
Akhundzadih, 131, 132
Aksu, Abdulkadir, 255
al-Assad, Bashar, 101
al-Azhar, Sheikh, 52
al-Azhar University, 75
al-Banna, Rajab, 61, 62
Albright, Madeleine, 275
Alexandria, 24; Copts living in, 24, 46
Alexandros, Pope, 48
al-Fath, 75
Algeria: *aârouch*, 207, 219, 221; anti-colonialism in, 200, 201; as Arab and Muslim, 195, 202; Arab culture and language in, 204; as Arabist, 222; Arabization policy, 209, 211, 214; Arab nationalism

and, 200, 202; attitudes toward Berber movement, 220; Berber question *and* Berbers of. *See* Berber movement of Kabylie *and* Berbers of Algeria; Berber Spring, 206; Citizen Movement, 208; citizenship in, 213; civic politics in, 217–18, 223, 225; definition of, 195–6; democratization of, 218, 223; demonstrations in, 207; diversity within, 223–4; economic problems, 196, 203; elections, 204, 206, 217, 220; elite in, 222, 223; France and, 195, 200, 208, 210, 214; freedom of association law, 204; Front of Socialist Forces (FFS), 205, 207, 219, 220; High Commission for Amazighity, 206; identity, 197; Idir el-Watani, 201; independence, 201, 202, 209, 211; independence war, 200; Islamic Front of Salvation (FIS), 204, 206; as Islamic state, 203, 222; Islam in, 202, 210; Islamism in, 203, 204, 206–7, 210, 214, 220, 222, 223; liberalization in, 203–4, 223; living conditions in, 203; Movement for the Triumph of Democratic Liberties, 201; multilingualism in, 201; National Democratic Rally (RND), 221; nationalism, 195, 200, 201–2; nationalism of, vs. Arabo-Islamic nationalism, 201; National Liberation Front (FLN), 202, 204, 221; new social contract, 223–4; Ottoman rule in, 210; Party of the Algerian People (PPA), 201; political crises, 196; Rally for Culture and Democracy (RCD), 205–6, 207, 219–20; rebellions in, 203, 204, 206–7, 220, 224; referendums in, 221; religious groups vs. state in, 195; religious organizations, 204; 1988 riots, 203; *shari'a* in, 203; social/economic stratification in, 209; social problems, 211; social upheaval in, 211; state control in, 196; Tamazight in, 218, 221, 222; terror years of 1990s, 206; villages in, 207; violent fighting in, 195; weakness of civic structures in, 216

al-Ghazzali, 170
al-Hajjaj b. Yusuf, 16
'Ali, 6
'Ali Muhammad Shirazi, Sayyid, the Bab, 132
al-Jahiz, 13
al-Khatib, Muhibb al-Din, 75
Al-Khousheh, 31
al-Manar, 75
Almohads, 168, 169, 171, 173
Almoravids, 168, 169–70
Al-Musawwar, 31
al-Qa'ida, 62, 273
al-Qardawi, Sheikh, 31–2
al-Shaybani, 16
al-Sisaya, 73
Amazight. *See* Berbers
Amnesty International, 138, 140, 149
Anatolia, 236
Anderson, Benedict, 59, 60, 75, 123, 128, 196
an-Na'im, Abdullahi, 10, 18–19
Ansar al-Islam, 273
Anthony, St, 53

Anti Atlas, 172, 176; Berbers in, 175
Aoun, Michel, 100
apostasy: of Baha'is, 139, 147, 151, 156, 157; of Berbers, 284; in Iran, 147, 148–9, 150, 151, 152
Appleby, Scott, 11
Aqa Khan Kirmani, Mirza, 131
Arabic language, 36, 171, 172–3, 183; in Algeria, 204; in Egypt, 25; in Morocco, 166–7; rise of, 13
Arabs: conversion to Berber, 171; as linguistic classification, 178; religious basis of authority, 166; in *umma*, 285
ARGK. *See* Kurdistan: Peoples Liberation Army of Kurdistan
Atatürk, Mustafa Kemal, 230–1, 233, 234, 235, 236, 250, 253–4
Ateş, Atilla, 248
Athanasius, Anba (Bishop), 43, 45, 51, 53
Athanasius (Patriarch), 48, 53
Atiya, Aziz Souriyal, 47
Atlas Mountains. *See* Anti Atlas; High Atlas; Middle Atlas
Australia: Coptic Church in, 60; Copts in, 103
Averroes. *See* Ibn Rushd

Bab, the. *See* 'Ali Muhammad Shirazi, Sayyid
Babism, 127, 131, 132
Baha'i(s): administrative order of, 134–5, 141; apostasy of, 139, 147, 151; as apostates, 155, 156, 157; authoritarianism in, 135; burial of dead, 142–3; capital cases against, 151–2; children of, 139, 156; citizenship of, 144, 152, 157, 158; civil death of, 157–8; control of members, 135; converts from Islam, 148; death sentences of, 158; demonization of, 137–8; discrimination against, 141; Eastern Orthodox Christians compared with, 130; education of, 141, 143; electoral system, 134–5, 141; emigration of, 138–9; employment of, 143, 146; espionage activities, 150, 151; excommunication of refugees, 139; extermination through attrition, 157; families, 156; globalization and, 132, 133; under Great Terror, 138; Gulpaygani document concerning, 143–4, 157; "hands of the cause," 135; harassment of, 141, 146, 157; history of, 131–2; industrialists, 136–7; ineligibility for compensation, 141–2; Inquisition, 135; intellectuals, 135; under Islamic Republic of Iran, 130; and Israel, 138, 144, 151, 156; judicial system and, 142; under Khamenei, 143–4, 157; under Khomeini, 137–9; leaving the religion, 136; marriage of, 156; marriages, 142; membership list, 137, 138; in military, 135; modernity and, 132; and Musaddiq crisis, 136, 137; numbers of, 131–2, 136, 139; Open University, 154–5; and Pahlevi regime, 138; peace and, 133; persecution of, 137–9, 142–3, 146, 154–5; pogroms against, 136, 158; as political movement, 134, 138, 144, 156; as political party, 128; present conditions for, 155–6; as prisoners, 138, 139,

141, 142, 151; proselytizing by, 141, 143; publications, 135; quietism of, 134, 135; reconversions of, 151–2; registered vs. unregistered, 139; relations with Iranian nation, 137; relations with shah, 136–7; as scapegoats, 148, 158; and separation of religion and state, 134; Shi'ites and, 134, 135–6, 137; and state bureaucracy, 142; and theocracy, 134; tolerated as individuals only, 143, 144; as traitors, 148; and universities, 141, 154–5

Baha'u'llah, 132–3, 134

Baluch language, 131

A Banquet for Seaweed, 91

Baring, Sir Evelyn. *See* Cromer, Evelyn Baring, Lord

Barzani, Masud, 255, 268, 269, 270, 271, 272, 276

Barzani, Mustafa, 267–8

Barzinji, Mahmud, 267

Bayly, C.A., 58

Ben-Dor, Gabriel, 11, 12, 58, 130, 159, 168

Benflis, Ali, 215

Bengio, Ofra, 11, 12, 58, 130, 159

Ben Kaddour, Abdaslam, 174

Beqa'a Valley, 94

Berber Cultural Movement (MCB), 205, 206, 207, 219, 220

Berber movement of Kabylie: and autonomy, 224; autonomy and, 208; and citizenship, 215; as civic movement, 213; clashes with state security personnel, 218, 220; demands of, 205, 207; and democratization of state, 205, 223; dialogue with state, 219, 220; discrediting of, 224; el-Kseur Platform, 207–8, 218, 219, 221, 223, 225; ethnicity as mobilizing factor, 210, 222, 223; ethnicity vs. civility of, 213; ethnicization of, 211–12; government reaction to, 211–12; and Islamism, 204–5, 205–6; isolation of, 224; lack of flexibility, 219; language issues, 222; nationalism and, 214–15; as persecuted minority, 224; problems underlying, 221–2; radical ethnicist vs. civil activist factions, 218–19; radicalization of, 217; secession and, 208; self-determination, 214

Berbers: of Algeria. *See* Berbers of Algeria; as apostates, 284; consciousness of, 167, 168; cultural identity of, 172; differences from other minorities, 166; dynasties, 168–9; egalitarianism among, 179, 182–3; empires of, 169; as ethnic group, 167; history of, 166–7; identity formation of, 63; language of cultural productions, 168; as linguistic classification, 178; as majority, 168; of Morocco. *See* Berbers of Morocco; origin of, 284; politics, 179; Sanhaja, 169; territorial nationalism and, 63; as tribal vs. ethnic, 167–8; in *umma*, 285

Berbers of Algeria, 63, 186; and Arabization policy, 211; and Arab majority, 216; as Christians, 203; civic view of, 217–18; clash with Algerian nationalists, 201; conflict against state, 195; cultural and linguistic demands,

211; culture of, 202, 206–7; discrimination against, 209; in elite, 222; ethnicist view of, 216–17; ethnicity of, 196, 213–14; geographic distribution of, 210; as imagined community, 196; internal migration of, 209; Kabyle question, 185; language, 202, 206–7, 208, 209; as leaders, 209; linguistic claims, 196, 202; May 2001 protests, 188; and mechanical solidarity, 179; as minority group, 216; as minority vs. majority of population, 208–9, 217; mixed marriages among, 208–9; mobilization of, 196, 219; and Muslim invaders, 202; as Muslims, 202; Mzab, 210; nationalism of, 200–1, 212, 216; particularism of, 208–10, 212, 214; parties of, 204; persecution of, 216; political consciousness, 196; political mobilization of, 210; politicization of ethnicity, 196; Qbayil, 210, 211. *See also* Berber movement of Kabylie; repression of, 202, 220, 224; secular character of movement, 203; Shawiyya, 210; Tamazight language, 206. *See also* Tamazight; Tuareg, 210

Berbers of Morocco, 63; activism of, 167, 172; in Anti Atlas, 175; Arabic language spoken by, 172–3; becoming Arab, 171; bilingualism of, 173; colonial-era discourse on, 171; consciousness, 186–7; culture, 164, 165, 177–8; *dahir* (1930), 188; discrimination against, 164; diversity of communities, 176–7; dynasties of, 167; in High Atlas, 175–6; human rights of, 172; identity, 178; and IRCAM. *See* IRCAM; languages, 171, 172–3. *See also* Tamazight; linguistic blocs, 172–3; in Middle Atlas, 174–5; number of speakers, 177; oppression of language and culture, 172; political consciousness of, 165; political-economic inequalities, 172; politicization of, 164, 171, 185; postcolonial discourse on, 171; poverty among, 185–6, 187; radical politics among, 187; relations with Arabs, 171; in Rif Mountains, 173–4; rural vs. urban, 183, 185, 187; segmentary organization, 174, 178–9, 181; status of, 164; tribes of, 178–9; tribe vs. language or state, 178–9; urban-rural variations, 172

Berber Spring, 206
Bhutto, Benazir, 118
Bhutto, Zulfikar Ali, 117–18
Bidlisi, Sharaf Khan, 264
Binational Fulbright Commission, 8
bin Laden, Osama, 273
Birand, M. Ali, 243
blasphemy, 120
Bosnian war, 284
Botiveau, Bernard, 72
Bourqia, R., 180
Bouteflika, Abdelaziz, 207, 219, 221
Britain: Charter Act, 111; in Egypt, 25–6, 38, 66–8, 71; in India, 111; protection of minorities, 71
Browne, E.G., 133
Bulliet, Richard, 13

Burujirdi, Ayatollah, 136
Bush, George W., 276
Buyids, 131

Cairo: American University, 47;
    Copts in, 24, 46; Muqattam hill,
    46; *zabbalin*, 46; Zawya al-Hamra
    incident, 27
caliphate: fall of, 18; Turkish, 237;
    Umayyad, 13
Capuchin friars, 113
Casablanca, 177, 184
Castells, Manuel, 35, 49
caste(s): converts as members of,
    114; economics and, 124; Jat, 114,
    115; loss of, 115; marriage and,
    116; missionaries and, 112–13,
    114; Muslims and, 116; of
    Pakistani Christians, 122–3;
    Rajput, 114, 115; scheduled, 114
Center for Religious Freedom, 61
Chaker, Salem, 167, 178, 212
Chamoun family, 96
Chatterjee, Partha, 75, 128, 158–9
Chiapuris, John, 182
children: circumcision of, 36, 40;
    in Coptic Church, 40–1; in
    Morocco, 184; naming of, 40
Christianity: of Copts, 59; differ-
    ences between groups, 88, 89;
    in mass media, 32; Muslim
    converts to, 113, 155; pressures
    on groups, 88; Sikhs and, 117;
    and television, 30, 35
Christianity Solidarity Interna-
    tional, 61
Christians: Berbers in Algeria as,
    203; Coptic. *See* Coptic Church;
    Copts; *dhimmi* status, 27; distinc-
    tions between, 102–3; in Egypt,
    23, 29–30, 32. *See also* Copts;
    evangelical, 61–2; evangelicals,
    148; in Iran, 129, 152, 156; in
    Iraq, 62; Islam and, 285; in
    Islamic countries, 31–2; in Leba-
    non. *See* Lebanese Christians;
    and Muslims, 17, 22, 25, 27, 29,
    33, 86, 155; nationalism, 103; in
    Pakistan. *See* Pakistani Chris-
    tians; as people of the Book, 5,
    32; in Punjab. *See* Punjabi Chris-
    tians; Rif liberated from, 173;
    television and, 35
Chuhra(s), 112–15, 122, 123–4, 125;
    baptism of, 113; conversion of,
    112–13; denial of background,
    114; education of, 113; harass-
    ment of, 113; as lowest members
    of Kammis, 114–15; as term
    describing work, 114
Church Missionary Society, 69
circumcision, female, 52, 66
citizenship: in Algeria, 213; of
    Baha'is, 144, 152, 157, 158; and
    Berber movement of Kabylie,
    215; of Copts, 28; in Ottoman
    Empire, 239; of Pakistani
    Christians, 122; in Turkey, 239
civic order, defined, 215
civility: defined, 215; ethnicity vs.,
    215–16; primordialism vs., 216
Clement of Alexandria, 53
Clinton, Bill, 275–6
Cohn, Norman, 284
Cold War, 198, 199
collective identity, vs. primordial-
    ism, 223
Collins, Jeffery, 67
colonialism, 25–6, 109; and ethnic
    groups, 12; legacy of, 199–200;

Index 325

and nationalism, 128; and tension between ethnicity vs. civility, 215–16
Combs-Schilling, Elaine, 181
communism, 285
conflicts: among minorities, 11; among religious groups, 85; ethnic, vii; international, 198, 199
Connor, Walter, 214
converts and conversions: baptism of, 114; and Christian evangelicals, 148; Chuhra, 112–13; families, 113; groups, 113; in India, 112; to Islam, 4, 6, 284; from Judaism, 156; Muslim to Christian, 155; from Orthodox Church to Coptic Church, 90; persecution of, 113; poor Indians, 113–14; reconversions, 151–2; Sikhs, 117; untouchables, 112–13
Coptic Centre for Social Studies, 42, 50–1
Coptic Church: action groups in, 42; in Africa, 47; in Australia, 60; baptism in, 65; Bishopric for Social and Ecumenical Affairs, 39; Bishopric for Youth, 39–40, 51; bishops in, 43–4, 45; calendar, 35, 37; in Canada, 60; children in, 40–1; Christian unity under, 89, 90; church construction, 92; churches outside Egypt, 24; Clerical College, 44–5; clericalization of, 38; community-development projects, 32; converts from Orthodox Church, 90; cooperation with regime, 92; dioceses overseas, 60; divorce and, 65; dominance in community, 77; as "easternized," 86; education and, 39, 74; Eucharist in, 44, 45; feminists in, 52; hierarchy within, 23, 92; holy and sacred places, 36; in international politics, 33; and Islamists, 42, 62; and Islamization, 76; leadership of, 23, 38, 44, 53; losses of members, 24; Maronites compared with, 102; marriage in, 65–6; *maulids* in, 45–6; monasteries, 27, 38, 44, 45, 91, 92; monastic movement, 94; monastic revival, 38, 44–7, 74; Muslims and, 23, 43–4; neomillet partnership with Egypt, 92, 94; nonterritoriality of, 93; Orthodox identity, 38; outside Egypt, 47; pastoral revival, 38, 41–4; patriarchate, 90, 94; pedagogical revival, 38; political activism, 76–7, 93; political alliance with state, 77; reform of, 25, 28, 49, 69, 70; religious councils, 68, 69, 76; as representative of all Copts, 74, 77, 92, 102; revival of, 37–40; rural-development projects, 49; rural diaconal project, 44–5; saints in, 45–6; schools, 32; seminaries, 24, 43; sense of belonging, 35; since Second World War, 70; social services to Copts, 77, 92; spiritual formation in, 45, 53; state policy toward, 93; *takris* in, 43; textual tradition, 35; as *umma*, 62; unity within, 94; universe of, 46–7, 53; in US, 60–1; in West, 47; women in, 41–2, 43; youth ministry in, 41–2

Coptic Encyclopedia, 47
Coptic identity, 53; as Egyptians, 79; formation of, 23, 25; markers with Muslim Egyptians, 24; for resistance, 49
Coptic Legion, 66
Coptic Orthodox Church, 24
Coptic studies, 47
Copts: activities of, 102; adaptation of expressions, 37; adoption of Muslim practices, 65–6; American Coptic Association, 61; and Anglican and Presbyterian missionaries, 69; Association of St Mark, 47; attacks on, 27–8, 30–1; in Australia, 103; baptism of, 40, 48; belonging to Egypt, 53–4; birth rates, 24; and British occupation, 66–8; children's education, 24, 26, 39; Christianity of, 59; as Christians, 64–5; circumcision of children, 36; as citizens, 28; clergy vs. secular in US, 61; communities outside Egypt, 47; community representation to outside world, 59–60; conversions to Islam, 64, 89; conversions to other denominations, 65; cross tattooed on wrist, 37, 40, 47, 54; *dhimmi* status, 25, 34, 64, 72, 86–7; dialogue with Muslims, 51–2, 54; diaspora of, 24, 47, 286; differences with Muslims, 25; discrimination against, 29–30, 67, 69–70, 70–1; dispute within community, 62, 71; dress of, 37; education of, 24, 38–9; and Egyptian nationalism, 66, 69; as Egyptians, 23, 32–3, 59, 71, 78, 102, 286; emigration from Egypt, 32; and evangelical Christians, 61–2; as exclusive community, 35–6; expatriate, 47–9; expatriate vs. Egyptian, 286; families, 24; food of, 37; geographical distribution, 24, 93, 101; as ghetto dwellers, 33, 34; golden age for, 68; human rights, 34; interfaith discussions with Muslims, 51; intermarriage with Muslims, 42; in Islamic milieu, 86–7; language, 33; Lebanese Christian groups compared with, 85–8, 88–9, 102; loss of wealth, 26; and martyrdom, 40, 41, 74; in mass media, 34–5, 50; migration by, 64; minority status, 61, 89–90; mixed marriages, 42, 48; and Muslim extremists, 34, 51; and Muslims, 69, 78; Muslim violence against, 72–3; names of, 37, 40; nationalism of, 48–9, 92; non-Orthodox Christians and, 36; as nonviolent civil-rights movement, 49; numbers of, 24, 64, 89–90, 93; origins of, 24; and other Christian minorities, 59; peaceful resistance of, 52–3; in People's Assembly, 93; persecution of, 59–60, 63; political involvement, 26, 30, 70, 76, 93; population growth rate, 24; poverty among, 24, 36; as prime ministers, 25; in private sector, 24, 26; in public life/service, 25, 30, 50, 54, 66, 67; relations with state, 77–8; religious education vs. modernization, 75; resistance to British colonialism, 25–6; restrictions on, 91–2; rites of passage, 40;

salawat al-tisht ritual, 40; in schools, 26, 50; self-renewal of, 49, 53, 73, 74, 75–6, 77, 91; shared experiences with Muslims, 36; and *shari'a*, 64; sharing national identity with Egyptian Muslims, 59; in social strata, 24, 33, 35; songs of, 37; status of, 63–4; studies of, 23; *subu'*, 40; Sunday schools, 38, 39, 41, 42–3, 91, 92, 94; two worlds of, 46–7; uniqueness of, 78; in US, 103; views on women, 36; violence against, 69, 77; in Wafd Party, 71, 73; websites, 61; in West, 33
Copts Digest, 48
Cottam, Richard, 136, 137
Coulter, Ann, 82n9
Council of Chalcedony, 48
Country Reports on Human Rights Practices, 29–30
Cragg, Kenneth, 86–7, 104
Cromer, Evelyn Baring, Lord, 69
cultural vs. religious minorities, 286
culture: and minority identities, 285; politics of, 188; print, 60, 75; tolerance and, 199. *See also* subheading culture *under names of groups and countries*

Dar al-Harb, 4, 5–6; conversion into Dar al-Islam, 15; migration from, 16; US as part of, 18
Dar al-Islam, 4; as "imagined community," 19; migration to, 16, 17; US as part of, 18
da'wa, 15
DDKD. *See* Kurds: Revolutionary Democratic Cultural Association
DDKO. *See* Kurds: Revolutionary Cultural Society of the East
DEHAP. *See* Turkey: Democratic People's Party
Demirel, Süleyman, 240, 248
democratization, 200, 224
Derija, 165
Dersim, 238
developing areas: authoritarian rule in, 198; economic disparities in, 198
Dhabihi, Kurush, 146
dhimmis, 5, 8, 9, 18, 87, 88, 103, 104; Christians as, 27; Copts as, 25, 34, 64, 72, 86–7; in Iran, 156; religious minorities as, 156
Dhulfaqari, Ramadan 'Ali, 147
Dimishqi, Arman, 146
Dinshaway incident, 68
discrimination, 70; against Baha'is, 141; against Berbers, 164, 209; against Copts, 29–30, 67, 69–70, 70–1; linguistic, 187; against minority identities, 67; in Morocco, 187; persecution vs., 71; religious, 70; tolerance vs., 71; against women, 29–30
Dreher, Rod, 82n9
Druze, 95, 101
Durkheim, Emile, 11, 179

Ecevit, Bülent, 253
ECHR. *See* European Court of Human Rights
Eddé family, 96
Edmonds, C.J., 263
ego formation, 283
Egypt: ambiguity regarding Christians in, 29–30; antidemocratic nature of state, 29; Arabic

language in, 25; Arab invasion of, 24–5; Arab nationalism in, 104; Arab socialism in, 26, 27; attitude toward Christians, 23, 32; British in, 25–6, 38, 66–8, 71; civil society in, 90–1; Constitution, 26, 33, 72, 91, 93; dissidents in, 29; employment of civil servants in, 31; feminism in, 52; independence, 26, 38, 71; *infitah*, 72; Islam as state religion, 28, 72; Islamic radicalism in, 91–2; Islamic religious education compulsory in schools, 26, 39; Islamism in, 23, 27, 28, 32, 34, 42; Islamization of, 76; Jews in, 28; land laws, 74; law of national unity, 239; Liberal Constitutionalist Party, 73; Liberal Nationalism, 26, 27; mass media, 32, 34–5, 50, 91; Ministry of Religious Affairs, 74; nationalism of, 66, 69; nationalization in, 60, 74; neomillet system, 92, 94, 100, 102; People's Assembly, 93; population, 24; protection of minorities by British, 71; religion in, 22–3, 27, 28, 49–50; repression in, 90–1; 1919 revolution, 25–6, 71; 1952 revolution, 26, 74; Revolution of Free Officers, 89; school curricula revision, 50; sectarian violence in, 30–1; *shari'a* in, 28–9, 72, 93; Shura Council, 30; Six Day War, 22, 27; State Security, 30–1; state violence in, 32, 33; Sunni Muslims in, 90, 101; symbolic geography of, 36; television in, 30, 35; tourists targeted by extremists in, 28, 32; trade with US, 72; Turkey and, 248; and *umma*, 35, 48; women in, 30; World Wars and, 26. *See also* Coptic Church; Copts

Elazığ, 237, 246

Elçi, Serafettin, 240, 252, 254

elites: in Algeria, 222, 223; in multi-ethnic states, 200; and power, 180

el-Khawaga, Dina, 76

en-naba'a, 91

Erbakan, Necmittin, 234, 238, 255

Erdoğan, Recep Tayyip, 255

Erdoğan, Rıza, 255

Eriksen, Thomas Hyland, 59

Erikson, Erik, 283

ERNK. *See* Kurdistan Liberation Front

ethnic groups, 12; Berbers as, 167; conflicts, vii; democratization and, 224; mobilization, 224; repression and, 224; self-renewal, 25

ethnicity, 59; civility vs., 215–16; and contiguity, 213; defined, 213; and democratization, 200; and "imagined community," 213–14; and nationalism, 128; nationhood and, 214; and primordial loyalties, 213; as rallying point for other unresolved problems, 208; relative deprivation and, 253; and self-government, 214–15

ethnic movements: autonomy of, 199; demands of, 199; evolution of, 230; inclusion of, 199; independence of, 199; recognition for, 199

Europe: colonialism of, 4; and Kurdish question, 252; Kurds in,

241, 244, 251; Muslims in, 19; relations with Iran, 153; trade with Iran, 151; and Turkey, 252
European Court of Human Rights (ECHR), 250
European Union (EU), 231, 244, 245, 250–1; Turkey and, 251–2
Evliya Chelebi, 264

Fez, 167
fiqh, 17
Fırat, Abdulmelik, 254
Firdawsi, 133
Fouad, Vivian, 52
Foucault, Michel, 180
France: in Algeria, 195, 200, 208, 210, 214; Berber militants in, 223; and Morocco, 173, 175; nationalist tradition in, 128; and Qbayil, 210–11; in Rif Mountains, 173
Franco, General, 173
Franjieh, Sulaiman, 96
Franjieh family, 99
Freud, Sigmund, 283
fundamentalism: modernization-conflictual approach, 11; as reaction against secularization, 11; religious minorities under, 137

Gama'a Islamiyya, 73, 91
Gandhi, Mahatma, 49
GAP. *See* Turkey: Southeastern Anatolia Project
Garden of the Monks, 45
Geertz, Clifford, 12, 108, 180, 213, 215
Gellner, Ernest, 167–8, 175, 178–9, 182
Gemayel, Bashir, 99
Gemayel family, 97, 98

Germany: Federation of Kurdish Organizations in Germany (YEM-KOM), 245; Kurds in, 251; PKK in, 246; relations with Iran, 151; stereotypes in Nazi race mythology, 284
Ghali, Boutros, 25, 68–9, 69–70
Giddens, Anthony, 180
Girgis, Habib, 39
globalization: and Baha'i, 132; and group demands, 199; and group rebelliousness, 198; and Iraqi Kurds, 286; and minority identities, 286; and social movements, 253; and standard of living, 182; and weakening of state, 198
Goan Catholics, 115–16, 122, 123
Gobineau, Joseph-Arthur, comte de, 131
Gorst, Sir Eldon, 67, 68, 69, 70
graveyards, 142–3
Greek Orthodox Church, 94–5, 97, 99, 236
Guermah, Massinissa, 207
Gulf War, 8, 266, 268
Gulpaygani, Sayyid Muhammad, 143–4, 148, 157, 158
Gunpowder Empires, 4
Gurr, Ted, 253

Habermas, Jürgen, 153
Haddam, Mansur, 146
HADEP. *See* Turkey: People's Democratic Party
Hadith, 15–16
Halabja, 268, 273
Hamayouni Decree, 25
Hamidiye Regiments, 235
Hammoudi, Abdellah, 180–1, 188
Hanafi jurists, 16, 17

Hanbali jurists, 17
Harakat-ul-Ansar Pakistan, 110
harbis, 6
Hariri, Francis, 273
Hart, David, 175, 182
Hasan, Sana, 27, 33
Hassanpour, Amir, 263
Haykal, Muhammad Husayn, 73
Hdidduland, 174
Helsinki Summit, 250
High Atlas: Berbers in, 175–6, 183; farming in, 176; Tashelhit spoken in, 172
Hijra, 5, 15
Hinduism: attitude toward Christian conversions, 113; caste system, 116; missionaries and, 112
historians: study of minorities, 9
Hizbullah, 247
Hobsbawm, Eric, 159
Hodgson, Marshall, 7
Hourani, Albert, 10
Hujjatiyyih movement, 134, 137, 141
human rights: of Berbers in Morocco, 172; for Copts, 34; Iranian attitude toward, 129; and Islam, 10; for Kurds, 245; for minorities, 19; traditional Islamic theological categories vs. modern frameworks, 10
Huntington, Samuel, 109
Husayn, Taha, 73
Husayn 'Ali Nuri, Mirza. *See* Baha'u'llah
Husayn-Aliy-i-Baha, Mirza, 149

Ibbetson, Sir Denzil, 112
Ibn Rushd, 17
Ibn Tumart, 169, 170–1
Ibrahim, Saad Eddin, 29, 60, 64, 65, 91
identity/identities: building of, 49; collective, 215–16; consciousness and, 167; formation of, 283; legitimizing, 49; material factors, 185; politics of, 165; project, 49; religious vs. secular state, 75; for resistance, 49. *See also* minority identities; religious identities
Ignatieff, Michael, 213, 215
İhsan Nuri Paşa, 237–8
Iklé, Fred, 62
imagined communities, 19, 59, 213
Imazighen. *See* Berbers
India: blasphemy laws, 120; British in, 111; canal colonies, 113–14, 115; cathedrals in, 111; land ownership in, 115; Malabar Coast, 16; missionaries in, 111; Muslim refugees from, 116; Partition, 116; schools in, 111, 112; social changes in, 112; untouchables of, 112, 115; war with Pakistan, 110
Indyk, Martin, 276
infidelity, 31–2
information technology and secular nationalism, 60
Institut Kurde de Paris, 244
l'Institut Royal de la culture amazighe. *See* IRCAM
international order, restructuring of, 198
Iran: Afghan refugees in, 130; apostasy in, 147, 148–9, 150, 151, 153; Aryan civilization of, 131; Baha'i attitude toward nation, 137; Baha'is under, 130; *basij*, 145,

154; Christians in, 129, 148, 156; civil identity, 134; clerical leaders, 129; Constitutional Revolution, 156; court system, 146; *dhimmi* status in, 156; economy, 140, 145, 153; elections, 145; espionage in, 150; ethnic minorities in, 138; and Europe, 151, 153; and *fatwa* against Salman Rushdie, 145; German relations with, 151; history of, 130–1; Hostage Crisis, 145; human-rights abuses in, 138, 140–1, 146; intellectuals in, 154; and international conception of human rights, 129; and Iraqi border concessions, 268; Islamic identity, 137; Islamic Republic of, 127; Jews in, 129, 152, 155, 156; under Khatami, 153–6, 159; under Khomeini, 137–9, 156; Kurdish nationalism in, 232; and Kurdistan, 276; Kurds in, 138, 267. *See also* Kurds of Iran; languages of, 131; and Lebanese hostage crisis, 145; legitimacy of, 267; liberalization of, 155; liberals in, 154; and Muslim conquest, 131; Muslim converts to Christianity in, 155; nationalism in, 127, 129, 145, 157; non-Armenian Christians in, 152; Pahlevi regime, 134, 138, 152; Pan-Islamism of, 138, 156; persecution of political opposition, 140; political prisoners, 138, 140; population, 139; pragmatic conservatives of, 144–5, 153, 158; privatization in, 140; radical theocrats in, 145; under Rafsanjani, 140, 144–6, 153, 154, 157; reactionary faction in, 145, 153; relations with US, 154; relations with West, 140, 146, 153–4; religious minorities in, 129–30, 140–1, 152, 153, 155; 1979 revolution, 137; shift to left in, 153; Shi'ism in, 128; Shi'ite Muslims in, 128–9; Shi'ite religion intertwined with, 148; student activists in, 154; Sunni Muslims in, 129–30; theocracy in, 127, 128, 129, 137–8, 140, 154; Tobacco Revolt, 132–3; Turkmen in, 138; war with Iraq, 139, 157, 266, 268; and World Bank, 146, 158; Zoroastrianism in. *See* Zoroastrianism

Iraq: *Anfal* campaigns, 268; Bagdinani-speaking area, 271; chemical attack on Halabja, 268; Christian evangelicals in, 62; creation of, 266–7; economic conditions, 271–2; fertile land in, 267; fresh water in, 267; Gulf War, 266, 268; Kurdish nationalism in, 232; Kurdistan Workers' Party (PKK) in, 270–1, 272; Kurds in. *See* Kurds of Iraq; Kurmanji-speaking area, 271; legitimacy of, 267; March Manifesto, 268; nationalism, 269; oil in, 271; oil reserves, 267; partitioning of, 269; Shi'ite Arabs in, 267, 278; Sunni Arabs in, 267, 278; UN Security Council Resolutions, 268–9, 270, 272–3; 1998 US bombing of, 275; US invasion of, 49; US war with, 276–7, 278; war with Iran, 139, 157, 266, 268; Washington Accord, 272

Iraqi National Congress (INC), 272

Irbil, 270, 272, 274, 275
IRCAM, 164, 167, 168; and Berber culture, 172, 177, 189; Berber issues over time, and, 171, 186; and education system, 183, 185, 187; establishment of, 164, 188; implementation of, 186, 189; and languages in rural areas, 184; mandate of, 164–5; significance of, 165; as symbol of emerging civil society, 188; uses of, 188
Islam: in Algeria, 202, 203, 210; Berbers and, 284; Christians and, 285; conversions to, 4, 6, 15, 24, 34, 46, 64, 284; Copts and, 25, 41, 89; expansion of, 4; human rights and, 10; Jews and, 285; and Kurdish nationalism, 235; and Kurds, 241; linguistic component, 166; meanings of, 7–8; and minority identities, vii-viii, xiii; as monolithic, 88; in Morocco, 171, 181–2, 187, 189; Muslims as legal majority, 4; nationalism and, vii; nation-states within, 285; non-Muslims in countries, 32; in Pakistan, 109; practice of, in non-Muslim lands, 16; radical, 62, 78, 91–2. *See also* Islamism; radicalization of, 285; religious pluralism within, 285; and rise of supreme leader, 285–6; as social force, 27; social theory, 8; in Spain, 203; as state religion in Egypt, 28, 72; taught to Coptic children, 26, 39; teachings on television, 30, 35, 37; in Turkey, 235, 236, 237, 238, 255
Islamic Jihad. *See jihad*

Islamic law: interpretations of, 17; nationalism and, 128–9
Islamic Republic of Iran. *See* Iran
Islamic Republic of Kurdistan. *See* Kurdistan
Islamism, 86, 103; in Algeria, 203, 204, 210, 214, 220, 222, 223; and Berber movement of Kabylie, 205–6; Coptic Church and, 42; in Egypt, 23, 27, 28, 32, 34, 42, 91–2; hard-line, 6; in Kabylie, 204–6; in Kurdistan, 273; in Pakistan, 118, 119, 123; as Seceders, 6. *See also* fundamentalism
Islamist National Outlook Movement, 238
Isma'ili, 7
Israel: Baha'i and, 138, 144, 151, 156; Coptic Church attitude toward, 33; Mossad, 151; Six Day War, 22, 27; Turkey and, 248
Ithna-'Ashara, 7
Izady, Mehrdad, 264, 265

Jama'at-i Islami, 109
Jama'at Islamiyya, 27
Jamiat-i-Ulema Islam, 110
Jerusalem: Coptic Church attitude toward, 33
Jews and Judaism: conversions from, 156; in Egypt, 5, 28; in Iran, 129, 152, 155, 156; and Islam, 285; as people of the Book, 32; persecution of, 283–4
Jhangavi, Haque Nawaz, Maulana, 110
jihad, 15, 73, 91, 173, 236
Jinnah, Mohammad Ali, 109
John Paul II, Pope, 48, 50
Joseph, John, 120, 123

Judaism. *See* Jews and Judaism
Julien, Charles-André, 209
Jund al-Islam, 273

Kabyles, 179
Kabylie, 196, 203; autonomy for, 212, 216, 219; Berber movement of. *See* Berber movement of Kabylie; Citizen Movement of, 219, 220; crisis, 220–1; ethnic mobilization in, 205, 211; French policy regarding, 210–11; Gendarmerie forces in, 220; independence for, 216, 219; Islamism in, 204–5, 205–6; Movement for the Autonomy of Kabylie (MAK), 212; repression in, 220–1; social upheaval in, 211, 220–1
Kadiri Sufi order, 231, 232, 234
Kadkhuda-Zadih, Ruhu'llah, 155
Kammis, 114–15
Karachi, 116, 119
Kardouchoi, 264
Karkai, Sarteed, 275
Kasravi, Ahmad, 134
Kassem, Abdul Karim, General, 268
Kemalism. *See under* Kurdish nationalism *and* Turkey; Atatürk, Mustafa Kemal
Kettani, Ali, 18
Khalajabadi, Kayvan, 141, 146–7, 150
Khamenei, 'Ali, Ayatollah, 139–40, 140, 143–4, 145, 154
Khani, Ahmad, 264–5
Kharijites, 6
Khatami, Muhammad, 129, 153–5, 159

Khomeini, Rohu'llah, Ayatollah, 128, 129, 137–9, 140, 141, 142, 144, 145, 148, 149, 156
Kiraza, 45
Kirkuk, 277
Kissinger, Henry, 268, 276
Kramer, Martin, 82n10
Kraus, Wolfganag, 174, 175, 179, 182
kuffar, 6
Kulta, Yuhanna, 51–2
Kurdish Human Rights Project (KHRP), 245
Kurdish identity: after 1980 coup, 241; fragmentation of, 233–4; nationalist vs. Islamic, 241; politicization of, 243; religious vs. secular forces, 233–4; secularization of, 239
Kurdish movements, 243–4, 253, 254. *See also names of individual groups*
Kurdish National Congress (KNK), 246, 255
Kurdish nationalism, 229, 241, 245, 251, 263; and economic deprivation of Kurdish regions, 252–3; feudal, 265; Hizbullah and, 247; in Iraq, 232; Iraqi nationalism and, 269; Islam and, 235; and Kemalism, 240; *Kurdayeti*, 266; and leftist movement, 242; and Pan-Kurdish state, 252; separatist, 242; state reaction to, 240–1; violence of, 241–3, 247
Kurdish National League, 237–8
Kurdistan, 247, 263, 264, 271; civil society in, 273; currency, 274; division of, 265–6; economic conditions, 272; elections in, 273;

as federal state, 269–70; honour killing of women in, 274; hospitals, 274; Iran and, 276; Islamic Republic of, 247; Islamists in, 273; landmines in, 274; Mahabad Republic of, 268; NGO contributions, 273; oil refinery, 274; oil revenues, 271–2; and OPC, 268; Patriotic Union of Kurdistan (PUK), 268, 270, 271, 272, 273, 274; Peoples Liberation Army of Kurdistan (ARGK), 249; political parties in, 273; population, 273–4; protection from Iraqi government, 275; Sheikh Mahmud as "king," 267; trade with Turkey, 274; Turkey and, 276; Turkish military strikes into, 271; united, 266; universities, 275; and US, 275–6

Kurdistan Democratic Party (KDP), 268, 269, 270, 271, 272, 273, 274

Kurdistan Liberation Front (ERNK), 245, 246

Kurdistan Workers' Party (PKK), 231, 241, 242, 244, 245–7, 248–50, 254, 255; in Iraq, 270–1, 272

Kurds: *ağas*, 265; autonomous status, 63; differences among, 265; economic deprivation of regions, 252–3; emirates, 264, 265; in Europe, 244, 245, 251; human-rights causes, 245; independence of, 270; Institut Kurde de Paris, 244, 265; in Iran, 138. *See also under* Iran; language of, 131, 265; library in Sweden, 244; March Manifesto, 268; as minority, 263; mountains and, 265; myths regarding origins, 264; as nation, 263; Newroz, 264; oppression of, 266; publishing houses, 244; religion of, 265, 266; Revolutionary Cultural Society of the East (DDKO), 240; Revolutionary Democratic Cultural Association (DDKD), 240; secession of, 267, 269; separatism, 267; sheikhs, 266; Sunni, 63, 266; transnational spaces, 244–5; tribalism of, 265; in *umma*, 285; in West, 275

Kurds of Iran, 267

Kurds of Iraq, 63; as allies of US, 276–7; autonomy for, 268; federalism of, 269–70; flight to mountains, 268; globalization and, 286; infighting among, 268, 272; interaction with Turkish Kurds, 243; and Iran-Iraq War, 268; percentage of population, 267; and Turkey, 270–1, 277–8; 1991 uprising, 268, 275. *See also* Kurdistan

Kurds of Turkey, 63, 272; adaptation of Turkish culture, 230; *ağas*, 232, 250; Alevi, 233–4, 238, 239–40, 253, 267; *asirets*, 232; assimilation of, 230, 233, 243; autonomy of, 233; in cities, 247; clans, 233; consciousness raising, 240, 242; costs of conflict in provinces, 246–7, 251; culture, 230; dialects of, 233; Diyarbakır Province, 234, 237, 241, 251; as ethnic entrepreneurs, 231, 232; in Europe, 241; Europeanization of issues, 231; and European role, 252; framing of resistance, by state, 238; geography of, 233;

homeland, 234; identity formation, 231; intellectuals, 231, 239, 244; interaction with Iraqi Kurds, 243; Islam and, 241; language of, 252; leaders, 232; leftist movement and, 242; marginalization of, 241; as nation, 233; nationalism of, vs. Turkish nationalism, 232; networks of, 242, 244, 245; Nurcus, 247; in Ottoman Empire, 63; particularism, 232; politicization of identity, 229, 230; provinces of, 234; secularization of identity, 231; separatism of, 241; *seyyids*, 232, 233, 234; socialism and, 239–40; tribal structures, 231, 232–3; tribes, 241; *umma* and, 241; university students, 242; in village-guard militia system, 246; villages of, 230, 246, 247; youth, 240, 242, 246–7; Zazas, 238
Kyrillos VI, Patriarch, 28, 37, 38–9, 44, 53, 92

Lahore Diocese, 116
languages: minority, 165; and minority identities, 285; reforms, 13. *See also subheadings* language *and* languages *under names of countries and peoples*
Laroui, Abdallah, 169
Larson, Warren, 62
Latin America, Muslims in, 182
Lausanne Treaty, 236
Lawrence, Bruce, 11
Layachi, Azzadine, 182, 184–5
Lebanese Christians: activities of, 102; Copts compared with, 85–8, 88–9, 102; creation of secular political movements, 96; decline in numbers, 96; in denominational groups, 96; dominance of parties, 101–2; dominance of state, 98; Maronites as representative of, 102. *See also* Maronites/Maronite Church; and militias, 99; under National Pact, 95–6; numbers of, 95; and parties of Lebanese Front, 99; and Phalange, 99–100; political activity, 100–1; role in government, 95; and secular-Christian state, 102; territoriality of, 97, 101; threats to, 87
Lebanese Forces militia (LF), 99, 100, 102
Lebanese Front, 87, 99
Lebanon: civil war, 97, 98, 99, 100, 101, 102, 104; confessional system, 96; creation of, 95; downfall of Christian-dominated parties, 97; Druze, 95, 101; European interest in, 95–6; Greek Orthodox Church in, 94–5, 97, 99; Guardians of the Cedars, 98; *hamula*-based political parties, 96–7; independence, 95, 101; Israeli invasion, 98; Liberal Party, 96; militias in, 98–9; *millet* system in, 95, 97, 101; monastic movement, 99; National Assembly, 95; National Bloc, 96; national identity of, 97–8; National Liberal "Tigers," 98–9; National Pact, 95–6, 99; neomillet system in, 102; numbers of Christians in, 95; Palestinians in, 86, 98, 100; parties in, 101–2; Phalange in, 96–7, 98–9, 99–100; political

failure of, 104; political parties in, 96; population, 95; religious communities of, 94; Roman Catholic Church in, 94, 96; Sabra massacre, 100; sectarian democratic system in, 95–6; Shatila massacre, 100; Shi'a in, 95; Sunni Muslims in, 95; Syrian intervention, 101; Syrian Orthodox Church in, 94–5; Ta'if Agreement, 100, 102; Ta'if regime, 89; Tanzim, 98
Leveau, Remy, 184
Lewis, Bernard, 7–8, 130, 159
liberal democracy, 199
liberalization, and political mobilization, 200
Lounes, Maatoub, 207
Lowery, Rich, 81n9
Luri language, 131

MacInnes, Rennie, 69
madrasas, 41, 118
Magalet Madaris Al-Ahad, 41
Maghraoui, Abdeslam, 184, 185
Maher, Vanessa, 174, 175
Mahrami, Dhabihullah, 147–50, 151–2
majlis al-milli movement, 68
majority/majorities: Arab, and Berbers, 216; Berbers as, 168; identities of, 283–4; Muslim, Coptic Church relationship with, 23; Muslim, minorities vs., vii; Muslims as legal, 4; primordial ties in, 284
Malik, Habib C., 87, 104
Malik b. Anas, 16
Maliki jurists, 17
Mamluks, 66

Mann, Michael, 229
Marais, Octave, 175
Marinids, 168
Mark the Evangelist, St, 24
Maronites/Maronite church, 86, 94, 98, 99, 100; Coptic Church compared with, 102; Council of Maronite Bishops, 101; history of, 94; numbers of, 94; patriarchate, 99, 100–1, 102; as representative of Lebanese Christians, 102; territories of, 97; Western influence vs. Easternism, 87
Marrakech, 170
marriages: Baha'i, 142, 156; and caste, 116; and conversions to other denominations, 65; in Coptic Church, 65–6; intermarriage with Muslims, 42; mixed, 42, 48
Marshall, Paul, 61
Martin, Maurice, 26–7
Marty, Martin E., 11
Marx, Karl, 11
Masih, Ayyub, 120–1
mass media: Christianity in, 32; Copts in, 34–5, 50. *See also* television
Matta al-Meskin, Father, 39, 45, 52, 53, 92
mawali, 6
Mawdudi, Mawlana Sayyid Abu 'l-'Ala, 109
Mayer, Ann, 155
Mecca, 16, 19n3, 32, 62
mechanical solidarity, 179
Medina, 5, 15, 19n3, 62, 284
MED-TV, 246
Meinardus, Otto, 65

Melchite Church, 94–5, 99, 284
Mesopotamia, 236
MHP. *See* Turkey: Nationalist Action Party
Middle Atlas, 174–5, 176; Berbers in, 182; Tamazight spoken in, 172
Middle East Council of Churches (MECC), 103
Middle East War (1967), 86
Mikhail, Kyriakos, 70
Miller, Susan Gilson, 180
millet system, 5, 89, 95, 97, 101, 104
minority identities: and discrimination against, 67; distinguishing features, vii-viii; and ethnic migration, 286; formation of, viii, xii; globalization and, 286; in nation-states, xii, 285; politicization of, vii; radicalization of, vii, 285; and secular ideologies, 285; theoretical model for, xii
minority/minorities: autonomy for, 286; classification of, 10; compact vs. diffuse, 130; conflict among, 11; Coptic attitude toward, 71, 78; Copts as, 89–90; cultural vs. religious, 286; defined, 12; demand for participation, 224–5; differentation of, 13; economic development and, 11; group formation, 11; historians' study of, 9; human rights for, 19; identification of, 3; identities of, 283–4; interaction with nation-states, 286; international accords and instruments, 9–10; Islamic concept of, 7; languages of, 165; literature on, 58; modernization theory, 11; Muslim ethnic, viii;

Muslims as, 14–17; numbers of, 10; opting out of states, 199; particularism-driven movements, 199; poverty and, 284–5; primordialism and, 12, 284; protection by British in Egypt, 71; religious. *See* religious minorities; religious tolerance for, 19; religious vs. cultural, 286; research on, 14; separation of, 286; and social change, 14; social identity, 11; social sciences study of, 9, 11, 14; and state ideology, 285; study of, 9–10, 11
minority status: of Copts, 61; definitions, 3–4, 13–14; determination of, 13; dominance and, 13, 14; ideology and, 14; power and, 13, 14; racism and, 14; and size of group, 12–13
missionaries: canal colonies, 113–14, 115; caste-consciousness of, 114; and caste system, 111–12, 113; Catholic, 113; in India, 111; in Pakistan, 117; schools, 113; United Presbyterian, 111–12
Mithaqi, Bihnam, 141, 146–7, 150
modernization: and Coptic Church renewal, 74–5; and Kurdish nationalism, 232; religious identities and, 78; theory, 11
Moghul Empire, 4
Mohajirs, 109
Mohammed VI, King, 164, 165
Mongols, 17
Montagne, Robert, 175, 182
Morocco: 'Aid al-Adha, 176; Arab consciousness in, 167; Arabic language in, 166–7; Arabs settled in, 166; armies, 169–70; Berbers

of. *See* Berbers of Morocco; children in, 184; colonial period, 173; controlled by Berber dynasties, 167; cultural models, 180–1; diversity in, 172; drug trade, 174, 176; economic conditions, 184–5, 187; education in, 185, 187; France and, 173, 175; hashish trade in, 174; health in, 184, 185; illiteracy in, 184; independence, 180; inequality in, 185; l'Institut Royal de la culture amazighe. *See* IRCAM; interrelatedness of people, 171; IRCAM. *See* IRCAM; Islam in, 171, 181–2, 189; languages in, 165, 183; linguistic discrimination in, 187; link to Prophet Muhammad, 164; literacy in, 187; marijuana production, 174, 176; migration within, 176; monarchy, 180, 187, 188–9; national independence, 174; poverty in, 184, 187; power in, 179–80, 180; protectorate period, 173, 174; Ramadan in, 176; Royal Institute of the Amazigh Culture. *See* IRCAM; rural conditions, 185; sectarian politics in, 189; social identity in, 183; Spain and, 173–4; state power in, 180, 181; structural adjustment in, 184–5; taxation in, 169; on UN Human Development Index, 184; villages in, 185; women in, 184, 185

Morqos, Samir, 42
Mosel, 277
Mount Lebanon, 94, 97
Mousa, Anba (Bishop), 35, 39, 42, 51

Mubarak, Husni, 27–8, 61, 63, 77, 90–1, 92
muhajirun, 15
Muhammad, Prophet, 52; successors of, 4; 64
Muhammad Ali, 25, 66
Muhammad Rashid Rida. *See* Rashid Rida, Muhammad
Mu'izz, Khalif, 46
Mujahidin-i Khalq, 137, 138, 140, 145
mu'minun, 6
Murji'ites, 6
Musaddiq, Muhammad, 136, 137
mushrikun, 4
Muslim Brotherhood, 23, 26, 27, 31, 35, 72, 74, 75
Muslim League, 109
Muslims: in Africa, 18; in America, 17–19; in Asia, 18; attitude toward Christian conversions, 113; and Berbers in Algeria, 202; Bosnian, 284; and British occupation, 66–7; and caste, 116; and Christians, 22, 25, 27, 29, 31–2, 33, 86, 115, 121, 122, 123–4; circumcision of children, 36; conquest of lands by others, 17; conquests by, 94, 131; converts to Christianity, 155; and Copts, 25, 42, 43–4, 49, 51–2, 54, 59, 65–6, 69, 78; dominance of, 13, 86; dress of, 37; in Egypt, 29, 32, 62; in Europe, 19; extremist, 29, 32, 34, 51, 62, 73. *See also* Islamism; feminists, 52; in Iberian Peninsula, 17; identities in US, 18; interfaith discussions with Copts, 51; intermarriage with Copts, 42; Latin American solidarity with,

182; as legal majority, 4; and *maulids*, 45; migration of, 15–16, 17; as minorities, 13, 14–17; in non-Muslim lands, 15–17; non-Muslim minority status in societies, 9; in North America, 19; oppression of, 15, 16; in Pakistan, 110, 116, 121, 122, 123–4; persecution of, 283–4; population growth rate, 24; poverty among, 36; and protection of minorities by British, 71; in public service, 67; and Punjabi Christians, 115; shared experiences with Copts, 36; *subu'*, 40; twentieth-century diasporas, 18; views on women, 36; violence against Copts, 72–3; in Wafd Party, 71; in the West, 18, 19
musta'min, 6

Nakşibendi order, 231, 232, 234, 237
Napoleon, 66
Nasser, Gamal 'Abd al-, 26, 27, 60, 72, 74, 76
nationalism: anticolonial, 75; in colonized world, 128; defined, 263; democratization and, 224; of Egypt, 66, 69; ethnicity and, 128; as excluding communities, 158–9; exclusionary, 128; indigenous groups and, 136; individual state, vii; information technology and, 60; in Iran, 127, 129, 145, 157; Islamic, vii; and Islamic law, 128–9; minority identities and, 285; and nation building, vii; pluralist, 128, 159; religion and, 85, 128, 159; religious minorities and, 136; repression and, 224; romantic, 131, 133; secular, vii, 285; spiritual, 75, 128; territorial, 63; theocracy and, 128; Turkish, 242
nation building, 35, 200; assimilation and, 230; and "nationalisms," vii
nation(s): construction of, 108; defined, 263; problems in, and majority vs. minority groups, 222–3
nation-states, 229, 284; authoritarian, 285; economic hardships within, 284–5; and international social ideologies, 285–6; Islamic, 285; minorities' interaction with, 286; minority identity formation in, xii; and religion, 285; secular nationalism of, 285; and *umma*, 285. *See also* states
neomillet system, 89, 92, 100, 102, 103, 104
Nezan, Kendal, 265
Ni'matu'llahi, 130
Nirenberg, David, 284
Nixon, Richard M., 276
Nursi, Said, 247

Öcalan, Abdullah, 231, 240, 242–3, 248, 249–50, 255
Öcalan, Osman, 249
OHAL. *See* Turkey: Regional State of Emergency Governorate
Omar, Tahani, 29
Operation Northern Watch, 270
Operation Provide Comfort (OPC), 268
oppression: of Berbers of Morocco, 172; of Kurds, 266; of language

and culture, 172; under Muslim leaders, 16; Muslims living under, 15, 16; of Pakistani Christians, 118–19

Orthodox Church: Baha'i compared with, 130; converts to Coptic Church, 90; fifth-century division, 90. *See also* Greek Orthodox Church

other, the: "aqaliat" as, 159; classification of Islam and, 4; Copts as, 78; *shari'a* and, 3; stereotypes and, 284

Ottoman Empire, 4; in Algeria, 210; centralization policies, 229, 231, 233, 234, 235; citizenship in, 239; collapse of, 252; ethnic identity in, 234–5; European colonial powers and, 235; Kurds in, 63, 230, 264, 265; Lebanon during, 95; *millet* system, 5, 89, 97; partitioning of, 235, 236; religious groups in, 235; treaty with Persian Empire, 265

Ouyahia, Ahmed, 215

Özal, Turgut, 246, 251

Pacini, Andrea, 58

Pagan polytheism, 4

Pahlevi, Muhammad Reza, Shah, 134, 136

Pahlevi dynasty, 134, 138, 152

Pakistan: *bastis* in, 117, 122; blasphemy laws, 119–21, 124; caste system in, 116; Christian evangelicals in, 61–2; civil war, 109; conditions following partition, 116–17; defining of, 110; electoral system, 121–2, 123, 124; groups in, 108–9; as homeland for Muslims vs. Islamic state, 110; as Islamic state, 110; Islam in, 109; Islamism in, 118, 119, 123; languages in, 108–9; *madrasas*, 118; under martial law, 119; migration to urban areas, 117; missionaries in, 117; Muslims in, 110; nationalization in, 117–18; Partition, 109, 116; population, 110; religion in, 109, 124; Roman Catholic Church in, 117; tolerance in, 109; *ulama* in, 109, 110; violence in, 119; Wahhabi Islam in, 110; war with India, 110

Pakistani Christians, 110–11, 117; and blasphemy laws, 119–21, 123; caste of, 122–3; citizenship status, 122; dress of, 119; education of, 124; employment of, 117–18; identity as Christians vs. Pakistanis, 125; marginalization of, 119, 124; Muslim relations with, 123–4; in National Assembly, 121–2; oppression of, 118–19; relations with Muslims, 121, 122; ridiculing of, 125; schools run by, 118; violence toward, 124; "Western" religion of, 124–5; and Zia coup, 118–19

Palestine: Coptic Church attitude toward, 33; defeat by Zionist forces, 26; national rights, 99

Palestine Liberation Organization, 99

Palestinians, in Lebanon, 86, 98, 100

Pan-Arabism, vii, 27, 86, 98, 103

Pan-Kurdism, 252, 255, 265

Paris: Institut Kurde de Paris, 244, 265; Peace Conference, 234

People of the Book, 5, 32
persecution: of converts, 113; discrimination vs., 71. *See also subheading* persecution *under names of groups and countries*
Persian Empire, 265
Phoenicians, 166
Pipes, Daniel, 82n10
PKK. *See* Kurdistan Workers' Party
pluralism: nationalism and, 128, 159; power and, 198; religious, 285
Polenz, Ruprecht, 151
Portuguese, 166
Powell, Colin, 276
power: elites and, 180; master and disciple *diagramme*, 180; pluralism and, 198; state-centred, 180
Presbyterians. *See* United Presbyterians
primordialism, 12, 109, 210, 213, 284; civility vs., 216; collective identity vs., 223
print: capitalism, 60, 168; culture, 60, 75
PUK. *See* Kurdistan: Patriotic Union of Kurdistan
Punjabi Christians, 115, 122, 123
Punjabi language, 113

Qadisha Valley, 94
Qajars, 131, 132
Qbayil. *See* Berbers of Algeria
Qur'an: Arabic of, 167; and Coptic school children, 26; equality of believers in, 182; on infidelity, 31–2; Islam in, 3; on Muslims living under oppression, 15; political activity and, 181–2
Qureish (Patriarch), 100
Qutb, Sayyid, 31, 73

Raboteau, Albert, 8–9
Rafsanjani, Hojjatu'l-Islam 'Ali Akbar Hashimi, 129, 140–1, 144–6, 157
Rahbarpur, Ghulam Husayn, 151
Raja'i, Muhammad 'Ali, 137
Ramadan: *iftar* gatherings, 44, 50; in Morocco, 176; in Pakistan, 119
Rashid Rida, Muhammad, 75
Rashidun period, 4, 5, 6
Ravani, Parviz, 152
Rawhani, Ruhu'llah, 154
religion: ascriptive, 104; and communal identity, 104; discrimination against, 70; free choice and, 104; fundamentalism. *See* fundamentalism; and "imagined community," 104; and nationalism, 128, 159; nation-states and, 285; in Pakistan, 109; pluralism within Islam, 285; politicization of, 103; and politics, 104
religious groups: classification of communities, 4; conflict among, 85; and nationalistic groups, 85; political activity, 85, 87; radical, 85
religious identities: cultural threats to, 75; and modernization, 74–5, 78
religious minorities, viii, 8–9; cultural vs., 286; and decline in secularism, 286; *dhimmi* status, 156; in Iran, 129–30, 140–1, 152, 153, 155; under Islam, 127–8, 137; nationalism and, 136; under theocracy, 129
resistance, 76
Reza Shah. *See* Pahlevi, Reza Shah
Rif Mountains, 173–4; Berbers of, 173–4, 175, 182; farming in, 176; Tarifit spoken in, 172

Roberts, Hugh, 185
Roman Catholic Church, 94; canal colonies, 114; in India, 114; Maronites in communion with, 94; in Pakistan, 117
Rose, Arnold M., 12
Rosen, Lawrence, 180
Royal Institute of the Amazigh Culture. *See* IRCAM
Ruhi, Kamyar, 146
Rumelia, 236
Rushdie, Salman, 120, 145

Saad, Stephanie, 167
Saadi, Said, 206
Sabet, Habib, 136
Sabi'ans of Harran, 5
Sadat, Anwar al-, 27, 63, 71, 72–3, 78, 91
Saddam Hussein, 233, 266, 268, 271–2, 276, 278
Safavids, 4, 131
Said, Edward, 105n9
Said, Rushdi, 50
Said, Seyh (Sheik), 237, 250
Saladin, 264
Salafiyya, 75
Salahaddin, 270
Salahaddin University, 275
Salamé, Ghassan, 96
Saljuqs, 131
Salman, Salih, 247
Samaan, Father, 46
Samaan, 46
Samandari, Bahman, 143
Samuel, Bishop, 39, 53
Sanasarian, Eliz, 159
Sangh, Rashtrya Swayamsevak, 159
Sao Paulo, Brazil, 184
SAVAK, 134

Scott, James C., 76
sectarianism, 6. *See also subheadings beginnning* sectarian *under names of groups and countries*
secularism, 5; appearance of secular states, 71; and Coptic Church renewal, 75; print culture and, 75
Seddon, David, 184
Sørensen, Ninna, 173
self-determination, 199
Sen, Amartya, 182–3
11 September 2001 terrorist attacks, 18, 31, 62, 85
Şerif Paşa, 236
Sevres Treaty, 236, 271
Şeyhs, 232, 234
Sfeir, Nasrallah Butrous, Cardinal, 101
Sha'arawi, Sheikh, 30, 52
Shafi'is, 17
Shamm al-Nasim holiday, 36
shari'a, 3, 6, 8, 19; in Algeria, 203; Copts under, 64; in Egypt, 28–9, 72, 93
Shatzmiller, Maya, 168–9, 171
Shaykhi, 130
Shenuda III, 28, 52, 53, 60, 61, 65, 76–7; banned to monastery, 27; Bible studies, 45; books on church affairs, 74; and breaking-of-the-fast gatherings, 50; on challenge of Islamic environment, 40; and church revival, 39; on Copts within Egyptian state, 62, 63; establishment of seminaries, 43; exiled to monastery, 92; exiling of, 29, 63; on female genital mutilation, 52; and Muslim assaults on Copts, 72–3; nominated for

UNESCO-Madanjeet Singh Prize, 29; ordaining of bishops, 43; reconciliation with Mubarak, 62, 77; relations with Sadat, 72–3; and religious councils, 68, 76; reshaping of church's hierarchy, 23; response to attacks on Coptic population, 93; on social services to Copts, 76–7; as successor to St Mark, 24; summary of al-Banna book, 61

Shi'a Islam, 6–7; and Baha'is, 134, 135–6, 137; branches of, 7; as infidels, 110; in Iran, 128–9, 148; in Iraq, 278; in Lebanon, 95; Mahdi of, 132; Sufi orders, 130, 155; Sunni separation, 6

shirk, 4–5

Shu'ubiyya, 13

Siebers, Tobin, 79

Sikhs, conversion to Christianity, 117

Sipah-e-Sahaba, 110, 121

Six Day War, 22, 27

Smith, Anthony D., 23, 25, 49, 64, 213, 232

socialism, 285

social sciences: ethnological/ethnographic research, 14; sociological research, 14; study of minorities, 9, 11, 14

Solomon, King, 264

Soviet Union, collapse of, 198, 199, 248

Spain: Civil War, 173; Islamization of, 203; linguistic communities, 173; Morocco and, 173–4; in Rif Mountains, 173

states: changes since Cold War, 199; collective identity, 215–16, 223; elites in, 200; minorities' opting out of, 199; multiethnic, 200, 216; multilingual, 216; new domestic order in, 199, 200; resistance to change, 199. *See also* nation-states

Stene, Nora, 41

stereotypes, 284

Sufism, 130, 155

Sulaymaniya, 274, 275, 277

Sunna, 3, 8

Sunni Islam, 4; in Egypt, 90, 101; in Iran, 129–30; in Iraq, 278; Kurdish, 63, 233–4, 238, 253, 266; in Lebanon, 95; Shi'a separation, 6

Suroush, 'Abdu'l-Karim, 154

Sweden, Kurdish Library in, 244

Sykes-Picot Agreement, 266

Syria, 236; separation of Lebanon from, 95; Turkey and, 248

Syrian Orthodox Church, 94–5

Talabani, Jalal, 255, 268, 269–70, 271, 272, 276

Taliban, 110

Talibi, Musa, 150, 151–2

Tamazight, 168, 172, 186, 187; in Algeria, 218, 221, 222; lexical standardization of, 165; in schools, 165

Tarifit, 172, 173

Tashelhit, 171, 172, 173

Tawhid, 273

television: Christianity and, 35; Islamic teachings on, 30, 35, 37

Tessler, Mark, 184

theocracy: Baha'i and, 134; in Iran, 127, 128, 129, 137–8, 140, 154; and nationalism, 128

Thomas, Edward, 188–9

Tin Mal, 170, 171
Tizi Ouzou, 207, 211, 220
tolerance: cultural, 199; discrimination vs., 71; in Pakistan, 109; political, 199; religious, 19, 199
Tumart, Ibn. *See* Ibn Tumart
Tunceli, 238
Turkey: anticentralization rebellions, 231; Armenians in, 236; assimilation policies, 230, 233, 243; attitude toward Kurdish state in Iraq, 272; caliphate, 237; citizenship in, 239; Constitutional Court, 246, 250; Constitutions, 239; 1971 coup, 240; 1980 coup, 240–1, 242, 244; Democracy and Peace Party, 254; Democratic People's Party (DEHAP), 245, 255; destruction of PKK, 248–50; economic development in, 240; and economic problems of Kurdish regions, 252–3; and Egypt, 248; elections, 240, 255; and EU, 231, 245, 250–1, 251–2; Felicity Party (SP), 255; framing of Kurdish resistance, 238; Initiative Commission for a New Political Formation, 254; Initiative Commission for Unity, 254; 1983 insurrection, 248; Iraqi Kurdish relations with, 277–8; Islam in, 235, 236, 237, 238, 255; and Israel, 248; Justice and Development Party (AKP), 255; Kemalism in, 236, 238–9, 253–4; Kurdish question/problem, 251, 254; and Kurdistan, 276; Kurds in. *See* Kurds of Turkey; Labour Party, 240; languages in, 252; leftist movement, 240, 242; legitimacy of, 267; linguistic policy, 252; martial law, 246; military forces, 248–9; *millet* system in, 237; modernization of, 229, 230–1, 234; Motherland Party, 251; Muslim population, 267; national identity, 237; nationalism of, 229, 236–7, 238–9, 242; nationalism of, vs. Kurdish nationalism, 232; Nationalist Action Party (MHP), 252; National Program, 252; National Security Council, 252; nation building, 231; as nation-state, 230–1, 231; and OPC, 270–1; People's Democratic Party (HADEP), 250, 254, 255; People's Republican Party (CHP), 255; rebellions against, 237–8; regional inequalities in, 253; Regional State of Emergency Governorate (OHAL), 246, 247; relations with Europe, 252; relations with US, 271; religion in, 235; Revenge Hawks of Apo, 249; secular nationalism of, 238–9; Seyh Said uprising, 250; social contract needed, 253–4; Social Democrat People's Party (SHP), 255; solutions for Kurdish question/problem, 251, 254; Southeastern Anatolia Project (GAP), 253; Sunni Muslims in, 267; and Syria, 248; trade with Kurdistan, 274; Turkism in, 229; *umma* in, 285; 1984 uprising, 241; and US, 248, 276, 277; war with Greece, 236
Turkish Historical and Language Society, 238
Turkmen, in Iran, 138

Ubeydullah, şeyh, 235
'Umar, 5
Umayyads, 6, 13
umma, 18, 285; Coptic community as, 62; Egypt and, 35, 48; Turkish Kurds and, 241
UNESCO-Madanjeet Singh Prize for the Promotion of Tolerance and Non-Violence, 29
Uniate Churches, 94
United Nations: Charter of 1945, 9; Declaration on the Elimination of Intolerance and Discrimination Based on Religion or Belief, 9–10; High Commission on Human Rights, 146; Human Development Index, 184; and Iraqi oil, 271–2; oil-for-food program, 273; Security Council Resolutions regarding Iraq, 268–9, 270, 272–3; Universal Declaration of Human Rights, 9
United Presbyterians, 111–12; conversion of untouchables, 112–13; difference from other missionaries, 112; education of, 112
United States: blacks as minority group, 13; Coptic Church in, 60–1; Coptic seminary in, 24; Copts in, 69, 103; *Country Reports on Human Rights Practices*, 29–30; discrediting of Middle East scholars, 62; Freedom from Religious Persecution Act, 61; image problem in Muslim world, 8; Information Agency, 8; invasion of Iraq, 49; Iranian relations with, 154; and Iraqi border concessions, 268; Iraqi Kurds as allies, 276–7; and KDP-PUK fighting, 272; and Kurdistan, 275–6; Muslims in, 17–19; nationalist tradition in, 128; Operation Northern Watch, 270; Operation Provide Comfort (OPC), 268, 270–1; as part of Dar al-Islam or Dar al-Harb, 18; pro-Israeli forces in, 61, 62; religious minorities in, 8–9; trade with Egypt, 72; Turkey and, 248, 271, 276, 277; war with Iraq, 276–7, 278
untouchables, 112–13, 115, 124
Urdu language, 113

van Bruinessen, Martin, 243
Venema, Bernhard, 174, 175

Wafd Party, 26, 27, 70, 71, 73
Wahba, Yusuf, 25
Wahhabi Islam, 110
Wakin, Edward, 64–5
Washington Accord, 272
West: Coptic churches in, 47; Copts in, 33; Iranian relations with, 153–4; Muslims in, 18, 19
Wigrams (missionaries), 263
women: Berber, 174, 175; in Coptic Church, 41–2, 43; Coptic views on, 36; discrimination against, 29–30; in Egypt, 30; honour killing of, 274; men's attitudes toward, 52; in Morocco, 184, 185; political representation, 30; religious, feminist discourse for, 52; rights groups, 49; and *takris*, 43
World Bank, 184, 185, 187
World Council of Churches, 103

Xenophon, 264

Yacine, Kateb, 168
Yazd, 142
Yazdani, Hozhabr, 136
Yazdi, Mohammed, Ayatollah, 150, 158
YEM-KOM. *See* Germany: Federation of Kurdish Organizations in Germany
Yılmaz, Mesut, 251
youth: in Coptic Church, 39–40, 41–2, 51; Kurdish, 240, 242, 246–7

Zaghlul, Saad, 71, 72
Zaydi, 7
Zia al-Haq, General, 110, 118–19, 120, 121
Zoroastrianism, 127, 129, 131, 136, 152, 156, 264